Therapeutic Jurisprudence and Victim Participation in Justice

International Perspectives

Edited by

Edna Erez

Michael Kilchling

Jo-Anne Wemmers

Carolina Academic Press

Durham, North Carolina

Library of Congress Cataloging-in-Publication Data

Therapeutic jurisprudence and victim participation in justice / edited by Edna Erez, Michael Kilchling, and Jo-Anne Wemmers.
p. cm.
Includes bibliographical references and index.
ISBN 978-1-59460-946-6 (alk. paper)
1. Therapeutic jurisprudence. 2. Law--Psychological aspects. 3. Restorative justice. I. Erez, Edna. II. Kilchling, Michael, 1958- III. Wemmers, Jo-Anne M., 1964-
K346.T44 2011
340.1'9--dc22

2011011870

Carolina Academic Press
700 Kent Street
Durham, North Carolina 27701
Telephone (919) 489-7486
Fax (919) 493-5668
www.cap-press.com

Printed in the United States of America

This book is dedicated to the memory of Bruce J. Winick—a pioneer of therapeutic jurisprudence, a fine scholar, and a caring human being.

Contents

Therapeutic Jurisprudence and Victim Participation in Justice: An Introduction

Edna Erez, Michael Kilchling & Jo-Anne Wemmers

Therapeutic jurisprudence (TJ) looks at various aspects of the law to determine whether or the extent to which substantive rules of law, legal procedures, and the roles or actions of legal actors are therapeutic. Conversely, it considers how the same processes can be non-therapeutic, or even anti-therapeutic. TJ emanated some two decades ago from mental health law, as scholars began looking at the positive and negative therapeutic aspects of proceedings leading to the involuntary civil commitment of mental patients (Wexler & Winick, 2001; Wexler 2008). TJ continues to develop into a conceptual framework that has applications in numerous areas of the legal milieu, such as informal interactions between various legal actors that result in formal actions, or how processes and outcomes are conveyed or presented to participants. The physical legal setting creates an additional level of complexity, and qualities inherent in such locations may either promote or depress TJ.

Although TJ originated within legal academia, it quickly gained a thoroughly interdisciplinary perspective. It has attracted the interest of social scientists including psychologists, criminologists, and community-minded researchers such as social workers, swiftly transitioning from an academic interest to a field of inquiry relevant to and applied by practicing professionals in diverse areas of U.S. law. What began as an American[1] exercise soon crossed international boundaries, especially in English-speaking countries—such as Canada, Australia, and New Zealand—and then beyond. The International Network on Therapeutic Jurisprudence website (INTJ, 2009) shows that TJ

1. The term "American" refers solely to the United States.

writing, while overwhelmingly in English, can also be found in Spanish, Portuguese, Italian, French, Japanese, Dutch, Swedish, Hebrew, and Urdu. A perspective that originated in the field of mental health law has evolved into a psychologically sensitive way to look at virtually all aspects of law and justice. Thus, TJ writings now inform the often-disparate proceedings involved in criminal, juvenile, family, personal injury, immigration, probate, and many other subfields of law. In this volume, we will extend the application of TJ principles and concepts to address an area that so far has received little attention in TJ literature—crime victims' participation in criminal justice around the world.

The application of TJ principles to substantive and procedural criminal law began with the agenda of improving the implementation of the law. TJ strives to accomplish harmonious functioning of the law by observing court proceedings and outcomes with an eye directed towards increasing therapeutic value for participants. A parallel agenda has impacted juvenile law, providing insights into ways to increase juvenile therapeutic benefits from participation in proceeding. With this general aim, TJ has addressed institutions such as "problem-solving courts," especially drug treatment courts (Winick & Wexler, 2003). TJ investigators looked at how courts can improve the compliance of defendants with orders of the court, and how courts can enhance long-term law-abiding behaviour even as their jurisdiction draws to a close. For example, "graduation ceremonies" are routinely held in drug treatment courts, providing participants with a memorable event that supports their transition to the next phase of their life, which will hopefully be free of both drugs and courts. In the criminal court context, the application of TJ is not limited to the arena of problem-solving courts. Indeed, TJ lends insights that can be used in criminal courts more generally, and to other juridical bodies that address victim harm and grievances in an attempt to achieve reconciliation. In criminal law, the TJ literature extends beyond the structure and function of courts to include the professional roles of lawyers. This is especially true of defence lawyers, as discussed in *Rehabilitating Lawyers: Principles of Therapeutic Jurisprudence for Criminal Law Practice* (2008), authored by workshop participant David Wexler. The emphasis on defence lawyers is indicative of the fact that, until now, the bulk of TJ work has focused on the rehabilitation of criminal defendants; the relevance and contribution of TJ for victims' issues has lacked a presence on centre stage.

However, that is not to say that TJ lacks the potential for making contributions to the area of victims, and to victimology. Indeed, using the phrase "victims of crime" to search the bibliography on the INTJ website reveals articles addressing TJ and victims, including perspectives from scholars in the United States, Canada, Australia, and India. These findings are probably the result of efforts such as the pioneering collection of articles edited by Wexler and Winick—*Law in a Therapeutic Key: Developments in Therapeutic Jurisprudence* (1996)—featuring a section on the "wide-angle lens of therapeutic jurisprudence." For example, a chapter by Richard P. Wiebe addresses "The Mental Health Implications of Crime Victims Rights" (Wexler and Winick, 1996, p. 213). With the high prevalence of mental illness in U.S. prisons (see, e.g., Human Rights Watch, 2009), and the greater prevalence and incidence of victimization of the mentally ill (see, e.g., Teplin et al., 2005), mental health was and still is an important topic to address. There may be as much to gain in rehabilitating victims as there is to gain from rehabilitating offenders, though an inability to achieve the latter should not discourage us from attempting to help the former, as victims are likely more amenable to rehabilitation than offenders.

In an attempt to encourage the study of potential impact of TJ approaches for victims, the Onati conference on TJ and victim participation in the criminal process broke important ground by addressing victim welfare and well-being during, and as a result of, participation in proceedings (e.g., Erez, 1999; Wemmers & Cyr, 2005). The next developmental steps in expanding the purview of TJ to important aspects of the law are being addressed through this collection. First, a major workshop on TJ and the role of victims in the criminal process brought scholars together to share their ideas, with interdisciplinary and international input. Next, the publication of the chapters in this book allows for the sharing of these ideas with a wider audience. Our hope is that the volume will serve to solidify the place of victims within the therapeutic jurisprudence research agenda.

Where victims are concerned, the TJ inquiries relate to the impact of proceedings on victim welfare. This includes measuring their level of satisfaction or dissatisfaction with the criminal justice procedure, beginning at the time of interaction with the police. The termination of the process can be hard to conceptualize due to high recidivism and re-victimization rates. Just as some offenders commit a disproportionate amount of crime, some individuals may be disproportionately victimized. The end of the process may involve alerting the victim(s) when the offender is released, paroled, or moved to another facility, a practice that has expanded rapidly in the U.S. since its inception in Kentucky fifteen years ago. A victim notification system is now employed statewide in 80% of states, and in some jurisdictions in 47 of the fifty United States (Halladay, 2009). Yet victim participation may take many forms, ranging from their physical presence at various events, through providing some input, to full-fledged participation and representation by counsel. When the TJ lens is focused on a particular area or problem, other perspectives will arise from the increased attention of creative researchers, and it is our hope that this will occur with attentive readers of this volume. For instance, one issue not directly addressed here but clearly important for future work relates to apology and its significance to victims. What types of victim interactions with offenders are most and least likely to prompt an offender to apologize? How can victim statements be used to help facilitate a meaningful apology?

To situate the formulation of answers to such questions, the first section of this volume addresses victim participation. Winick (this volume) begins this section with a discussion of how TJ can contribute to our understanding of the plight of victims of crime, with a focus on how the legal process can be re-imagined to facilitate their healing and human potential. Winick provides an overview of TJ perspectives as an interdisciplinary framework to examine victim participation and input in proceedings. Envisioning law as an instrument of healing and rehabilitation, he argues that rules of law, legal processes, and the roles played by those who apply the law—judges, lawyers, police officers, and court personnel—should be the focus of attention when we address victim participation in justice. According to Winick, TJ can play a vital role in transforming legal proceedings at all levels so that victims may purposefully evolve into survivors. Such a focus would help ameliorate and minimize the secondary victimization that victims often experience as a result of existing practices within the criminal justice system.

The second article in this section presents empirical research examining victim participation through a TJ lens. Erez, Ibarra, and Downs (this volume) provide an American perspective on victim participation reforms and welfare based on interviews with criminal justice professionals and victims-turned-activists. They examine the outcomes of some of the reforms that were instituted in attempt to improve victim status, reporting that they have had some positive or therapeutic effects. The chapter attempts to provide a framework for further analysis for reforms that warrant additional exploration and evaluation. Still, this dataset offers unique insight into the process described by Winick (this volume), demonstrating how victims transition into survivors and activists.

Providing an even more diverse array of viewpoints, Kury and Kilchling, (this volume) discuss research on the legislation and implementation of accessory prosecution in Germany. Based on interviews with victims and various criminal justice professionals (judges, public prosecutors, defense lawyers, victim lawyers acting as accessory prosecutors, and victim support workers), they relate that the mere presence of the victim lawyer can significantly change the atmosphere in the courtroom, thus affecting the willingness of the defense to treat the victim more respectfully. The utilization of victim lawyers, which continental law allows, is a concept that should be further explored in other legal systems as a potential new tool for victims seeking therapeutic outcomes.

The chapter by Wemmers (this volume) details the perspectives of Canadian judges, prosecutors, and victim support workers on therapeutic concerns for crime victims. While lamenting that victims in Canada are currently largely excluded from the criminal justice process, the author concedes that victim exclusion from the system does to some extent shelter them from the offender. Faced with this reality, based on her interviews, Wemmers attempts to answer the question: when is participation helpful or therapeutic for victims, and when is it harmful or anti-therapeutic? Though the voices of victims are not included, their experiences are relayed through the sentiments of key actors in the criminal justice proceedings who interact with victims on a daily basis. It would be interesting to know if their viewpoints coalesced with the perceptions of victims.

The second section of this volume considers victims and the law. First, Wexler (this volume) outlines a proposal for law school victim legal advisor clinics. Wexler proposes that students affiliated with a law school clinic could offer capable and legally knowledgeable accompaniment to victims who may need help understanding the proceedings. This proposal takes the position that by better informing victims of how the criminal justice works their frustration with the system could be tempered. As Wemmers (this volume) finds in her interviews with criminal justice professionals, lawyers, prosecutors and judges often find that victims often do not understand the system and misinterpret normal criminal procedure as a personal attack on their integrity. This proposal would bring victims into the court without compromising the rights of the accused. Furthermore, such a role could afford law school students with counselling experience while sensitizing them to the needs of victims. This kind of tool will augment measures currently practiced in legal settings to improve the victim's lot in proceedings. In this way, the creation of new tools begets the need for even newer tools, as the potential for growth within the area of victim TJ is only matched by the need to examine current applications more closely.

Second, Walther (this volume) works to enumerate victim rights in Germany as a means of creating new applications. Walther notes that in Germany, no doctrinal or particular constitutional framework exists from which specific victim's rights could be developed. Therefore, the creation of a conceptual constitutional framework would itself be a new tool for TJ, ensuring that rights are no longer a matter of "simple" law codified in the German criminal procedure code. Instead, the role of the victim as witness, accessory prosecutor, and interested party should conform to five specific central rights: 1) The right to make evidentiary motions, 2) the right to ask for an expansion of the accusation, 3) the right to ask questions at the taking of evidence and make statements,

4) the right to have the support of an attorney, if necessary at the expense of the state, and 5) the right to be informed and to have the assistance of interpreters. While delineation sometimes equates to limitations, victims' rights should provide a number of channels leading towards active participation, including the right to pose questions, to oppose orders of the court, and to challenge questions (Walther, this volume). Such guidelines would provide new applications specific to the German system, but it becomes apparent that analogous delineations in other legal contexts could provide similar opportunities for analysis.

The third article in this section addresses the role of the victim in Austrian criminal procedure. Based on victim surveys, Sautner and Hirtenlehner focus on victim satisfaction with legal procedures. The survey is especially timely, as the Austrian system has undergone fundamental reforms of procedural law aimed at strengthening the victim's position. These alterations mark a paradigm shift that upgrades the victim from a pure witness to a full process party, so the survey's aim was to find out how satisfied the victims were with their role in criminal proceedings at that time, and the extent to which they approve of the new rights they will be given. The article addresses both substantive issues related to changes in victim role in proceeding and with methodological considerations on how to study such changes and avoid some potential research pitfalls. Their contemplation of prospective applications of similar methodologies allows for a smooth transition to the third section of the book: new applications and tools in TJ.

In the third section—addressing TJ in the context of restorative and transitional justice—Gal and Shidlo-Hezroni (this volume) elucidate the case of child victims, followed by Buntman's analysis (this volume) of the victims of apartheid in relation to the South African Truth and Reconciliation Commission. Gal and Shidlo-Hezroni focus on child victims within the criminal justice system, examining the idea of restorative justice as reflective of a TJ approach. Situating their analysis within a discussion of young victims' vulnerability in the current legal system, the article explores restorative justice and its main principles, theories, and supportive movements. This allows for careful consideration of the different ways justice officials can provide child victims with better therapeutic outcomes.

Whereas Gal and Shidlo-Hezroni's chapter discusses a specific population, Buntman (this volume) discusses a unique legal body. The Truth and Reconciliation Commission (TRC) was created in the 1990s as a quasi-judicial body with both legal and political mandates intended to substantially contribute to healing victims, both individually and collectively, from the wounds and violence that accompanied apartheid. This was accomplished through a "therapeutic investigation," though Buntman notes that whether or not the TRC is judged to have been therapeutic for victims depends significantly on whom the victims are understood to be. Therefore, Buntman considers four categories of victims: 1) victims who came forward to the TRC, 2) victims as defined by the TRC's legislative authority but who did not come forward to the TRC, 3) victims of apartheid who were not victims of gross violations of human rights, as defined by the law, and 4) the conflict-ridden, divided, and torn South African society emerging from apartheid and into democracy. Using this framework, Buntman discusses successes (e.g., established the rule of law) and limitations (e.g., narrow definition of victims) of the TRC, extending the analysis by examining five internal or implicit logics of reconciliation—pragmatism, Christian notions of grace and forgiveness, African communalism, positivism, and law—that have impacted how TJ has functioned in this setting. Buntman's analysis details how diverse intersecting powers can influence TJ, revealing why careful attention should be given to definitional considerations of victims within any TJ framework. Without precise definitions that accept the disparate motivations inherent when distributing victim conscious criminal justice, it becomes possible to inadvertently create new victims.

The fourth section contains three chapters addressing the controversies and limits arising from affording victims special TJ considerations. The first chapter asks, "Is revenge therapeutic?" (Van Stokkom, this volume). Pemberton and Reynaers (this volume) continue by discussing how victim impact statements mitigate the rights of suspects, a sentiment echoed by Hoyle (this volume) in her chapter considering how victim emotions and impact statements may lead to more punitive sentencing. Despite our optimism for the positive potential of TJ, in order to stay informed and avoid unintended negative consequences, it is important to consider some controversies and limitations.

In questioning the therapeutic value of emotions such as anger, resentment, and resultant revengeful desires, the first chapter (Van Stokkom, this volume) in the section on controversies and limitations addresses potential adverse implications of increased victim participation. The author notes that such reflection is especially relevant given political pressure to impose severe sanctions. Meanwhile, the public seems to be increasingly more aware of the failures of correctional systems to reduce recidivism, and the high proportion of crimes committed by individuals with criminal histories. But is the public also becoming more aware of victims? Here Van Stokkom comments on what happens when victims take centre stage, resultant emotions of both defendants and victims, and the role of TJ within restorative and criminal justice frameworks. The discussion works to tease out an answer to the question: is revenge therapeutic? By building upon Van Stokkom's methodology, conclusions, and references, it becomes possible to create an empirical framework for providing additional outcome measures to determine how revenge impacts therapeutic settings. This chapter suggests new ways TJ scholars could look at their datasets, and new interactions to observe. Meanwhile, the next chapters detail the therapeutic benefits and limitations of a tool that is already firmly entrenched as a focus of TJ researchers: the victim impact statement.

Pemberton and Reynaers (this volume) proffer that victim impact statements may adversely affect the rights of suspects and the impartial nature of the trial, and, despite the relative wealth of scholarship on the subject, need still greater scrutiny. Moreover, they suggest that the therapeutic focus of victim integration reforms is alien to the criminal justice process, making victim impact statements a less than effective participation measure. The authors contend that better articulation of the envisioned therapeutic benefits and closer inspection of the therapeutic literature will reduce the tension with established criminal justice principles, while simultaneously providing a more fruitful base for conducting research into the effectiveness of victim impact statements. This new emphasis on the victim is also likely to lead to TJ scholarship on the role of the prosecutor, an area just now emerging (Wexler, in press), and closely related to victim rights. If prosecutors are to play a more therapeutic role, it will likely be easiest for them to begin with their relationships with victims. In fact, one of the contributions in this volume (Erez, Ibarra, & Downs) notes how a prosecutors' friendliness with defense attorneys and informal exchanges in the courtroom before the court convenes, described as the "work group" phenomenon (Eisenstein & Jacob, 1977), have baffled and offended victims (Erez, Ibarra, & Downs, this volume). As we keep in mind such interesting nuances that are ripe for observation and systematic scrutiny, the final chapter in the book again reminds us of the potential for negative consequences when victim participation in criminal justice settings is non-therapeutic, or anti-therapeutic.

Hoyle (this volume) details the transition of criminal justice in the U.S. and U.K. from a private to a State-led process, a shift that has altered the role of victims. Rather than some victims (e.g., wealthy) going on the offensive through available legal channels, states now seek justice in the form of punishing an offender. In some systems, it seems punishing the offender is more important than "rewarding" the victim, or at least returning them to their status quo, which has motivated victims' rights movements aimed at enhancing the place of victims in the criminal process. As we have noted, one such method now available in some legal systems is the victim impact statement. In this chapter, Hoyle reminds us that the timing of the victim impact statement is worthy of careful consideration. She suggests that post-sentence victim impact statements would preserve the principle of just deserts, and allow judges and juries to return to their prior reliance on more objective sources to judge a crime's severity. This provides an example of a way to limit victims' rights, while providing a clear locus for their assertion. Interestingly, while many of the chapters have focused on the TJ context as a place, this article reminds us of the importance of time and timing. If researchers are to observe and record the processes involved in TJ, they should be prepared to then provide evidence-based suggestions for how to improve the order of operations. And maybe the place can also be altered. For example, perhaps there should be TJ courts, where citizens seeking therapeutic recourses to victimization can have a different kind of day in court.

The contributions in this volume address various ways in which victims are incorporated into TJ. This includes instances in which the alleged victim's interests can conflict and compete with the defendant's interests and adequate protection by the law. The use of the term 'alleged victim' (Walther, this volume) underscores the complexities inherent in providing victims with rights before the defendant has been definitively found to be the offender. Research and real world experiences have shown that eyewitness statements are not always accurate, so involving the victim may lead to more defendants unjustly being found guilty. This necessitates careful consideration of the role of human emotions in criminal trials and reinforces the need to weigh the potential benefits for victims with the impending consequences for defendants.

It is our hope that this collection will stimulate interdisciplinary TJ activity centering on the role of victims, launching a major new direction of TJ research and practice. TJ criminal law writing, which has traditionally focused on courts and their relationship with criminal defendants, is now poised to mature and to branch into other areas. The role of TJ in the work of criminal justice professionals, such as prosecutors, is just beginning (Wexler, in press), and coincides with the new emphasis on TJ and victims spearheaded by this volume. TJ research is growing diverse enough in scope to provide a more complete reality that will inform a convergent framework based on the experiences of all actors involved in the legal process.

References

Beloof, D. and Cassell, P. (2005). 'The Victim's Right to Attend Trials: The Reascendant Consensus,' 9 Lewis and Clark Law Review 481.

Burke, K. and Leben, S. (2007). 'Procedural Fairness: A Key Ingredient in Public Satisfaction' (a White Paper of the American Judge Association), available at http://aja.ncsc.dni.w/htdocs/AJAWhitePaper9-26-07.pdf.

Eisenstein, J. and Jacob, H. (1977). *Felony Justice: An organizational analysis of criminal courts.* Boston: Little & Brown.

Erez, E. (1999). 'Who's Afraid of the Big Bad Victim? Victim Impact Statements as Victim Empowerment and Enhancement of Justice,' Criminal Law Bulletin 545.

Halladay, J. (2009). Victim-Notification Systems Marks 15 Years. USA Today.

Hartley, C.C. and Petrucci, C.J. (2004). 'Practicing Culturally Competent Therapeutic Jurisprudence: A Collaboration Between Social Work and Law,' 14 *Washington University Journal of Law and Policy* 133.

Human Rights Watch (2009). Mental illness, human rights, and US prisons: Human rights watch statement for the record: Senate judiciary committee subcommittee on human rights and the law. Retrieved November 30, 2009, from www.hrw.org/en/news/2009/09/22/mental-illness-human-rights-and-us-prisons.

International Network on Therapeutic Jurisprudence website, at (www.therapeuticjurisprudence.org).

National Crime Victim Law Institute website, at (www.ncvli.org).

Teplin, L.A., McClelland, G.M., Abram, K.A., and Weiner, D.A. (2005). Crime victimization in adults with severe mental illness: Comparison with the National Crime Victimization Survey. Arch Gen Psychiatry, 62:911–921.

Wemmers, J. and Cyr, K. (2005). 'Can Mediation be Therapeutic for Crime Victims? An Evaluation of Victims' Experiences in Mediation with Young Offenders,' 47 Canadian Journal of Criminology and Criminal Justice 527.

Wexler, D.B. (in press). 'Therapeutic Jurisprudence, Legal Landscapes, and Form Reform: The Case of Diversion,' *Florida Coastal Law Review.*

Wexler, D.B. (2008). *Rehabilitating Lawyers: Principles of Therapeutic Jurisprudence for Criminal Law Practice.* Durham, NC: Carolina Academic Press.

———. (2008). Two Decades of Therapeutic Jurisprudence, 24 *Touro L. Rev.* 17.

———. (2006). 'Therapeutic Jurisprudence and Readiness for Rehabilitation,' 8 Florida Coastal Law Review 111.

———. (2005). 'A Tripartite Framework for Incorporating Therapeutic Jurisprudence in Criminal Law Education, Research and, Practice,' 7 *Florida Coastal Law Review* 95.

Wexler, D. and Winick, B. (1996). *Law in a Therapeutic Key.* Durham, NC: Carolina Academic Press.

Wexler, D. and Winick, B. (1991). *Essays in Therapeutic Jurisprudence.* Durham, NC: Carolina Academic Press.

Winick, B.J. (2007). 'A Legal Autopsy of the Lawyering in Schiavo: A Therapeutic Jurisprudence/Preventive Law Rewind Exercise, 61 *University of Miami Law Review*, 595.

Winick, B.J. and Wexler, D.B. (2006). 'The Use of Therapeutic Jurisprudence in Law School Clinical Education: Transforming the Criminal Law Clinic,' 13 *Clinical Law Review* 605.

Section 1:
Victim Participation

1

Therapeutic Jurisprudence and Victims of Crime

Bruce J. Winick

Abstract

Therapeutic jurisprudence is an interdisciplinary scholarly approach that asks us to envision law as an instrument of healing and rehabilitation, and to examine on this dimension rules of law, legal processes, and the roles played by those who apply the law—judges, lawyers, police officers, and court personnel. This chapter addresses how therapeutic jurisprudence can contribute to our understanding of the plight of victims of crime and how the legal process can be reimagined to facilitate their healing and human potential. It addresses how therapeutic jurisprudence can help the legal system to turn victims into survivors, and to ameliorate and minimize the secondary victimization that many experience as a result of existing practices within the criminal justice system.

1. Introduction

Therapeutic jurisprudence focuses attention on the emotional well-being of those who come into contact with law and the legal system (Winick & Wexler, 2003; Stolle, Wexler & Winick, 2000; Wexler & Winick, 1996; Wexler & Winick, 1991). It is an interdisciplinary field of legal scholarship that calls for theoretical and empirical analysis of law's therapeutic impact. In addition, it has a law reform agenda. It suggests that law's antitherapeutic effects should be minimized, and when consistent with other justice values, that law's potential for increasing the emotional well-being of the individual and society as a whole be increased. It asks us to envision law as an instrument of healing and rehabilitation, and to examine on this dimension rules of law, legal processes, and the roles played by those who apply the law—judges, lawyers, police officers, and court personnel. Therapeutic jurisprudence has produced numerous proposals for reshaping the law and how it is applied, and has identified many empirical questions for social science exploration (Winick, 2006).

What can therapeutic jurisprudence contribute to our understanding of the plight of victims of crime and how the legal process can be re-imagined to facilitate their healing and human potential? How can therapeutic jurisprudence help the legal system to turn victims into survivors? The criminal process and the way police, judges, court personnel, prosecutors, and defense lawyers play their roles with regard to the victim of crime should be animated, in important part, by a concern for the needs of the victim. Crime, particularly violent crime, disrupts the emotional equilibrium of the victim. It can produce in the victim strong feelings of anxiety, fear, depression, humiliation, anger, powerlessness, and betrayal. It can reduce the individual's sense of self-esteem and self-efficacy. When the crime has been perpetrated by someone the victim knows, a trusted employee, a neighbor, a relative, or an intimate, for example, the experience can shatter the victim's sense of trust and willingness to have close relations in the future. Some victims of crime, especially if the crime is of a repetitive nature, such as domestic violence, develop a form of learned helplessness. This is a psychological syndrome that can limit effective performance in a variety of areas, inhibit motivation, and produce feelings of helplessness, hopelessness, and emotional reactions that mirror clinical depression (Seligman, 1980; Seligman, 1975; Walker, 1977). Some victims acquire a form of post-traumatic stress disorder (American Psychiatric Association, 2000, pp. 463–68; Herman, 1997; Wilson, 1989; McGruder-Johnson et al., 2000).

What do victims of crime need and want from the criminal justice system? How can legal actors in the criminal justice process help to ameliorate their suffering and psychological damage? How can they avoid further exacerbating their psychological harm? To the extent that existing practices impose on the victim further damage, producing a form of secondary victimization, how can they be reshaped to avoid or minimize these effects? These are the questions that therapeutic jurisprudence poses.

2. Meeting the Victim's Needs: Some Therapeutic Jurisprudence Suggestions

What do victims of crime need and want? They may need immediate medical or emotional attention, and police and other first-responders should be trained in how these needs can be met. The victim will feel violated and fearful of being re-victimized. As a result, the police should focus on providing information and reassurances that can help to restore their sense of security.

In general, victims need to get in touch with the strong feelings that the crime has produced in them, expressing them rather than suppressing or repressing them. Victims need to understand what has happened and the impact it has had on them. They need sympathy and understanding, not blame. They need to reframe their experience. They need to reassert a sense of control over their lives. They need to have the opportunity to tell their story to listeners who will be sympathetic and not judgmental. All of those within the criminal justice process with whom the victim will relate should receive training to sensitize them to these needs and how to meet them.

All participants in the legal and judicial process need to understand the various types of psychological damage that being victimized by crime can produce. All need to learn how to act in ways designed to facilitate their amelioration rather than their exacerbation. The training they receive should include sessions conducted by psychologists or social workers designed to increase their sensitivity to these issues and to the do's and don'ts of victim interaction. They need theoretical understanding, but also skills training that should include modeling and role-play exercises.

In addition to sensitizing them to the typical emotional reactions that victims of crime experience and how to deal with them, these legal actors should be educated about appropriate resources in the community to which they can be referred. Indeed, when feasible, the police and the courts should employ social workers that can provide rapid intervention when needed. In appropriate cases, individual or group counseling should be made available, at governmental expense, to those in need and who feel that they would benefit from it.

The education and training provided to all participants in the legal and judicial process should also cover the more esoteric psychological reactions that crime victimization may produce. They need to understand that those victimized by crime can experience a feeling of loss of control in their lives that can produce serious psychological consequences. If they attribute this loss of control to personal shortcomings and feel that it reflects a global rather than a limited deficiency on their part that is permanent rather than changeable, they may acquire feelings of learned helplessness (Garber et al., 1980. pp. 154–55; Abramson et al., 1980; Peterson & Bossio, 1989, p. 237–38). Police in court procedures should attempt, whenever possible, to empower the victim rather than to perpetuate his or her sense of not being in control (Dutton, 1992, pp. 94–95; Gondolf, 1998, pp. 96–97; Herman, 1997, p. 133; Waites, 1993 pp. 89–90). They need to communicate to them that they do not bear responsibility for their victimization and teach them ways of helping to prevent future victimization.

To the extent that victims suffer from a form of post-traumatic stress disorder, police, judicial, and legal proceedings should encourage them to "open up" about their experiences and how they feel about them (Pennebaker, 1990). This could be accomplished by designing intake and other processing forms to enable victims to write out a description of what occurred to them and what feelings they experienced. Some victims will have language or literacy deficits that will make writing difficult. Others, because of their cultural background, will be reluctant to put their statements in writing. For these and perhaps other victims who might find a writing requirement objectionable, the court process could use a court official to interview victims and fill in the forms for them. At a minimum, victims should be encouraged to do this on a voluntary basis and told that such descriptions will be helpful for improving police and judicial proceedings in these cases, for public understanding of these problems, and for helping other victims. Such written descriptions should be shared with other victims and the public on an anonymous basis, and the victim should be assured of privacy in this respect. Psychologist John Pennebaker, in his book *Opening Up* (1990), has shown that people suffering a variety of traumas, including war trauma, natural disasters, or being victims of crime or accidental injury, gain significant psychological benefits from telling their stories to others, particularly if in writing. Police, prosecutorial, and judicial processes should thus encourage such opening up by the victim whenever possible. Another way of accomplishing this is by having the victim complete a victim impact statement that can be used at sentencing.

When police, prosecutors, and court officials interview victims who seem reluctant to tell their full story and uncertain about whether to report the crime or ambivalent about the perpetrator, helping them to describe their feelings might succeed in helping them to resolve them. Victims also can be told that sometimes even testifying at a deposition or in court about their story may have a healing effect (Mills, 1999, p. 575). Sometimes the victim will be reluctant to proceed based on fear of having to again confront the perpetrator, either at a deposition or at trial. Indeed, such a confrontation may provoke high stress, anxiety, and fear, causing the victim to relive the emotional trauma of the crime episode. To avoid the victim's apprehension about such a confrontation with the perpetrator, and to reduce the psychological pain and distress it might produce, police and prosecutors can suggest that alternative approaches, such as the use of video-taped or one-way closed circuit television testimony, might be possible and may not violate the defendant's right to confront the witnesses against him (*Maryland v. Craig*, 1990).

Too often, the criminal justice system treats victims in ways that are emotionally distressing and disempowering (Herman, 2003). Trial procedures are designed to protect the rights of the accused, whose liberty is sought to be taken away. Little attention is given to the rights and interests of the victim, with the result that victims often experience the criminal process as unfair, disempowering, disrespectful, and an affront to their dignity. They have little or no say in determining what the defendant will be charged with and in how the case will be made against him. These are tasks for the prosecutor, who rarely consults the victim. Although the need to protect the defendant's rights will predominate over the sometimes conflicting interests of the victim, more attention needs to be given to the victim's needs and interests at every phase of the proceedings. We must be sure not to re-victimize the victim through court procedures that are distressing and further disempowering.

In this connection, police, judges, court personnel, and state attorneys need to understand the lessons of the literature on the psychology of procedural justice (Lind & Tyler, 1988; Thibaut & Walker, 1975; Tyler, 2006; Lind et al., 1990). This literature shows that when litigants are treated in ways that accord them a sense of participation and dignity, and are given the feeling that court actors have good intentions, they respond with higher satisfaction to judicial proceedings and the results of such proceedings, even if unfavorable. Victims need to be accorded a sense of "voice," the ability to tell their story, and "validation," the sense that what they have to say is taken seriously. They should be treated with dignity and respect by police and court officials who convey to them a sense that what is being done is in their best interests and done with good rather than bad intentions.

Victims often experience the criminal justice process as coercive. Treating them in accordance with the insights drawn from the procedural justice literature also will diminish the extent to which they feel coerced and will give them a sense of voluntary choice even in inherently coercive contexts. People that are given a choice, rather than made to feel coerced, respond better and with greater satisfaction, more motivation and effective performance (Winick, 2005). Indeed, experiencing choice and a sense of self-determination is often vital to an individual's sense of her own locus of control, and may be essential to emotional well-being (Winick, 1997, pp. 68–83; Winick, 1992, pp. 1755–68). Treating victims with procedural justice thus can help to ameliorate their psychological stress and restore their emotional equilibrium.

Judges, court personnel, police, and prosecutors thus need to be given training in these techniques. Providing victims with procedural justice does not mean transferring to them decision-making authority about the criminal charge, plea bargaining, or the presentation of the evidence at trial. These are decisions for the prosecutor, but the prosecutor can consult with the victim concerning them, and provide the victim with the reasons for the decisions he or she may make in these regards. The victim should be given a voice, not a veto. But if victims are treated with dignity and respect, are listened to and taken seriously, and have had their dignity respected, they may be more able to accept the prosecutor's decision, even if they disagree with it. If treated in these ways throughout the criminal justice process, victims may be more able to accept its outcome. By contrast, when victims feel that their sense of voice, validation, and dignity have not been respected, they are more likely to resent both the outcome and the process and hold on to their feelings of anger, vengeance, and anxiety. Such acceptance of the outcome, which procedural justice can help to achieve, can be the beginning of healing.

Police, prosecutors, judges, and court personnel also need training in how to be good listeners and to convey sympathy, empathy, and understanding. This will increase victims' trust and confidence in these officials and in the criminal justice process generally. It will reduce the resentment that victims frequently experience, and create a climate in which they will feel freer to express their feelings about the crime. All of this can help victims to get past their emotional reaction to the crime and to begin healing.

Much of the distress experienced by victims in the criminal justice process relates to their failure to understand how the process works and why. They may not understand the various stages of the process, and the inevitable delays that will occur. This lack of understanding can further contribute to their anxiety, fear, and depression. The remedy is for all criminal justice personnel to provide victims with increased information about the process and to express a willingness to answer their questions. This is described in the social cognition literature as "information control" (Fiske & Taylor, 1984, p. 122; Sydeman et al., 1997, p. 211). Understanding the process will reduce victims' stress, fear, and anxiety, and help them to manage their expectations concerning what will occur. Such information can be provided orally, through written materials, or through offering the victim the opportunity to view a videotape orientation to the criminal process.

The criminal justice process should make more use of restorative justice models. Unlike the retributivist focus of many criminal justice systems, this model gives greater recognition to the fact that a crime has harmed the victim and upset the equilibrium of the community, and seeks to address these through victim/offender conferencing (Bazemore & Schiff, 2001; Braithwaite, 2002; Strang & Braithwaite, 2001). Such victim/offender conferencing typically includes family and other support group members of both victim and offender (Bibas & Bierschbach, 2004). It provides victims an opportunity to describe to the offender the harm they experienced as a result of the crime and the feelings it produced. This sometimes provokes feelings of empathy in the offender and sometimes an apology. An acknowledgement of wrongdoing and a genuine apology can allow victims to heal (Petrucci, 2002). When the defendant pleads not guilty and seeks a trial to contest the charges, such victim/offender conferencing would likely be unavailing and it may not be possible to compel the defendant to participate. However, when the defendant has pled guilty and is facing a future sentencing, such conferencing with the victim might provide the defendant with an incentive to apologize and provide the victim with a healthy opportunity to express feelings. Similarly, if the defendant is convicted at trial, a post-verdict and pre-sentencing victim/offender conference will provide these incentives and opportunities, and will not compromise the defendant's rights.

One way of allowing a victim to have a voice is through Victim Impact Statements. Typically, these statements include a description of the physical and/or emotional harm that a victim or family member suffered following the commission of a crime (Arrigo & Williams, 2003). Victim impact evidence recognizes the victim's status as the injured party in the prosecution and empowers the victim with an opportunity to participate in the criminal justice system (Tobolowsky, 1999). The victim expresses his or her perspective or feelings about the effect of the crime, and this expression constitutes a form of communication between the victim and the offender, as well as between the judge and the offender (Roberts & Erez, 2004). Ideally the victim is best suited to sensitize the offender to the consequences of the crime, and presentation of the victim impact statement by the victim may therefore be preferable to having prosecutors convey impact information, as the offender would be able to relate to what a victim conveys more than to impact details presented by a legal professional who has the role of prosecuting the case. As most victims and offenders are laypersons rather than criminal justice professionals, and are often unfamiliar with legal jargon, a direct appeal by the victim to the offender may be a more effective route to encourage offenders to accept responsibility (Erez & Roberts, 2006).

3. Conclusion

This Chapter makes a number of suggestions drawn from therapeutic jurisprudence that are designed to reduce the psychological harm that the crime has produced for the victim and to avoid the victim's secondary victimization by the criminal justice system. These proposals are somewhat theoretical, applying to this context principles of psychology and psychological theory developed in other areas. Whether these proposals would succeed in bringing healing to the victim and reducing the antitherapeutic effects of the criminal justice process presents an empirical question in need of social science research. Social scientists interested in the criminal justice system and in the plight of victims are encouraged to conduct empirical research on what victims want and need and on what legal responses bring greater satisfaction and healing.

A basic insight of therapeutic jurisprudence is that how legal actors play their roles can have therapeutic and antitherapeutic effects even in the absence of legal change. In the way they deal with victims of crime, police, prosecutors, judges, and court personnel all are therapeutic agents. Understanding this basic insight can itself be transformative for these public officials. Once they understand that the way they communicate and act with crime victims can further exacerbate their distress and suffering or help to bring about their healing, this will change their behavior and provide motivation for them to receive training and education in this regard. Moreover, not only will this reframing of their professional roles predictably produce greater satisfaction and healing on the part of the victim, but it also can increase their own professional and personal satisfaction (Hora & Chase, 2003/2004; Chase & Hora, 2000).

References

Abramson, L.Y., Garber, J., and Seligman, M.E.P. (1980). Learned Helplessness In Humans: An Attributional Analysis. *In* Garber, J. and Seligman M.E.P. (Eds.), *Human helplessness: Theory and applications.* New York: Academic Press.

American Psychiatric Association (2000). *Diagnostic and statistical manual of mental disorders: DSM-IV-TR.* Washington, DC: American Psychiatric Association.

Arrigo, B.A. and Williams, C.R. (2003). Victim Vices, Victim Voices, and Impact Statements: On the Place of Emotion and the Role of Restorative Justice in Capital Sentencing. *Crime Delinquency.* 49:603–626.

Bazemore, G. and Schif, M. (Eds.) (2001). *Restorative community justice: Repairing harm and transforming communities.* Cincinnati, OH: Anderson Publishing.

Bibas, S. and Bierschbach, R.A. (2004). Integrating Remorse and Apology into Criminal Procedure. *Yale Law Journal,* 114:85–148.

Braithwaite, J. (2002). Restorative justice and therapeutic jurisprudence, *Criminal Law Bulletin*, 38:244–62.

Chase, D.J. and Hora, P.F. (2000). The Implication of Therapeutic Jurisprudence for Judicial Satisfaction, *Court Review*, 37:12–19.

Dutton, M.A. (1992). *Empowering and healing the battered woman: A model for assessment and intervention.* New York: Springer Publishing Company.

Erez, E. and Roberts, J.V. (2006). Victim participation in the criminal justice system. In *Victims of Crime.* Robert C. Davis, Arthur Lurigio, and Susan Herman, Eds. (3rd Edition), p. 277–298. Sage Publications.

Fiske, S.T. and Taylor, S.E. (1984). *Social Cognition.* Reading, MA: Addison-Wesley Publishing Company.

Garber, J., Miller, S.M., and Abramson, L.Y. (1980). On the distinction between anxiety and depression: perceived control, certainty, and probability of goal attainment. *In Human helplessness: Theory and applications.* Judy Garber and Martin E.P. Seligman, Eds. New York: Academic Press.

Gondolf, E.W. (1998). *Assessing woman battering in mental health services.* Thousand Oaks: Sage Publications.

Herman, J.L. (1997). *Trauma and recovery.* New York: BasicBooks.

Herman, J. (2003). The Mental Health of Crime Victims; Impact of Legal Intervention. *Journal of Traumatic Stress,* 16:159–166.

Hora, P.F. and Chase, D.J. (2003/2004). Judicial Satisfaction When Judging in a Therapeutic Key, *Contemporary Issues in Law,* 7:8–38.

Lind, E.A., Kanfer, R., and Earley, C.P. (1990). Voice, control, and procedural justice: Instrumental and noninstrumental concerns in fairness judgments, 59 *Journal of Personality & Social Psychology,* 59:952–959.

Lind, E.A. and Tyler, T.R. (1988). *The social psychology of procedural justice.* New York: Plenum Press.

Maryland v. Craig, 497 U.S. 836. (1990).

McGruder-Johnson, A.K., Davidson, E.S., Gleaves, D.H., Stock, W., and Finch, J.F. (2000). Interpersonal violence and post-traumatic symptomatology: The effects of ethnicity, gender and exposure to violent events. *Journal of Interpersonal Violence,* 15:206–16.

Mills, L.G. (1999). Killing her softly: Intimate abuse and the violence of state intervention. *Harvard law review,* 113:550–614.

Pennebaker, J.W. (1990). *Opening up: The healing power of confiding in others.* New York: W. Morrow.

Peterson, C. and Bossio, L.M. (1989). Learned Helplessness. *In* Rebecca C. Curtis (Ed.), *Self-defeating behaviors: Experimental research, clinical impressions, and practical implications,* pp. 237–38. New York: Plenum Press.

Petrucci, C. (2002). Apology in the criminal justice setting: Evidence for including apology as an additional component in the legal system. *Behavioral Science and the Law*, 20:337–362.

Roberts, J.V. and Erez, E. (2004). Communication in Sentencing: Exploring the Expressive Function of Victim Impact Statements. *International Review of Victimology*, 10:223–244.

Seligman, M.E.P. (1975). *Helplessness: On depression, development, and death.* San Francisco: W.H. Freeman.

Seligman, M.E.P. (1980). *Human helplessness: Theory and applications.* New York: Academic Press.

Stephen, J., Williams R., Yule, W. (1997). *Understanding post-traumatic stress: A psychosocial perspective on PTSD and treatment.* Chichester, NY: J. Wiley.

Stolle, D.P., Wexler, D.B., and Winick, B.J. (2000). *Practicing therapeutic jurisprudence: Law as a helping profession.* Durham, NC: Carolina Academic Press.

Strang, H. and Braithwaite, J. (Eds.) (2001). *Restorative justice and civil society.* Cambridge, UK: Cambridge University Press.

Sydeman, S.J., Cascardi, M., Poythress, N.G., and Ritterbrand, L.M.(1997). Procedural Justice in the Context of Civil Commitment: A Critique of Tyler's Analysis, *Psychology, Public Policy & Law*, 3:207–221.

Thibaut, J. and Walker, L. (1975). *Procedural justice: A psychological analysis.* Hillsdale, NJ: Erlbaum Associates.

Tobolowsky, P.M. (1999). Victim Participation in the Criminal Justice Process: Fifteen Years After the President's Task Force on Victims of Crime. *New England Journal on Criminal and Civil Confinement.* 25:21–105.

Tyler, T.R. (1990, 2006). *Why people obey the law.* Princeton, NJ: Princeton University Press.

Waites, E.A. (1993). *Trauma and survival: Post-traumatic and dissociative disorders in women.* New York: Norton.

Walker, L.E. (1977). Battered women and learned helplessness. *Victimology* 2:525–534.

Wexler, D.B. and Winick, B.J. (1996). *Law in a therapeutic key: Developments in therapeutic jurisprudence.* Durham, NC: Carolina Academic Press.

Wexler, D.B. and Winick, B.J. (1991). *Essays in Therapeutic Jurisprudence.* Durham, NC: Carolina Academic Press.

Wilson, J.P. (1989). *Trauma, transformation, and healing: An integrative approach to theory, research, and post-traumatic therapy*, New York: Brunner/Mazel.

Winick, B.J. (2006). Therapeutic jurisprudence: Enhancing the relationship between law and psychology. *In* B. Brooks-Gordon and M. Freeman, (Eds.),

Law and Psychology: Current Legal Issues, pp. 30–48. New York: Oxford University Press.

Winick, B.J. (2005). *Civil Commitment: A Therapeutic Jurisprudence Model.* Durham, NC: Carolina Academic Press.

Winick, B.J. (1997). *Therapeutic Jurisprudence Applied: Essays on Mental Health Law*. Durham, NC: Carolina Academic Press.

Winick, B.J. (1992). On Autonomy: Legal and Psychological Perspectives, *Villanova Law Review*, 37:1705–1777.

Winick, B.J. and Wexler, D.B. (2003). *Judging in a therapeutic key: Therapeutic jurisprudence and the courts.* Durham, NC: Carolina Academic Press.

2

Victim Welfare and Participation Reforms in the United States: A Therapeutic Jurisprudence Perspective*

Edna Erez, Peter R. Ibarra & Daniel M. Downs

Abstract

The adversarial process of the criminal justice system does not consider victims as a party to proceedings, which contributes to victims' alienation and dissatisfaction with justice proceedings. Efforts to alleviate the psychological harm to victims include the provision of rights to provide input into proceedings, among other recent victim-centric reforms. Victim impact statements and other participatory rights have been designed to increase victims' sense of inclusion in proceedings, thereby serving as a catalyst for healing psychological and emotional injury. In this study, we examine accounts describing the impact of these reforms on crime victims in two jurisdictions in the U.S. The data are comprised of in-depth interviews with criminal justice professionals (N = 27) who have close contact with victims in the course of their daily work, and with victims-turned-activists (N = 7). The findings suggest that victim-centric reforms are associated with therapeutic effects that

* The study was conducted with support from the Transcoop Program of the Alexander von Humboldt Foundation, the Ohio Office of Criminal Justice Services, and Kent State University Office of Research and Sponsored Programs. Points of view are those of the authors and do not reflect the views of the funding agencies. Linsey Britz transcribed the interviews and Julie Globokar provided insightful suggestions and editorial assistance. This is an expanded version of a paper presented on March 8–9, 2007 at a workshop on "Therapeutic Jurisprudence and Victim Participation in Justice," at the Onati Institute for the Sociology of Law, in Onati, Spain.

emerge as a result of participation in the criminal justice system, including validation, vindication, and empowerment. However, anti-therapeutic effects may also result from participation, particularly when victims provide court testimony or learn about plea agreements from which they have been excluded.

1. Background

Whether and to what extent victims should participate in criminal justice proceedings has long been a point of dispute in adversarial legal systems. In the adversarial model of justice, the focus of the criminal trial is centered on a conflict between two presumably equal adversaries, the prosecution and defense, played out before an impartial adjudicator—the judge. Historically, a crime victim's role has been to file a complaint about his or her victimization, leaving it to authorities to pursue the case and bring the offender to justice. Victims in adversarial legal systems have traditionally been unable to participate in criminal trials for a number of structural and normative reasons (Doak, 2005). Being viewed as 'private parties' whose role should be confined to that of witnesses, there is reluctance to accord them participatory rights. Such rights for "third parties" (Sebba, 1996) are perceived as a threat to the objective and public nature of the criminal justice system. Their role is at best that of passive participant; she or he would appear if called to testify and respond to examination in direct and cross-examination.

Over the past three decades, adversarial justice systems have experienced significant changes in the policies and practices related to the role of victims in criminal justice proceedings, beginning with the arrest of a suspect and continuing through the offender's release from prison. Most Western countries with adversarial legal systems have passed legislation pertaining to victims' participatory rights throughout the justice process (Hall, 1991) and created a wide range of services for crime victims (e.g., the right to receive information about the status of "their" case, receive financial and psychological assistance, freedom from harassment or intimidation). Despite the restricted role that adversarial proceedings have typically allowed victims, participation now includes a range of rights regarding victim consultation and expression, if not outright control over some steps in the process (Edwards, 2004; Roberts & Erez, 2004).

The victim's role has been transformed from one of passive witness to that of active participant. While still lacking full "standing" as a party to the proceedings, victims are informed, consulted, and invited to participate more than ever before. Traditionalists (e.g., Ashworth, 1993) consider this evolution an unwelcome threat to core values central to the adversarial model. Concerns have also been raised that victims are invoked as a potent rhetorical device or symbolic tool to buttress demands for harsher punishment: "victims in the service of severity" (Ashworth, 2000). Opponents of victim participation rights have also enumerated possible negative effects of participation in proceedings on victims (e.g., Reeve & Mulley, 2000; Sanders et al., 2001), claiming that victims should be sheltered from the burden of determining penalties (Reeve & Mulley, 2000), and from other harms that may result from participation in adversarial proceedings (Erez, 1994).

From the perspectives of victims' rights advocates, the new reforms are viewed as evidence of victims' progress toward the ultimate goal of full participation in the criminal process (Cassell, 1999; Erez, 1994; O'Hara, 2005), as well as a means for enhancing the therapeutic potential of participation while limiting the anti-therapeutic dynamics victims sustain during proceedings (e.g., Erez, 1999; Roberts & Erez, 2004; Chalmers, Duff & Leverick, 2007). Critiques continue to question these reforms, arguing that they are accomplished at the expense of defendants' rights, or are inherently in violation of due process (e.g., Hoyle, in this volume).

Research hitherto has seldom examined the impact of victim-centric reforms on victims, or examined how victims perceive the new participatory schemes of criminal justice. Applying a therapeutic jurisprudence perspective, this study attempts to shed light on how victims in the US experience their participation, input and expression rights against the backdrop of adversarial legal proceedings.

2. Victim Participation and Therapeutic Jurisprudence

The recent victim-centric initiatives are rooted in concerns about victims' invisibility or, more recently, their status as "ambiguous participants" (Edwards, 2004) within the exigencies of adversarial proceedings. Two major dimensions have dominated concerns with the welfare of victims who participate in proceedings: first, the fairness with which the justice system handles victims' interests and needs *vis a vis* the rights and preferences of offenders; and second, the impact that participation has on victims' psychological well-being.

Regarding fairness concerns, it is argued that crime victims—the parties who have suffered the brunt of harm in the criminal event—should have similar rights as those that accrue to offenders; in particular, victims should have a voice in proceedings (e.g., Erez, 1990; 1994) that goes beyond providing testimony or responding to closed questions (Herman, 2003). Exclusion from participation has long been a source of frustration for victims (Erez, 1994), who feel they have been denied "procedural justice"—the ability that litigants have to present their case to authorities (Lind & Tyler, 1988; Wemmers, 1996). Regarding the impact that various aspects of participation in proceedings have on victims' psychological well-being, victims have long complained about the burdens stemming from exclusionary criminal procedures, inadequate resources, organizational constraints, and criminal justice objectives that may conflict with their aims or needs (see Erez & Roberts, 2007).

This brief review suggests that victim well-being and satisfaction with justice are simultaneously affected by lack of participation and, where partaking occurs, the structure and terms of participation. It may be the case that reforms that provide for victim involvement in justice exposes them to procedures, interactions and experiences that are helpful and empowering, but also to those that prove onerous and disempowering. In the spirit of therapeutic jurisprudence (Wexler & Winick, 1996), therefore, we examine accounts describing the impact of recent victim-centric reforms, as related by criminal justice professionals and victims-turned-activists.

The experience of criminal justice proceedings is differentiated by both personal attributes of victims and the type of victimization sustained. Yet, the people with whom we spoke noted many common themes regarding the various effects associated with participation, irrespective of such differences. These themes highlight how the adversarial justice system can work to enhance victims' experiences with participation in proceedings, although—as we note in our conclusion—the extent to which such enhancements can occur will likely always be constrained by the adversarial practices that organize justice settings and proceedings.

3. Methodology

The data are derived from in-depth interviews with criminal justice professionals (N = 27) who have close contact with victims in the course of their daily work, and with a sample of victims-turned-activists (N = 7). The majority (88%) of the justice professionals handles criminal cases in a major urban jurisdiction in a Midwestern state and the remainder in a midsize town of the same state; the victim activists conduct their activities throughout this state. The professionals serve in different capacities in the criminal justice system and include three judges, eleven prosecutors, five probation officers, and eight court-based victim advocates. The latter collect victim impact statements (VIS), attend to victims' needs during the VIS presentation (or exercising the right of allocution) in court, and respond to victims' questions regarding their role in the court. At the time of the interview, the professionals' experience on the job ranged between twenty months to twenty years, with a median of six and a mean of eight years.

The professionals were contacted directly by the research team or were invited by their respective administrators to participate in a discussion about their observations of, and encounters with, crime victims in the justice system. Those who were willing to participate were interviewed in individual or focus group sessions that lasted between one and a half to five hours. Interviews were semi-structured, consisting of open-ended questions about how victims fare during the various stages of the criminal justice process; emphasis was placed in documenting how present day (reform era) victims compare with those of the past where participation is concerned. Interviewees were encouraged to raise any issues and offer contrastive scenarios depicting the range of victim welfare issues in the justice system.

The victims-turned-activists included the surviving family members of persons who had been murdered as well as victims of domestic violence. These interviewees were instructed to tell the story of their personal experiences with the justice system, which often entailed a narrative of disillusionment as well as one of seeking structural changes in the system conducive to a more victim-sensitive approach in the prosecution of criminal cases.

Interviews with both groups (i.e., professionals and activists) were recorded, transcribed and analyzed for recurrent themes that most typify how criminal justice proceedings, outcomes, and situational contingencies may be helpful or harmful to victims.

4. Results

The criminal justice professionals as well as victims-turned-activists with whom we spoke acknowledged that victim participation in adversarial systems of justice can result in both therapeutic and anti-therapeutic experiences. While most interviewees believe that participating in proceedings might be beneficial to the well-being of victims, the parameters envisioned in these scenarios vary; some argue that victim participation should be complete and unconditional, while others hold that participation might do more harm than good under certain circumstances. As the discussion below demonstrates, some of the underlying issues determining whether victim participation is helpful or harmful are endemic to adversarial proceedings; others are related to the victimization involved, the situational contingencies of proceedings, or the individual attributes of victims. The professionals we spoke with, however, could not specify a type of victim who would *most* benefit from participation in proceedings. Most thought that it was a personal matter that varied by the individual victim. In the words of one prosecutor:

> I personally don't think there is a demographic or a crime or any other variable like that that drives (the effect of participation on a victim). I think the victim drives that. I think it's determined by where the victim is emotionally.

4.1 Therapeutic Aspects of Victim Participation

The notion that justice professionals should view victim input as important to their decision making—a standard worth striving for—was subscribed to by interviewees from all groups. The therapeutic potential of victim involvement centered on three themes: victim empowerment, validation, and "moving on." These themes in turn were associated with direct participation, filing victim impact statements, and access to victim advocates.

4.1.1 Victim Voice and Empowerment

Following victimization, crime victims often feel that they have lost control over their lives. Empowerment pertains to victims regaining power and a sense of control, which can be facilitated by participation in the justice process and having one's voice heard. Opportunity for input can provide victims with a sense of agency and control that may have been damaged by the victimization. Knowing that their input is sought and valued by decision-makers in the case is likewise assuring, helping victims feel they are party to the proceedings, such as when someone in the prosecutor's office requests their input on a pending plea agreement.

Participation may result in self-insight regarding one's victimization, which can be in its own way empowering, allowing victims to look at their past victimization in a different light, and to re-interpret the experience and make changes in their lives. One prosecutor expressed the point in terms that were echoed by others:

> I think that the empowering thing that victims can get from working through the system is the appreciation that the system can be a tool and, even if it fails them, it is an experience which illustrates to them that the solving of the problem of the presence of violence in their lives is not dependent upon what someone else is necessarily going to

> do for them, but it's a matter of their coming up with a strategy that utilizes the tools that are available to them.

Allowing victims to play a role in the justice system not only provides them with a greater *sense* of agency; it can also empower them to influence the system's processing of cases in substantive ways. Victim involvement has the potential to prospectively influence the practices of personnel; knowing a victim's outcome preference can shape how a prosecutor handles a case at earlier stages. At the same time, prosecutors can use such conversations early in the case to align victims' preferences more closely with what is considered realistic or plausible within the terms of the law and the court culture. Indeed, the very notion that some outcomes are viewed as implausible or unrealistic may galvanize some victims to try and shape matters on an even larger scale, using their experience as victim-participants to seek broader changes in the justice system, such as through legislative activities, the pursuit of which may also prove empowering.

While most interviewees appreciated the potential that input into proceedings has for victim welfare, concerns were raised about how this practice might affect principles of criminal law in adversarial legal system, including the presumption of innocence. Victim voice and empowerment were not viewed as absolute. There are legal as well as strategic limitations that ought to be taken into account throughout the process; explaining the logic of these limitations often constitutes one of the more challenging encounters that occur between victims and justice professionals, as victims' built-up expectations about the extent of their voice and empowerment may have to be scaled back.

4.1.2 Validation and Vindication

An essential consideration determining victim welfare concerns the extent to which victims' experiences are validated, that is, recognized and taken into account. Attendance at court proceedings provides victims with a variety of symbolic and visual cues that help them sense whether their complaint is being taken seriously. Presence in court or at parole board hearings allows victims to observe their violator being addressed as a defendant and/or as a prisoner. Scenes such as the defendant being brought in wearing a jail/prison uniform, accompanied by law enforcement agents, or taken out of the courtroom in handcuffs, all serve to validate the victim complaint. Especially important for validation is hearing how the judge or the prosecutors "handle your story," i.e., relate what the defendant did (or is alleged to have done) to the victim. As one prosecutor put it:

> You have the prosecutor, all the people in the courtroom seeing what happens and it's like "Hey, they believed me." Because I think for a lot of victims there is the doubt. Even though they know they're telling the truth, other people don't really quite buy what they're saying and I think that does help victims a lot, more so than hearing about it.

Validation is particularly important for vulnerable victims such as children. One prosecutor provides the following example to describe the benefit of being present during court hearings:

> In all my child sex cases I would have the parents bring the children back down, especially if they are scared of the defendant, so they can see him being led away in handcuffs. Even if he was only doing time in the [county jail], they didn't understand that, I think just seeing the person in hand cuffs and walking away at the close of it, closes things for them.

The professionals also mentioned that victims who are present during sentencing hear the judges' sentencing remarks about convicted offenders, remarks that confirm the offenders' guilt, acknowledge the harm the victim has sustained, and support the victims' version of events.

Vindication is related to, but not coterminous with, validation. Vindication entails obtaining a sense of justice having been served by virtue of how the process moved forward and culminated in "just deserts," a standard that is itself subject to continually modified adjustments in victim expectations. While justice professionals are well aware that participation may pose emotional demands for victims, they also believe that at the end of the process victims will feel rewarded if the offender is found guilty. One prosecutor explains this sense of vindication:

> My observation would be that it was a difficult thing for them to do what they accomplished—you know it's like running a marathon race and getting to the end—it was a very difficult, tough thing for that witness to do, but they did it and as a result of what they did there was an evil person convicted and now he has to face the consequences. Sometimes I think it's retribution for what they had to sit through.

However, victims need not have a sense of vindication undone by virtue of a disposition or sentence with which they disapprove. Experiencing therapeutic effects through involvement in proceedings can also grow from continued involvement with the case, enabling the victim to acquire an understanding of "the rules of the game." Continued involvement with the case, a heightened understanding of locally relevant considerations that enter into justice decisions and practices, exposure to how one's story is being handled, and observations of the hardships that the defendant may have faced by virtue of the charges all shape a victim's sense of vindication.

4.1.3 Moving On

Although it is often said that one of the purposes of contemporary justice proceedings is to restore a sense of balance and help victims attain "closure," the professionals and victims with whom we spoke seemed wary of using the term closure in an unqualified way, preferring to talk in terms of helping victims "move on." Closure in this limited sense, professionals and victims agreed, is important and has therapeutic value for victims; closure in the sense of "getting over" victimization is more problematic. Criminal proceedings can influence how one moves on, but moving on need not be tied to a sense of vindication; it may be facilitated by the passage of time itself. In such circumstances, the mere finality of the case functions as a signal that this stage of their life is indeed over. As one prosecutor notes:

> It seems that with most of the victims, whatever point and whatever they're doing independent of the criminal case, they have a sense of moving on with their life; and you can tell the point at which someone—I'm no expert—but there's a point at which they need to move on with their life because what we do is not going to determine how or whether they move on with their life. Whether it's a sexual assault—and I do rapes and all that kind of stuff too, or a shooting or something like that—when they've moved on, the finality of the proceedings is the most important thing for them.

At times, the victim may have moved on before the case has been completely disposed. For these victims, involvement with proceedings may represent a reopening of semi-healed wounds; hence proceedings might disturb the sense of finality. A prosecutor relates such a story:

> I just had a case last week that had been going on for two years. By now this victim was—I don't mean to say she was cavalier about it, but—she has moved on so far from this being a factor in her life and the only thing she wanted was to not testify. Not because she was afraid or worried about the outcome or the chances of success or anything

> like that, but she had so clearly moved on from this that it would be a step back to have a trial for her.... so the finality, using that clear example, was obviously much more important than anything we did.

The notion that one might have passed a point where attaining finality took priority above all else, including vindication, was confirmed by a victim turned activist who said, "I think at that point I just didn't care no more. I didn't care what nobody thought. I just wanted this to be over with."

The passage of time can thus serve to re-orient how victims experience their encounters with professionals and justice settings, as their emotional evolution reshapes their sense of the means and ends of their involvement. One victim advocate describes what this progression can entail:

> My experience is the closer [in time] to the event, the angrier they are. The further they are removed from the incident itself, generally speaking, the more practical they become. They then begin to want to move on with their lives.

"Closure," therefore, must be understood in all its complexity, against the backdrop of a number of shifting considerations, ranging from victims' own changing internal states to the justice processes that are contemporaneous with the in and out of court experiences that victims are encountering.

4.1.4 Victim Impact Statements

The victim impact statement (VIS) is a vehicle through which many of the processes described above are expressed. The VIS (or its counterpart in England and Wales, the victim personal statement) allows victims to provide input into sentencing. In it, the victim describes the impact of the crime on his or her life, including physical, social, psychological, and financial harms. The VIS may be delivered either in writing, orally, or visually (in countries or jurisdictions that allow victim allocution or presentations through a video). Judges are encouraged, or in some jurisdictions required, to take the victim impact statement into account when determining sentence. Given the opportunity it provides for victims to voice their experiences, and its placement near the end of the justice process, the VIS has the potential to support empowerment, validation, and moving on; still, these outcomes are not guaranteed for those providing a VIS.

The VIS was mentioned by the interviewees as an important venue for the expression of victim voice. There was a consensus that it was therapeutic for the victims to tell their story and have a chance to explain the impact that a crime had on their lives. A probation officer who assists victims in writing the VIS notes that

> It gives them the opportunity to express themselves and let the judge know what happened in their own words—the judges get to hear their side of the story. If you have been injured, part of the empowerment is probably coming to court and telling your story.

Especially highlighted in statements by professionals is the idea of the VIS as a moment of confrontation between victim and offender, a moment of expressive truth, as it were, one in which the victim can state for the record, in a face-to-face encounter, the extent of the harm that the offender's actions have done. The importance of this expressive element can be combined with an empowerment aspect, as characterized by a judge:

> Sometimes they want to get it out, they want to just come up and look at the perpetrator/offender straight in the eye and say, "You did this to me and this was wrong and I'm not going to let you overwhelm me."

In cases where the victim and defendant are related, the VIS can be a method for conveying the concern that the former has for the latter. A prosecutor describes the spirit of this kind of encounter:

> Here is a grandmother-granddaughter misuse of credit card type of case. So the grandmother is the victim of the misuse of credit card. Granddaughter stole the credit card and used it for some reason. That grandmother pressed charges, wants to know that the granddaughter did something wrong—maybe it was for a drug habit or maybe it was for a boyfriend or something else—they oftentimes in there, they also have a chance to say, "I just love her and she needs to ..." this, this and that.

In this kind of circumstance, the VIS is offers a method for reaffirming the victim's hope that the offender will receive some kind of help that will "straighten them out." The victim can affirm that prosecution was pursued in the spirit of "tough love," and not to punish the offender, nor to extract a measure of compensation. The VIS functions like an extension of family counseling sessions at such poignant moments.

The VIS presentation takes on a more serious and heightened significance in cases resulting in a victim's death. When a victim dies, the right to speak is extended to the deceased's family members. The victim's family often uses this opportunity to express their rage about their loss and communicate with the person that has taken the life of their loved one. One mother whose daughter was five months pregnant at the time she was shot and killed by her husband, and who became an activist as a result of her experiences, described how she felt while providing victim impact information:

> I felt very strong that day, being able to say for the first time what we wanted to—I felt very strong. I got to say what I needed to. I think giving the impact statement just empowered us.

Professionals agree that it is important for relatives of deceased victims who feel the need to voice their anguish. In addition, the VIS is a mechanism through which they can speak *for* the departed victim, in a sense enabling his or her voice to be heard. A prosecutor describes how the families of murdered victims use the opportunity in this way:

> They talk about their loved one, if they've lost a loved one. They talk about how much that person meant to them. In one case they talked about how she grew up and how she impacted so many peoples' lives, what a good student she was, an athlete, a good sister, a daughter, a daughter with a grandchild and how devastating it was for them. A lot of times they want to represent the victim, they want that judge to know what that victim was all about.

A family of victim-activists reported creating a "memory book" that functioned both as VIS (it featured remembrances written about the murder victim by friends and family members that spoke to what the loss meant to them), and as archive, to be read long after the memoirists had passed:

> In forty years, all of us who are in the second generation are going to be gone, but our words will still be here. You're dealing with three generations here. Our parents—grandparents are still alive, but our daughter also has siblings, she has a niece behind, and younger cousins … We have a promise to all these younger siblings that as our generations pass, they are the ones who have to make sure [the murderer] is behind bars for forty years. They will be there for us and they know that these books are here. [The victim advocate] keeps one on record. [The state capitol] keeps one on record and they've promised us that. Parole has one, [the prosecutor] has one. They promised us that if there are not family or friends that can at that time be there, no matter what reason, they will have our words and there will be voices there for [our daughter].

In such cases, the VIS offers solace to the victims that their advocacy will have constituted an enduring legacy, both for surviving kin and for the criminal justice system. It represents the fruits of a project that should be preserved, a permanent presence to be taken into account in any future action that may arise in conjunction with the case.

While a few professionals highlighted that some victims may be "frustrated by having to tell their story again and again," the professionals agreed that most victims are interested in submitting a VIS and that few victims reject an opportunity for input into sentencing. A probation officer avowed:

> I don't even know that I've had anybody refuse. You tell them that they don't have to do it, but nonetheless they all do it. They want the judge to know how it's impacted them. A lot of times you don't know the impact of the injuries.

Nevertheless, an interesting gender imbalance was noted by our interviewees. Most professionals agree that women (who are often more verbal and emotionally expressive compared to men) are more likely to verbalize and submit a VIS. We were told that it is often angry women who want to speak, and that it is women who often ask that the violator be helped rather than penalized.

The professionals highlighted some problems that may arise when victim are speaking in court. While they are supportive of the empowerment that such appearances provide victims, some professionals want to avoid tensions that are produced when victims confront offenders. One prosecutor explains how judges attempt to defuse the confrontational moment that can accompany the voicing of a VIS:

> ... by avoiding the personal element of speaking directly and challenging somebody, the judge, I think—that's what he is attempting to do—controlling any personal challenges, anything like that. The atmosphere in a homicide sentencing or in a serious felonious assault sentencing is so tense, that I think by making them address a neutral party the judge is trying to dial down the level of tension.

The judicial exercise of control over the potentially cathartic moment in this way suggests that victims cannot take for granted their own expectations for empowerment, validation, and "closure" will be obtained in court, because ultimately court proceedings are subject to the judge's discretion, the exercise of which may appear unfathomable to the victims involved. Such judicial constraints may attenuate the therapeutic value of exercising one's right to allocution, particularly for victims who were not apprised of the possible admonition before preparing for their appearance.

4.2 *Anti-Therapeutic Effects of Victim Participation*

Although a number of therapeutic benefits may accrue from victim involvement in proceedings, our interviewees acknowledged that many aspects of participation have at times been harmful rather than beneficial for victims. Common procedures and contingencies identified as likely to prove onerous include: victim testimony, cross examination of the victim, plea agreements and sentencing. Process-based aspects that can have adverse effects on victims pertain to delays and continuances, overburdened court dockets and the pressure to move cases along, the complexity of the system and the victim's less than full understanding of the structure and procedures associated with the career of a criminal case in an adversarial legal system. Additional difficulties may also arise because of special relationships between the victim and offender, and owing to particular offender attributes.

4.2.1 Speaking in Court

Victims who become involved as parties to proceedings will often have to tell their stories again and again to different people in different circumstances—they may, as one prosecutor put it, "feel like it's the system giving them the run around, 'Geez, I just told the cops this, now I've got to tell you.'" This repeated, serial narration may in itself be "painful" to victims, because each re-telling entails revisiting the victimization, an especially onerous experience when the crimes center on sexual assault, according to the professionals who spoke with us.

Of the many auspices under which victims verbalize their experience with, and the impact of, the crime event, speaking in court is possibly the most emotionally fraught encounter according to the professionals we interviewed. Victims generally speak in court under two types of circumstances, either to offer sworn testimony or to offer a VIS. Taking the stand (to testify or to undergo cross-examination) was singled out as especially likely to "re-injure" victims, but the various forms of speaking in court should be viewed along a continuum of risk for anti-therapeutic effect, a continuum that corresponds to the intensification of adversarial discourse.

Although the giving of a VIS runs contrary to the usually adversarial nature of court proceedings, it can nonetheless prove to be a difficult or unsettling experience for victims. The professionals suggested that for some victims a VIS written before sentencing, whether to be read aloud or just read by the judge, was likely to be most helpful. Writing a VIS in itself is cathartic for victims and helps to address victim concerns about making a presentation in court; for those who prefer oral statements, it was suggested that having a written statement prepared may help reduce the stress of speaking in court. The hardships involved in presenting one's statement in court were described by one victim turned activist, though this hardship appeared to be tempered by the awareness that the VIS was primarily an expressive exercise:

> Once you get up there—like I'm stumbling with you—you can't do that in court. You've got to have your statement ready and get it over with. That intimidated me; I didn't want to take forever. But it didn't matter; I didn't have to worry about it too much because they were already saying what they were going to do.

The moment in time at which the VIS is given suggests that the matter is in a sense a *fait accompli.* Guilt will have been established independent of the VIS, although sentencing may have been influenced by it. Taking the stand to recount one's story under direct or cross examination by an attorney, when a finding of guilt has yet to have been established, and when the telling of one's story is structured through a series of questions, probes and responses, is a more freighted and burdensome endeavor. One is both reliving a difficult experience that one might rather not revisit, *and* one is having one's every utterance assessed for veracity and consistency. That one is forced to look eye-to-eye to the source of one's harm does not ease the burden.

Cross-examination can be especially unsettling for victims. Although there is protection from hostile cross-examination, the nature of the adversarial legal system gives this element of the process the potential to be deeply distressing. According to interviewees, defense attorneys will often use cross-examination to establish that victims are embellishing their testimony and/or failing to be truthful in their statements. Cross-examination procedures also require victims to respond to questions that they may find offensive or inappropriate. One judge explained:

> I think I've seen victims who were very uncomfortable with the examination of a defense attorney because the defense attorney's questions were suggesting that the victim was either exaggerating or manufacturing the testimony. The victims might look up and ask, "Do I have to answer that question?" And usually I say, "Yes you do, because it's relevant."

One victim advocate pointed to the very tone of proceedings as potentially harmful to victims:

> Cross is usually a lot more traumatizing (than direct) … the prosecutor calls the victim to the stand and the defense attorney gets up to

> question the victim; it's a lot more traumatizing usually because the tone of voice a lot of times is a lot more stern or harsh. The prosecutor will get up and kind of walk up over near the witness stand and kind of stand closer and use a tone of voice—have more of a dialogue, whereas the defense attorney will get up—most times—and state, "You said this, you did that, didn't you do ...?" you know, its just a lot more stern ...

Prosecutors, who are well aware of the heightened adverse effects of cross examinations on victims, expressed feeling helpless in preventing this practice and unable to protect victims from defense attorneys.

4.2.2 Plea Agreements/Sentencing

Court outcomes are often disappointing to victims. Offenders, in the judgment of many victims, are let off too easy or "get away with murder." Especially irksome to victims, in the experience of justice professionals, are plea agreements, often sprung on victims as "done deals." From the system's point of view, plea agreements are often called for because of the strength of evidence, and prosecutors may pursue such negotiations precisely to avoid disappointing victims, who might otherwise witness the offender's acquittal. Another consideration for prosecutors is that plea bargains may promote the benefit of precluding the need for victims to appear at trial:

> I have an idea what is the potential for beneficial therapeutic intervention and what is the potential for some traumatic outcome. There are cases where the victim is simply too fragile to proceed, in which case I'm going to try it and do everything I can to negotiate a plea.

The plea bargain might then be presented to a victim as the best possible, or most logical solution, rather than one that is being done for his or her emotional well being. When presented with the plea agreement in such terms, victim input may seem less integral and more perfunctory to proceedings, which can itself be upsetting to victims who have been led to believe that their preferences and injuries would be taken seriously.

The specificity and complexity of relevant sentencing guidelines that constrain prosecutors' plea bargaining strategies can further exacerbate the sense of injustice that victims feel when learning of the plea deal. As one prosecutor explained:

> How do you explain to a juror—to a victim, let's say somebody's son has been hit over the head with a 2 × 4, and they've been made com-

> atose, basically. For lack of a better term they're a vegetable. Now the most we can get them on is felonious assault, attempted murder has the same penalty, so it's not that big a deal. How do you explain to that person that the most they're going to be able to get is eight years in prison? When you can go into my house and try to steal my stereo and you get ten years, for an aggravated burglary, and nobody got hurt, I wasn't home. How do you explain that to them? I think that kind of thing is very frustrating for a victim. There's all kinds of rules as to—the rules have gotten much more convoluted and confusing in sentencing than it used to be.

In spite of the difficulty with which victims are coaxed into participating in the process, everything can come undone should the judge determine that the nature of the offense is not commensurate with the filed charge or negotiated plea. A prosecutor recalls such a memorable case:

> A domestic violence (DV) victim was afraid to be involved. Finally, after some time, she made a stand to be involved in the case, but because of this particular judge who doesn't think much of DV cases, the case was reduced; he said that if he tried it, it would be a not guilty. So it was reduced and the guy was given credit for time served and that was it. So here you have a person who has been a victim and there's several people who have been victims of this person, and finally they reach a point where they want to take a stand and then you have a Judge who kind of pooh-poohs it, saying "Oh well, I'm not going to take this seriously because I don't think DV is much of a crime." And this to someone who'd had her jaw broken on both sides? This side completely shattered so she had a steel plate in her face because he kicked her with his "clean work boots," is the way his son described it. And the judge actually said in sentencing "If this weren't domestic violence I'd send you to the penitentiary."

Even if the victim observes that the court delivers a sentence that is in keeping with the victim's sense of what is just, it is possible that the victim may experience a sense of guilt over it. Court officers we spoke to stated that they found this was most likely to happen with members of stigmatized minorities, who might feel torn between loyalty to an aggrieved population, and a need to see that justice is delivered:

> I see this particularly with minority women, it's very difficult—having the responsibility of putting another black man in the penitentiary, that responsibility—that's a lot of responsibility to lay on

> someone. These people willingly take this responsibility—"This is my fault that another black man is going to the penitentiary." It's a lot of pressure that's placed on victims.

For many victims, the VIS can carry special import in cases resolved through a plea bargain. Compared to a case that goes to trial, the plea bargaining process is not as likely to reveal all of the relevant facts for purposes of punishment. The VIS provides victims with the opportunity to have their physical and psychological injuries acknowledged, while also providing judges with a vehicle for understanding the injury or loss incurred by the victim, thereby informing whether the judge aligns with the terms of the plea negotiation. One judge explains:

> I rely a lot on what the victims tell me as far as the nature of the offense, especially in a plea situation, where we don't have a trial so I don't hear all the facts. Also, if I say it's likely that the sentence I'm going to give you is probation with no incarceration and then I hear from the victim or I read the victim impact statement and I say, whoa, this was a much more severe situation than you explained to me, I feel they have to go to prison.

4.2.3 Hardships Emerging from Participation in Proceedings

Participation in proceedings creates a number of potential burdens for victims in the United States. Having agreed to participate as a witness, often reluctantly and at times with fear of retaliation, victims confront logistical issues that can test their resolve and patience. One victim advocate offers an example from the more practical end of the hardships continuum:

> Prosecutors ... are out of touch with the fact that—because they get paid to come here and they have a place to park already—[ordinary] people are intimidated by coming downtown, people are inconvenienced by coming downtown, people lose time from their jobs to come downtown, people have to get childcare to come downtown, and then you ask for a continuance or things get disrupted and you just cavalierly say you have to come back again, as though that is just no big deal.

Adjustments in personal schedules and uncompensated monetary sacrifices do not exhaust the nature of the hardships victims confront once they become active in a case. The very complexity associated with case processing is itself demoralizing to victims, who can be at a loss to understand the legal constraints, justice requirements, and legalistic terminology that characterize a criminal case. Indeed, a limited understanding of the process is often behind victim dissatisfaction with their justice experiences. Victims develop an impression that "nothing is happening" owing to the lack of forward movement despite numerous court dates. Continuances were singled out as a major source of despair for victims. One prosecutor explained the ordeal that continuances represented for victims as follows:

> If a case is set for trial tomorrow and I'm the victim, I'm preparing myself now to testify. Then when you get in and find out the case is going to be delayed for another month, it is an emotional let down. They prepare, they go through it mentally what their testimony is going to be and then all the sudden, they don't have a chance to tell their story. It's frustrating for them.

Continuances can occur for a large number of legally justifiable reasons, but victims often feel demoralized by them, seeing them as yet another mark of how the "system" is unresponsive to victim concerns or overly concerned with the rights of defendants.

The court's social world provides another vector through which victims encounter situations that underline the distance between themselves and justice professionals. The court is an institution where justice professionals interact as "work groups" (Eisenstein & Jacob, 1977) exchanging information about everyday concerns, addressing each other in an informal manner, conversing amiably about mundane issues, and inadvertently displaying shared membership in a culture to which victims are outsiders. Such exchanges may be perceived by victims as indicative of an indifference or lack of respect towards the seriousness of the victim's plight. One victim activist notes therein

> (D)isrespect by defense attorneys and judges and prosecutors, speaking to one another in a familiar tone. That is so disrespectful to the families sitting there, that they refer to each other on a first name basis and that they even discuss something in the courtroom like a family vacation—that is so disrespectful.

Victims contrast such easygoing jocularity with their own sense of feeling shut out and unwelcomed by the system, as they experience court officers who seem rushed and disinclined to take the time to discuss the case with them in the detail they feel is merited.

The processing of cases through the justice system is subject to organizational objectives and constraints for which victims may lack appreciation. The strain resulting from the large number of cases processed through the contemporary criminal justice system necessitates that professionals work to "move the cases along" even as they interact with victims and their advocates. Consequently, in some instances a case will be plea bargained without any effort being made to solicit victim input. Pressure to move a case along can culminate in a less than sensitive approach to prosecutors' encounters with victims; victims are not imagining an aloof or emotionally distant orientation toward them at the hands of the prosecution. As one prosecutor put it:

> There still is quite a bit of bullying of victims that goes on. There is to a certain extent the necessity, I think, in the jobs that we have, to objectify the process and the crime and the victim. You cannot get emotionally involved in every one of these cases—even in any one of these cases to the degree that you might if you didn't have to do this everyday. Where, on the other hand, because we do this all the time, we do tend to get, sometimes, sort of jaded to the process.

Professionals, however, recognize that too overt an effort to solicit victim input can be counterproductive and prove stress-inducing for victims in certain circumstances—cases involving intimate partner violence, for example—where the victim may not want to be viewed as responsible for the prosecution's strategies. Thus, victims struggle with how low-key or how much of an activist they should appear to be during proceedings, especially since the defendant and the defendant's friends and family may be observing the victim's conduct in court. Victim participation, therefore, does not cease from being a stressful experience once the decision has been made to become involved; the unease simply is reframed in response to the particularities of the situations in which their participation plays out.

Some professionals are pessimistic about the potential for the system to better accommodate the needs of the victims, with some even suggesting instead that victims might be best advised to limit their involvement in proceedings. As one prosecutor put it, "I think the way to make it less traumatic or the easiest thing on the victims is having them here as little as possible."

5. Responding to the Challenge: The Function of the Victim Advocate

Justice professionals who interact with victims during proceedings have long felt the need to address the emotional aspects of victim participation in justice and to provide victims with necessary support. The introduction of victim advocates in the criminal justice process was one step toward this goal. Training justice professionals (prosecutors and judges) about victims' emotional concerns and justice related needs was another. Victim advocates within prosecution offices are specifically expected to "handle" victim emotions and alleviate prosecutors of this "burden." The legal system's incorporation of victim advocates and the emphasis on justice professionals' increased sensitivity to participating victims was uniformly supported by the interviewees as beneficial to all parties involved, and to the justice system as a whole.

Prosecutors and judges reacted to our broaching of the topic of therapeutic jurisprudence and victim participation by immediately citing the victim advocate, typically asking "Have you spoken with the victim advocates yet?" The professionals noted the multitude of services that victim advocates provide to victims and the justice system: Victim advocates serve as a resource to victims of crime, providing them with information, support, referral and advocacy; and they act as intermediaries with law enforcement and the criminal justice system to gather case processing information for victims. As one judge put it, "Just the fact that we have a victims' division now maybe made us more aware of what the victims go through. I think that really helped."

Prosecutors and judges alike noted the importance of providing victims with information about their legal rights or the availability of resources for victims, such as compensation and referrals, or explaining to them basic terminology regarding court structure, procedures or documentation:

> The advocates are a great innovation. I think what the victims want the most is to understand what's going on, the ability to see and hear what's happening, to have somebody explain to them what the process is all about, to be able to anticipate what's going to happen next. I think if you've been victimized and you're put into a position where you don't understand what's going on, it's like being victimized all over again. So I think it is important for them to understand the process and how it's going to affect them as they go through it and this is what victim advocates do.

The assignment of victim advocates to individual victims can provide a sense of constancy to victims as their case moves through the system, something many professionals believed to be particularly important in cases where victims suffer serious trauma, such as those involving rape. Such constancy may work to mitigate the bureaucratic impersonality that can often prove demoralizing to victims.

Victim advocates also benefit the prosecutors by helping to fulfill a role for which the prosecutors are not well-equipped, namely developing rapport-based relationships with victims, often referred to by prosecutors as "bonding." For their part, victim advocates agreed with this characterization of themselves as having a central role to play in softening the often harsh or cold realities of the courtroom. The victim advocates with whom we spoke, and who were spoken of by others, believed in the importance of working on behalf of individuals who were likely to have negative or distressing experiences with the law, thus playing an instrumental role in increasing therapeutic and mitigating anti-therapeutic outcomes, in spite of sometimes insurmountable or strained circumstances.

6. Discussion and Conclusion

Victim invisibility in the US criminal justice system has increasingly been addressed by various reforms that institutionalize victims' rights to information, protection, consultation and voice in proceedings. As our interviewees have noted, present-day victims are provided assistance in addressing the financial and emotional aspects entailed by their victimization; agencies and organizations both inside (e.g., victim assistance programs in the prosecutor's office) and outside the justice system (e.g., victim service-based NGOs) implement such assistance, and legal professionals (prosecutors, judges) are accountable to follow law and policy concerning victim participation and input. Victims are also informed about proceedings and justice officials consult them about their preferences or concerns, providing them opportunities to express their feelings about the violation and harm they sustained (see also Erez, 1999; Herman, 2005). Victim advocates within the justice system offer an important source of support and guidance for victims, and they often serve as an important buffer between the impersonal or "clinical" (Erez & Rogers, 1999) nature of prosecutorial case-handling and the victims' need for personal attention, acknowledgement, and validation.

Yet, while the reforms have alleviated many of the justice system's traditional drawbacks concerning victims, major sources of anti-therapeutic effects remain deeply rooted in the adversarial justice process, as was recognized by the professionals and victim-turned-activists who participated in this study. Although victim impact statements can be utilized without an actual victim appearance in court, victims are required to testify and submit to cross-examination—standard procedures of justice. Even benign questions during direct examination can produce stress and anger in victims; confrontational or hostile cross examinations by defense attorneys can be much more distressing. Victims who want their offenders to be held responsible for the victimization ordinarily cannot escape these procedures.

The organizational context of justice, with overburdened dockets and pressures to move cases along creates an additional source of frustration and dismay to victims, as do court practices (such as continuances) and legal terminology that victims find incomprehensible. Participation in justice proceedings requires victims to navigate these contingencies while they still manage the consequences of the traumata.

It is evident that three decades of activities on behalf of victims have made a difference for victims who participate in justice, reducing many of the antitherapeutic tendencies entailed by involvement in proceedings. However, to completely eliminate onerous experiences for victims, the legal system would have to abolish its adversarial justice principles. The narrow scope of experimentation with alternative justice models (e.g., restorative justice) in the United States, and the preliminary results regarding their effects on victims' welfare, suggest that such a development is highly unlikely to occur and that the new pains of participation in justice are likely to remain undisturbed for some time to come.

References

Ashworth, A. (1993). Victim impact statements and sentencing. *Criminal Law Review,* July:498–509.

Ashworth, A. (2000). Victims' rights, defendants' rights and criminal procedure. In A. Crawford and J. Goodey (Eds.), *Integrating a victim perspective in criminal justice: International debates* (pp. 185–204). Aldershot: Dartmouth.

Blumenthal, J.A. (2005). Law and the emotions: The problems of affective forecasting. *Indiana Law Journal,* 80 (2):155–238.

Cassell, P.G. (1999). Barbarians at the gates? A reply to the critics of the Victims' Rights Amendment. *Utah Law Review,* 1999(2):479–544.

Chalmers, J., Duff, P., and Leverick, F. (2007). Victim impact statements: Can work, do work (for those who bother to make them). *Criminal Law Review,* May:360–379.

De Hann, W. and Loader, I. (2002). On the Emotions of Crime, Punishment and Social Control. *Theoretical Criminology,* 6:243–353.

Doak, J. (2005). Victims' rights in criminal trials: Prospects for participation. Journal of Law and Society 32 (2):294–316.

Douglas, R., Laster, K., and Inglis, N. (1994). Victim of efficiency: Criminal justice reform n Australia. *International Review of Victimology, 3,* 95–110.

Edwards, I. (2004). An Ambiguous Participant: The Crime Victim and Criminal Justice Decision-Making. *British Journal of Criminology,* 44:967–982.

Eisenstein, J. and Jacob, H. (1977). *Felony justice: An organizational analysis of criminal courts.* Boston: Little, Brown and Co.

Erez, E. (2004). "Victim Voice, Impact Statements and Sentencing: Integrating Restorative Justice and Therapeutic Jurisprudence Principles in Adversarial Proceedings" *Criminal Law Bulletin*, Sept.–Oct.:483–500.

Erez, E. (1999). Who's Afraid of the Big Bad Victim? Victim Impact Statements as Victim Empowerment and Enhancement of Justice. *Criminal Law Review*, July:545–556.

Erez, E. (1994). Victim Participation in Sentencing: And the Debate Goes On ... *International Review of Victimology*, 3:17–32.

Erez, E. (1990). Victim participation in sentencing: Rhetoric and reality. *Journal of Criminal Justice, 18*, 19–31.

Erez, E. and Roberts, J. (2007). Victim Participation in Criminal Justice. In Robert C. Davis, Arthur Lurigio, and Susan Herman (3rd Edition) *Victims of Crime.* Newberry, CA: Sage publication.

Goodrum, S. (2007). Victims' rights, victims' expectations, and law enforcement workers' constraints in cases of murder. *Law and Social Inquiry*, 32 (3):725–757.

Henderson, L. (1985). The wrongs of victims' rights. *Stanford Law Review, 27*, 391–430.

Herman, J.L. (2003). The Mental Health of Crime Victims: Impact of Legal Intervention. *Journal of Traumatic Stress*, 16(2):159–166.

Herman, J.L. (2005). Justice from the Victim's Perspective. *Violence Against Women*, 11(5):571–602.

Karstedt, S. (2002). Emotions and Criminal Justice. *Theoretical Criminology*, 6(3), 299–318:299–301.

Lind, E.A. and Tyler, T. (1988). *The Social Psychology of Procedural Justice.* New York, NY: Plenum Press.

O'Hara, E.A. (2005). Victim Participation in the Criminal Process. *Journal of Law and Policy*. 13:229–247.

Orth, U. (2002). Secondary victimization of crime victims by criminal proceedings. *Social Justice Research, 15*, 313–326.

Orth, U. (2003). Punishment goals of crime victims. *Law and Human Behavior, 27*, 173–186.

Petrucci, C. (2002). Apology in criminal justice setting: Evidence for including apology as an additional component in the legal system. *Behavioral Science and the Law, 20*, 337–362.

Pizzi, W. (1999). Victims' rights: Rethinking our "adversarial system." *Utah Law Review* 1999*(2)*, 349–367.

Reeves H. and Mulley, K. (2000). The New Status of Victims in the UK: Opportunities and Threats (pp. 125–145) in A. Crawford and J. Goodey (Eds.) *Integrating a Victim Perspective in Criminal Justice.* Aldershot: Dartmouth.

Roberts, J.V. and Erez, E. (2004). Communication in Sentencing: Exploring the Expressive Function of Victim Impact Statements. *International Review of Victimology*, 10:223–244.

Rose, M.R., Nadler, J., and Clark, J. (2006). Appropriately upset? Emotion norms and perceptions of crime victims. *Law and Human Behavior*, 30 (2):203–219.

Sanders, A. (2002). Victim participation in criminal justice and social exclusion. In C. Hoyle and R. Young (Eds.), *New visions of crime victims* (pp. 171–22). Oxford: Hart.

Tobolowsky, P. (1999). 'Victim Participation in the Criminal Justice Process: Fifteen Years After the President's Task Force on Victims of Crime,' *New England Journal on Criminal and Civil Confinement*, 25(1):21–106.

Wemmers, J. (1996). Victims in the Criminal Justice System. Amsterdam: Kugler Publications.

Wexler, D. and Winick, B. (Eds.), *Law in a therapeutic key: Developments in therapeutic jurisprudence.* Durham, NC: Carolina Academic Press.

3

Accessory Prosecution in Germany: Legislation and Implementation[1]

Helmut Kury & Michael Kilchling

Abstract

The chapter describes the German system of accessory prosecution (Nebenklage) that provides the tool to integrate victims in criminal proceeding and allows victims to benefit from provisions on victim assistance, protection and restitution. It then analyzes the implementation of accessory prosecution in the country, and the perceptions by and the impact on those involved in such cases, with a particular focus on the victims. The results of interviews with victims, judges, public prosecutors, defense lawyers, victim lawyers acting as accessory prosecutors, and victim support workers (N = 18) on victim participation are then reported. In general, all professional groups expressed their satisfaction with the present procedural options available for victim participation in Germany. Interviews of victims reveal an explicit interest in their offenders' conviction and satisfaction with the possibility for attending the full procedure. The authors come to the conclusion that there is considerable evidence that the Nebenklage can contribute to reducing or even preventing secondary victimization in the course of the prosecution process. Both the presence of the (personal) lawyer as a supportive figure and the (enhanced) status of a process party can have protective function delivering feelings of relative security. It seems that in such a setting that is protective and symbolic at the same time, even traumatized victims can have the possibility to attend the trial and to participate on an advanced status that privileges the victim compared to other ('mere') witnesses.

---

1. The authors would like to express their gratitude to Stephan Bischoff and Erika Koch for carrying out the interviews of the study.

1. Introduction

Until the middle of the 19th century, the status of the victim in criminal proceedings had been marginalized in conjunction with the increasing governmental monopolization of prosecution and sanctioning of the offender. In the course of this development, the role of the victim had been gradually reduced to that of the witness who was needed only as a piece of evidence during trial and prosecution (Weigend, 1989: 93 et seq.). In Germany, however, this deficit had already been taken notice of rather early when the *Reichsstrafprozessordnung* ("Code of Criminal Procedure of the German Empire") was passed in 1877. As a consequence, particular legal instruments such as, in particular, accessory prosecution ("*Nebenklage*"), private prosecution (applied in cases of defamation mainly) and the procedure to force the prosecution to make a charge ("*Klageerzwingungsverfahren*"), were introduced, which allowed the victim to participate more actively in the criminal proceedings. Still to date, these are the main victim-related instruments, amongst which accessory prosecution developed to become the most relevant one.

It should be noted, however, as has been clearly pointed out by Weigend (1989: 97 et seq.), that these instruments have to be considered as largely coincidental products, results of clashes of interest, sporadic (but hardly rationalized) historical reminiscences and if nothing else, "parliamentary compromises". Representing the (former) absolute penal power of the 19th-century state and its absolute penal theory (Kilchling, 2002: 58), the legislature's intention at the time was quite obviously not a fundamental reinforcement of the injured party within the criminal proceedings. Weigend (1989: 131 et seq.) notes that "the *Nebenklage* as implemented in the Code of Criminal Procedure of 1877 merely had an accessory function in conjunction with the private prosecution and the *Klageerzwingungsverfahren*, two legal institutions which by themselves had little practical relevance."

Whereas the private prosecution intends to keep victims of petty crime off the public prosecution system, the purpose of the *Klageerzwingungsverfahren* is to safeguard the functioning of the traditional German principle of mandatory prosecution ("principle of legality") in general rather than the interests of the individual victim. In other words, it is another instrumentalization of the victim for the system's sake. Seen from such a perspective, the concept of accessory prosecution, in the course of the modern victim movement, has radically changed into an instrument that is clearly provided as *the* main participatory option for victims interested in *actively* contributing to the trial of their criminal.[2] In recent years, not only was the list of crimes that qualify for accessory prosecution further expanded (see below, 2.); also in court practice it gained increasing significance (Kilchling, 2006). Meanwhile, other continental jurisdictions have similar instruments, such as the *acusación particular* in Spain or the *partie civile* in France.[3]

In the following, the legal development of the accessory prosecution will be briefly illustrated, previous research findings will be outlined and, in the main part, the results of our own explorative survey will be presented, concluded by a discussion.

2. Legal Developments

It is certainly an effect of the emergence of victimology of the late 20th century that the development of legal institutions such as accessory prosecution was increasingly promoted. In the past, the status of victims of crime was not considered to be a serious issue, neither in research nor in practice (Kaiser, 1996: 1055). However, in the course of the growing attention to the victims, the necessity to prevent secondary victimization during preliminary proceedings and trial became evident (Hirsch, 1989: 700). As a consequence, the protection of victims has been strengthened, for example during interrogation. The development was accompanied by a general improvement of procedural rights such as accessory prosecution. Thus, victim policy in Germany was never reduced to the issue of victim protection; it also includes, as an additional element, legal options (so-called subjective rights) for active victim involvement. For a while, these participatory elements as provided by the *Nebenklage*, were even deemed to be insufficient. As Kaiser (1996: 1057) once emphasized, the "[existing form of] accessory prosecution [...] doesn't sufficiently bring to bear the interests of the victim within the criminal proceedings. A generally improved victim status would make it entirely superfluous."

This has drastically changed. According to Hassemer & Reemtsma (2002: 85), "*Nebenklage* today is the legal institute in which legislature has put the highest hopes during recent years in its efforts to fortify the rights of crime victims."

In Germany as well as in many other countries, the increasing interest in the victims' perspective also included the issue of state compensation. With

---

2. Cf. the shift from Hans von Hentig's (1948) notion of "the criminal and his victim" to Hans Joachim Schneider's (1979) "the victim and his criminal" ("*Das Opfer und sein Täter*").

3. For further comparative perspectives, see Brienen & Hoegen (2002).

reference to the principle of solidarity, the German legislature recognized the necessity, as has been the case in other countries before, to financially support victims of serious crimes and felonies. This led to the introduction of the first Victim Compensation Act of 1976[4]—long before European jurisdictions were obliged by European framework legislation to implement such rules.[5] Since then the law has been modified several times. The latest amendment was enacted in 2009[6] when the territory principle, according to which victims can only receive state compensation if victimized within the country, was abolished at least for victims of terrorism.[7] In 2005, 22,794 applications were filed, though 9,195 of these claims have been declined (Schwind, 2009: 434).

In December, 1986, the so-called Victim Protection Act was passed, which came into effect on April 1st, 1987.[8] The law's objective is "to guarantee the victim an assured procedural position" (Böttcher, 2007: 72). The primary achievement of this new piece of legislation was the detachment of accessory prosecution from private prosecution. Thereby, accessory prosecution evolved from its original status "as a mere 'accessory' to private prosecution and the *Klageerzwingungsverfahren*" (Weigend, 1989: 159) into an "independent legal institution" (Barton, 2006: 211). In addition, the possibilities for victims to sue the offender for payment of financial restitution in the immediate course of the criminal trial—so-called adhesion procedure—were revised and improved.

The respective provisions allow for a better standing of the victim during criminal proceedings, for instance concerning protection from questions regarding privacy and intimacy, concerning the removal of the accused from the courtroom and the exclusion of the general public, access to the case files, assignment of an attorney during preliminary proceedings and the trial, and the active participation in the trial as *Nebenkläger* ("accessory prosecutor"). As accessory prosecutor, the victim has the role that is comparable to that of a joint plaintiff, i.e., autonomous from the public prosecutor as well as from any other

---

4. Law Concerning the Compensation of Victims of Violent Crimes ("*Gesetz über die Entschädigung für Opfer von Gewalttaten—OEG*") of 15.5.1976, BGBl. I, p. 1181.

5. Cf. European Convention on the Compensation of Victims of Violent Crimes of 24.11.1983; E.U. Framework Decision 2001/220/JHA of 15.03.2001 on the Standing of Victims in Criminal Proceedings, O. J. L 82, p. 1; E.U. Directive 2004/80/EC of 29.4.2004 Relating to Compensation to Crime Victims, O. J. L 261, p. 15.

6. Third Act Amending the Victim Compensation Act ("*Drittes Gesetz zur Änderung des Opferentschädigungsgesetzes—3. OEGÄndG*") of 25.6.2009, BGBl. I, p. 1580.

7. For further details, see Albrecht & Kilchling (2009).

8. [First] Victim Protection Act (Law Concerning the Improvement of the Victims' Status in Criminal Proceedings—"*Opferschutzgesetz*") of 18.12.1986, BGBl. I., p. 2496.

participants in the trial. Early research suggests however, that the implementation initially brought little practical change to the status of the victim (Kaiser, 1992: 13 et seq.). This was mainly due to the unsatisfactory resolution of the question of costs (Staiger-Allroggen, 1992: 134; Rieß, 1984: 130 et seq.; Weigend, 1984: 791; Schünemann, 1986: 200). According to the 1986 act, all legal costs of the accessory prosecutor, including the attorney fees, are considered as regular procedural costs that are borne with the offender in case of conviction only. Therefore, the victim has to bear the financial risk of acquittal (unless he or she is poor and qualifies for legal aid).

A further consolidation of the victims' position came in 1998 when the Witness Protection Act was enacted.[9] A major goal of the law was to improve the possibilities to protect particular witnesses—so-called victim-witnesses, including indirect victims, and other witnesses as well—during interrogations. A number of spectacular trials dealing with cases of sexual abuse of children in the course of which demands for a better protection of such witnesses were voiced had a considerable influence on the elaboration and implementation of the law. Especially children and juveniles are supposed to benefit from the new provisions. In particular, proxy interrogations via CCTV as well as support and the possibility for assistance to witnesses and victims were introduced, the latter providing, for the first time, the possibility to make use of a constant, so-called psycho-social care by victim assistance agents, including escort during testimony in the courtroom. Combined concepts of legal assistance plus extra-legal attendance and care were developed in particular for victims of sexual and other violent crimes.[10]

In 2004, the [First] Victim Rights Amendment Act[11] came into effect. In particular, the afore-mentioned option for legal and extra-legal assistance was transformed into a real subjective right entitling the victim to be accompanied by a support person at any time. In addition, the adhesion procedure for obtaining compensation was further consolidated, the regulations concerning videotaping of interrogations were further amended, and a provision was added which allows victims to claim for advance information about release or earlier release of offenders in custody, their relocation into an open facility or other forms of (temporary) leave. Last, but not least, the 2004 act introduced the new figure of the so-called 'privileged victim attorney' which is of particular im-

---

9. Law Concerning the Protection of Witnesses during Criminal Proceedings and the Amelioration of Protections of Victims ("*Zeugenschutzgesetz*") of 30.4.1998, BGBl. I, p. 820.

10. For more details, see Kilchling (2006).

11. Law Concerning the Fortification of Victims' Rights during Criminal Proceedings ("*Opferrechtsreformgesetz*") of 24.6.2004, BGBl. I, p. 1354.

portance in our context here. Based on this amendment, a privileged subgroup of the victims who are formally eligible for accessory prosecution[12] now have the exclusive right to have their attorney officially assigned, at the expense of the state. Hence for the first time, a select group of victims really have the free choice to enjoy all of their procedural rights without any further financial risk. As a first step, this position was granted to victims of sexual crimes, victims of attempted homicide, bereaved relatives in cases of homicide, victims of selected other felonies, and all victims below 16 years of age. Through the Second Victim Rights Amendment Act of 2009[13] this group of privileged victims was slightly enlarged. Most significant is the increase of the age limit which now includes all juvenile victims younger than 18. The amendment also includes a general extension to all victims who are unable to exercise their procedural rights without professional legal counseling, or victims for whom non-eligibility would actually be unbearable, independent of the concrete type of crime.

After a long and controversial political conflict, finally, accessory prosecution was also made available, under certain conditions, in criminal proceedings against juvenile offenders.[14] For a long time, this had been deemed unreasonable in light of the strong educational rationale of the German youth justice system. Simultaneously, additional crimes against personal integrity and liberty such as stalking and forced marriage were included in the catalogue of crimes that qualify for *Nebenklage.*

After all these various amendments, the following victims are currently eligible to exercise their rights as an accessory prosecutor:

> (1) All victims of sexual crimes, human trafficking, assault, robbery and other violent offences against personal integrity including attempted homicide, all major crimes against personal liberty including extortion, kidnapping and hostage-taking, aggravated coercion and indecent assault including forced marriage, stalking, and some status offences in the context of the Protection of Violence Act;[15]

---

12. Literally speaking, and contrary to the formal terminology, it is the victims (!) who are privileged here, not their attorney …

13. Second Law Concerning the Fortification of Victims' Rights during Criminal Proceedings ("2. *Opferrechtsreformgesetz*") of 29.7.2009, BGBl. I, p. 2280.

14. Introduced by the Second Law Concerning Modernization of Criminal Justice ("2. *Justizmodernisierungsgesetz*") of 22.12.2006, BGBl. I, p. 3416.

15. Law Improving Civil Protection against Violence and Stalking and Regulating the Removal from the Marital Home ("*Gewaltschutzgesetz—GewSchG*") of 11.12.2001, BGBl. I, p. 3513.

(2) close family members of victims who were killed, i.e., the most affected group of indirect victims;
(3) all those who successfully passed a *Klageerzwingungsverfahren*;[16]
(4) all other victims when exceptional circumstances apply; this general clause explicitly specifies cases in which the victim suffers from serious consequences.

Not included are any crimes against property. As a consequence, victims of burglary are not eligible.[17] From a victimological perspective, this exclusion which is based on the assumption that material damage should be exclusively covered by private insurance companies appears more than questionable. It neglects the impact of this type of victimization, in particular the significant psychological consequences.[18] It has to be monitored if the courts will make use of the afore-mentioned new general clause (4) in order to admit victims in such cases as well.

3. The *Nebenklage*

Before evaluating in more detail the potential therapeutic impact of the *Nebenklage* on the participants and particularly, the victims, let us add just a very short outline of the general concept of accessory prosecution. Based on the inquisitorial process model, civil law jurisdictions such as Germany can easily integrate a third process party without disturbing the balance between prosecution and defense[19] which is an inviolable element of the common law trial.[20] And in fact, the position of the accessory prosecutor can be characterized as a quasi party status. Unlike in the context of the victim impact statement, which can be seen as a mere symbolic tool that leaves the structural exclusion of the victims untouched, the accessory prosecutor is, more or less fully, integrated in the entire proceeding (see *Figure 1* below).

More generally, the possible extent of integration of the victim in the procedural setting is influenced by the basic process model applied in a certain jurisdiction. As is further visualized in the figure below, the direction of com-

16. See above, 1.

17. According to art. 243 of the German Criminal Code, burglary is an aggravated from of theft. Under such a concept, the breach of privacy which often is the most burdening factor for the victims more or less fades away.

18. For more details, see Kilchling (1995).

19. For more details, see Brienen & Hoegen (2002).

20. For more details, see Erez & Wemmers, in this volume.

*Figure 1: Adversarial versus Inquisitorial Process Structure**

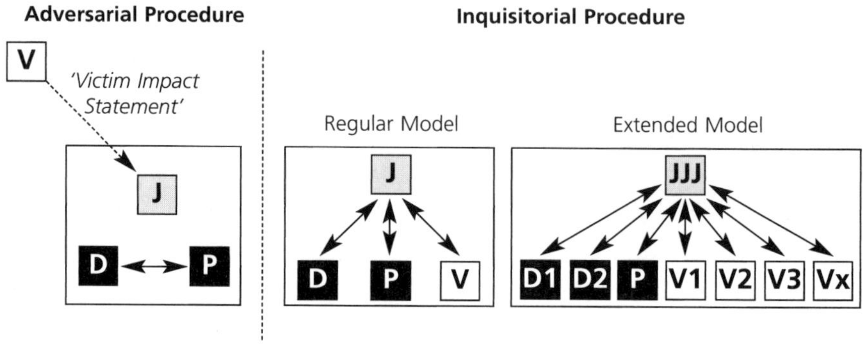

* The different roles of participants: (Defense, Judge, Prosecution and Victim).

munication is one of the most significant differences between the two models. In contrast to the horizontal courtroom action of the common law procedure, the inquisitorial (civil law) process is vertically structured. This setting allows a more flexible arrangement of parties, also for extended situations with more than the 'regular' number of individuals participating. From its basic design, the inquisitorial model ideally allows for an unlimited number of participants; limits may only arise from aspects of controllability and practicability (in terms of limited courtroom space, etc.[21]). In the big Nazi trial against *John Demjanjuk* who was tried in Munich in winter, 2009/10, for having contributed to the murder of 27,900 Jewish prisoners in the former concentration camp of *Sobibor*, some 40 surviving victims were admitted as accessory prosecutors.[22] In all such cases, it is the responsibility of the presiding judge to balance out the rights and actual contributions of the parties.

The accessory prosecutor can exercise his or her rights personally, or together with an attorney, or fully represented by the attorney. They have by and large the same pre-procedural and procedural rights as the prosecutor; only the post-procedural rights are somewhat limited. More concretely, victims acting in that role have full access to all case files at the pre-procedural stage, including all pieces of evidence. During trial their privileged position becomes also visible with their own desk placed in the front part of the courtroom, close

21. If necessary it can happen that trials are relocated from the court building into a city hall, congress center or other premises allowing for adequate placing of more than the regular number of process participants on stage.

22. FAZ of 22.12.2009.

to the magistrates' bench, right beside the public prosecutor, and face-to-face to the defense desk. Unlike other victims and witnesses, they have the right to be permanently present during the trial, even before they have given their own testimony. They can fully participate in and contribute to the proceedings, in particular during the examination and cross-examination of the accused, of other witnesses, and authorized experts. They can ask questions at any time, and file procedural motions. And finally, they have the right to make their own final pleading including proposal of a concrete sentence, after the prosecutor's and before the defense's; even a final reply to the defense plea is possible. After the verdict they have the right to make an appeal, independent from prosecution and defense. However, remedy is limited to the extent that the reclamation has to be based on legal considerations; a non-substantiated plea for a different (harsher) sentence alone is not admitted. *Nebenklage* action can be initiated at any time, and stage. It is still possible even after the trial, just for the purpose of remedy. It is the victim's free choice to exercise this right and he or she can chose to abstain from any such action.[23]

4. Previous Studies on Accessory Prosecution

Despite the increased significance of accessory prosecution the current state of research is unsatisfactory. Hardly any research on the action of the accessory prosecutors' attorneys is available in the criminological literature. In the past, the *Nebenkläger* quite often was wrongly regarded as an 'auxiliary' to the public prosecutor and supposed to have the same interests, i.e., the enforcement of the public demand and power to punish. Others emphasize the significance of the *Nebenklage* in protecting the victim from further, secondary victimization. According to Barton (2006: 217) it is largely unexplained what the *Nebenkläger* attorney is supposed to achieve during criminal proceedings. The role of the attorney appears to be "burdened with conflict and can implicate problems of acceptance, including with fellow attorneys" (Barton, 2006: 218).

In his study based on the analysis of case files, Kühne (1986: 98) concluded that accessory prosecution serves primarily as a preliminary to pressing civil claims. It appears to have no major influence on the probability of a conviction or the sentence.

Since for a long time accessory prosecution held, as shown above, only a peripheral status to the point of considering its abolishment altogether, nowa-

23. For more details, see Kilchling (2006).

days its significance has risen significantly. Hüsing (1983: 91 et seq.) found in her study, also based on analysis of case files, that in approximately one out of three cases eligible for *Nebenklage* (32.8%) it was actually exercised by the victims. It was most frequently used by victims of bodily injury caused by negligence and relatives of victims of involuntary manslaughter. Moreover, in trials concerning bodily injuries caused by traffic violations accessory prosecution is frequent. In about two thirds (64.3%) of the examined cases with accessory prosecution the cause was in fact a traffic accident. The more serious an injury proved to be the more readily accessory prosecution was exercised by the victim. Like Kühne, she also did not find any verifiable influence of accessory prosecution on the outcome of the trials. In 99% of the examined proceedings, the accessory prosecutor employed the service of an attorney. He accessed the records in 80% of the cases, participated otherwise rather passively in the proceedings, contributed hardly any evidence, and legal remedies were initiated extremely rarely. The scope of defense of the accused remained largely untouched. The additional financial burden for the defendant caused by the legal costs of the *Nebenklage* however was considerable.

Kuhlmann (1982: 311 et seq.) also found in his study that the accessory prosecution had hardly any affect on the outcome of the trial. At the same time, the author alludes to the increased financial burden for the accused. His analysis of records showed that a motion to take evidence originated in only 4.8% from the *Nebenkläger* attorney. The pleading didn't differ from that given by the public prosecutor in none of the trials examined. Schulz (1982: 130 et seq.) analyzed the official criminal court statistics from 1971 to 1979 and came to the conclusion that the frequency of attendance of accessory prosecutors at trials indicates a strong interest among victims in active participation. In addition, he found that within the scope of accessory prosecution influence on the trial is exercised to a great extent. The right to make a motion to take particular evidence has been made ample use of. The respective motions were generally accepted by the courts. He further observed a prolongation effect of *Nebenklage* on the trials at local courts, though the difference is only slight. Sessar (1980: 331) too, found in his analyses that attorneys of accessory prosecutors did not have significant influence on the courts' ruling on serious crimes. He even concludes that the sentence in cases with accessory prosecution were more lenient than in the control group.[24]

According to information released by the Federal Statistical Office concerning trials at criminal courts during the period from 1982 to 1998, the frequency of accessory prosecution at local courts decreased from about 3% in 1982

---

24. For further details of the studies referred to here, see also Barton (2006).

to approximately 1% in 1998. In contrast to this, during the same period the frequency regarding accessory prosecution at the district courts increased from 9.4% to 18%. In the range of serious crimes the increase is significant, in trials concerning sexual offenses and attempted homicide, accessory prosecution has been on the rise since the passing of the 1987 Victim Protection Act. The number of victims of sexual harassment and rape as well as relatives of victims of intentional and involuntary manslaughter who participate in the trial as accessory prosecutor is well above average: Every second trial concerning rape was the subject to accessory prosecution (Federal Statistical Office, 1982–1998; Niedling, 2005). Even after 1998, accessory prosecution at district courts has further increased significantly. In recent years, in more than 20% of all district court trials *Nebenkläger* (attorneys) were present (Barton, 2006; Kilchling, 2006). In absolute figures, this was the case in some 2,400 of ca. 11,400 such trials of 2008 (Federal Statistical Office, 2008). And this is in fact the most relevant statistical figure since the more serious crimes which make the main part of crimes that qualify for accessory prosecution, go directly to the district courts in first instance. Considering further that only a part of the trials conducted there include an eligible crime it can be assumed that the actual percentage of victims exercising their right as *Nebenkläger* is considerably higher (Kilchling, 2006). It is also interesting to look at the origin of the legal remedies: of ca. 54,500 first instance appeals in 2008, about 49,700 were filed by the accused, some 11,300 by the public prosecutor, and only 358 by the *Nebenkläger* (Federal Statistical Office, 2008).

Due to the notable legislative changes implemented in recent years, the earlier studies referred to above cannot be transposed directly to the present situation. However, more recent studies are rare, and they focus on isolated issues mostly. Staiger-Allroggen (1992: 157) found a considerable victim dissatisfaction in regard to the commitment of their attorneys. Observation of trials showed an "insignificant" role of the accessory prosecutors' attorneys. Kaiser (1992: 246 et seq.) examined the victims' status within criminal proceedings right after the implementation of the 1987 Victim Protection Act and conducted interviews with lawyers and *Nebenkläger*. As could be expected at that time, accessory prosecution was more popular with attorneys than with judges and public prosecutors. The latter viewed accessory prosecution as a factor of delay of the proceedings and additional workload. Positive aspects such as greater satisfaction of the victims and positive effects on the sentences were found as well. However, of the victims interviewed, more than half did not express any interest in active participation in the proceedings, about 28% expressed a general interest in active participation, and only 14.3% of the respondents had actually joined the trial as *Nebenkläger*.

Dölling et al. (2000: 126 et seq.) analyzed the records of district court trials from 1994 and found that in more than 11%, one or more *Nebenkläger* had joined the suit and most of them were represented by an attorney. Only in exceptional cases did more than one victim act as accessory prosecutor. According to this study, accessory prosecution led to a lengthening of the trial. In a more recent study, Niedling (2005) examined records of the district court of Nürnberg/Fürth of 1997 and conducted additional interviews with the victims. Barton (2006) judged these data as "notedly heterogeneous" and "of little substance." Important criticisms are especially the lack of representativeness and the fact that the results don't reflect the status quo of legislation. In summary, Barton concludes his overview on the state of *Nebenklage* in Germany that its legal reality is empirically explored on a rudimentary level at best. "Criminological research has not yet embraced the issue: The professional practice of accessory prosecution presents itself as a terra incognita on the map of criminologists" (Barton, 2006: 222).

In Albrecht's (2005) comprehensive overview of current research relating to criminal proceedings, no relevant piece of empirical research on accessory prosecution is recorded.

5. Explorative Study

In our new explorative study, we analyzed how far the intentions of the different initiatives of the German legislature concerning the protection of the victim within criminal proceedings have reached their goal. In other words, how far they effectively contributed to the satisfaction of the victim. It is a qualitative study. Three representatives of each of the relevant participants in a trial with accessory prosecution were interviewed: 1) judges, 2) public prosecutors, 3) defense counsels, 4) *Nebenkläger* attorneys, 5) representatives of victim support organizations, and 6) victims themselves. In all, 18 people were interviewed. The interviews were guided by a half-standardized questionnaire and conducted by two students in winter, 2005/06. All interviews were completely recorded on audiotape and evaluated by content analyses.[25] Anonymity was guaranteed to all of the respondents. The density and openness of the responses is a strong indication of the validity of the findings. The analysis has been conducted in southwest Germany (Freiburg and vicinity), results may thus be influenced by a regional practice. The victims were a woman who was

25. For more details on methodology, see Früh (2004), Brosius & Koschel (2003), Rössler (2005) and Bischoff & Koch (2006: 68 et seq.).

victimized by aggravated assault and two men, one of them victim of an attempted homicide, the other victim of a homosexual rape.

In the following the most essential findings of the explorative study will be presented.

5.1 *Assessment of the Psychological Benefits of Accessory Prosecution for the Victim in Practice*

According to all respondents, it is possible for a *Nebenkläger* attorney to assist his or her client during criminal proceedings in many ways. In doing so, emotional assistance, transfer of information regarding procedure and backgrounds of the trial as well as protection against attacks by the defense are of psychological benefit for the victim. The participatory status connected with accessory prosecution, which grant the victim the status of subject to the proceedings, can give him or her a feeling of control, reduce feelings of helplessness and incapacity and can thus prevent secondary victimization. It has been clearly pointed out from different sides that the victim in a trial formally eligible for accessory prosecution should be actively informed about this right, but that the decision whether or not to exercise this right should not be influenced by them. Basically, participation of the victim is considered to be useful especially in cases of serious offenses. Most attorneys and representatives of victim support organizations, however advise every eligible victim to take legal action in terms of accessory prosecution. They also hold the view that accessory prosecution cannot have a negative impact on the victims psyche. The other groups in this study expressed more reserved views about this.

5.2 *Assessment of the Impact of Accessory Prosecution in This Study on the Course of the Trial*

Nebenkläger attorneys and staff of organizations concerned with victims' assistance assume a lengthening effect on trials due to accessory prosecution. This assumption, however, is not shared by the other groups. A delay of the trial and additional workload for the court is seen especially when an attorney becomes active in the trial. Judges consider the additional workload as insignificant. A large majority of the respondents consider that the *Nebenklage* offers few possibilities to exercise a concrete impact on the trial while significantly greater costs are deemed to be a regular result from the victims' participation.

5.3 Assessment of the Impact of Accessory Prosecution on the Sentence

The majority of respondents assessed impact on the concrete sentencing outcome of the trials as rather insignificant. At the same time, however, as emphasized especially by attorneys and judges, the impact of emotional appeals by the victim party is hardly to be measured and could well have a subtle influence on sentencing.

5.4 Assessment of the Danger of Secondary Victimization during the Trial

The jurists questioned unanimously felt that German judges knew about and felt attentive to the dangers of secondary victimization. The intention of improving the protection of the victim seems to have arrived in legal practice. What remains unclear, however, is how far this knowledge is put into practice in individual cases. The questioned parties reported on consequences they personally drew regarding their own behavior during trial. Victims support organizations also reported a significant improvement of the relations between justice agents and victims in the context of criminal proceedings. At the same time jurists participating in the proceedings point out the principal limitation of victim protection with regard to the task of ascertaining the truth during the trial.

5.5 Assessment of Behavioral Patterns of Participants with a Positive Impact on Victims Participating

When asked for concrete behaviors that may have a positive impact on victims participating in the trial, the following aspects were explicitly mentioned: During preliminary proceedings the victim should be questioned only once and, if possible, by a competent person. Furthermore, the interrogation should be videotaped. Faulty investigations and mistakes by the police should be avoided. In suitable cases, the possibility of plea bargaining transactions between judges, public prosecution and defense should be used to avoid a testimony by the victim. According to the current procedural rules, neither the victims nor their attorneys have to be heard in advance, nor do they have the right to participate in the decision. At the moment, this is certainly the most problematic deficit in the *Nebenklage* powers (Kilchling, 2002: 61, with further references). During the interrogation in the course of the trial aggressive and intrusive questioning should be avoided; should it happen anyhow the judge should intervene. During interrogations of victim witnesses the meaning and necessity of questions should be explained. Furthermore, they should have the possibility to give an extensive report on their victimization and not only a short version or, even worse, being forced to remain silent about all of those details that seem to be of no formal-legal relevance. Also the exclusion of the public was considered to be helpful. And finally, all judicial decisions should be comprehensible for nonprofessionals or explained. All in all, the respondents acknowledge the balancing position of the judge between impartiality, the desire to unveil the truth and the duty to care for the victim as a very difficult task. In addition, a general trend towards victim-friendly strategies of defense counsels is seen. It seems as if nowadays, such victim-friendly defense behavior is exercised in the expectation that it might be beneficial for the client.

5.6 Assessment of Behavioral Patterns of Participants with a Negative Impact on Victims Participating

Public prosecutors and criminal judges couldn't identify many of such negative factors. It doesn't come as a surprise that especially actions initiated by the defense counsel are being named here, like the challenging of the credibility of victim witnesses, or the allegation of a share of responsibility for the victimizing event, or the trivialization of the crime and, respectively, the consequences.

5.7 Efforts by Judges, Prosecutors and Attorneys to Minimize the Burden for the Victim

Especially on part of the prosecution several points are mentioned that can reduce the burden on the victim. For example, the prosecutors desire more personal contact with the victim during preliminary proceedings; this includes, in particular, the possibility to conduct the interrogations in person, to inform the victim about the continuation and progress of the proceedings, and to arrange contacts to social institutions. This is in contrast to the excessive burden of work of the prosecutors. A further conflicting aspect is the common practice of day-wise trial presence according to which prosecutors normally have to represent cases before court for which they were not responsible before—also confronting them with victims they've never met, and vice-versa. Only in major trials such as the afore-mentioned cases of large sexual child abuse,[26]

26. See above, 2.

or murder cases, a thorough responsibility is the practice. Regarding the style of questioning of victim witnesses during the trial, it has been pointed out that it should not be conducted like an interrogation, even in light of the fact that critical questions principally cannot be avoided. In case of aggressive questioning by the defense, intervention appears necessary. In this respect, judges articulated more careful opinions by pointing out that the tolerance with aggressive questioning should not be limited unnecessarily. Judges also consider information of the victims about the trial as a core issue. In addition, the victim should always be given the opportunity to report on the consequences of the crime. On the part of the defense attorneys, it is mentioned that a professional attitude would generally avoid any unnecessary burdening of the victim.

5.8 Considerations of Jurists about Adequate Participation of the Victim in Trial

The majority of the respondents, including all representatives of victim support organizations, appreciate the current degree of participation of the *Nebenkläger* in the trial. However, one of the public prosecutors considered the participatory rights as too extensive. In his opinion, the work of the prosecution would sufficiently take care of the interest of the victims. Not surprisingly, it is mainly the defense counsels who felt that the victims' rights are too extensive.

5.9 Victims' Reasons for Exercising Accessory Prosecution

All three victims questioned stated that they joined the proceedings in order to ensure their interest in a harsh punishment of the offender. It has to be taken into consideration, however, that all three victims were injured through very serious crimes. Such a punitive interest cannot be assumed for victims in general. Furthermore, it was important for the victims questioned to have the right to participate actively in the trial.

5.10 Psychological Consequences of Accessory Prosecution for the Victims

Which psychological consequences were reported by the questioned victims, and how do they finally assess the behavior of the other participants? All three victims reported that their participation in the trial as accessory prosecutor, including the confrontation with the defendant, have had a positive impact on the coping with the crime. Only one victim was disappointed that in his case, the victim was found criminally incapable; not surprisingly the sentence was considered too mild. The majority of the victims described the prosecutor as being very dedicated to the case and apparently exerted to bring the offender to justice. In general, the prosecution seems to be perceived by the victims as a procurator of their interests. It also seems to be important for the victims that their testimony concerning the circumstances of the crime and the damages caused by the crime are depicted and recognized adequately. All victims voiced positive feelings towards the behavior of the judges. Even the behavior of the defense counsel was, all in all, experienced as not being offending. Less surprisingly, all victims expressed appreciation for their attorneys' activities and valuated it to be beneficial for their own psychological wellbeing. Particular emphasis is given by all victims to the relieving function of the attorney, inside and outside of the court. Pointed out especially was the preparation for the trial and the explanation of the legal context of the case and the formalities of the procedure. All the statements by the victims can be summarized and generalized insofar that especially the institution of the *Nebenklage* attorney was considered to be explicitly helpful.

5.11 The Actors

Statements of the prosecutors can be summarized as follows: they strive to burden the victim as little as possible while the case still has to be cleared up, although in this particular phase, at least some burdening of the victim is considered unavoidable. From a general perspective, protection of the victim seems to be quite compatible with the role of the prosecution. At the same time, it is made clear by the prosecution that they don't want to be perceived as procurators of the interest of satisfaction of the victim. The questioned prosecutors report on good and bad experiences with accessory prosecution, depending especially on the person of the attorney. One public prosecutor dismissed this legal institution as unnecessary, his reason for this being especially "activism on part of the accessory prosecutor's attorney."

Also the judges obviously feel committed to the protection of victims. However, conflicts are being identified with regard to their self-perceived task of being a negotiator committed to neutrality. In particular they always have a fear in mind not to deliver reasons to the defense because of prejudice due to lack of distance to the victim. It is also evident that the judges' efforts to avoid secondary victimization have to stand back behind their obligation to come to find the truth and clarify the case respectively. From the judges' side, the legal institution of accessory prosecution is appreciated without any reservations. Supposedly it is considered as an equipoise to their own restrictions mentioned here.

The defense attorneys rightly emphasize their role in the trial as a lobbyist of the defendant whose ambition has to be the best possible outcome of the trial for the client. In consequence of this they have to establish at least doubts about his guilt by challenging the charge including the victims. According to the results of the interviews, efforts concerning the protection of victims are nevertheless perceived to be not completely incompatible with this role. In the case of a guilty plea or other proof of guilt, such efforts are even considered of key importance since they can have a positive impact on the sentence and are thus in the original interest of the defendant. Since judges meanwhile have been sensitized about the issue of victim protection, victim-sensitive behavior is seen as an essential component of effective defense. Quite obviously, victim protection in such a context is fueled by strategic reasoning. Nevertheless, within the scope of a defense counsel's function, it is obviously unavoidable to back off victim protection in certain cases although, in general, thoughtful treatment of the victim during the trial is found compatible with a professional defensive strategy. Consequently, attorneys neither have principal reservations towards accessory prosecution—in another case they can also be beneficiaries of the very same role.

As could be expected before, the responding *Nebenklage* attorneys unanimously considered this as a reasonable possibility of victim participation in criminal proceedings. In the interviews they upheld the interests of crime victims even in somewhat biased manner. This might be due to the fact that two of the three questioned experts were obviously entirely committed to the issue of victim protection. The third respondent however emphasized that in spite of the great importance of victim protection a higher priority should be given to the truth-finding function of the criminal process. At the same time she feels that the danger of secondary victimization of victims in a trial is very small today.

The representatives of victim support organizations, too, strongly advocate accessory prosecution. They usually advise their victim clients to exercise their *Nebenklage* rights whenever these are formally eligible. Accordingly, very little negative effects for the victims are being seen. This is the view of representatives of victim's interests who show great commitment for victims and sometimes demand for harsher treatment of the offenders than the victims themselves. Two of the three representatives questioned admitted openly to viewing their participation in this study as publicity for victims' concerns. Their answering behavior was considerably less differentiated and significant than that given by the representatives of all other groups.

Regarding the questioned victims, their desire for harsh punishment of the offender is striking, although this is, as mentioned above, related to the grave victimization of the respondents. In this respect, their plea is plausible and understandable, and in a way also typical for victims interested in exercising their rights as *Nebenkläger*, i.e., a group which is characterized by victimization patterns which regularly are much more serious than those of the average victim. This also explains the fact that two of the *Nebenkläger* questioned were not satisfied with the concrete sentence; at the time of the interview one of those victims still felt anger about the 'mild' sentence. Little significance concerning the emotional and psychological wellbeing of the victims was found with regard to the behavior of their respective judges, prosecutors and attorneys. They mostly report on short term emotional and psychological reactions to the behavior of the other trial participants. Further analyses of this outcome will certainly have to consider that the victims, at the same time, regarded their treatment as fair—negative experiences would certainly bring contrary effects here. This leads to the preliminary conclusion that the behavior of other parties in the trial intending and attempting to avoid secondary victimization apparently has a relatively small impact on the wellbeing of the victim, at least in a long term perspective. It seems as if positive experiences scale differently, and impact less clearly, than do negative ones. Of great importance, however, is the behavior of the accessory prosecutor's attorney. Both aspects, protection and support of the client, are significant. The attorney is an important support figure for the victim throughout the trial who can exercise emotional assistance and possibly absorb harmful effects.

6. Discussion

In conclusion, the statements of the respondents give clear evidence that it is possible for judges, prosecutors and attorneys to foster the idea of victim protection in criminal proceedings, without being able to completely avoid stress and strain for the victim. The majority of the respondents differentiate explicitly or implicitly between necessary and unavoidable, and unnecessary and avoidable burdening of a victim during the trial. Some interventions of the participating parties which explicitly stress the victim are considered unavoidable since they are imperative for the purpose of establishing the truth or for the efforts to sow justified doubts regarding the guilt of the accused. Other practices such as the multiple repetition of the same question even though an answer has already been given are clearly unnecessary and avoidable. Defense attorneys clearly recognize that it is often in the best interest of their client to treat the victim with as much care as possible anticipating that in case of conviction, a respectful treatment of the victim can have a mitigating effect, while putting unnecessary pressure on the victim can be counted as an aggravating circumstance. The majority of judges, prosecutors and attorneys think that victim protection cannot only be realized through abstaining from behavior which can lead to an unnecessary burden for the victim, but also via active assistance. Judges and prosecutors clearly recognize that a verdict of not guilty or an intensive questioning of the victim due to doubts about the offender's guilt can be stressful factors for the victim. On the part of the defense, on the other hand, it was emphasized that victim protection is not the concern of the defense and will thus be applied only if beneficial to the offender. Nevertheless, the questioned victims by no means considered the behavior of the defense counsel during their trial as offending, on the contrary, as respectful. Thus it can not be assumed that the behavior of the defense counsel has a (strongly) negative impact on the emotional and psychological wellbeing of the victim.

It becomes apparent from the questioned jurists' statements that the concept of victim protection as such is generally endorsed. But they also admit difficulties in practicing victim protection in everyday work life since the search for the truth in general and the rights of the accused in particular have to have, in case of conflict, higher significance than the protection of the victim—which is certainly reasonable. The primary purpose of criminal proceedings is not to protect the victim but to filter out the truth as far as possible and to reach a verdict which is 'just' for all participants. Victim protection has its limits at court. Therefore, the goal can only be to keep emotional and psychological stress and strain for the victim at the lowest possible extent—which the parties questioned for our study obviously attempted to do. It is difficult to determine the degree of knowledge of the jurists about secondary victimization and victim protection in general. It is likely to differ from person to person. Still, to date, the topic of victim protection is not part of law education in Germany.

Another obvious conclusion from our findings is that the treatment of the victim before the court has seen a significant change in the last two decades. The treatment of the victim obviously became more respectful. Obviously, the spirit inherited in the legislature's concept of victim protection has by and large arrived in practice. Nevertheless, it cannot be assumed to be an absolute routine matter yet. This is also mirrored by the most recent legislative activities such as the First and Second Victim Rights Amendment Acts of 2004 and 2009. Thus, there is still some gap between victim protection in theory and its implementation in legal practice—and it cannot be eliminated entirely.

This gap includes the problem of sentencing expectations, too. As mentioned before, the victims questioned gave high priority to harsh punishment.

Victims of less serious crimes would probably have given lesser importance to the aspect of sentencing. This is suggested by the results of several victim surveys conducted in Germany. Sessar (1992) for example found that the majority of respondents of a survey conducted in the city of Hamburg voiced greater support for compensatory forms of punishment, like material damages, or restorative options, including community service, rather than for punishment in its traditional sense. Kilchling (1995: 427 et seq.) found quite similar preferences: of all victims questioned nationwide, only about 8% opted for an unconditional prison sentence for their offender. This is of course more or less exactly the group that qualifies for accessory prosecution. Amongst other groups of probands, however, the majority pursued the objective of recovering lost objects or receiving damages through the complaint; punitive reasons were supported only by about 20% of the victims; and punishment loses most of its significance in cases in which the victim has been compensated for their damages (Sessar, 1992: 248). During the personal interviews with the victims about the aims of punishment, it was discovered that most respondents especially regarded imprisonment as inhumane, ineffective or fostering rather than preventing recidivism. Punitive attitudes of the victims, if present, were related to prevention and protection of society from further crime (Sessar, 1982: 249; for methodological objections, see Kury, 1995).

From a psychological point of view, evidence suggests that the legal institute of accessory prosecution can contribute to avoiding or at least reducing secondary victimization during the trial and facilitate the coping process. No evidence, however, was found that it might have an explicit satisfactory function; especially victims who regard accessory prosecution as a guarantee for harsh punishment are likely to be disappointed. From a psychological point of view, the most important advantages of accessory prosecution are, in particular, the legal representation of the victim which appears to be the norm, better information about the theoretical background and the procedural rules of the trial, and emotional assistance before the court. The official role of a process party adds a kind of particular authority to those victims that provides the space to participate in a procedural setting that is protective and symbolic at the same time. It seems that on the basis of such an—institutionally enhanced—procedural status that privileges the victim, compared to other witnesses, even the negative situational effects of testimony and cross-examination can be prevented. Interestingly, one of the victims felt additional protection and affirmation from the fact that a second victim party, represented by another victim lawyer, was present in that trial. Already the presence of a legal advisor and a rough idea about the proceedings can give a sentiment of relative security to the victim and make it possible for the traumatized victim to attend the trial and not be exploited just as a witness. A victim who feels protected, supported and accepted as a legitimate participant has a much lower risk of feeling exposed again to uncontrollable forces like during the victimization than when left all to him or herself. Under such preconditions, the confrontation with the offender can be beneficial to the coping process in the medium and long term, even if the encounter and examination momentarily produce strain and challenge the physical and psychological capabilities of the victim.

In addition to these subjective perceptions, a further objective consequence of accessory prosecution which was explicitly emphasized on part of the judges is remarkable: obviously the mere presence of the *Nebenklage* attorney can change the atmosphere in the courtroom to a degree that the willingness to treat the victim respectfully increases significantly without any further action taken by the attorney. In addition, practice as accessory prosecutor offers attorneys who usually represent the defense a possibility to experience the victims' perspective which can probably have an impact on their future behavior as a defense counsel.

In light of the possible positive impact of accessory prosecution, victims should be informed about the possibility to join action in any case that is formally eligible. According to the Second Victim Rights Improvement Act of 2009, police and judicial authorities are explicitly obliged to do so. Likewise, voluntariness is essential. It must be left to the victim to make use of this possibility or not. In no case should he or she be pressured by third parties including victim support agents. Another psychologically essential precondition for a beneficial impact of the exercise of accessory prosecution is an adequate performance by the *Nebenklage* attorney. He should focus on informing the victim appropriately and grant emotional relief and protection inside and outside of the courtroom. This requires active use of available rights like the filing of motions to counteract attempts by the defense to blame the victim. However, these competences should not be used to raise unrealistic expectations through activities such as, in particular, the plea for an unjustified extent of punishment or the voicing of speculations that cannot be proven later. The victim representative should further avoid polarizing during the trial in an inadequate manner since an objective course of the trial will be beneficial for his client. In such regard, aggressive accessory prosecution can have similar negative effects to an aggressive, conflict-oriented defense strategy. It has been rightly suggested by judges to offer more advanced training for *Nebenklage* attorneys in the future.

Under these preconditions, *Nebenklage* is clearly beneficial for a victim who decided to join action after thorough consideration of personal expectations, advantages and disadvantages, including the financial risk, which for many of the victims is not to be underestimated.

References

Albrecht, H.-J. (2005). *Rechtstatsachenforschung zum Strafverfahren. Empirische Untersuchungen zu Fragestellungen des Strafverfahrens zwischen 1990 bis 2003.* Neuwied: Luchterhand.

Albrecht, H.-J. and Kilchling, M. (2009). Victims of Terrorism Policies—Should Victims of Terrorism be Treated Differently? In: M. Wade and A. Maljević (Eds.): *A War on Terror? The European Stance on a New Threat, Changing Laws and Human Rights Implications.* Dordrecht etc.: Springer, pp. 221–241.

Barton, S. (2006). Nebenklagevertretung im Strafverfahren. Ein neuartiger, aber kriminologisch vergessener Bereich der rechtsberatenden Praxis. In: T. Feltes, C. Pfeiffer, G. Steinhilper (Eds.), *Kriminalpolitik und ihre wissenschaftlichen Grundlagen. Festschrift für Hans-Dieter Schwind zum 70. Geburtstag.* Heidelberg: C.F.Müller, pp. 211–224.

Bischoff, S. and Koch, E. (2006). *Nebenklage in der Praxis—Opferschutz oder sekundäre Viktimisation? Eine inhaltsanalytische Studie zu den Erfahrungen Prozessbeteiligter.* Unveröffentlichte Diplomarbeit, Universität Freiburg.

Böttcher, R. (2007). Das Recht des Opfers auf Erhalt von Informationen im deutschen Strafprozess. In: R. Moos, U. Jesionek, O.F. Müller (Eds.), *Strafprozessrecht im Wandel. Festschrift für Roland Miklau.* Innsbruck: StudienVerlag, pp. 67–89.

Brienen, M. and Hoegen, E. (2000). *Victims of Crime in 22 European criminal Justice Systems.* Nijmegen: Wolf Legal Productions.

Brosius, H.-B. and Koschel, F. (2003). *Methoden der empirischen Kommunikationsforschung. Eine Einführung.* Wiesbaden: Westdeutscher Verlag.

Dölling, D., et al. (2000). *Die Dauer von Strafverfahren vor den Landgerichten.* Köln: Bundesanzeiger.

Fabricius, D. (1994). Die Stellung des Nebenklagevertreters. *Neue Zeitschrift für Strafrecht*, pp. 257–263.

Früh, W. (2004). *Inhaltsanalyse. Theorie und Praxis.* Konstanz: UVK.

Hassemer, W. and Reemtsma, J.P. (2002). *Verbrechensopfer.* München: C.H.Beck.

Hentig, H. v. (1948). *The Criminal & His Victim.* New Haven: Yale University Press.

Hirsch, H.J. (1989). Zur Stellung des Verletzten im Straf- und Strafverfahrensrecht. Über die Grenzen strafrechtlicher Aufgaben. In: G. Donseifer, et al. (Eds.), *Gedächtnisschrift für Armin Kaufmann.* Köln etc.: Heymanns, pp. 699–721.

Hüsing, D. (1983). *Die Rechtswirklichkeit der Nebenklage.* Göttingen: Univ. Diss.

Kaiser, G. (1996). *Kriminologie. Ein Lehrbuch.* Heidelberg: C.F.Müller.

Kaiser, M. (1992). *Die Stellung des Verletzten im Strafverfahren. Implementation und Evaluation des "Opferschutzgesetzes."* Freiburg: edition iuscrim.

Kilchling, M. (1995). *Opferinteressen und Strafverfolgung.* Freiburg i.Br.: edition iuscrim.

Kilchling, M. (2002). Opferschutz und der Strafanspruch des Staates—Ein Widerspruch? *Neue Zeitschrift für Strafrecht*, pp. 57–63.

Kilchling, M. (2006). Die Rechtslage zur Opferbegleitung in Deutschland. In: U. Jesionek u. M. Hilf (Eds.): *Die Begleitung des Verbrechensopfers durch den Strafprozess.* Innsbruck/Wien/Bozen: Studienverlag, pp. 139–164.

Kühne, H.-H. (1986). Die tatsächliche Bedeutung von Opferrechten in der Deutschen Strafprozessordnung. *Monatsschrift für Kriminologie und Strafrechtsreform*, pp. 98–102.

Kuhlmann, G.J. (1982). Die Nebenklage—eine Sinekure der Anwaltschaft. *Deutsche Richterzeitung*, pp. 311–312.

Kury, H. (1995). Wie restitutiv eingestellt ist die Bevölkerung? Zum Einfluss der Frageformulierung auf die Ergebnisse von Opferstudien. *Monatsschrift für Kriminologie und Strafrechtsreform*, pp. 84–98.

Niedling, D. (2005). *Strafprozessualer Opferschutz am Beispiel der Nebenklage. Bestandsaufnahme und Ausblick nach sechzehn Jahren Opferschutzgesetz.* Münster: LIT-Verlag.

Rieß, P. (1984). Die Rechtsstellung des Verletzten im Strafverfahren. Gutachten C für den 55. Deutschen Juristentag. *Verhandlungen des 55. DJT*, Bd. I, C 9. München: C.H. Beck.

Rössler, P. (2005). *Inhaltsanalyse.* Konstanz: UVK.

Schneider, H.J. (1979). *Das Opfer und sein Täter—Partner im Verbrechen.* München: Kindler.

Schünemann, B. (1986). Zur Stellung des Opfers im System der Strafrechtspflege. *Neue Zeitschrift für Strafrecht*, pp. 193–200.

Schulz, J. (1982). *Beiträge zur Nebenklage.* Berlin: Duncker & Humblot.

Schwind, H.-D. (2009). *Kriminologie. Eine praxisorientierte Einführung mit Beispielen.* 19th edition. Heidelberg: Kriminalistik Verlag.

Sessar, K. (1980). Rolle und Behandlung des Opfers im Strafverfahren—Gegenwärtiger Stand und Überlegungen zur Reform. *Bewährungshilfe*, pp. 328–340.

Sessar, K. (1992). *Wiedergutmachen oder strafen: Einstellungen in der Bevölkerung und der Justiz.* Pfaffenweiler: Centaurus.

Staiger-Allroggen, P. (1992). *Auswirkungen des Opferschutzgesetzes auf die Stellung des Verletzten im Strafverfahren.* Univ.Diss. Göttingen.

Weigend, T. (1984). Viktimologische und kriminalpolitische Überlegungen zur Stellung des Verletzten im Strafverfahren. *Zeitschrift für die Gesamte Strafrechtswissenschaft*, pp. 761–793.

Weigend, T. (1989). *Deliktsopfer und Strafverfahren*. Berlin: Duncker & Humblot.

4

Victims in the Criminal Justice System and Therapeutic Jurisprudence: A Canadian Perspective*

Jo-Anne Wemmers

Abstract

Research with crime victims suggests that victims seek participation and recognition in the justice system (Shapland et al., 1985; Kilchling, 1995; Wemmers, 1996; Erez, 1999). However, victim participation in the criminal justice system is a point of debate among scholars (Ashworth, 1993; Erez, 1999). Participation can take various forms: it can mean an active decision-making role or merely consultation and consideration (Edwards, 2004; Wemmers and Cyr, 2004). In addition, there is the question of how victims are affected by their participation. While victims in Canada are currently by and large excluded from the criminal justice process, their being outside the system does, to some extent, shelter them from the offender. This raises the question: when is participation helpful or therapeutic for victims and when is it harmful or anti-therapeutic? Based on interviews with judges, public prosecutors and victim support workers in the province of Quebec, this study presents the perceptions of these three key groups of professionals.

* The study was made possible by grants from the *Transcoop Program* of the *Alexander von Humboldt Foundation* and the *Fondation pour la Recherche Juridique au Canada*. Points of view are those of the authors and do not reflect the views of the funding agencies.

1. Introduction

For decades victimologists have been telling us that victims want to participate in the criminal justice system. However, just how victims want to participate and the consequences of their participation in the criminal justice system have been and continue to be fervently debated (Ashworth, 1993; Erez, 1999; Edwards, 2004). Some authors emphasize the balance of rights between victims and the accused and believe that victim participation encroaches on the rights of the accused (Ashworth, 1993; Roach, 1999). Others argue that law is a social force that affects people's lives and emphasize the impact of laws and legal procedures on the individuals that they touch (Austin and Tobiasen, 1984; Wexler and Winnick, 1991). Authors such as Wexler and Winnick (1996) and their model of *therapeutic jurisprudence*, and Sherman (2003) with his model of *emotionally intelligent justice*, are examples of what can be called a growing movement to recognize the impact of legal intervention on the emotions of victims, offenders and communities.

1.1 Therapeutic Jurisprudence

Therapeutic jurisprudence views legal rules, legal procedures, and the roles of legal actors (such as lawyers and judges) as social forces that produce behaviors and consequences, which are sometimes therapeutic and sometimes anti-therapeutic for the persons affected by the law (Wexler and Winick, 1991; Wexler and Winick, 1996; Winick, 1996; Winick, 2000). This approach draws our attention to the emotional and psychological side of law and the legal process. It is not a theory but a way of looking at the law. Therapeutic jurisprudence calls for the study of these consequences in order to identify them and to ascertain whether the law's antitherapeutic effects can be reduced, while enhancing its therapeutic effects, without subordinating due process and other justice values (Winick, 1996).

Therapeutic jurisprudence was originally developed in the area of mental health law (Wexler and Winick, 1991). Later, it was expanded to include defendants in criminal cases (Wexler and Winick, 1996). It is only recently that therapeutic jurisprudence has taken the next logical step, namely applying it to victims of crime. While the term therapeutic jurisprudence it is relatively new in victimology, the idea that victims are affected by their experiences in the criminal justice system is not at all new. But instead of calling it therapeutic jurisprudence, victimologists have used the term secondary victimization, to refer to how insensitive reactions by officials can augment the victim's suffering (Symonds, 1980; Maguire, 1991).

According to therapeutic jurisprudence, lawmakers and those who apply the law must be aware of its effects on the mental health of those involved (Wexler and Winick, 1991; Winick, 2000). As Herman (1992; 2003) points out, a court of law is particularly effective for provoking intrusive post-traumatic symptoms. However, satisfaction with the criminal justice system has been found to be positively associated with post trauma adjustment among victims of violence (Byrne et al., 1996). Several authors suggest that fair procedures may be therapeutic (Waldman, 1998; Wexler and Winick, 1991). In other words, when victims feel that they have been treated fairly, this would help their recovery from their victimization.

Just how legal actors and procedures affect victims, is addressed by Procedural Justice Theory. According to this theory, fairness is important because it communicates to people that they are valued and respected members of their group (Van de Bos et al., 2001). Wemmers (1996) has established the relevance of procedural justice for victims of crime and found that victims' fairness judgments affected their faith in the criminal justice system. In particular, when victims felt that police and public prosecutors had shown an interest in them, had given them an opportunity to express their wishes and had taken their wishes into consideration, victims were more likely to feel that they had been treated fairly (Wemmers, 1996). Because of the message procedures send to participants about their standing in the group, fair procedures impact victims' healing or recovery (Tyler and Lind, 1992; Wemmers and Cyr, 2005).

1.2 Victim Participation

What is victim participation? The victimological literature distinguishes between two types of victim participation, namely active participation where the victim has decision-making power and passive participation where victims have no power over decisions but are consulted and informed of the developments in their case (Wemmers, 2003). Edwards (2004) identifies four types of victim participation. The first type of participation that Edwards distinguishes is *control*. According to Edwards, control implies that criminal justice authorities are obliged to seek and apply the victim's preference. This type of participation is essentially the same as active participation where the victim is the decision-maker. Edward's second type of participation is *consultation*. This type of participation obliges criminal justice authorities to seek and consider victims' preferences. Consultation coincides with what is also referred to as passive participation. The third type of participation identified by Edwards is *information provision*, in which authorities are obliged to seek and consider victim information. According to Edwards, this type of participation obliges victims to supply information and does not give them an option. This type of participation is essentially the role of the witness in criminal justice: victims are obliged to testify if requested. Edward's fourth type of participation is *expression*. Here, victims have the option of supplying information or expressing emotions and authorities are obliged to allow victim expression but they are not obliged to consider it.

Victim participation of some kind is now a requirement of legal proceedings according to the United Nations Declaration of Basic Principles of Justice for Victims of Crime and Abuse of Power (1985), the Council of Europe Recommendations for Victims of Crime (R (85) 11) and more recently, the Council Framework Decision of the European Union (2001/220/JHA). The latter is a binding decision which requires that Member States ensure that victims have a real and appropriate role in its criminal legal system (Art. 2) and safeguard the possibility for victims to be heard during proceedings (Art. 3). However, these instruments are written in abstract terms in order to apply to a variety of legal systems and thus, they fail to specify exactly what victim participation means. In its simplest form victim participation gives victims a voice or an expressive role, while in its most elaborate form, victim participation gives victims a role in decision-making. Following these recommendations and decisions enunciated by the various international and national organizations, the right for victim participation is no longer questioned. As Sanders et al. (2001) assert, victim participation is here to stay. The question is, however, how should victims participate?

1.3 Canadian Criminal Justice

Before presenting the study, we need to briefly describe the Canadian criminal justice system and victims' role in it. Canada shares the common law legal tradition. In common law, victims are essentially witnesses to a crime against the State. Outside of their role as a witness to the crime, Canadian victims have no special legal standing. The criminal trial is an adversary procedure, which pits the State against the accused. The State has the task to prove beyond a reasonable doubt that the accused committed the crime for which he is accused. In practice, most cases are plea-bargained. This means that the State, or the Crown as it is called in Canada, will reduce the charges in exchange for a guilty plea by the accused.

Should the case go to trial, the victim may be called upon to give testimony. Victims do not have a choice when it comes to testifying. They are either called upon by the Crown or by the defense and should they be requested to give testimony, they are legally obliged to comply. Moreover, when testifying, victims are not at liberty to say whatever they want. Instead, they are expected to reply to the questions that are asked of them. They cannot refuse to answer a particular question and they cannot include information that they think is important unless it is asked of them.

The word victim did not enter the Canadian Criminal Code until 1989 when legislation for Victim Impact Statements (VIS) was introduced (Laurin and Viens, 1996). The VIS is a written statement by the victim that is presented to the judge at sentencing. In a VIS victims may include information about the consequences of their victimization that they believe are relevant for the judge. Since they were first introduced at sentencing, VIS have been introduced at federal parole hearings, allowing victims a voice at multiple stages of the criminal justice system.

Besides the VIS, there are some other special provisions in the Code for witnesses who are also victims. However, these measures are only available for certain crimes such as sexual assault or when the victim is a minor. Available measures include publication bans protecting the identity of the victim and the mandatory legal representation of the accused when cross-examining the victim in order to ensure that the victim will not be directly questioned by the accused (Laurin and Viens, 1996; Wemmers, 2003). The VIS is the only available measure that is specifically intended to give victims a voice in the criminal justice process.

The division of powers in Canada is as such that the Criminal Code is under federal jurisdiction. However, the provinces in Canada are responsible for the administration of justice and therefore the development and implementation of victim policy. Thus, law making is done centrally by the federal government and its application is delegated to the provinces. In the province of Quebec, a victims' Bill of Rights, the *Loi sur l'aide aux victimes d'actes criminels* was adopted in 1988. This law outlines victims' right to information, reparation and support. The law specifies that victims have the right to be informed of their rights and of their role in the criminal justice system. Victims have a right to support, to be informed of the progress of their case and to present their views at appropriate stages of the criminal justice process. In 1995 the *Ministère de la Justice, Québec* introduced the INFOVAC program in order facilitate victim notification by the police and the courts.

In a study on victims' experiences in the Quebec criminal courts, Wemmers and Cyr (2006) found that victims were not systematically informed about the services available to them. Most victims were not asked by police if they wanted information about victim support and most did not know where to go for help or information. This might not be an issue if the victims in this study were not affected by their victimization, but almost three-quarters of respondents were victims of violent crime and most victims said that they were affected by the crime. In all, 45% of the victims who participated in the study showed symptoms of PTSD. Yet, almost half of the victims of violence said that they had not received information about the provincial compensation program. Not surprisingly, many victims were dissatisfied with the information they received about services and their dissatisfaction grew over time. In addition to the lack of information about services, most victims were not informed of the developments in their case. Almost all victims (91%) said that they wanted to be notified about the developments in their case. Over 70% of victims were dissatisfied with the information they received about up-coming court proceedings and their dissatisfaction grew over time.

With respect to VIS, Wemmers and Cyr (2006) found that most victims said that they had made a written victim impact statement. The victim impact statement was introduced in the Criminal Code in order to provide victims with a systematic opportunity to inform the court of the impact of the crime. While two-thirds of victims felt that the victim impact statement allowed them to say what was important, one-third felt that it did not. Victims were not particularly satisfied with the victim impact statement. When asked if they would submit a victim impact statement again in the future, one quarter said that they would probably not. Moreover, as their cases progressed through the criminal justice system, victims were less inclined to feel that the victim impact statement was important. These findings suggest that the victim impact statement is not satisfying victims' need for recognition and participation in the criminal justice process. This raises the question, when and how is victim participation therapeutic for victims?

The present study sought to better understand the potential for healing of victims of crime in the criminal justice system by examining victim participation and its perceived impact on victims. Criminal justice professionals were interviewed to determine their views about victim participation in the criminal justice system and its impact on victims. Firstly, the study asks when is participation therapeutic and when is it anti-therapeutic for victims? Secondly, it looks at the different stages of the criminal justice process and asks which stages are particularly therapeutic and which as anti-therapeutic. Thirdly, it considers what could be done to make victim participation more therapeutic and less harmful for victims.

2. Method

As the influence of the criminal justice system on the process of victim healing has been relatively unexplored, a qualitative method was used for this study.

The study explores the perceptions of actors in criminal justice actors with respect to victim participation. The samples do not need to be representative at a national level because this is an exploratory study.

The study used in-depth interviews of the parties involved in legal proceedings, as well as the legal and allied professionals who interact with victims and who have first hand experience in observing or attending to participants' emotional reactions or needs. Thus prosecutors, defense lawyers, judges, and victim assistance personnel were interviewed about their experiences with procedures, legal decisions and remedies regarding victim input that have proved to be helpful, empowering and therapeutic and those that have had adverse or antitherapeutic effects on participants. Most interviews were conducted one-on-one, however, in one interview two victim support workers were interviewed together.

The interviews address the common therapeutic issues associated with participation. Questions about the difference in therapeutic effects between offence categories will be included in the interviews of the legal and allied professionals in the relevant jurisdiction. By including input from all the various professionals involved in proceedings, the research may identify previously unrecognized factors that enhance or detract from participants' welfare. Contingencies and circumstances of therapeutic and antitherapeutic effects are explored.

The interviews were conducted in French and lasted on average 90 minutes. The quotations presented in this paper were translated by the researcher for the purpose of this paper.

2.1 Recruitment

Professionals who participated in the study were recruited in the geographical area of Quebec. A request was made to the local authorities and professional organizations in the greater Montreal area for their collaboration with the study. When this did not lead to sufficient volunteers, professionals were approached on an individual basis and invited to participate. In all, 3 judges, 8 prosecutors and 11 Victim Support workers were interviewed.

2.2 Sample

Among the 11 victim support workers who were interviewed, two were directors of victim support offices and nine were victim support workers. Three people interviewed were male and eight were female. Their years of experience varied from one and a half to thirteen years. The average number of years of experience for the sample was five and a half years. All of the respondents worked in victim assistance offices (*Centre d'aide victimes d'actes criminels, CAVAC*) in the province of Quebec: four worked in the city of Montreal, five in the Laval and one in Longueuil.

The eight public prosecutors who were interviewed had on average 21.6 years of experience, the minimum number of years of experience was three and the maximum was 33 years. In all, four were female and four were male. All of the respondents worked as Crown prosecutors in the province of Quebec: three worked in Montreal, two worked in Laval and three worked in Val d'Or.

The three judges who participated in the study were all from Montreal. There was one woman and two men. On average they had 20 years of experience as a judge and prior to becoming a judge they had worked as a public prosecutor.

2.3 Data Analysis

Interviews were taped and transcribed verbatim. The transcripts were then analyzed for patterns and common themes following grounded theory. The data provide rich descriptions of the how victim participation in criminal justice proceedings may be helpful or harmful to victims and what criminal justice professionals believe can be done to reduce the risk of secondary victimization.

3. Results

3.1 Voice

A common theme in the interviews was the therapeutic value of speaking out about what had happened. Voice was considered potentially cathartic at any stage in the criminal justice process: from reporting the crime to the police to delivering a victim impact statement at sentencing. However, the most important stage in the criminal justice process from a therapeutic perspective is the first time that victims denounce their aggressor publicly and report the crime to the police. Many respondents felt that voice allowed victims to take back a sense of control over their lives.

> "It's reporting the crime to the police. To openly declare that they were the victim of a crime." ENT5-Prosecutor
>
> "It's the trial.... When I consider the point of view of victims of sexual violence, it's testifying.... Each time, for her, it's as if it permits her to reassert herself with respect to what happened." ENT19-CAVAC

While later stages, such as testifying in court, were considered by some to be therapeutic, others saw them as a source of stress for victims. Rather than liberating victims and providing them with a renewed sense of control, these stages removed control from victims. In particular, having to repeat and relive their victimization and all of the emotions associated with it was viewed as traumatizing for some victims.

> "I would say reporting the crime to the police. After that, the victim is faced with so much stress that they often wonder whether they made the right decision to go to the police. However, I think that at least when they report the crime, in a crisis situation, I think that this helps them." ENT17-CAVAC
>
> "It is clear that having to relive certain events is very traumatizing.... I sense that it is very difficult to relate, not just for the first time but the many times, our system what her to retell her story to the detective, to the community police officer, to the special investigator, to the Crown prosecutor and again later in the trial. This repetition of the event is disagreeable and I think that it could be difficult...." ENT24-Judge

It is interesting to note that victim impact statements, while available in Quebec since 1989, were not spontaneously mentioned in the interviews as a therapeutic stage in the criminal justice process. Thus, while these statements may be meant to provide victims with a voice, the criminal justice actors who were interviewed did not see them as a means of expression for victims that was worthy of mentioning.

3.2 Respect and Recognition

Another main theme found in the data is respect and recognition of the victim by authorities. Repeatedly, professionals argued that how victims were treated was key and that signs of recognition and respect had a therapeutic affect on victims. Essentially, respect and recognition meant that victims felt they had been listened to and that people heard what they had to say and believed them.

> "... it means to be treated with respect, to be listened to by the prosecutor and the police, to be understood, to give time to the victim." ENT13-CAVAC
>
> "I have never yet met a victim who did not appreciate meeting with the prosecutor." ENT2-Prosecutor

> "... to be believed.... Their biggest fear is that they won't be believed" ENT9-CAVAC2

Conversely, the respondents felt that when an attitude of respect and recognition was lacking, this was anti-therapeutic for victims. In particular not caring about the victim, ignoring the victim, not showing any concern for the victim and his/her rights, these were all things believed to be harmful for victims. Repeated delays were seen as a gesture of disrespect for the victim that left them feeling unimportant and discouraged.

> "The worst thing for victims is the way that they are treated or mistreated by the justice system. One often has the impression that they came for nothing, that no one takes care of them.... treating victims like suspects." ENT2-Prosecutor
>
> "The indifference of the justice system.... The police tell the victim that if anything happens they will contact her. But it doesn't happen like that. They give the victim false information, which leads to a feeling of injustice." ENT16-CAVAC
>
> "I personally think that it is the feeling of not having been consulted. I think that is anti-therapeutic. When one doesn't consider or, even worse, ignores the victim...." ENT15-JUGE

Many respondents stressed how important it is for victims that they feel they are believed. But how can victims be believed if the whole purpose of the criminal justice process is to determine whether or not the defendant actually committed a crime against the victim? After all, in legal terms we talk about the *presumed victim* and only use the word victim after the defendant has been found guilty. Different actors employ critical questioning, however, cross-examination of victims by the defense is notoriously difficult for victims. The respondents mentioned that critical questioning, especially cross-examination, was particularly painful because it could undermine the victim and suggest that he/she should not be believed.

> "Well, it's cross-examination. There, all victims leave it feeling victimized. They were questioned, they were doubted, they were not respected ... they relive the crime too ..." ENT13-CAVAC
>
> "It's the cross-examination that is often the worst. That lawyer has something to prove. He has to raise a doubt...." ENT5-Prosecutor

Although cross-examination was generally felt to be anti-therapeutic for many victims, it was also believed to be an important part of the criminal justice system and one that could not easily be removed. Does this mean that it is impossible to recognize the victim in the early stages of the criminal justice process? Is it reasonable for victims to expect to be treated with dignity and respect in an adversarial system? While the respondents felt that being believed was important to victims, they also talked about recognition of the person behind the victim and his/her human needs. Their responses suggest that being believed does not just mean recognizing the offender's guilt. Feeling like one is believed is about an attitude in which the victim's humanity is recognized.

> "It's how things are done ... if victims have the impression that they were treated with a minimum of courtesy, attention, respect ... it's a question of attitude...." ENT9-CAVAC
>
> "I will explain to the victim. It is my decision and I have to accept the fact that they will not agree with it. I will try to the best of my knowledge and my ability to explain it to them.... But I think that it would be more frustrating for a victim to go to court and feel that the judge didn't even see him, to not have the judge explain anything to him and to learn that the case was delayed or to think that the offender got off lightly." ENT15-Judge

Criminal justice professionals also felt that the negative impact of cross-examination was amplified by victims' lack of understanding of the workings of the criminal justice system. The respondents emphasized that while respect and recognition are about how victims were treated, it is also about how victims *perceive* the way in which they were treated. It is a subjective appraisal by the victim and one that is influenced by the information that is available to them. Several respondents stressed that critical questioning or even an acquittal did not necessarily mean that the victim had not been believed. They felt that if victims only understood how criminal law worked, they might be less at risk of secondary victimization.

> "In criminal law, the role (of the judge) is not just to believe.... The proof has to be beyond reasonable doubt ... So one can believe the victim and be obliged to acquit. And if victims perceive an acquittal as not being believed by the judge, then I think that this is too bad ... Maybe one should find an alternative. Maybe.... prevent and explain the role ... I am talking about the system because you don't only have the judge, you have the prosecutors and the police. I think that it's because it hasn't been explained very well that one risks re-victimizing the person." ENT24-Judge
>
> "Feeling like you're not believed.... Frustration regarding the criminal justice system ... Not understanding what is the role of the po-

lice, the Crown, and juries is frustrating and not very therapeutic ..." ENT4-Prosecutor

3.2 Outcomes

In addition to how victims were treated, many respondents mentioned the outcome of the criminal justice process as something which could either add or subtract from the therapeutic impact of the criminal justice system. These respondents stressed the significance of punishment of the offender and compensation with respect to validation and recognition of the victim. An acquittal was generally viewed as anti-therapeutic because it sent a message to victims that they were not believed.

> "To have followed the criminal justice process to the end and then have the judge give a reasonable sentence that he explains to the accused and to the victim. This person will leave the court feeling that the system works and that can be therapeutic." ENT5-Prosecutor
>
> "The verdict, if it is an acquittal. Feeling like you're not believed.... Frustration regarding the criminal justice system ..." ENT4-Prosecutor

Some respondents viewed sentencing as therapeutic because it signified the end of the criminal justice process. For these respondents, healing didn't really begin until the criminal trial was over.

> "Knowing that justice was done.... Finally being able to turn the page ..." ENT12-Prosecutor

3.3 How to Improve the Therapeutic Impact of Criminal Justice

Respondents were unanimous that victims needed better information and that this would reduce the risk of secondary victimization. Communicating with victims and providing them with information about the criminal justice process and their case was something that the respondents did, which they felt was therapeutic for victims.

> "In the first place, information.... Emotionally, this is helpful because the people will feel anxious with respect to the justice process. But because we inform them they feel some relief. We also tell them what they can do. We offer them choices ..." ENT18-CAVAC

> "To keep them informed of all the steps of the judicial process. For victims there is nothing like knowing where they are going...." ENT8-Prosecutor

However, some legal professionals felt that it was not their job to look after the victim and that there were limits on what they could do for victims.

> "It is not our role to bother about the victim. Our role is to represent society. We have a role to inform (victims) but not to manage victims' emotions.... We are not psychologists ..." ENT4-Prosecutor
>
> "It is always a question of a very delicate balance. Because the judge who is too receptive towards the poor victim, I think that he would not be playing his role. He is not a therapist. It is very delicate...." ENT24-Judge

Respondents were asked if victims should have their own legal representation in the criminal justice process. Would it reduce the risk of secondary victimization if victims were provided with someone who would be responsible for them and who could explain the criminal justice process? After all, respondents did believe that victims' poor understanding of the criminal justice system made things worse for victims and led them to misinterpret legal decisions and actions as personal attacks. But their responses to the idea of introducing a lawyer for victims were mixed; seeing both advantages and disadvantages.

Some of the advantages that were mentioned were that victims might have better information and be treated better. Victims would finally have someone who listens to them and whose job is to represent their interests. Their legal representative could explain the criminal justice system to victims which would help victims understand what was happening and why.

> "Therapeutic. Victims would undoubtedly have the impression that they were much better listened to, to be represented, to always have someone who takes care of their interests ..." ENT8-Prosecutor

Disadvantages included the costs (who would pay?), the addition of yet another burden on the system and concern that the introduction of another lawyer would disturb the balance in the adversarial system. Moreover, some respondents doubted whether legal representation would give victims the feeling that they were listened to.

> "But, on the other hand, if I look at the treatment of victims of conjugal violence who have cases before the civil court regarding the custody of children. There is a lot of dissatisfaction regarding the lawyers....

> Well, for example, the lawyers are not available often enough, they are there to do their job. Victims expect to get more understanding and empathy from someone who they hire. So, there too there is perhaps a lack of information. Not understanding a system that goes beyond their comprehension. 'I can't even call my lawyer because it costs me money. I receive bills for everything.' So, the costs as well." ENT16-CAVAC

4. Discussion

When is participation therapeutic? The response to this question is unequivocal: participation is therapeutic for victims when they are shown recognition and respect. Conversely, victim participation is considered anti-therapeutic when respect and recognition of the victim are absent. These findings converge with research on crime victims that recognition and respect are associated with victim satisfaction (Shapland et al., 1985; Wemmers, 1996) and associated with post trauma adjustment among victims of violence (Byrne et al., 1996). Victims seek validation and they are helped when they find it.

The finding that recognition and respect are crucial for victims' participation in the criminal justice system to be therapeutic corresponds with the research on procedural justice. When victims are validated, respected, considered and consulted, they will find that they were treated fairly by authorities (Wemmers, 1996). Fair procedures are therapeutic for victims (Waldman, 1998; Wemmers and Cyr, 2005). However, when victims are excluded, not respected or recognized, not consulted or considered, they will feel that they were treated unfairly (Wemmers, 1996). Unfair procedures are anti-therapeutic for victims because they have a negative impact on the victim's well-being (Wemmers and Cyr, 2005). A key feature of procedural justice is that when people feel that they were fairly treated, this provides a cushion of support, making unfavorable decisions more palatable (Lind and Tyler, 1988; Tyler, 1990; Wemmers, 1996). In other words, if a prosecutor treats the victim with dignity and respect and is able to gain the victim's confidence, then the victim will still feel thay they were treated fairly, even when the prosecutor makes an unpopular decision. This is particularly important in the criminal justice system where prosecutors and victim support workers cannot guarantee victims favorable outcomes.

Participation is also considered therapeutic when it provides the victim a voice. Voice is considered to have a positive impact on victims when it allows them to assert themselves, denounce their aggressor and regain a sense of control over their lives. However, when testifying is not by choice or when critical questioning follows it, this is considered anti-therapeutic. Sources of secondary victimization include having to relive their victimization when testifying and being doubted or not believed. It is curious that the respondents did not spontaneously mention victim impact statements in relation to victim participation. This measure, which was intended to give victims a voice, was introduced in Quebec almost 20 years ago. Their failure to mention this suggests that victim impact statements are not considered important.

Like voice, sentencing was considered a double-edged sword. Sentencing could be therapeutic when it validated the victim, confirming their victimization and the offender's responsibility. However, it could also be anti-therapeutic when it failed to validate the victim. The worst was an acquittal, which sent a message to the victim that they were not believed. However, the negative impact of sentencing could be cushioned when professionals communicated with victims, explaining their decision. In terms of procedural justice theory, by recognizing and respecting the victim, fair procedures can cushion the negative effects of an unfavorable outcome.

In terms of what victim participation means, Edwards (2004) describes several different types of participation ranging from simple information to consultation, to active decision-making. The present findings do not suggest that victim participation should mean that victims be given an active role in decision-making. This conclusion coincides with that of Wemmers and Cyr (2004), following interviews with victims of crime. When victim participation means respect and recognition, as the respondents in this study have expressed, it does not put victims at increased risk of exposure and confrontation. Instead, it cushions the possible negative impact of confrontation and cross-examination without limiting the rights of the accused. Edwards (2004) suggests that victim dissatisfaction with participation may be because victims and authorities have different expectations with respect to the role of victims. He offers that victims may expect an information-provision or consultative role, whereas authorities see victim participation simply as expressive. The importance that some of the respondents in this study placed on voice coincides with Edwards' suggestion victim participation is viewed primarily as expressive. However, the respondents in this study also recognized the therapeutic impact of information and consultation. The present findings suggest that authorities do seem to understand victim participation in terms of consultation and information. They simply do no always act accordingly.

Emotionally intelligent justice uses information and communication with victims to facilitate the therapeutic effects of the criminal justice system and reduce the risk of secondary victimization. But whose job is it to look after victims? Judges and prosecutors can provide victims with information, and their responses indicate that they could do more for victims. However, there are limits on just what they can do for victims. An obstacle preventing legal professionals from communicating more with victims is their role in the criminal justice process. Judges are obliged to remain neutral. Public prosecutors represent the State and not the victim. While the Prosecutor will consider the impact of the crime on victims, this is not the only factor that they must consider when deciding on how to handle the case. Sometimes the interest of the victim may conflict with the interests of the State. For example, whereas the State may be served by a speedy disposal of the case and therefore plea bargain, this may not do justice to the wishes of victims who seek validation and recognition of their suffering. However, none of the respondents argued that it was impossible to consider the victims' feelings in the courtroom setting. Therapeutic jurisprudence argues that we consider how people are affected by the law and that we use this information to enhance the law's effectiveness. This does not mean that victims should not be confronted and cross-examined but rather, that victims should be provided with information and support so that they can put questioning into context and not view it as a personal attack or disbelief.

The respondents in this study did not embrace the possibility of introducing legal counsel for victims in the adversarial procedure. Reactions were mixed. On the one hand, concerns were raised about who would pay for such a service, and what role would they serve. On the other hand, it was felt that legal representation for victims could improve the information given to victims, explaining the criminal justice process to them and thus having a positive impact on how they perceived the criminal justice procedure. While a lawyer for victims may have no formal role in the criminal justice process, victims could benefit from a better understanding the justice system.

Clearly, it's the job of victim support to look after victims. Their key function is to provide information to crime victims. However, a study conducted among crime victims in Quebec shows that most are not told about victim support and most do not know where to go for help (Wemmers and Cyr, 2006). Thus, victims will often not have access to victim support. In addition, victim support workers are not lawyers. They tend to come from the social and human sciences. While many will have a rudimentary understanding of the criminal justice system, their main task is to provide support for victims and not legal counseling. Perhaps the introduction of legal counsel in the victim support offices is worthy of further exploration.

While the findings are instructive as an exploratory study, they cannot be generalized to other settings. One must bear in mind that the present study is based on a small, non-representative sample. Further research with a larger and representative sample is needed in order to better understand how professionals view the impact of law, as a social force, on victims.

In order for victim participation to be therapeutic, victims should be consulted and considered. There is no evidence that the structure of the criminal justice system needs to be changed before it can become therapeutic. However, we do need to provide the necessary resources to allow better information and communication with victims.

References

Ashworth, A. (1993). "Victim impact statements and sentencing." *Criminal Law Review*, July: 498–509.

Austin, W. and Tobiasen, J.M. (1984). Legal Justice and the Psychology of Conflict Resolution. In: Robert Folger (Ed.). *The Sense of Injustice: Social Psychological Perspectives* (pp. 227–274). Plenum Press, NY.

Byrne, C., Kilpatrick, D., Beaty, D., and Howley, S. (1996). Has Victims Rights Legislation Improved CJS Treatment of Crime Victims? Poster presented at the 12th Annual Meeting for the *International Society for Traumatic Stress Studies*. November, San Francisco.

Council of Europe, (2006). *European Committee on Crime Problems. Explanatory memorandum to the Recommendation Rec (2006) on assistance to crime victims*. 967 Meeting, 14 June.

Edwards, I. (2004). An Ambiguous Participant: The Crime Victim and Criminal Justice Decision-Making. *British Journal of Criminology*, 44, 967–982.

Erez, E. (1999). Who's Afraid of the Big Bad Victim? Victim Impact Statements as Victim Empowerment and Enhancement of Justice. *Criminal Law Review*, 545–556.

Herman, J.L. (1992). *Trauma and Recovery*. New York, NY: Basic Books.

Herman, J.L. (2003). The Mental Health of Crime Victims: Impact of Legal Intervention. *Journal of Traumatic Stress*, 16;2, 159–166.

Kilchling, M. (1995). *Opferinteressen und Strafverfolgung* (Victim Interests and Criminal Prosecution) Freiburg im. Br.: Max-Planck-Institut fur auslandisches und internationales Strafrecht.

Laurin, C. and Viens, C. (1996). La place de la victime dans le sytème de justice pénale. In: J. Coiteux, P. Campeau, M. Clarkson, M.M. Cousineau (Eds.). *Question d'équité: L 'aide aux victimes d'actes criminels* (pp. 109–134). Montréal: Association québécoise Plaidoyer-Victimes.

Lind, E.A. and Tyler, T. (1988). *The Social Psychology of Procedural Justice*. New York, NY: Plenum Press.

Maguire, M. (1991). The Needs and Rights of Victims of Crime. In: Michael Tonry (Ed.) *Crime and Justice: A Review of the Research* (pp. 363–433). Chicago, IL: University fo Chicago Press.

Poupart, L. (1999). La victime au centre de l'intervention. Montreal: Association québécoise plaidoyer victimes.

Roach, K. (1999). *Due Process and Victims' Rights: The new law and politics of criminal justice.* Toronto: University of Toronto Press.

Sanders, A., Hoyle, C., Morgan, R., and Cape, E. (2001). "Victim Impact Statements: Don't Work, Can't Work." *Criminal Law Review*, June: 447–458.

Shapland, J., Willmore, J., and Duff, P. (1985). *Victims in the Criminal Justice System.* Aldershot: Gower Publishing.

Sherman, L. (2003). Reason For Emotion: Reinventing Justice with Theories, Innovations and Research—The American Society of Criminology 2002 Presidential Address. *Criminology*, 41:1, 1–38.

Symonds, M. (1980). The Second Injury. *Evaluation and Change, Special Issue.* pp. 36–38.

Tyler, T. (1990). *Why People Obey the Law.* New Haven: Yale University Press.

Tyler, T. and Lind, E.A. (1992). A Relational Model of Authority in Groups. In: M.P. Zanna (Ed.) *Advances in Experimental Social Psychology, Vol. 25* (pp. 115–191). San Diego, Academic Press.

Van den Bos, K., Lind, E.A. (2002). Uncertainty Mangement By Means of Fairness Judgements. *Advances in Experimental Social Psychology*, 34, 1–59.

Van den Bos, K., Lind, E.A., and Wilke, H. (2001). The Psychology of Procedural and Distributive Justice Viewed From the Perspective of Fairness Heuristic Theory. In: R. Cropanzano (Ed.) *Justice in the Workplace: From Theory to Practice, Vol. 2.* (pp. 49–66) Mahwah, NJ: Lawrence Erlbaum Associates Publishers.

Waldman, E.A. (1998). The Evaluative-Facilitative Debate in Mediation: Applying the Lens of Therapeutic Jurisprudence. *Marquette Law Review,* 82, 155–170.

Wemmers, J. (1996). *Victims in the Criminal Justice System.* Amsterdam: Kugler.

Wemmers, J., *Introduction à la victimologie.* Montreal: Les Presses de l'Université de Montréal, 2003.

Wemmers, J. and Cyr, K. (2004).Victims' Perspectives on Restorative Justice: How much involvement are victims looking for? *International Review of Victimology*, 11, 1–16.

Wemmers, J. and Cyr, K. (2005). Can Mediation be Therapeutic for Crime Victims ? An Evaluation of Victims' Experiences in Mediation with Young Offenders. *Canadian Journal of Criminology and Criminal Justice, 47* (3), 527–544.

Wemmers, J. and Cyr, K. (2006). *Victims' Needs Within the Context of the Criminal Justice System.* International Centre for Comparative Criminology, University of Montreal.

Wexler, D. and Winick, B. (1991). *Essays in Therapeutic Jurisprudence.* Durham, NC: Carolina Academic Press.

Wexler, D. and Winick, B. (1996). *Law in a Therapeutic Key: Developments in Therapeutic Jurisprudence.* Durham, NC: Carolina Academic Press.

Winick, B. (1996). The Jurisprudence of Therapeutic Jurisprudence. In: D. Wexler and B. Winick. *Law in a Therapeutic Key: Developments in Therapeutic Jurisprudence.* Durham, NC: Carolina Academic Press.

Winick, B. (2000). Redefining the Role of the Criminal Defense Lawyer at Plea Bargaining and Sentencing: A Therapeutic Jurisprudence/Preventive Law Model. In: D. Stolle, D. Wexler and B. Winick (Eds.) *Practicing Therapeutic Jurisprudence: Law as a Helping Profession* (pp. 245–308). Durham, NC: Carolina Academic Press.

Section 2: Victims and the Law

5

Victim Legal Clinics and Legal System Victim Impact Statements: Addressing the Therapeutic Aspects of Victim Participation in Justice

David B. Wexler

Abstract

One way that victims can better participate in the criminal justice system is if they are accompanied to court by a legally knowledgeable person who can explain the proceedings. This chapter proposes that students affiliated with a law school clinic could ably perform that function. In addition, that role could give the students some counselling experience and sensitize them to the needs of victims. Another proposal of the chapter is that the students could interview the victims and then prepare a Legal System Victim Impact Statement, a statement focusing not on the impact of the crime on the victim (a matter covered by the traditional Victim Impact Statement) but rather of the impact on the victim of the legal process itself—from the first encounter with the police until the tail end of the process. This type of statement would allow for reform of the system itself, and would produce lawyers sensitive to a therapeutic jurisprudence look at the law.

1. Introduction

How can lawyers—and the legal system generally—become more aware of and responsive to crime victim needs? That is the therapeutic jurisprudence inquiry underlying this chapter.

The inquiry led me to focus on the formation of lawyers—on the process and content of legal education, particularly in the increasingly important area of clinical legal education. What better way to see things from a victim's perspective than to have a lawyer in-training have personal contact with a victim and to accompany the victim to court proceedings? At the same time, the law student role should provide emotional support to the victim as well and help dissipate the frightening mystery of the legal proceedings.

Such a step, I believe, will begin to create a bar much more sensitive to victim issues. But to reform the system, much more is needed. Law students counseling victims, and involved in crafting Victim Impact Statements, will surely learn much about how criminal acts affect victims—physically, emotionally, economically. But a broader victim-centered education would sensitize law students to ways in which the legal system itself affects victims, and that purpose is very much a part of the chapter's proposal for a Legal System Victim Impact Statement. The preparation of such statements can give victims a voice regarding a wider range of issues. It can also educate law students and other functionaries in the system, and can result in a real reform of practice. Let us, then, look at the specifics of these two related proposals, set forth in a step-by-step format:

1. Law school clinical programs are plentiful, at least in the U.S., and Therapeutic Jurisprudence (TJ) is of growing interest to law school clinics (Winick & Wexler, 2006; St. Thomas Law Review Symposium, 2005).
2. Legal clinics have traditionally emphasized litigation, but are increasingly interested in imparting interviewing and counseling skills (Winick & Wexler, 2006).
3. Law students could offer support and legal information to victims of crime in pending criminal cases. In fact, a handful of victim legal clinics already exist, assisting victims in state courts and in one case in federal court as well. (National Crime Victim Law Institute website). Some of those clinics seem to emphasize litigation issues. The kind of clinic I have in mind, however, would focus on providing legal information, advice, and counseling. In jurisdictions with well-staffed Victim Witness Assistance programs, many of the functions described here are in fact provided by the program. But law student involvement can provide additional cost-free resources to such programs, and law students may add their developing professional expertise and knowledge of criminal procedure to the mix of talents. Of equal importance, these programs offer a superb TJ training opportunity for law students to improve their interpersonal communication skills in sensitive settings, to enhance their ability to work with allied professionals, and to improve their knowledge of legal and courtroom procedures.

4. The proposed clinic would allow students to observe courtroom proceedings (itself an important educational objective) and, at the same time, would provide the students with actual client contact in an interviewing and counseling context.
5. Since such a clinic would involve counseling, but would not technically involve actual in-court client representation, such a clinic could be open to students who are not yet in their final year of law school (in the U.S., a typical requirement for engaging in limited, supervised, in-court representation).
6. Such clinics could seemingly operate in any jurisdiction, although they would provide students a more robust role in jurisdictions—like the U.S. federal jurisdiction (United States Code) and many states (Beloof & Cassell, 2005)—that basically permit victim presence throughout the proceedings, as opposed to those that may treat the victim as a mere "witness," subject to rules governing witness sequestration during trial.
7. The precise role of the clinic will need to be fleshed out, and will also depend somewhat on the local legal landscape, but some functions might include:
   a. Explaining to the victim the legal proceedings and legal terminology (e.g., no contest plea, not guilty by reason of insanity, allocution): what just happened, what is happening, what is supposed to happen next?
   b. This function might also include a discussion whether the victim would desire to be present or absent from an upcoming portion of the proceedings, e.g., one that might be disturbing or one that might be dry, technical, and deadly dull.
   c. Accompanying the victim when the prosecution interviews and prepares the victim for direct and cross examination. The presence of a familiar figure—the clinic student—should render the meeting with the prosecutor less frightening for the victim, and the observational opportunity should provide an excellent educational experience for the law student.
   d. Working with a victim support service to hook the victim up with available, appropriate services—a function that will be of obvious value to the victim and will be valuable to the law student by providing an opportunity to learn about social services and to work with social service professionals, matters of increasing importance in the work of today's criminal and poverty lawyers (Wexler, 2005).
   e. Supporting the victim in the preparation of a written or oral Victim Impact Statement, explaining the substance and procedure of sen-

tencing, and generally preparing the victim for allocution (Wexler, 2006).

f. Explaining the judges' sentencing decision and underlying reasons (Wexler, 2006).

g. Helping the victim prepare a Legal System Victim Impact statement (as described more fully below).

8. A Victim Legal Advisor Clinic could, of course, provide its services in criminal cases generally. But, especially if the law school clinic operates in affiliation with an established and broad-based Victim Witness Assistance Program, the law school clinic might limit its participation to certain categories of cases.

   For example, one excellent opportunity for learning and providing service might be a victim clinic limited to the specialized area of federal Indian law cases. These are serious criminal cases that, had they occurred outside the boundaries of Indian nations, would be heard in state court. But because of their special status, these cases are prosecuted in federal court, a forum often regarded—by defendants and victims alike—as distant, foreign and frightening (Washburn, 2006). Students participating in a Federal Indian Victim Legal Advisor Clinic could bring to their work (and further develop) a heightened cultural competence, an attribute that ought to be much appreciated by the clinic clients (Hartley & Petrucci, 2004).

   Another specialized area in federal court practice—one typically (but incorrectly) thought of as only a state court matter—is domestic violence (Raeder, 2006). Of course, specialized knowledge and sensitivity would be crucially important to those clients as well, and a law school clinic might limit itself to such cases.

9. The proposal for a Legal System Victim Impact Statement (LSVIS) (see 7(g) above) is sufficiently important to warrant separate attention here. The traditional Victim Impact Statement speaks to the impact of the *crime* on the victim. The victim is given "voice" and that voice might influence the court's sentencing decision. But given the serious problems of "secondary victimization" and the often anti therapeutic impact of the legal system itself, why should we not also have a *Legal System Victim Impact Statement,* told from the victim's perspective? Such a statement can serve an important expressive function, and can provide the victim with further "voice." Some might argue, however, that, in contrast to the traditional Victim Impact Statement, a Legal System Victim Impact Statement would have no possibility of influencing the outcome of the victim's case, and that it would be "patently unfair" to "solicit an opinion from someone

who has *no* potential to affect the outcome" (Burke & Leben, 2007, p. 12). But a Legal System Victim Impact Statement may "pacify the need to speak and participate" (id.) *and* have real world impact, albeit in the *future*. A Legal System Victim Impact Statement might indeed serve a legal system reform function, and many victims would no doubt be interested in providing their feedback if such might yield value to others in time to come.

Ideally, a LSVIS could be prepared in stages—following police interviews, after cross-examination, following the imposition of sentence, and the like. In any case, a LSVIS could be prepared after the case, perhaps as a component of a detailed exit interview with a Victim Witness Program and its affiliated law school Victim Legal Advisor Clinic.

Therapeutic jurisprudence has, in a number of contexts, made effective use of the preventive law pedagogical "rewind" technique, where a scenario is re-wound to a time in the past and consideration is given to what might have been done differently to have avoided the eruption of a troublesome legal issue or the accompanying emotional turmoil (Patry, 1998; Winick, 2007). The LSVIS can be looked at as a type of rewind exercise—one we might learn from so as not to repeat mistakes in the future.

The LSVIP will help to identify some difficulties encountered by victims in the adversary process itself (e.g., cross examination). Consider an actual example given by Erez and Downs (2007) (this volume) of how disrespected victims might feel when, before or after a formal court session, but in the courtroom and in the presence of the victim, informal conversations take place among defense attorneys, judges, and prosecutors about such mundane matters as family vacation plans and the like. The actual case documented by the above researchers involved just such a casual conversation in the presence of parents awaiting the adjudication of a case involving the murder of their child.

Such conversations likely occur without any disrespect intended. But if the offensiveness of such conduct is later called to the attention of those individuals, perhaps in the form of a LSVIS, my guess is those legal actors would think twice before having a similar conversation in the future.

A LSVIS could be prepared by a victim with the support and assistance of a student legal advisor. Involvement of a law student in the statement preparation should serve to increase the future lawyer's sensitivity to the emotional and interpersonal consequences of the legal system and its functionaries—a matter of utmost importance but traditionally neglected by legal education.

The LSVIS should emphasize both good and bad behaviors by various actors, beginning with the police and continuing throughout the process.

It is indeed important to include the good in order to reinforce that type of behavior by system participants and to move toward the eventual development of "best practices" in the area.

A completed LSVIS could be distributed by the clinic student to the relevant actors. Indeed, a legal clinic might even collect and compile LSVISs and prepare a year-end report summarizing victim views of proper and improper behaviors. Such a report might lead to reforms of practice or even of the law itself, and the report and underlying statements can constitute a rich resource for researchers.

A preliminary form for a LSVIS could profitably be drafted by a team of Victim Witness Assistance Program professionals and researchers, based on their considerable combined knowledge of the types of behaviors and processes of importance and concern to crime victims.

10. A Victim Legal Advisor Clinic has the advantage of bringing resources into the system without appreciable cost to the system itself. Of course, law school clinics will cost something to run, but law schools are always looking for good, interesting, and effective ways of educating their students, and a victim legal clinic could do so while serving an important social function. Students exposed to such a clinic will take enhanced interpersonal skills and a TJ perspective with them into practice. And that practice may be in criminal law—leading to prosecutors with greater interpersonal understanding and sensitivity, and to criminal defense attorneys who employ a TJ lens. Indeed, if students participate in a Victim Legal Advisor Clinic before their final year, they might indeed cap off their clinical experience with a final year stint in a prosecutor or defense clinic.

2. Conclusion

These comments and proposals were triggered by the research reports presented at the workshop and now published in this volume. The comments may now be taken full circle: The existence of Victim Legal Advisor Clinics and a chronological collection of Legal System Victim Impact Statements would also provide a major evaluation research opportunity—to see, among other things, whether and how much this type of victim participation will make a difference. If the results are positive, the research would likely provide important ammunition for increased public funding of victim participation in justice. Moreover, the enterprise will stimulate interdisciplinary TJ activity centering on the role of victims, launching a major new direction of TJ scholarship. TJ criminal law writing, which has traditionally focused on courts and their relationship with criminal defendants, is now poised to mature and to branch into other areas. The role of TJ in the work of prosecutors is just beginning (Wexler, in press), and coincides perfectly with the new emphasis on TJ and victims (for earlier work, see Erez, 1999; Wemmers & Cyr, 2005) spearheaded by this volume.

References

Beloof, D. and Cassell, P. (2005). 'The Victim's Right to Attend Trials: The Reascendant Consensus,' 9 Lewis and Clark Law Review 481.

Burke, K. and Leben, S. (2007). 'Procedural Fairness: A Key Ingredient in Public Satisfaction' (a White Paper of the American Judge Association), available at: http://aja.ncsc.dni.w/htdocs/AJAWhitePaper9-26-07.pdf.

Erez, E. (1999). 'Who's Afraid of the Big Bad Victim? Victim Impact Statements as Victim Empowerment and Enhancement of Justice,' Criminal Law Bulletin 545.

Erez, E., Ibarra, P.R., and Downs, D. (2009). 'Victim Participation in Justice and Therapeutic Jurisprudence: The American Perspective' (this volume).

Hartley, C.C. and Petrucci, C.J. (2004). 'Practicing Culturally Competent Therapeutic Jurisprudence: A Collaboration Between Social Work and Law', 14 Washington University Journal of Law and Policy 133.

National Crime Victim Law Institute website, at www.ncvli.org.

Patry, M.W. et al. (1998). 'Better Legal Counseling Through Empirical Research,' 34 California Western Law Review 440.

St. Thomas Law Review Symposium on Therapeutic Jurisprudence in Clinical Legal Education and Legal Skills Training. (2005). 13 St. Thomas Law Review 403.

Raeder, M. (2006). 'Domestic Violence in Federal Court: Abused Women as Victims, Survivors and Offenders,' Federal Sentencing Reporter.

United States Code, 18 U.S.C. 3117 (a) (3).

Washburn, K.K. (2006). 'Federal Criminal Law and Tribal Self-Determination,' 84 North Carolina Law Review 779.

Wemmers, J. and Cyr, K. (2005). 'Can Mediation be Therapeutic for Crime Victims? An Evaluation of Victims' Experiences in Mediation with Young Offenders,' 47 Canadian Journal of Criminology and Criminal Justice 527.

Wexler, D.B. (in press). 'Therapeutic Jurisprudence, Legal Landscapes, and Form Reform: The Case of Diversion,' Florida Coastal Law Review.

———. (2005). 'A Tripartite Framework for Incorporating Therapeutic Jurisprudence in Criminal Law Education, Research and, Practice,' 7 Florida

Coastal Law Review 95 (2006), 'Therapeutic Jurisprudence and Readiness for Rehabilitation', 8 Florida Coastal Law Review 111.

Winick, B.J. (2007). 'A Legal Autopsy of the Lawyering in Schiavo: A Therapeutic Jurisprudence/Preventive Law Rewind Exercise, 61 University of Miami Law Review 595.

Winick, B.J. and Wexler, D.B. (2006). 'The Use of Therapeutic Jurisprudence in Law School Clinical Education: Transforming the Criminal Law Clinic,' 13 Clinical Law Review 605.

6

Victims' Rights: Procedural and Constitutional Principles for Victim Participation in Germany

Susanne Walther

Abstract

In Germany, no doctrinal, in particular constitutional framework exists from which specific victims' rights could be developed. Recent European Law mandates that victims will be met with adequate dignity. However, the setting is unique as the alleged victims' interests can conflict and compete with the defendant's interests to be adequately protected by the law. Currently protected interests of the victim attach to her role as witness, as a collateral prosecutor, and as an interested party. With regard to the role as witness, an emerging right not to have to appear repeatedly deserves special mention. In giving testimony, the victim has a right to first render her narrative. Special rules apply with regard to intimate subjects. While closed-circuit-technology is available, complete anonymity of the victim is not allowed. The role of the victim as accessory prosecutor (Nebenkläger), particularly in cases of sex crimes and crimes against physical integrity, is a limited one but provides a number of active participation rights including the right to pose questions, to oppose orders of the court and to challenge questions. In cases of particular seriousness or complexity, the victim can be assisted by a state-paid attorney. It is argued here that Nebenklage is a useful instrument that should be extended to a broader set of crimes. As regards the status of current law, within the rubric of the victim simply as an 'interested party,' security, reparations and restitution of property are high on the agenda in Germany. Yet, finally, what is needed for the future is a conceptual, constitutional framework so that rights are no longer a matter of 'simple' law codified in the German criminal procedure code. Two basic rights guaranteed by the German constitution are useful: Human dignity and fair trial. Human dignity stands for the proposition that just like the offender, the victim must be treated as a subject to the proceeding. What emanates from this is an original participation right, especially a right to be heard. Fair trial for the victim, on the other hand, implies to see that justice is done. Author argues that five specific rights should be central: The right to make evidentiary motions, the right to ask for an expansion of the accusation, the right to ask questions at the taking of evidence and make statements, the right to have the support of an attorney, if necessary at the expense of the state, and the right to be informed and to have the assistance of interpreters.

1. Introduction

Today, it is beyond dispute that victims of crime deserve special legal recognition and protection. One could expect, therefore, to find articles on victims' rights in the constitution or at least in constitutional discourse. While the passage of a Victims' Rights Amendment has been discussed for long in the United States,[1] in Germany no such discussion exists. There is a conspicuous lack of a doctrinal, in particular constitutional framework from which specific victims' rights could be developed. Victims' rights are not mentioned in the German constitution of 1949 and neither in the European Convention of Human Rights of 1950. The law books and commentaries are void of references to constitutional guarantees when it comes to victims' rights, especially victims' rights during the criminal justice process.

I did find a reference to 'dignity', however, in a recent legal act by the European Union. The European Council, in 2001, passed a framework decision on the position of the victim within the criminal justice process.[2] It mandates better protection for victims of crime regardless in which member state they are located. The member states are bound to harmonize their laws and regulations on the criminal justice process in order to provide the following guarantees:

- The right to be heard and to present evidence
- Early access to information relevant for victim's interest

1. For the text of the proposed amendment of Jan. 2003, see 19 Fed. Sentencing Reporter 2006, p. 57.

2. Framework Decision of 15 March 2001 on the standing of victims in criminal proceedings, O.J. L 82 22 March 2001, p. 1.

- Adequate forms of translation and communication
- The right to participate during the proceedings and access to legal advice, including, if necessary, legal counsel free of charge
- The right to reimbursement of court costs
- Adequate protection with regard to security, privacy and public reputation
- The right to reparation
- For out-of-state victims, adequate options to participate in the proceedings via video- or telephone-conference.

In addition the member states guarantee that throughout the criminal justice process victims will be met with adequate respect of their dignity and that particularly vulnerable victims receive adequate protection.

While this program deserves, in principle, full support, complications can arise within the special framework of the criminal justice process. It is one of the central purposes of the criminal justice process to protect the accused, not only against private acts of revenge by the victim and his family but also against undue acts of prosecution by the state. In particular, it is the purpose of the criminal justice process to make sure that the truthfinding and sentencing processes remain governed by the law, and not governed by politics. In the same breath this means that the criminal justice process is a process which must be dominated by experts, not by lay persons. Taken seriously, this means that the victim's role must remain a limited one—his or her generalizing hostilities against 'criminals of this kind' cannot be allowed in. Within the procedural setting of criminal prosecution, it seems even questionable to use the term victim: The defendant enjoys the presumption of innocence, which means that the person injured is, strictly speaking, only the alleged victim. The full-fledged legal status of 'victim' attaches only upon a final verdict that the defendant has been found guilty, in a process governed by the law, of the crime in question. In other words, as long as the criminal justice process is on-going, the alleged victims' interests can conflict and compete with the defendant's interests to be protected, particularly against biased judges, fabricated evidence and unfair procedural tactics. At the same time, there's a person who claims to have been injured and typically can prove to have been injured, and who therefore demands protection in various ways. It is a very unique setting that deserves to be kept in mind when we demand better protection of victims' rights.

In the following, I will first describe the status quo, in Germany, of victim participation during the criminal justice process. In doing so, I will concentrate on major aspects, such as the victim as witness, the victim as a accessory prosecutor, and the victim as an interested party. In the final section, I will discuss the need for a conceptual, constitutional framework.

2. Currently Protected Interests of the Victim during the Criminal Justice Process

2.1 The Victim as Witness

First of all, within the criminal justice process the alleged victim will usually be needed by the prosecutor as an accusatory witness. The state expects the victim, just as it expects any other citizen, to be ready to serve as a witness. Traditionally, this witness duty can result in a heavy burden: The victim may be asked several times throughout the proceedings to appear and to be subject to interrogation. He or she may be exposed to the defendant and the public, either when giving testimony in court or upon entering or leaving the court room. While some persons will not mind this kind of exposure, or even desire to get a chance to personally confront the defendant in the public courtroom, oftentimes, especially in cases of family or sexual violence, the victim will want to be protected as best as possible against exposure, and especially against repeated exposure.

In the German criminal justice system, the witness' first basic duty is 'to appear' when summoned by a prosecutor or by the court (there is no duty to appear and testify when summoned by the police, but in practice, police interrogation is the rule). In this respect two questions arise: Does the victim-witness have a right to be spared from having to appear repeatedly? More specifically, the question is whether an emerging right should be recognized to have testimony recorded as early as possible, so that it may be preserved to be displayed later in court. The second question is: Can the victim-witness insist on being called as a witness at trial? In Germany, none of these rights are generally recognized.

Several innovations in criminal procedure, however, point in the direction that the right to not have to appear repeatedly could be viewed as an emerging right. First of all, it is a rule today that the testimony of young witnesses shall be recorded via audio-video-technology. The same applies for witnesses who may be unavailable at trial.[3] If the witness is unavailable at trial, recorded testimony can be used as evidence at trial. Unavailability may be due to ill-

3. §58a of the German Criminal Procedure Code, StPO.

ness, but also due to physical endangerment.[4] Whereas the traditional rule was that only testimony taken by a judge could be entered via audio-video-recording, nowadays it is recognized that police interrogation as well may be used.[5] However, it is not sufficiently recognized, in Germany, that the psychological burden of giving testimony in court as such can make the witness 'unavailable.' A special rule applies in cases of sex crimes, crimes against life or crimes against dependants. In such cases, the video-recording of judicial testimony by a young person under 18 years of age may even be used when the witness is available.[6]

What about the opposite right, the right to be called as a witness at trial? In Germany, the question of which witnesses will be called is a matter of evidence, and for the court to decide.[7] Motions to hear the victim as a witness can be filed by all parties, including the victim herself if she acts as a an accessory prosecutor (so-called *Nebenkläger* according to §§395 et seq. StPO), i.e., an additional prosecuting party to the proceedings. The request to call a witness can be turned down by the court only in a limited set of circumstances,[8] for instance, when the fact in question can be considered as already proven. When the victim appears, it can be viewed as very essential for the protection of respect and human dignity of the victim during testimony, the victim has a natural interest first to tell 'her story'. The German Constitutional Court recognized that the witness has a fundamental right of fairness which includes the right to render her testimony first in narrative form.[9] In fact, the German criminal procedure code provides for a specific rule on how witness testimony is to be taken. First, the witness must be asked to give a so-called 'report' in her own words.[10] Further questioning is appropriate only if it is necessary for the purposes of clarification, completion or for examination of the foundations of the witness' knowledge.[11] These rules must not only be respected by the court, but also by prosecutors and the police during the investigation stage.

Moreover, the witness will be interested to be protected, as much as possible, against having to give information on intimate subjects, and against being confronted by the defense. The law requires that witnesses respond to questions

---

4. Cf. Meyer-Gossner (2009: §251 annot. 20).
5. §§255a, 251 [1] StPO.
6. §255a [2] StPO.
7. §244 [2] StPO.
8. §244 [3] StPO.
9. BVerfGE 38, pp. 105, 117 [decisions of the Constitutional Court Vol. 38]; see also RGSt. 74, pp. 35 [decisions of the *Reichsgericht* Vol. 74].
10. §69 [1] StPO.
11. §69 [2] StPO.

when interrogated by a prosecutor or by a judge (again, there is no such duty in police interrogations). Similarly, witnesses have to respond to questions when interrogated by defendants and their counsel at trial.[12] Special rules apply for young witnesses under 18 years of age; their testimony is taken exclusively through questioning by the presiding judge; the prosecutor, the defendant and his counsel may ask the presiding judge to pose certain questions.[13] Endangered witnesses may be allowed to not give personal information on their identity and place of dwelling.[14] Questions on facts that might be offensive to the witness shall, as a rule, not be asked.[15] Moreover, witnesses and victims in particular, have a right to be accompanied by counsel.[16] Victims can also have legal counsel who can help them seek protective measures. Where the accusation involves a felony, a serious sex crime or an organized crime, the victim—like any other witness—can have counsel at the state's expense. For other offenses the cost will be carried by the state if victims cannot afford counsel and the case is too complex for victims to handle their interest themselves. In addition, victims can ask that another entrusted person be present when they are interrogated as a witness.[17] The victim's attorney may exercise the right to object to certain questions and may ask to have the public excluded.[18] The victim's wish not to be physically confronted with the defendant or with the entire courtroom setting can be met in certain cases by closed circuit technology. Where grave endangerment of the witness can be shown, the judge, during the phase of investigation, can hear and preserve the witness testimony outside the presence of other parties.[19] During trial, the defendant may, in certain cases (particularly endangerment of a young witness) be temporarily excluded.[20] In many respects, particularly with regard to potential grounds of appeal (see Weigend, 1998: C 53), it is today considered preferable by prevailing practice to make use of closed-circuit television and order the witness to be interviewed at a different location.[21] The testimony shall be recorded if the witness might be unavailable at a future hearing. Still, all these precautions do not allow for complete anonymity of the victim as witness. In particular, the victim's face,

12. §240 [2] StPO.
13. §241a StPO.
14. §68 StPO.
15. §68a StPO.
16. §68b, §406f [2] StPO.
17. §406 f [3] StPO.
18. §406 f [2] StPO.
19. §168e StPO.
20. §247 StPO.
21. §247a StPO.

physical appearance and voice may not be completely obscured.[22] Moreover, the preservation of testimony for future use at trial requires, according to the prevailing view, that the testimony be taken by a judge;[23] there is, at present, not sufficient trust in the objectivity of police interrogations.

2.2 *The Victim as Accessory Prosecutor*

Whether the victim appears as a witness or not, he or she may have a broader interest in becoming a prosecutorial party to the process, and, thus, play an active role. In the German criminal justice process, as a rule, it is not the victim but an official prosecutor who functions as the accuser. There is however, an exception for so-called 'private claim crimes.'[24] These are minor crimes such as, for instance, trespassing, insult, or simple assault. In such cases, the victim can act as a 'private prosecutor'. In practice, such private prosecutions are extremely rare. Clearly, the costs of acting as a prosecutor are high and it is no surprise, therefore, that victims prefer a professional prosecutor to vindicate their interests. One of the costs is the risk to pay the court fees and the costs of the defense if the accused is acquitted.[25] Another option has, however, become more popular: Certain victims may join the process as so-called *Nebenkläger* [accessory prosecutors]. The relevant code section particularly lists sex crimes and crimes against physical integrity.[26] The declaration to join the prosecution must be in writing, and it becomes effective at the time when the state prosecutor files the accusation with the court.[27] Nowadays, victims join the proceedings in around 20% of the more serious cases which are handled at first instance by the district courts (Barton, 2006: 213–214). The accessory prosecutor's financial risk is, however, not completely eliminated: She has to pay her own expenses if the accused is acquitted and with some likelihood even if the case is dismissed.[28] In case of an unsuccessful appeal, she can also be ordered to pay the defendant's expenses.[29]

The role of the accessory prosecutor is limited: She does not file her own instrument of accusation, but instead 'joins' the state prosecutor as an accessory

22. See BGHSt 32, 115, 124; critized by Weigend (1998: C 42 et seq.).
23. §§162, 168 et seq. StPO.
24. §§374 et seq. StPO.
25. §471 StPO.
26. §395 StPO.
27. §396 [1] StPO.
28. §472 [1 & 2] StPO.
29. §473 [1] StPO.

and then has a number of active participation rights. First, it is useful to file the declaration to join as early as possible. Although participation rights officially attach only at a later time (after the official accusation), in practice the victim will have opportunities to influence the course of investigations, and, as a consequence, the scope of the accusation that is to be filed with the court if she appears as an accessory prosecutor early on. Once the accusation is filed, the accessory prosecutor has no right to have it amended (for instance, to have the defendant accused of 100 instead of 30 acts of rape).[30] The rights of the 'accessory prosecutor' include the right to be present throughout the trial, even if he or she will also be called as a witness.[31] He or she can appear with counsel, or be represented by counsel.[32] With regard to important procedural decisions, of which the prosecutor must be informed, the accessory prosecutor must be informed as well and has a right to allocution.[33] Most importantly perhaps, the accessory prosecutor has a right to discovery which she can exercise through her attorney. Moreover, she has a right to challenge judges and expert witnesses, a right to pose questions, and to oppose orders of the court as well as questions. The victim can also influence the investigation by requesting that specific evidence be gathered and can make formal declarations, including a closing statement.[34] It is of central interest to victims, of course, to enjoy the support of a professional attorney. The Code of Criminal Procedure provides, in certain cases where the charge is particularly serious, that the victim be assisted by counsel paid by the state.[35] Otherwise, counsel will be paid by the state if she cannot afford the costs and the case is too complex to be handled on her own.[36] In any case, the victim's expenses for the accessory prosecution have to be carried by the accused if he is convicted of a crime that concerns the victim.[37]

It is, of course, a central question, what purposes are legitimately served by allowing the alleged victim to join the prosecution. Scholarly opinion cites the interest in 'satisfaction'. The accessory prosecutor is thought to pursue primarily immaterial interests in seeing the offender convicted and punished. With regard to punishment, however, the Code provides for an interesting limitation: The victim cannot appeal a conviction based on the argument that the de-

30. See the so-called '*Stephanie*' case which was tried in Dresden in 2006; for more details, see www.dw-world.de/dw/article/0,,2284333,00.html.

31. §397 [1] StPO.

32. §§397, 378 StPO.

33. §§397 [1], 385 StPO.

34. This includes the plea for a particular sentence.

35. §397a [1] StPO.

36. §397a [2] StPO.

37. §472 [1] StPO.

fendant should receive a harsher sentence or be convicted of a crime which would not allow the victim to join the proceeding in the first place.[38] The German *Nebenklage* seeks to strike a delicate balance: The question of punishment is considered to be a matter for expert judges, assisted by the lay jurors. Punishment is not to be considered a matter for the people. It is seen as legitimate, however, that the victim pursues his or her interests in truth-finding, in reparations that ought to be served for instance when the offender is eligible for probation, and also in the expression of punishment and security interests. In addition, the accessory prosecutor can influence the course of investigations and exercise a certain control over the criminal justice process. The accessory prosecution is an important institution that allows the victim to be a 'subject' in the proceeding, not an object. In this capacity, it serves directly to guarantee the protection of human dignity of the victim. In my opinion, the *Nebenklage* is a useful procedural institution. It is questionable, therefore, that the Criminal Procedure Code limits the options to join the proceeding to a still rather narrow set of crimes. Recently, however, the law has been extended to cover, for instance, as well crimes of burglary, robbery, and extortion.

Another way of becoming a party to the criminal justice process is the filing of a civil tort claim which will be 'attached' to the criminal justice process.[39] The injured party or his or her heirs can file a tort claim for damages based on material or immaterial losses (pain and suffering). The criminal court will decide whether or not the accused must pay damages to the victim but not on the amount of damages to be paid. If parties are unable to agree on the amount then, with the criminal court's decision in hand, they can request a civil judge to determine the amount of damages owed to the victim. Despite this option this so-called 'adhesion proceeding' is not very popular with the legal practitioners. Supposedly, the criminal justice process is seen as incompatible with issues that are of a purely 'civil' nature.

2.3 The Victim as an Interested Party

Yet even where the victim cannot or does not join the proceedings as an accessory prosecutor the law makes clear that he or she deserves a particular status. This status has been described as that of an independent party. A special, amended section of the Code of Criminal Procedure[40] assembles 'other rights of the injured person.' First, victims need help and support from the police. While

38. §400 [1] StPO.
39. §403 et seq. StPO.
40. §§406d et seq. StPO.

this aspect is not addressed by the Code of Criminal Procedure, it is today common practice that the police maintains special victim support units. It is the task of these units to provide effective psychological and practical support, including information on public institutions and private organizations that offer help for victims of crime.

Second, the victim has the right to be informed on the status of criminal proceedings.[41] Upon their request, the victim must be informed of the outcome of the court proceedings. The Code also provides a right to be informed of all dispositions relating to the custody of the defendant, throughout the criminal justice process, including the execution of sentence.[42] Thirdly, the victim can, through his attorney, ask for discovery, a right that comes into play as early as the investigation stage.[43] Of great importance is the right to be supported or represented by an attorney. In this respect, the law differentiates between victims in general, and victims who could (but do not) file a motion to join the proceedings as Nebenkläger. Victims generally enjoy the right to counsel; victims who are entitled to file a motion as accessory prosecutors can, in severe or complex cases, even ask for an attorney if they cannot afford one.[44] The law allows, with regard to support and representation by counsel, far-reaching participation rights during investigation and trial.[45] The costs of this participation will be carried by the accused if he is convicted of a crime that concerns the victim.[46] Finally, the law provides that the victim shall be informed of his or her rights.[47] This information should be provided to the victim as early as possible, ideally when the victim files a complaint with the police or prosecutor, otherwise when he or she is first interrogated as a witness.

Aside from the interest to gain information during the proceedings and to have a certain influence on the proceedings, the victim will often be interested in security, reparations and the restitution of property. With regard to reparations in the German criminal justice system, the promotion of victim-offender mediation has been high on the agenda during the past two decades. A special section of the Penal Code addresses the option of abstention from punishment where the offender has achieved to make amends.[48] However, only re-

41. §406d [1] StPO.
42. §406d [2] StPO.
43. §406e StPO.
44. §§406g [3], 397a StPO.
45. §406g [2] StPO.
46. §472 [3] StPO.
47. §406h StPO.
48. §46a of the Criminal Code, StGB.

ally serious cases are excluded. In serious cases, voluntary reparations, particularly in the form of a 'communicative process' between offender and victim, can and usually will be credited by the court by granting mitigation of punishment. The prevailing policy today is to investigate, as early as possible, whether the case in question is amenable to reparation. The Code of Criminal Procedure contains special provisions that oblige both the prosecution and the court to explore, at 'any stage of the proceedings,' whether the case in question is amenable to efforts of reparation, particularly victim-offender mediation. If the answer is yes, which requires that the victim consents, the case may be referred to a specialized agency.[49] The Code of Criminal Procedure also provides for a special type of dismissal when the case is less serious and the offender has made early, voluntary and comprehensive reparations.[50] Other options include reparation orders either in the context of a dismissal[51] or, as a collateral sanction, in the context of probation, parole or court warning.[52] Finally, as already mentioned, the victim may also file a formal civil tort claim with the criminal court, by way of a so-called 'adhesion' proceeding.[53]

This regime of reparation should, however, be simplified in the future. A general 'reparation order' by the court should simply be possible whenever the offender is found guilty or has accepted responsibility for the crime in question. This is not presently the case.

At present, in cases of crimes against property, such as theft, robbery or extortion, the victims are often interested in restitution of specific property values. Aside from this specific interest, victims are generally interested in reparation of other financial losses, and oftentimes in damages for pain and suffering. It is therefore in the interest of both the victim and the public that with regard to proceeds of crime the state can issue forfeiture warrants in favor of the victim of crime. So far, however, forfeiture is not possible where victim claims exist.[54] Ironically, this limitation was considered to protect victims' rights. The idea was that forfeiture of proceeds of crime would rank the states interests higher and thus hurt the property interests of the victim. In practice, however, non-confiscation by the state often works against victims' interests, for instance, where the victims are unknown or, for whatever reason, did not file claims. In such cases, the proceeds of crime remain in the hands of the offender. The Code of

49. §§ 155a, 155b StPO.
50. § 153b StPO.
51. § 153a StPO.
52. §§ 56, 56b, 57, 59 StGB.
53. §§ 403 et seq. StPO.
54. § 73 [1] 2 StGB.

Criminal Procedure does allow, however, the issuance of seizure orders in order to secure property in favor of victims' claims (so-called recovery assistance).[55] Movable items, for instance, a car or jewelry that was taken from the victim by way of theft or robbery, must be returned to the owner, provided there are no other claims and the items are no longer necessary for the criminal proceeding.[56] Yet, the victim may have a further interest in property items obtained by the offender as proceeds of crime, for cause of reparations that go beyond restitution of specific property. In this respect, the law now does accept that the victims' reparation claims deserve priority over the state's claims to forfeited proceeds of crime. This principle, and the principle that the state must assist the victim in gaining full reparation, has recently been reaffirmed by the legislature.[57] In the future, a seizure order issued in the context of recovery assistance will remain effective for a period of three years after the conviction. When the victim abstains from filing (or fails to file) a claim within this period, the seizure will transfer automatically into a confiscation order, and the state will become the owner of the frozen asset(s) (so-called substitute acquisition of ownership); in this case, the victim has to sue the offender.[58]

Still, the relevant norms do not serve to fully alleviate the victims' burden of formally pursuing a civil tort claim. Further simplifications are possible and desirable. For example, upon proof taken by the criminal court itself, the court should be able to simply declare forfeiture in favor of the victim or, more practically perhaps, in favor of a victims' fund.

Closely related to the topic of reparations is that of prevention of future attacks. Especially in cases of family or dating violence, the victim is concerned with issues of prevention. As of January 2002, the German legislature has enforced a specific Violence Protection Act [*Gewaltschutzgesetz*].[59] It allows the court to issue preventive orders that forbid further contact with the victim. The perpetrator may be ordered to temporarily stay away from shared dwellings, even where he is the owner of the apartment or house. The violation of a court order based on the Violence Protection Act is a crime punishable by up to one year imprisonment or a fine.

---

55. §111b [5] StPO.

56. §111k StPO.

57. Law Improving Restitution and Confiscation of Crime Proceeds [*Gesetz zur Stärkung der Rückgewinnungshilfe und der Vermögensabschöpfung bei Straftaten*] of 24.10.2006, BGBl. I, p. 2350.

58. §111i [2 & 3] StPO.

59. Law Improving Civil Protection against Violence and Stalking and Regulating the Removal from the Marital Home [*Gewaltschutzgesetz, GewSchG*] of 11.12.2001, BGBl. I, p. 3513.

3. The Need for a Conceptual, Constitutional Framework

As we have seen, the victims' interests are protected in the German criminal justice process in multiple ways. As mentioned in my introduction, however, it is unclear what the legal status of these rights is. Are they simply a matter of legal policy that could be changed at any time? Could, for instance, the right to present witness evidence first in narrative form be abolished by legislative fiat? Could the right to join the process as Nebenkläger and thereby become a party to the process be done away with if the legislator decided, for instance, that this institution should be thrown out as an obstacle to better efficiency? Could reparation be declared as a matter that should be exclusively dealt with in a civil proceeding?

My thesis is that we cannot develop rational answers to such queries unless we develop a conceptual framework that allows to develop specific victims' rights, and to evaluate rights that are of now guaranteed as matters of 'simple' law codified in the German criminal procedure. Such a conceptual framework must be developed on the level of constitutional law. I see two basic rights from which to develop victims' rights.

(1) The first basic right is *human dignity* (art. 1 GG[60]). Taking, as a starting point, the majority view that subscribes to the 'object-formula', it can be asserted that just like the offender must be treated as a subject to the proceeding, so must the victim. The victim, in particular, must not be treated as mere evidence, but she must be regarded as a subject with personal, individual and independent standing at the criminal trial. The victim has an original, legally protected interest in having the accusation examined by the court in a fair proceeding aimed at just sanctions. Because of this right to participate, the victim has a right to be heard. This right which in Germany is guaranteed in a separate constitutional article (art. 103 [1] GG), is the most important derivative of human dignity. As a minimum, the right to be heard implies the right of the victim to tell her own story with regard to the accusation in question, and to be taken into consideration by the court. Each victim must be provided the opportunity to address the court with a victim impact statement. Victims should also be heard before the court disposes of a case without trial, or enters into a plea agreement.

(2) The second basic right is the right to a *fair trial* for the victim. This right, too, has a connection to human dignity. Just as for the defendant, the

60. Art. 1 of the German Constitution [*Grundgesetz, GG*].

right to a fair trial is, in Germany, developed on the basis of an integrated view including, in pertinent part, articles 1 [1] and 2 [1] GG in combination with the rule of law, art. 20 [3] GG, and art. 6 [1] 1 of the European Convention of Human Rights (ECHR),[61] so should be a fair trial right for the victim. Even though the victim has no liberty interests at stake at trial—unlike the defendant—, it would be wrong to conclude that it is only the defendant's trial and not the victim's. For the victim, to see that justice is done can be an important factor in coming to terms with victimization. In recent scholarly discourse it has been said that not only the offender, but the victim as well must have the right to rehabilitation. Of particular importance is the truthfinding process and to have officially recognized that the offender's deed was wrongful (Hörnle, 2006: 950 et seq.).

In order that victims achieve active participation rights, the following rights for victims should be central:

- The right to make evidentiary motions
- The right to ask for an expansion of the accusation
- The right to ask questions at the taking of evidence and make statements
- The right to have the support of an attorney at the expense of the state
- The right to be informed and to have the assistance of interpreters.

If we are ready to recognize such a fair trial right for the victim, it is, of course, also necessary to consider inherent limits. As I mentioned in the introduction, the criminal justice process is a unique process that is governed by experts. It is important, therefore, to stress that this process must be foreclosed to populist sentiment. I see no obstacles, however, to an integration of the victim as an individual party, into the criminal justice process. Admitting, via the victim, the people at large with its hostile, generalizing sentiments into the process would, however, destroy the protective procedural setting that the state owes to the defendant. The criminal justice process operates in the name of the people, but it must not be run by the people.

References

Barton, S. (2006). Nebenklagevertretung im Strafverfahren. Ein neuartiger, aber kriminologisch vergessener Bereich der rechtsberatenden Praxis. In: T. Feltes, C. Pfeiffer, G. Steinhilper (Eds.), *Kriminalpolitik und ihre wis-*

61. Cf. BVerfG, *NJW* 2001, p. 2245; Beulke (2004: annot. 28).

senschaftlichen Grundlagen. Festschrift für Hans-Dieter Schwind zum 70. Geburtstag. Heidelberg: C.F. Müller, pp. 211–224.

Beulke, W. (2004). Strafprozessrecht. 7th edition, Heidelberg: Müller.

Hörnle, T. (2006). Die Rolle des Opfers in der Straftheorie und im materiellen Strafrecht. *Juristenzeitung*, pp. 950–958.

Meyer-Gossner, L. (2009). *Strafprozessordnung*. 52th edition, München: C.H. Beck.

Weigend, T. (1998). Gutachten C. In: *Verhandlungen des 62. Deutschen Juristentages Bremen 1998*, Vol. I. München: C.H. Beck, pp. C 1–C 131.

7

Victims on the Threshold of More Participation in the Austrian Criminal Justice System: Results of a Victim Survey in the Context of an Alteration of Procedural Law

Lyane Sautner & Helmut Hirtenlehner

Abstract

This chapter deals with the role of the victim in Austrian criminal procedure. In the dawn of a fundamental reform of Austrian procedural law that aims at strengthening the victim's position—the reform marks a change of paradigm that upgrades the victim from a pure witness to a full process party—a victim survey was conducted. The goal of the survey was to find out how satisfied the victims were with their role in criminal proceedings at that time and to determine the extent to which they approve the new rights they will be given. The article concludes with methodological insights on the use of standardized mail surveys to study victim samples provided by the police.

1. Introduction

The role a victim plays in the criminal justice system is influenced by various factors. The so-called criminal law theories play an important role here. Although they are seldom mentioned in positive law, as it is the case in sanction law, for example, which takes into consideration the general and special preventive necessities of punishment,[1] it can be assumed that the criminal law theories are the principles behind the criminal justice system. Criminal law theories which do not have the victim as a focus,[2] as it is the case in the idealistic retribution and the classical prevention theories, leave little room for the victim in the criminal justice system.

Besides these very basic considerations, there are also practical considerations which are relevant when defining the role of the victim in the criminal justice system. They generally concern the criminal procedure law, which establishes the way in which the victim has to participate in the criminal procedure and how the victim can realise his/her own interests within this process. Thus rules which regulate the adjudgement of damages within the criminal procedure have often been directed by thoughts of procedural economy. Regulations dealing with the protection of victims in criminal procedure result from the recognition that certain groups of victims, particularly victims of sexual offenses, often cannot be expected to participate at court in a regular way as this would mean to confront him or her with the offender again. A theory-based criminal law approach to the role of the victim on the one hand, and a practical approach on the other, are not necessarily opposing ideas. Many small steps taken by the legislator to improve the victim's position in the legal system can lead to a new understanding of the meaning of the victim in the criminal justice system. Such a change in understanding—which could mean a new criminal law theory is emerging—will, in the best case, affect positive law sooner or later.

Just such a development is currently emerging in the Austrian criminal procedure law. As the position of the victim has gradually improved in the criminal justice system since the end of the 1980s,[3] a clear change of paradigm has

1. Cf Austrian law, for example art 37 StGB (imposition of a fine instead of imprisonment), art 43 StGB (conditional sentence) and art 46 StGB (conditional release from imprisonment).

2. The fact that the victim does not play any role in the theory of retribution is quite obvious, because according to this, criminal law acts only on a metaphysical understanding of justice and applies this solely to the offender (cf. Prittwitz 2000: p. 59 f). The meaning of the victim in preventive justice is not so easy to understand. Positive, general prevention (so-called integrated prevention) has the aim of strengthening the social and ethical norms after the law has been broken; this actually refers to the general public, but recently the interests of the victims have been considered more strongly as a method of reaching this general aim. For more details on the relationship between the positive, general prevention and a restorative justice, see Hilf (2006a: p. 16).

3. The Criminal Law Reform Act 1987 (BGBI 1987/605) and the Criminal Proceedings Reform Act 1993 (BGBI 1993/26) implemented many regulations which prevent secondary victimisation, such as the right to refuse to give evidence, and the right to appoint a person of confidence (Jesionek, 2006: p. 214 f).

been completed. With the new law dealing with preliminary proceedings[4] which came into force on 1 January 2008, the victim of a criminal offense is recognized now as a subject of the criminal proceedings, independent of his/her damage claims, and is given a number of rights.

This change in the legal situation was the reason why a survey of victims was carried out in Linz,[5] the capital of Upper Austria, in 2006. The aim of the survey was to find out how satisfied the victims of criminal offenses were with their current role in criminal proceedings. Additionally, if the roles did not conform to expectations, then it should be possible to find out if the victims would approve the changes in the Austrian criminal procedure law.

2. The Position of the Victim in Austrian Criminal Procedure

The position of the victim in the Austrian criminal procedure was—and still is—characterized by the victim's obligation to give evidence and in connection with this, the aim to protect and consider the victim during the proceedings. This results in various rights such as, for example, the right to be freed from the obligation to give evidence,[6] the right to be protected while giving evidence[7] or to give evidence anonymously[8] or the right to have a person of confidence present while being questioned[9]—these are only a few of the rights. The dominance of the role as witness makes it understandable that any definition of a victim which would mean further participation in the pro-

---

4. Criminal Procedure Reform Act, BGBI I 2004/19. Regulations of the Criminal Procedure Reform Act are referred to as 'StPO-new.'

5. Limiting the research to Linz was done for practical and economic reasons. See the description of the methods at the end of the paper.

6. The right not to give evidence is given to victims of sexual offenses and victims who are under fourteen at the time of their questioning according to art 152 (1) no. 2a and 3 StPO. The requirement in both cases is that a so-called contentious hearing, that is questioning in the presence of both parties, has taken place. According to art 153 (2) StPO victims of sexual offenses have also the right to refuse to answer questions on highly personal particulars of their life or on details of the offense if this would be unbearable for them.

7. Art 162a StPO.

8. Art 166a StPO.

9. It is the right of a victim to be accompanied by a person of confidence according to art 162 (2) StPO, but, according to art 162 (3) StPO, it is obligatory for a victim who is not yet 14 at the time of the questioning, or who is mentally ill or who has a mental handicap, if this is in their interests.

ceedings was not covered in the former code of procedure.[10] Terms such as 'injured person' or 'aggrieved person' which are used in the criminal procedure are mostly used in civil law. Most of the rights to obtain information deal with protection and consideration of the victim. There are only few rights connected with participation. The victim has the possibility to join in the proceedings as a private participant in order to assert his/her civil law claim to compensation.[11] Although claiming for compensation is not participation to the criminal procedure in its real sense, the victim acting as a private participant at least has the right of access to records; he/she can provide the examining magistrate with any evidence that helps to reach a conviction of the accused;[12] he/she may participate in contentious hearing[13] and has the right to request that witnesses and experts are summoned.[14] As a private participant, the victim can conduct his/her affairs himself/herself or use the services of a counsel for the defence, a recognized victim protection organisation or any other authorized representative.[15] His/her rights of appeal are limited in general to appealing against the decision on their civil claims.[16] Additionally, as a private participant the victim has the right to represent the public prosecution as subsidiary prosecutor[17] if the public prosecutor does not prosecute the suspect or drops the case. However, subsidiary prosecution is of no practical importance, as the victim has to bear the risk of costs. At this point it should be pointed out that some of the regulations of the Criminal Procedure Reform Act relevant for victims already came into effect on 1 January 2006. This particularly concerns legal and psychosocial support of the victim throughout the criminal proceedings. Although care of the victim during the proceedings is already reality in Austria, I would like to deal with it in connection with the Criminal Procedure Reform Act because it is a part of the victims' 'packet.' With this we come to the legal situation since 1 January 2008.

To estimate the effect of the new legal position of the victim it is necessary to see it in the context of the reform of the preliminary proceedings. The Criminal Procedure Reform Act has distributed the roles played by the court, public prosecution, criminal police and accused in a completely new way. The

10. Höynck & Jesionek (2006: p.102) refer to the symbolic meaning(s) of the use of the word 'victim.'

11. Art 47 StPO.

12. Art 47 (2) StPO.

13. Art 162a StPO.

14. Art 222 (1) StPO.

15. Art 50 (1) StPO.

16. Arts 283 (4), 344, 283 (4), 465 (3) StPO.

17. Arts 48 f StPO.

court, which at present controls the procedure from the point of preliminary trial onwards, becomes an organ of control which mainly decides whether the law has been broken or not and approves the use of serious force. The public prosecution now is the head of the procedure, the field of responsibility of the criminal police is legally defined (and extended), and the legal position of the accused is strengthened. Within this circle of participants in the criminal proceedings the victim yet became subject of the proceedings. The importance of these reforms is reflected in the fact that the rights of the victim to participate in the criminal proceedings are laid down as a principle of the procedure.[18] In accordance to this is the obligation of the criminal police, public prosecution and court to consider the rights and interests of the victims and to inform them about their rights in the proceedings and the possibility of claiming compensation or receiving aid.[19] Restitution is included in the basic principles of procedure as in decisions about ending the proceedings the compensation of the victim always has to be investigated and the greatest possible amount supported.[20]

The key provision for all the victims' rights is the definition of the victim[21] which has been introduced by the reform of criminal procedure. According to this, a person is a victim if he/she has suffered damage through a criminal act or could otherwise be affected in his/her rights which are protected by criminal law. In addition to this very wide definition of a direct victim, within certain limits also indirect victims are recognized by the reform.[22] These include "the spouse, partner, direct relatives, the brother or sister of a person whose death may have been caused by the criminal act, or other relatives who were witnesses of the act."

The victim's position has changed through the reform in that his/her rights concerning protection and consideration during the proceedings have been extended. The same is true for the right to obtain information and the right to be automatically informed. The victim must be informed about the progress of the proceedings and, in particular, when the accused is released.[23] The most obvious change is in the victim's participation in its narrowest meaning. The rights given to the victim by the Criminal Procedure Reform Act include,[24]

18. Art 10 (1) StPO-new.
19. Art 10 (2) StPO-new.
20. Art 10 (3) StPO-new.
21. Art 65 (1) no. 1 StPO-new.
22. Art 65 (1) no. 1b StPO-new.
23. Most of the rights to obtain information came into force on 1 January 2006.
24. These rights belong to the victim independent of any civil law claims.

among others, the right to be represented,[25] the right of access to records,[26] the right to participate in contentious hearing as well as in taking evidence,[27] the right to question witnesses and experts as well as the right to have claims heard.[28] Completely new is the psychosocial and legal support to the victim throughout the proceedings.[29] All victims who could be subject to violence or serious threat through a premeditated act, or who could be injured in their sexual integrity, as well as the above-mentioned indirect victims, i.e., certain relatives of the person whose death may have been caused by the criminal act, have the right of such support. Of course the victim still has the right to participate in the proceedings as a private participant. The authority to pursue subsidiary prosecution is somewhat limited in favour of an application to the Court[30] to proceed with the investigation. Little has changed concerning the power to appeal in relation to the former law. The victim can appeal if his/her subjective rights[31] are injured or can lodge a complaint with the court[32] if his/her rights are violated during the investigations but the rights of the victim are not secured with respect to an appeal against the verdict. This can be seen as a deficit, as the whole responsibility for observing the rights of the victim lies within the power and goodwill of the court (Jesionek, 2006: p. 227). It also becomes obvious that it is not the aim of the law to give equally strong weapons to the victim, the accused and the public prosecutor. This ties in with the fact that the victim has no right to apply for evidence, except in civil claim suits.

This is very briefly the legal background to the survey of victims conducted in Linz.

3. Method

The empirical basis of this study is a standardized mail survey with people who have identified themselves as victims of criminal acts by reporting offenses to the police. The standardized mail survey method was selected in order

25. Art 73 StPO-new.
26. Art 68 StPO-new.
27. Art 66 (1) no. 6 StPO-new.
28. Art 66 (1) no. 7 StPO-new.
29. Art 66 (2) StPO-new.
30. Art 195 StPO-new.
31. Art 106 StPO-new.
32. Art 87 StPO-new.

to allow as large a group of victims as possible to reply, and so to get a representative picture of the prevailing opinions. The survey was done by post mainly because this is much cheaper than face-to-face interviewing.

The sample used for the survey were persons who had reported a crime to police stations in Linz[33] between 1 July 2004 and 30 June 2005 which led to an investigation by the criminal investigation department. An electronic record of the cases dealt with is kept by the criminal investigation department in Linz. The names and addresses of victims who had reported crimes were taken from this register.

The list of victims obtained from the police is not representative for all the victims of crime. In fact, there is a considerable bias concerning the severity of the offenses. Many victim surveys show that the crimes which are actually reported are far from representative of the crimes which are not reported[34] (Kesteren et al., 2000; van Dijk et al., 1991). A further source of bias can be found concerning the severity of the crime: criminal investigation departments prefer to work on serious crimes and on crimes which are relatively easy to solve (Kunz, 2004: p. 239; Steffen, 1976). This means that the list of victims used in the survey is biased towards more serious crimes.[35]

The group of victims registered in the electronic records of the police was further reduced in the next step. The following groups were excluded for methodological and substantive reasons: legal persons,[36] victims of sex

33. Linz is the capital of Upper Austria, has about 200,000 inhabitants, and is known for many types of industry and the good labour market situation. The unemployment rate was 3.7% in June 2005 (Electronic data system of the Upper Austrian Labour Market Service, http:www.ams.or.at/neu/ooe/1400.htm, downloaded 18 June 2006).

34. There are generally good reasons for not reporting a crime. The reason most often given, 'too little damage,' shows that these offenses tend to be less serious or intrusive. For information on selective reporting of offenses and the resulting bias of crimes registered with the authorities see Kesteren et al. (2000), Schwind (2003: p. 388 ff) and van Dijk et al. (1991).

35. Personnel from the Upper Austrian Executive confirm that petty crime plays a subordinate role in police records. Minor offenses such as theft with low value, shoplifting, bicycle theft, or minor damage to property are relatively under-represented in their daily work.

36. Behind this is the idea that the managers of enterprises which have been subject to damage through criminal acts (e.g., the manager of a supermarket which has been burgled) have not really suffered personal injury. Such persons are said not to show as much emotional and intellectual concern as persons who have been the victims of crime personally. This is probably why officials of victimized enterprises have a greater distance to any possible sentences. According to Kaiser (1993: p. 314) enterprises have a 'volatile victim characteristic.'

offenses,[37] persons who had been victimized by a family member (a close relative), victims of traffic offenses,[38] celebrities, victims of offenses where the police had noted 'not suitable for the press,'[39] and offenses concerning underage youth.

At the end of this selection process, the police named 1,646 victims who had been recorded between 1 July 2004 and 30 June 2005 in the electronic data system of the police criminal investigation department in Linz. A self-administered questionnaire was sent to these people at the beginning of February 2006. Four weeks later, a reminder was sent, together with a second copy of the questionnaire. The questionnaire was sent out by the police in both cases.[40]

A total of 694 persons filled in and returned the questionnaire, giving a return rate of 42%. 95% of the respondents said they had personally been the victim of a criminal act. 5% named another person as the real victim (generally a relative). As the idea behind the questionnaire was to find out the opinions of persons who had been directly affected by the crime; indirect victimization was not relevant. After the indirect victims had been removed from the study, the data set consisted still of 659 persons. Table 1 shows the sociodemographic profile of the respondents.

The subject of this work is the role of the victim in criminal procedure. As it concentrates on the experience of the victim in court it is necessary to limit the data sample to the victims who have reported a crime which has already been dealt with by criminal proceedings. This is true of about a fifth of the respondents. 18% of them (105 persons)[41] said that court proceedings had already taken place in connection with the crime they reported and that these proceedings had already finished.[42] If not otherwise specified, the findings in con-

37. Victims of sexual offenses were excluded through police sensitivity. The police authorities wanted to prevent the victim of a sexual crime from being confronted with the incidents again when it could be avoided.

38. These are persons who suffered injuries in traffic accidents where the other person involved was charged with bodily injury caused by negligence. It can be assumed that someone injured in a traffic accident does not usually see himself as the victim of a crime. This would lead to traffic victims having different needs concerning criminal law to the majority of 'classical' victims.

39. According to the police authorities, this is just a very small group. Less than 1% of offenses are classified as 'not suitable for the press.'

40. Data protection regulations did not allow the names and addresses of victims to be passed on to a university research institute.

41. 68 persons did not answer the question on how the proceedings had been carried out. If these persons are subtracted, there is a remainder of 591 on which the findings are based.

42. As victims generally have the status of lay persons in legal matters, we can assume that the question elicited information about the first instance of the criminal proceedings.

Table 1: Sample Description (N = 659)

Age	Percent
19–29 years	24%
30–39 years	21%
40–49 years	23%
50–59 years	14%
60 years and over	18%
Sex	
Male	55%
Female	45%
Nationality	
Austrian	94%
Other Nationality	6%
Residence	
Linz	70%
Outside Linz	30%

nection with the victim's role are based solely on the victims whose reporting of an offense led to court proceedings which have already ended.

4. Results

In the following we want to show how the victims of crime in Austria see their position in the judicial procedure, what kind of support is available for them, to what extent they make use of their rights, and which additional legal possibilities they would like to have.

4.1 Legal Advice and Social Support

According to the present legal situation, victims in Austria can claim different forms of support. These are especially: representation of their interests by a lawyer in the case of private participation, legal aid and psychosocial support from a lawyer and organisation for victim support respectively during the whole criminal procedure, as well as the right to appoint a person of confidence of their choice (friend or relative).

Most often, victims of crime find support and help in their private circle. 4 out of 10 victims with court experience said that a person of confidence had been present during questioning and proceedings, 23% always, 17% sometimes. A quarter (25%) had legal representation during the proceedings. 9% had taken advantage of the services of a victim support organisation.

In order to understand the findings it is necessary to realise that the sample of victims used here, and particularly in cases which went to court, had generally been subject to serious offenses. The victims in cases ending with a conviction had been subject to violence in 48% of the cases, or were the victims of burglary in 29% of the cases. With this background it becomes clear why 25% of the victims required a lawyer and 9% care from a victim support organisation.[43]

Among those persons who did not take advantage of their right to legal representation or support during the proceedings, there is certainly potential to extend the aid offered. 35% of the victims who did not have a lawyer during the proceedings would have liked to have legal representation. 23% of the victims who did not have support during the main proceedings would have liked to have it. Help was sought from victim support institutions mainly by the victims of violence.[44] 39% of the victims of violence would have liked to have support from a victim support organisation. The rates of respondents asking for victim support were much lower for victims of burglary (0%) or theft (13%).

4.2 Giving Evidence as a Witness

The interest of the court in finding out the truth corresponds to the obligation of all those subject to law who are summoned to court to give evidence about what they have observed. The victim, who if not even the only one, is often the main witness has this obligation like any other person. In order to reduce the danger of secondary victimization through giving evidence, there are various instruments to protect the victim. Among others these include the right not to give evidence, the possibility of considerate questioning and the exclusion of the public from court proceedings.

Almost two-thirds (64%) of the victims surveyed had given evidence in judicial proceedings. 36% had not acted as a witness in the court proceedings.

A comparison of the groups of offenses shows that it is particularly required from victims of violent crime to give evidence.[45] 92% of these victims gave ev-

43. Although the right to support during the proceedings only became law on 1 January 2006, and therefore was not available to the victims in this form, they nevertheless had the opportunity to have support during the proceedings from the victim support organisations.

44. Cramer's V = .43; $p \leq .01$.

45. Cramer's V = .54; $p \leq .001$.

idence personally during court proceedings. This is only true for 53% of theft victims and 36% of burglary victims.

Victims who gave evidence in court were asked how they had experienced the situation. There were roughly the same number of victims with positive experiences as negative ones. Just over half (52%) of the victims found the experience pleasant. Almost the same number (48%) found the experience stressful. Just as in the offense specific answers above, this evaluation of the witness situation was dominated by victims of violent crime. Two thirds (67%) of the victims who gave evidence personally had reported either bodily harm or robbery.[46]

Only 2% of the victims who gave evidence reported that the accused had to leave the room during their statement.[47] 98% said this was not the case. However, a third of the victims (33%) would have preferred the accused to leave the room. The remaining 65% gave evidence in the presence of the accused without this disturbing them.

Only 2% of the victims who had given evidence were able to do this outside the courtroom.[48] 27% would have preferred to give evidence in a special room. The remaining 71% gave evidence in the courtroom without this disturbing them.

In summary, the results of the findings show that about half of all victims found the giving of evidence an unpleasant situation. A third had preferred the accused to leave the room during their testimony; a quarter would prefer to give evidence outside the courtroom. These points of criticism cover the feelings of unpleasantness only partly.[49] There are other factors which make it difficult for victims to give evidence, but they could not be defined in this particular study.

4.3 Private Participation

Private legal claims arising from criminal acts (compensation for damage to property, for pain and suffering) are to be dealt with during court proceedings after an appeal by the victim. This means that the victim can participate in the proceedings up to the beginning of the court hearing in order to ensure

46. The number of theft and burglary victims is too low to evaluate their experience of being a witness separately according to offense.

47. Naturally these were the victims of violent offenses.

48. As expected, these were the victims of violent offenses.

49. 48% of the victims who acted as witnesses, and who found this unpleasant, did not want the accused to leave the room and neither did they wish to give evidence in a separate room.

his or her civil law claims are considered.[50] This kind of participation means that the victim becomes a private participant. A civil claimant has further opportunities to influence the proceedings—he has a right to see the records and the right to question the accused. Somewhat less than half of the victims (46%) whose cases ended with a decision of the court took part in the proceedings as a civil claimant. 54% waived this possibility.[51]

Participating as a civil claimant in criminal proceedings does not always appear to remove the necessity of conducting civil proceedings. 42% of the civil claimants surveyed reported that they were nevertheless referred to civil proceedings.

4.4 Wish for Influence

The extensions of the procedural rights of the victims of crime is based on the assumption that the victims would like to have some kind of influence on the progress of the criminal proceedings. More than half of the victims who have experienced court proceedings reject this idea. 54% were satisfied with the opportunities they had for bringing in their interests during the proceedings. 46% would have liked more opportunities to influence the course of the proceedings.[52]

The findings that almost half of the victims of crime who have experience of court proceedings would like to have more opportunity to influence the course of these proceedings raises the question of how these persons see the ideal position of the victim in procedural law. In the next step they were asked what additional rights they would have liked to have (independent of whether they would have availed themselves of these rights or not). Figure 1 illustrates the victim's profile of claims.

Victims who have already experienced proceedings ending with a court decision would primarily like to have the right to pose questions during court proceedings. A quarter of these victims would like to question the accused, the witnesses and the authorities personally. A fifth would like to participate in ascertaining the facts of the case, have access to the records of the case or be able to participate in decisions on whether the case is to be continued or not.

50. This right to join in is for ‚anyone whose rights are infringed through a crime or an offense which must be pursued by the authorities'. The only exceptions are victims of offenses which are not to be followed up by the authorities.

51. Different rates of private participation according to offense could not be observed (Cramer's V = .15; $p > .05$).

52. The wish to have influence is independent of the offense (Cramer's V = .22; $p > .05$).

Figure 1: Desired Rights in Criminal Proceedings (N = 101)

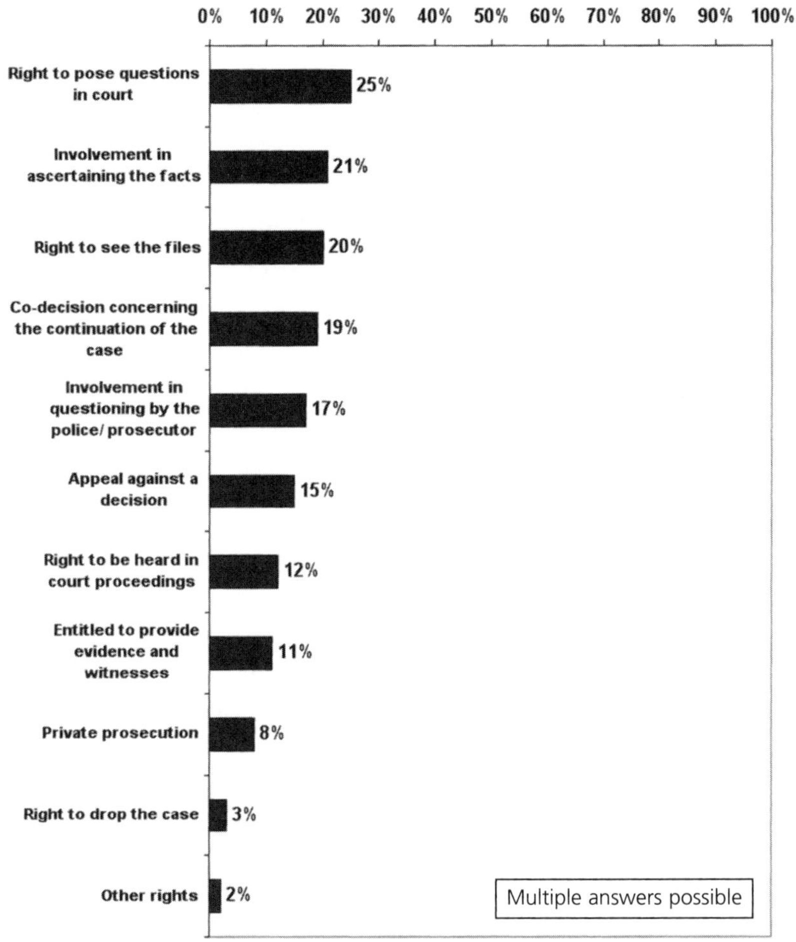

A sixth would like to participate in the questioning of the accused by the police or the public prosecutor. The opportunity to appeal against a court judgement was desired by 15% of the victims. The right to be heard by the court independent of their role as witness, and the right to request witnesses and experts independently were given with decreasing frequency. One in twelve victims would like to appear as their own prosecuting counsel. The possibility to stop the proceedings at any time or prevent them taking place at all was only desired by 3% of the victims.

Table 2: Satisfaction with the Legal Position of the Victim (N = 86)

	Percent
Very satisfied	16%
Fairly satisfied	48%
Fairly dissatisfied	24%
Very dissatisfied	12%
Total	100%

4.5 General Evaluation of the Victim's Standing in Criminal Justice Proceedings

An analysis of the victim's standing in criminal procedure not only requires an evaluation of their individual interests and how they utilise their current opportunities for participation and exerting influence, but also should provide information about their basic satisfaction with their role in the proceedings. To find this out, victims with court experience were asked to look back and consider how satisfied they were with their role (Table 2).

Looking back on criminal proceedings which resulted in either a conviction or acquittal two thirds of the victims gave a positive evaluation. 36% considered the position of the victim during the proceedings to be unsatisfactory.[53]

Those who were dissatisfied with the legal position of the victim were asked in an open question to give the reasons for their dissatisfaction. A glance at the points of criticism they gave shows that their dissatisfaction mostly arose from a lack of information and insensitive treatment by agents of the criminal justice system. Many victims would like more and better information about their rights during the criminal proceedings and also about the outcome of the case. Additionally, it seems that agencies of criminal justice should increase their sensitivity for the situation and needs of victims.

Some victims also criticized that it was not possible to claim damages or compensation for pain during the criminal proceedings. The inaccessibility of compensation during criminal proceedings means that the victims are referred to civil procedure. Many victims feel that the necessity to begin civil proceedings in order to protect their interests is an unpleasantness that could be avoided.

---

53. The evaluation of the role of victim in the criminal proceedings is independent of the type of offense ($\eta = .12; p > .05$).

5. Conclusions

In the survey of victims, the questions chosen and the findings concern all aspects of (possible) participation of the victim in the criminal justice procedure (cf Löschnigg-Gspandl, 2004: p. 161). For example, the questions on giving evidence deal with the victim's obligation to cooperate in finding out the truth, and on the other hand they also show the victim's need for protection and consideration during this procedure. Questions dealing with the victim as private participant concern the victim's interest in restitution; questions on the desire for more influence concern the victim's real participation. Questions on legal aid and social support play a part in all the sections mentioned.

If we are to analyse the findings of this survey of victims with criminal law in mind, there are different levels to be considered. 1) Firstly, there is the question how far the Criminal Procedural Reform Act actually meets the needs and interests of victims, as the aim of this reform is to provide for more consideration of the victim during the criminal proceedings. This means that the wishes and needs of the victims during criminal proceedings will be the benchmark against which the positive law is measured. 2) Based on this, the points of conflict which arise from considering the victim's interests throughout the criminal procedure should be pointed out. This concerns the balance between the needs and interests of the victim in relationship to guaranteeing a fair trial for the accused. 3) Finally, there is the sphere of penal doctrine, where the question is what can be gained from the findings of a victim survey for restorative justice.

Let us turn to the Criminal Procedure Reform Act. Giving evidence was found to be unpleasant by about half the victims and pleasant by the other half. The improvements which victims would like were mainly the removal of the accused from the courtroom while they were giving evidence and a more considerate and sensitive approach when being questioned. Here it must be noted that the Criminal Procedure Reform Act which regulates preliminary criminal proceedings has taken over sensitive questioning from the current law.[54] If it should be the case that, in future criminal procedures, the regulations on considerate questioning in the preliminary proceedings are to be applied to the main trial,[55] then the Austrian criminal procedure on one hand

54. Art 165 StPO-new.

55. Currently art 250 (3) StPO requires that art 162a (2) StPO (contentious hearing in preliminary proceedings) is applied in the main proceedings. Up to now such referrals have not been aligned with the regulations in the Criminal Procedure Reform Act.

has a legal instrument with which the victim's wish for more considerate questioning in the court proceedings can be satisfied, as the requirements for the use of these methods are relatively elastic; on the other hand the victim has no right of appeal that makes sure that a considerate questioning really takes place.

About half of the victims surveyed stated that they had participated in the criminal proceedings as a private participant in order to validate their civil law claim to compensation. As about half of these were then referred to civil law proceedings anyway it becomes clear that only for about a quarter of the victims it was possible to satisfy their wish for material compensation. Looking at this from the perspective of the Criminal Procedure Reform Act, the legal institution for civil participation not only meets this, but also tries to increase its effectiveness through a whole range of new regulations. Among these[56] are the right to call for evidence in the preliminary proceedings,[57] the possibility to appeal against a court decision to stop the proceedings,[58] and the basic procedural principle that on a decision to terminate the proceedings the victim's interest in restitution is always to be examined and to the highest possible amount supported.[59] Therefore the legal instrument to consider the victim's claims to compensation to a greater extent than before is included in the Criminal Procedure Reform Act.

The wish to participate in the proceedings, meaning to have more influence on them, plays a smaller role amongst the victims surveyed. Not even half of the victims were interested in having more rights to participate. The rights that they did mention concerned the right to obtain information, meaning either the right to ask questions during trial or the right of access to records, or to participate in finding out the truth. 'Hard' participation rights, such as the right to act as one's own prosecuting counsel or to file an appeal against the sentence, are not popular. Looking at these findings, it seems that the Criminal Procedure Reform Act has found an adequate solution by introducing many 'soft' participation rights, but also by not implementing the right of an accessory prosecution, the right to call for evidence or the right of appeal against the sentence (Höynck & Jesionek, 2006: p. 94).

The Criminal Procedure Reform Act definitely satisfies the wishes of the victims for legal aid and support throughout the criminal proceedings. The net of services has become more comprehensive through the introduction of

56. It is not possible to deal with all the reforms in this work. Cf, in detail, Hilf (2006b).
57. Art 67 paragraph 6 StPO-new.
58. Art 67 paragraph 6 StPO-new.
59. Art 10 paragraph 3 StPO-new.

psychosocial and legal support,[60] through the possibility to be represented independent of the exercise of civil claims[61] and to use the free services of a lawyer in certain circumstances as a private participant.[62]

All in all it can be said that the Criminal Procedure Reform Act accommodates the needs and interests of victims.

More rights for the victims would come into conflict with the rights of the accused. At the beginning of the criminal proceedings it is generally obvious that the injured party was the victim, particularly if he/she has suffered visible damages. In contrast, it is the criminal procedure itself which serves to ascertain whether the accused is guilty or not guilty. In other words, it is first necessary to find out whether the accused is responsible for the fact that the other party has become a victim. From this viewpoint it does not make much sense for both the victim and the accused to have the same weapons, as the accused then is confronted by two parties—the public prosecutor and the victim—both of whom are more interested in getting a conviction than a judgement of acquittal, although for different reasons. This makes the legislator's decision to reject 'hard' rights of participation for victims even more convincing. The other rights of the victim to participate are also somewhat problematic concerning the rights of the accused and the basic principles of the criminal procedure. It should be mentioned here that the publicity of proceedings, the immediacy of the proceedings and the principle of investigating the material truth could be endangered through the protection of, and consideration for, the victim. Just how far a limitation of these basic principles is acceptable is a question of balancing these against what is understood to be the legitimate needs and interests of the victim. However, one thing is certain; criminal justice without a reasonable consideration of the victim is no longer enough to satisfy today's legal requirements.

The conclusions that can be drawn from the results of the victim survey concerning criminal law theories are firstly that the interests of the victims which have been discussed in this connection by others (Kilchling, 2002: p. 59 ff; Hilf, 2006a: p. 16)—that is, protection and consideration, participation and compensation for the material and non-material damage—have been confirmed. However, not all of these fields are equally interesting for the victims. What stands out is that the desire to have more participation in the criminal proceedings seems not to play a large role in Austria.[63] If we try to give a mean-

60. Art 66 paragraph 2 StPO-new.

61. Art 73 StPO-new.

62. Art 67 paragraph 7 StPO-new.

63. This has already been explained above.

ing to the results of the survey, then we see in it the expression of a criminal justice culture in which the victim was only an object in the proceedings—the victim's role was limited to giving evidence. Only as a civil claimant could the victim make good his civil law claims against the accused. The change to a new understanding of criminal proceedings, in which the victim is a subject, has just begun in Austria. In other words, it can be assumed that the hesitant attitude of victims to more rights is partly caused by the fact that, for them, active participation of victims in the criminal procedure is not yet a matter of course. This would, however, be a precondition that victims can deal with the issue of active participation in depth. It can be assumed that the victims prefer to waive their rights in the proceedings because they do not understand the role well enough to be able to identify themselves with it. For the idea of a restorative justice, this could mean that the participation of the victim in the proceedings should not be underestimated because the victims have still to learn about their identity as active participants in judicial proceedings.

6. Methodological Excursus: Lessons to Be Learned from Our Study

A range of experiences were shared during the survey of victims presented here, and these could be of use to other academics concerned with victimology for the design and conducting of their studies, especially in the planning of the study and the use of mail survey in victim research.

The most important factor for getting a representative survey is the availability of a complete record of the total population in question from which an undistorted sample should be taken. In Austria no details of victims exist, neither on a national nor on federal state level. Lists of victims are only kept by local police authorities. Our original intention was to carry out a representative survey for the whole of Austria, but we had to give up this idea because collecting the relevant data from each of the local police stations would have meant an unjustifiable amount of research work.[64]

In recent years, the executive authorities have been subject to wide-ranging reforms which have led to rivalry and conflict between the police au-

64. Not all police authorities have a systematic data bank with details of victims. The registration of victims is not always done electronically, the registers are not organized in the same way, and are sometimes spread between different police stations. Even if the highest police authority had given instructions for them to cooperate, lack of personnel in the police force would have made it very difficult for them to provide support.

thorities. Research projects which need the support of different units of the police authorities can easily fall between the fronts. As the direct interest of some of the police authorities in the research project is rather low, victimological studies offer an arena for a conflict whose origin is elsewhere. Conducting such a study can be made very difficult, or even prevented, just because one gets between two different police authorities who are in conflict with each other.

When it is finally possible to carry out the study, the police authorities show considerable self-initiative. In this study it was agreed with the police authorities in Linz that they should take a random sample from the total number of reported crimes over a defined period of time. Only legal persons, persons who were under age and the victims of sex offenses were excluded. This sampling plan was then changed by the police themselves on their own initiative. The sample was taken only from the crimes dealt with by the criminal investigation department in Linz, and further groups of victims were excluded. The research team only discovered this by happy coincidence. The reasons behind this can only be guessed at. A motive for this modification of the sampling plan could have been the noble idea of ensuring that the results of the study were based on a group of clients who were more familiar with criminal justice because they had been more involved. Another motive could have been the desire to have a positive evaluation. Looking at the consequences of the sample design which was finally realized, we have to note that our sample of victims is distorted towards those who have suffered more serious offenses, and whose criminal proceedings are further advanced than is usually the case for the majority of offenses reported. There is evidence for both consequences.

Table 3 shows the distribution of offenses in the sample and their relationship to the official crime figures in Linz. It becomes clear that burglary is overrepresented in the sample here and the amount of violence is also higher than normal.

During the period of time set for the survey, 18% of the victims said that the crimes they had reported had already been dealt with by the court. 38% of the crimes had been cleared up and 18% of the accused had been convicted. However in total only 7% of the crimes in Austria lead to a conviction.[65] This difference is too great to be accounted for solely by the practice of acquittal.

65. The total crime detection rates for Austria for 2004 were taken from the Police Criminal Statistics of the Republic of Austria. The conviction rate was also calculated for the year 2004. The number of convictions shown in the Court Crime Statistics of the Republic of Austria was related to the number of suspects given in the Police Crime Statistics 2004. The product of the two values gives a conviction rate of 7%.

Table 3: Crime Structure

	Victims Participating in the Survey		Offenses Reported in Linz 2004*	
	Persons	Percent	Number	Percent
Burglary	290	47%	4.986	23%
Theft	183	29%	6.669	31%
Bodily harm	83	13%	1.809	8%
Robbery	26	4%	137	1%
Other offenses	40	7%	8.066	37%
Total	622	100%	21.667	100%

* Criminal acts according to the Criminal Code.

Source: Special analysis of police crime statistics 2004 for the City of Linz from the Federal Police Authorities.

Every survey of victims has to deal with the great problem of anonymity and data protection. Victims of crime want their case be dealt with confidentially. In our case, we were able to dispose of such worries by having the police authorities choose the sample and send the questionnaires. The university department conducting the research only appeared as the recipient of the questionnaires, which had been completed anonymously.

The question of how applicable mail surveys are for researching victims can also be discussed in the light of our experience. We would like to begin with the attainable rate of participation. The way the survey was organized led to a return rate of 42%. First, the police authorities sent the questionnaire twice together with a pre-stamped envelope to be sent in return directly to the university. This high return rate is particularly impressive considering that victims are very often from the lower educated classes (Kiefl & Lamnek, 1986; Lea & Young, 1993) and these groups participate less often in mail surveys than the upper educational classes (Diekmann, 1995: p. 361).

26% of the addressees returned the questionnaire in the first wave, another 16% in the second. This shows that the reminder had a substantial effect on the return rate and also leads to the assumption that having the police having written to them more than once also motivates people to participate who otherwise would not do so. It is also possible to gauge the level of compliance from looking at the questionnaire. The rate of missing values resembles an inverted U-form—on the first page, questions on the circumstances of the criminal act and why the victims reported the crime were answered by almost all the respondents. After that, the rate of questions answered on the legal position of the victim in the criminal proceedings gradually declines.

Some items on the standing of the victim in the proceedings and the exercise of his rights were not usable owing to the high no-response rate.[66] In the final third of the questionnaire there was a rapid increase in compliance again as more questions were answered. Questions with everyday formulations on the prominence of various sentencing goals were answered by almost all respondents. They were Likert-based measurements of the victims' attitude to the various sentencing goals, which had to be filled in using a seven-step rating scale. A high rate of answers was also given at the end of the questionnaire in a socio-demographical section, which was no problem for the respondents to answer.

To sum up our experience with a mail survey, we can only say that some parts did work, others not. Access to the personal data of victims is very difficult to obtain, and the researcher is dependent on the discretion of the relevant police authorities. Even if police can be convinced to cooperate, the practical organisation is often difficult.

As a researcher, one is well advised to anticipate a certain self-initiative in the police authorities, and not to misjudge their inherent dynamism that is difficult to control from the outside. The researcher should check constantly whether the activities of the police correspond to what was originally planned. Nevertheless, a representative, well-directed survey is hardly possible without their help, which is why we must be grateful for their cooperation at all.

Our decision for a mail survey was partly right and partly wrong. It depends on the form of measurement and the subject of the survey. Likert-based measurements of attitude which are formulated in every-day language seem to work well even when the questionnaires are self-completed. Information on the standing of the victim in the criminal proceedings seems to need more careful consideration, perhaps even special knowledge of legal matters and court proceedings is necessary. The answers are not easy for the respondents to provide, which results in a high non-response rate. If the necessary finance is available, surveys on the standing and role of the victim in criminal proceedings are better done face-to-face, when the interviewer can help the interviewee to avoid missing out questions which have such difficult content.

---

66. For the evaluations in this work the no-response rate was significantly below 10%. Only two of the items used showed a rate of missing values between 10 and 20%: these were the rate of private participation and the total evaluation of the role of the victim in criminal proceedings.

References

Diekmann, A. (1995). *Empirische Sozialforschung. Grundlagen, Methoden, Anwendungen.* Reinbek bei Hamburg: Rowohlt.

Hilf, M. (2006a). Der Strafrechtszweck der Restoration. In: U. Jesionek and M. Hilf (Eds.), *Die Begleitung des Verbrechensopfers durch den Strafprozess.* Innsbruck: Studienverlag, pp. 13–22.

Hilf, M. (2006b). Aktuelle Fragen der Privatbeteiligung. In: U. Jesionek and M. Hilf (Eds.), *Die Begleitung des Verbrechensopfers durch den Strafprozess.* Innsbruck: Studienverlag, pp. 61–72.

Höynck, T. and Jesionek, U. (2006). Die Rolle des Opfers im Strafverfahren in Deutschland und Österreich nach den jüngsten opferbezogenen Reformen des Strafverfahrensrechts: Österreich als Modell? *Monatsschrift für Kriminologie und Strafrechtsreform*, 89, pp. 88–106.

Jesionek, U. (2006). Die Entwicklung der Opferrechte im österreichischen Strafprozess. In: R. Moos, U. Jesionek, O. Müller (Eds.), *Strafprozessrecht im Wandel.* Festschrift für Roland Miklau zum 65. Geburtstag. Innsbruck: Studienverlag, pp. 211–227.

Kaiser, G. (1993). *Kriminologie.* Heidelberg: Müller.

Kilchling, M. (2002). Opferschutz und der Strafanspruch des Staates—Ein Widerspruch? *Neue Zeitschrift für Strafrecht*, 22, pp. 57–63.

Kesteren, J. v., Mayhew, P., and Nieuwbeerta, P. (2000). *Criminal Victimisation in Seventeen Industrialised Countries. Key Findings from the 2000 International Crime Victim Survey.* The Hague: DOHC.

Kiefl, W. and Lamnek, S. (1986). *Soziologie des Opfers.* München: Fink.

Kunz, K.L. (2004). *Kriminologie.* Bern: Haupt.

Lea, J. and Young, J. (1993). *What is to be done about law and order?* London: Pluto.

Löschnig-Gspandl, M. (2004). Das Recht des Opfers auf Wiedergutmachung. In: A. Dearing and M. Löschnig-Gspandl (Eds.), *Opferrechte in Österreich.* Eine Bestandsaufnahme. Innsbruck: Studienverlag, pp. 157–179.

Prittwitz, C. (2000). Opferlose Straftheorien? In: B. Schünemann, and M. Dubber (Eds.), *Die Stellung des Opfers im Strafrechtssystem. Neue Entwicklungen in Deutschland und in den USA.* Köln: Heymann, pp. 51–73.

Schwind, H.D. (2003). *Kriminologie. Eine praxisorientierte Einführung mit Beispielen.* Heidelberg: Kriminalistik Verlag.

Steffen, W. (1976): *Analyse polizeilicher Ermittlungstätigkeit aus der Sicht des späteren Strafverfahren.* Wiesbaden: Bundeskriminalamt.

Van Dijk, J.M., Mayhew, P., and Killias, M. (1991). *Experiences of Crime across the World. Key Findings from the 1989 International Crime Survey*. Deventer: Kluwer.

Section 3:
Restorative and Transitional Justice

8

Restorative Justice as Therapeutic Jurisprudence: The Case of Child Victims

Tali Gal & Vered Shidlo-Hezroni

Abstract

Therapeutic jurisprudence is the study of the role of the law as a therapeutic agent. It looks at the law as a social force that may produce therapeutic or anti-therapeutic consequence. Such consequences may flow from substantive rules, legal procedures, or from agents of the criminal justice system such as lawyers and judges. In fact, the task of therapeutic jurisprudence is to identify relationships between legal arrangements and therapeutic outcomes and to examine ways the law should be applied to support, or at least not to harm, those it affects (Wexler, 1992). This chapter focuses on child victims within the criminal justice system and examines the idea of restorative justice as reflecting a therapeutic jurisprudence approach. Following a discussion of young victims' vulnerability in the current legal system and the idea of restorative justice including its main principles, theory and supportive movements, this article suggests the different ways justice officials can provide child victims better therapeutic outcomes. In particular, the article reveals the importance of child participation in the legal process as a desired therapeutic outcome that will benefit children, families and communities.

1. Introduction

Therapeutic jurisprudence is the study of the role of the law as a therapeutic agent. It looks at the law as a social force that may produce therapeutic or anti-therapeutic consequence. Such consequences may flow from substantive rules, legal procedures, or from agents of the criminal justice system such as lawyers and judges. In fact, the task of therapeutic jurisprudence is to identify relationships between legal arrangements and therapeutic outcomes and to examine ways the law should be applied to support, or at least not to harm, those it affects (Wexler, 1992). This chapter uses a therapeutic jurisprudence (TJ) perspective to critically examine how the criminal justice system treats child victims; it further examines the idea of restorative justice (RJ) as reflecting a therapeutic jurisprudence approach toward victims in general and child victims in particular. Following a discussion of young victims' vulnerability in the current legal system, and the idea of RJ including its main principles, theory and practice, this chapter considers the concerns, as well as potential benefits, of RJ for victimized children.

2. The Vulnerability of Child Victims in the Criminal Justice System

Children and youth[1] are at increased risk of becoming victims of crime (Finkelhor, 2008), and consequently are likely to become involved in the criminal justice process that follows their victimization. When examining Western, adversarial criminal justice systems from a TJ perspective, it becomes clear that child victims can only rarely benefit from processes following their victimization. Commonly, child victims are in fact further traumatized, disempowered, and alienated from the process, and those who are victimized in their homes suffer most (Morgan & Zedner, 1992; Fortin, 2003; Herman, 2003; Zedner, 2004). The negative experiences of child victims in the criminal justice process result from the very nature of the criminal justice system. The major participants are the state, represented by the prosecutorial authority, and the offender. Whether mature or minor, victims' role is limited to that of witnesses. Victims, even when invited to present their opinions, are not considered parties to the process. In many cases, the process ends with a plea bargain, leaving no role at all for the victims; in other cases victims have only a passive role when they are called to give testimony. Even in the latter case, victims of all ages and of various crimes often are not given opportunities to tell their stories on their own terms, to ask questions that bother them or to talk about the aftermath of their victimization (Herman, 1992). Moreover, subjective feelings and impressions of the victims are typically excluded from the legal process and the

1. In this chapter we regard all young people under the age of 18 as children, in accordance with the legal definition of "a child" in many jurisdictions and international documents, in particular the UN Convention on the Rights of the Child.

victims are required to ignore some parts of their story and even change their testimony to comply with evidentiary rules. It is also argued that victims tell their stories in an extremely hostile environment only to provide the defense opportunities to find inconsistencies and portray them negatively (Scheppele, 1989; Taylor, 2004).

When the victim is a child, there are additional difficulties that make the criminal justice process particularly disturbing.[2] Due to young victims' limited knowledge and experience, their understanding of the process, its importance and the rationales behind various procedural rules is very limited. Therefore, children often experience greater anxieties, resent the need to testify, or believe that they are the ones being judged. Furthermore, taken away from their natural environments of school and home and needing to communicate with a large number of unfamiliar adults, many of whom are often not trained or used to speaking with young people, child victims in this adult oriented environment might feel even more alienated and scared.

Another stressful factor for child victims is the problem of language. Professional jargon, while often threatening and unclear to many adults, is particularly threatening for children whose vocabulary has not fully developed. Even words that professionals think are not 'jargon' might be unfamiliar and enhance the anxiety of young victims. In addition, childhood victimization carries with it some specific characteristics that make the process harder for children. Often, a large number of professionals are involved (such as child protection and education officials) that are not involved in crimes against adults and multiple interviews of the young victim are required. Combined with their limited understanding of the process, children often think that their reports are somehow wrong or that they are the ones under investigation. Finally, since children are often considered less reliable witnesses, they are regularly faced with either the acceptance of a plea bargain, or a particularly harsh investigative process in court (Morgan & Zedner, 1992).

---

2. Despite evidence regarding the stress associated with children's involvement in the criminal justice process following their victimization, it is important to remember that not everything is negative in that process, and not all children experience it as stressful or traumatic. Thus, for example, a positive outcome arising from the criminal justice process is the finding of guilt related to feelings of vindication and that justice was done. A finding of guilt also delivers a message of trust in the child's testimony, an acknowledgment of the wrong done to him or her, and a public message of denunciation. Other positive elements for child victims in the criminal justice process may be a feeling of empowerment as a result of being able to testify against the perpetrator and a cathartic experience since the young victims finally confronted their past and put it behind them (See: Peters et al., 1989; Cashmore, 1995; Ghetti et al., 2002).

Not surprisingly, the criminal process itself has been notoriously known as being re-victimizing, or causing a 'secondary victimization' for many child victims (Morgan & Zedner, 1992; Fortin, 2003; Herman, 2003; Zedner, 2004). The following are some of the most stressful events in the criminal justice process for young victims: testifying in court, waiting for testimony, being at the courthouse and some specific issues in family abuses cases.

Testifying in court has consistently been found as a stressful task for children (Eastwood & Patton, 2002; Ghetti, Weede & Goodman, 2002; Whitcomb, 2003; Malloy, Mitchell, Block, Quas & Goodman, 2006). Increased anxiety during testimony has been linked with being under cross examination, having to face the accused, discussing personal events in public, the formality and unfamiliarity of the process, and the need to testify multiple times (Cashmore, 1995; Ghetti et al., 2002, Malloy et al., 2006). Repeated testimonies and harsh cross examinations are correlated with greater distress during testimony as well as with higher risk of trauma in the longer term, including in adulthood (Ghetti et al., 2002; Whitcomb, 2003; Malloy et al., 2006). In Australia, for instance, children who were interviewed following their cross examination said that the cross examination, which could take hours and days, was particularly stressful. They described it as horrible, confusing and upsetting, and many felt they were being accused of lying (Eastwood & Patton, 2002).

Delays in the trial and particularly in the child's testimony can also be stressful for children and at the same time may add evidentiary difficulties as children's memory can fade (Fortin, 2003). In Australia, in-depth interviews of child victims and their parents revealed that long periods of waiting (lasting an average of 18 months) prevented children from being able to move on with their lives. They were expected to maintain their memory about what happened, were not allowed to discuss it with their families and supporters and their psychological treatment was put on hold. Typically they spent their time worrying about the upcoming trial. Children also reported having nightmares, feeling depressed, feeling great fears, not being able to concentrate at school, as well as feelings of self hatred and suicidal behavior (Eastwood & Patton, 2002).

The mere presence at the courthouse can also be stressful for child victims. In some jurisdictions child witnesses still have to wait (often for long hours, even days) in waiting rooms or corridors that are not geared for children. Often children are worried about meeting the offender and the offender's supporters. Sometimes they are not allowed to leave the room, either for their protection (to prevent an unwanted encounter with the defendant) or for fear of contaminating their testimony. These waiting periods are stressful for children, especially when there are no child friendly facilities (Whitcomb, 2003; Malloy et al., 2006).

When allegations of sexual abuse occur within families, there are additional difficulties. First, reporting the abuse carries the potential of separation from the family, which is a great source of stress and uncertainty for abused children (Ghetti et al., 2002; Malloy et al., 2006). Second, these children might find themselves testifying and being interviewed in multiple proceedings, each of them stressful: in the criminal court for questions of guilt and penalty, in the juvenile court for protection measures, and in the family court as part of divorce proceedings (Myers, 1994). Finally, the need to testify against their caretaker is particularly difficult since this is often someone whom they still love and hope to be loved by, despite the victimization (Fortin, 2003). In the specific case of interfamilial crimes, which, until the age of 7–8, are the most common crimes against children (Finkelhor, 2008, pp. 40–42), children may also incur direct financial and emotional consequences as a result of the defendant's incarceration and the family breakdown.

To summarize, the empirical findings reviewed here present a concerning situation from a TJ perspective, which seeks to uncover the emotional impact of the legal process on its participants beyond the specific context of the case and its outcomes (King, 2008a).

The findings support arguments regarding the stress related to the involvement in the justice process for child victims, especially with regard to the child's own testimony. While most or all children who testify endure anxiety during their testimony, many still suffer emotional difficulties which continue in the following weeks and months after the trial, especially after being interviewed numerous times and being required to go through unpleasant cross examination. In extreme situations, testifying in court has been correlated with long term mental health problems which continue into adulthood, particularly if the child did not have maternal support and when the trial ended with acquittal (Whitcomb, 2003; Malloy et al., 2006).

In the last three decades many jurisdictions have legislated various child-victims' reforms in order to better address the difficulties they face in the criminal justice system. These reforms include: expedited proceedings, special waiting areas, reduced formality (i.e., taking off wigs and robes and changing seating arrangements), exemptions from corroborating evidence requirements in cases of child testimony, the use of video cameras for early interviews, the use of Closed Circuit Television (CCTV) to enable children to testify from another room during the trial, the use of screens to prevent eye contact when CCTV is not available or undesirable, prohibitions on defendants from conducting cross examinations, the use of support persons to sit next to children testifying in court, and special children's courts for sexual abuse cases (See: Morgan & Zedner, 1992; Eastwood & Patton, 2002; Fortin, 2003; Whitcomb,

2003; Malloy et al., 2006; Burton, Evans & Sanders, 2006). It is important to note, however, that the implementation of these reforms has been limited (Groenhuijsen, 2004), and there is no empirical evidence that the emotional healing of victims has improved in jurisdictions where reforms have been introduced (Herman, 2003).

First, despite their availability, some of these reforms are only rarely used, either because of questions regarding the defendant's due process rights,[3] or because of the prosecution's concerns that the use of an alternative to the child's live testimony in court will reduce the credibility of the child's testimony, and as a result impair the prospects of proving the case (Goodman et al., 1998; Eastwood & Patton, 2002; Ghetti et al., 2002; Whitcomb, 2003; Malloy et al., 2005). In particular, the U.S. Supreme Court stated that the use of CCTV has to be balanced with the defendant's constitutional right to confront the accuser. Accordingly, CCTV can only be used in the U.S. if there is proof that the child will be so affected by confronting the accused in court that they will not be able to reasonably communicate while testifying (Ghetti et al., 2002; Malloy et al., 2006). This narrow ruling makes it difficult to use CCTV in most cases. Indeed, only a small minority of victimized children in the U.S. are allowed to give their testimony through CCTV (Myers, 1994; Whitcomb, 2003). This is also the case in the UK, where even though comprehensive reform has granted all child victims a 'status' of vulnerable witnesses deserving special measures of protection, CCTV is used only in a minority of cases, either because of due process considerations or due to assumptions regarding the capabilities of older children to testify in court (Burton et al., 2006).

Videotaped forensic interviews are yet another example: in the United States, they are only used in 17 percent of child sexual abuse trials (Malloy et al., 2006). In the UK, they are employed only in about a quarter of cases involving child witnesses, despite the statutory presumption for the use of video recorded interviews (Burton et al., 2006). Furthermore, even when such interviews are videotaped, they are usually additional to the child's live testimony and not an alternative to it, a fact that defeats the purpose of reducing the number of interviews the child has to go through (Malloy et al., 2006). Indeed, there is no evidence that the use of tape-recorded interviews reduces the number of interviews child victims have to endure (Cashmore, 2002).

Other measures are used even less. The removal of wigs, for instance, is used only in 15 percent of identified vulnerable witnesses in the UK (Burton

3. This is the case particularly in the U.S., where the right to due process has a constitutional status.

et al., 2006). In New South Wales, where a specialized Children's Court for sexually abused children was piloted, a recent evaluation found that despite specific training and child friendly regulations, not much has changed for child victims of sexual crimes. In particular, cross examination was still experienced as a stressful, unfair process and judges varied in their motivation and effectiveness in controlling defense attorneys. Additionally, delays often still occurred and technical problems with the equipment emerged (Cashmore & Trimboli, 2005).

Even support persons, although welcomed in theory, did not always escort the child witness to court, for various reasons, such as being required to testify at a later stage (Cashmore, 1995). In fact, trained volunteers or staff who accompanied the child as supporters did not resolve this difficulty. From a child's perspective, a victim services volunteer, who the child has met only shortly before the trial, does not address their need to be escorted by someone they are familiar with and trust (Plotnikoff & Woolfson, 2004).

Beyond the limited implementation of the above-mentioned reforms, a closer look at the way children experience them reveals that even when practiced, they do not offer a full remedy for victimized children. For example, even tape recorded interviews may be experienced as stressful by children (Fortin, 2003). Moreover, often technical difficulties emerge when certain techniques are being used. For example, when screens were used in Australia as an alternative to CCTV in order to prevent eye contact between the testifying victim and the defendant, problems arose because children could still hear the accused and see body parts (Cashmore, 1995; Eastwood & Patton, 2002). Even CCTV, which seems to be clearly a positive aid for young victims who need to testify, is not always used to children's satisfaction. There is evidence that some child victims would prefer to be present in the courtroom to tell their story in the defendant's presence and see him or her being punished. At a minimum, children would prefer to be consulted regarding the use of CCTV beforehand (Wade, 2002). This is not the current practice, at least in the UK, despite existing legislation (Plotnikoff & Woolfson, 2004; Burton et al., 2006).

The use of CCTV presents other limitations that surface when children are asked directly about the subject. In particular, children who testify through a CCTV are not allowed to have a family member as a supporter. Consequently, children state that, if informed, they might have preferred to give testimony in court, perhaps behind a screen, where they could have a familiar support person sitting next to them (Plotnikoff & Woolfson, 2004). Furthermore, these innovations are typically aimed at child victims of sexual and severe violent and intra-familial crimes. Other child victims are required to participate at the trial as any other witness, without any support (Whitcomb, 2003). Even when reforms are comprehensive and include all child victims, such as in the UK, in reality, as already mentioned, children who are not sexually assaulted, as well as older children are only rarely provided with special protection measures (Burton et al., 2006).

The use of Victim Impact Statement, a victim oriented practice providing victims with opportunities to tell courts about the way they were affected by the crime before sentencing, raises particular difficulties with young victims. In a study of child witnesses conducted by Cashmore (1995), court hearings in New South Wales, Australia regarding child sexual assaults during a 12 months period (1991–1992) were surveyed, totaling 517 cases. VISs were completed in only 23.4 percent of convictions, but only 13.8 percent were considered by the court. Younger children (aged 5 to 11) were more likely to complete a VIS in comparison with older children, and the researcher speculated that this was due to higher refusal rate by children aged 12 and older.

Another widely accepted reform is the preparation of children for court through age appropriate explanations of the court process, visits to the courtroom and the distribution of child friendly brochures describing the court experience. Enhancing children's understanding of the process has been found effective in decreasing their anxiety and improving their testimony. At the same time, these preparations are considered less controversial in terms of defendants' rights and the prosecution's interests, as long as they do not involve rehearsing or coaching the child (Morgan & Zedner, 1992; Ghetti et al., 2002; Whitcomb, 2003; Malloy et al., 2006). Yet, empirical examinations reveal that even this seemingly simple innovation is not implemented uniformly across jurisdictions and that some preparation programs are unsatisfactory. For example, children testifying in one Crown Court in England said that the preparation program did not provide them with sufficient information about their role in the trial, and some complained that in fact it even heightened their anxiety (Wade, 2002). Similarly, Burton et al., (2006) found that British children could not make informed decisions as to their preferred method of testifying since they had not had a court preparation visit at the stage of making those decisions, and therefore did not have a real understanding of how the various measures work.

It seems then that despite the introduction of child-friendly reforms in various jurisdictions, in practice the experience of most child victims in the criminal justice process is negative (Plotnikoff & Woolfson, 2004; Cashmore & Trimboli, 2005; Burton et al., 2006). First, important reforms such as CCTV, videotaped interviews and expedited proceedings are typically implemented only in cases of family and sexual abuse of children. Many other young victims, while still vulnerable due to their young age, are often required to testify in court as adults. Second, even in cases of sexual and family abuse, very often prosecutorial considerations and legal constraints lead to the decision not to apply stress reducing techniques, exposing victims to live testimony in court in front of the defendant. Thirdly, the effectiveness of these reforms has not yet been proved and seems to vary among jurisdictions. To use TJ terminology, in many cases child victims experience the criminal justice process as anti-therapeutic. Efforts to change this situation have not made significant changes. Children still see the process as alienating, frightening, disempowering and distressing (King, 2008a).

There is no doubt that there is much room for improvement in the criminal justice process, in the directions that many reforms have already taken. It is clearly demonstrated that when certain techniques are practiced, much of the stress experienced by child victims in the criminal justice process can be eliminated or at least reduced, and the satisfaction of the young victims with the process may be increased (Eastwood & Patton, 2002). These reforms are all derived out of a therapeutic approach aiming to reduce the stress endured by children involved in the criminal justice process. Nevertheless, even in ideal child friendly frameworks some aspects of the criminal justice process will not change, since it is based on fact finding and punishment. These are in conflict with some broader needs and interests of all victims, but perhaps child victims in particular, to tell their stories on their own terms, have their harms acknowledged and behavior validated, and to experience a sense of control and empowerment during the criminal justice process (King, 2008a). To positively address these interests of child victims, perhaps there is a need for a radically different approach. One promising direction is restorative justice and its implementation as an alternative to the criminal justice process. The following section presents the RJ approach.

3. Restorative Justice

Born out of disappointment with both the retributive and rehabilitative justice paradigms (Strang, 2002), RJ has emerged as a 'third lens,' according to which:

> *"Crime is a violation of people and relationships. It creates obligations to make things right. Justice involves the victim, the offender, and the community in a search for solutions which promote repair, reconciliation, and reassurance" (Zehr, 1990, p. 181).*

Restorative justice can be defined either as a process, or as a theory encompassing specific values and principles (Braithwaite & Strang, 2001). Marshall

(1999 p. 5) provided the most widely accepted definition of the procedural aspects of RJ, according to which it is " ... *a process whereby parties with a stake in a specific offence collectively resolve how to deal with the aftermath of the offence and its implications for the future.*"

According to Braithwaite (1999) the parties with a stake in the offence are typically victims, offenders and the affected community and the damage to be restored is whatever the stakeholders see as needing to be restored. The United Nations' *Basic Principles on the Use of Restorative Justice Programmes in Criminal Matters (2002)* provide a similar definition. Accordingly, 'restorative process' is defined as:

> "... *any process in which the victim, the offender and/or any other individuals or community members affected by a crime actively participate together in the resolution of matters arising from the crime, often with the help of a fair and impartial third party. Examples of restorative justice process include mediation, conferencing and sentencing circles" (Article I (3)).*

As to the principles underlying RJ, Morris and Maxwell (2001) argue that the critical values of RJ are:

> "... *the primacy of victims, offenders and communities of care through their inclusion in decision-making processes about how to deal with the offending and its aftermath; acceptance by victims, offenders and communities of some community or collective as well as individual responsibility for the offending and/or the reasons underlying it; an increased understanding on the part of victims, offenders and communities of care of the reasons for the offending and its impact on others; respect for all the parties involved in the process and the avoidance of stigmatic shaming; acknowledgment of responsibility for the offending through making amends; the reduction of reoffending; the reintegration of offenders and victims within their communities of care; and healing victims' hurt.*"[4]

Other critical RJ values identified in the literature are: Participation (Marshall, 1999; Moore & McDonald, 2000; Roche, 2003); reparation (Sherman, 2000; Roche, 2003); community involvement (Marshall, 1999; Sherman, 2000); crime as belonging to individuals (Morris & Maxwell, 2001; Roche,

---

4. *Id.*, at 267–8.

2003); deliberation (Moore & McDonald, 2000; Sherman, 2000); flexibility of practice (Marshall, 1999); equality (Moore & McDonald, 2000; Sherman, 2000; Braithwaite, 2003); forward looking approach (Marshall, 1999); and victims' involvement (Sherman, 2000). Nevertheless, respect is the most important value of RJ, and the reason behind other values such as participation, equality and reparation. Respect is perhaps also what differs RJ from the criminal justice process most. In the criminal justice process victims are not treated as individuals, subjects of their on rights, but rather as evidentiary objects (Wemmers, 2009). The treatment of victims and offenders as individual, separate subjects of the law is critical in the understanding of the therapeutic force of RJ. Indeed, RJ programs lead to substantially greater victim satisfaction across different jurisdictions, crimes, and programs (Shapland et al., 2007, Strang, 2002).

One of the central forces in the development of RJ has been the victims' movement, which advocated increasing services and financial restitution for victims (mainly in Europe) and for more participation and other procedural rights in the criminal process (particularly in the United States) (Van Ness & Strong, 1997; Strang, 2002). The victims' rights movement has been instrumental in uncovering the financial, physical and emotional impacts of crime on victims. It also identified the needs and wishes of victims that are, despite common stereotypes, far from retributive: When offered, victims prefer to receive material and symbolic reparation from their offenders; they want to be treated fairly and with respect and they want informal processes in which they can have a say (Shapland, 1984; Strang, 2002).

As 'emotionally intelligent' practice (Sherman, 2003; King, 2008b), RJ addresses each of the above-mentioned wishes of crime victims. It promotes individual participation and empowerment through a shift from professional decision-making; it emphasizes the importance of emotional and material reparation to the victim; it puts victims' needs at the center and provides space for storytelling and respectful listening (Hudson, 2003). The recurring notions of empowerment, active participation and non-domination apply to all participants, but importantly in the current context they apply to victims, including vulnerable ones as child victims.

4. Restorative Justice in Practice

The three practices most considered as restorative are Victim Offender Mediation (VOM), Conferencing, and Circles (Strang, 2002; Schiff, 2003). They are all 'restorative' in both values and process, and involve a direct dialog between victims and offenders (Shapland, 2003). They are also designed to put victims at the center, to encourage them to tell their stories, and to provide them with the opportunity to gain some control over the outcomes of the process. In most of these processes victims are also able to hear their family members and the offender's family condemning the crime and acknowledging their harm.

In mediation, the offender and the victim meet, with the support of a mediator, and discuss the crime and its aftermath. A restitution agreement is then reached. The mediator plays an active role in negotiating this agreement with the victim and the offender. The completion of the agreement is monitored in the follow-up phase (Umbreit, 1999).

Conferencing involves more participants. Typically, a conference involves the offender, the victim, and their respective communities of support, including usually family members and friends, teachers, spiritual leaders or others who have meaningful relationships with them. A facilitator provides the setting and leads the discussion, but otherwise leaves as much as possible of the discussion for the participants to work out for themselves. Other professionals, such as police and social workers, may also be present to provide information. The objective, however, is for the decisions to be made by the stakeholders, not the professionals. In some programs, such as in Family Group Conferences (FGC) or Family Group Decision Making Conferences (FGDM), an important part of the process is family private time, where professionals and other stakeholders leave the room and the offender and his or her family remain to decide on a plan. After an agreement has been reached, the other participants are invited in and the plan then needs to be approved.

Circles are yet a broader forum of decision-making, in the sense that they create opportunities for involvement of a whole indigenous community and its traditions. Sentencing circles are post-conviction mechanism designed as an alternative to a sentencing hearing. They are practiced largely in Aboriginal communities in Canada and in the United States and in some jurisdictions in Australia as a means to rehabilitate offenders, reduce recidivism, and empower the community. The participants in sentencing circles are the victim and the offender, their families, community elders and other community members, as well as state officials such as the sentencing judge, defense attorney, public prosecutor, and often the social worker or probation officer. The participants sit together in a circle and talk about the offence and the desired outcome, until a consensus is reached regarding the disposition. The final decision, however, is typically made by the sentencing judge, who can also decide to return the case to court. Sentencing circles hold political significance, as they are perceived as an opportunity for Aboriginal communities to regain their independence in controlling crime within their own community and reduce the numbers of incarcerated Aboriginal offenders (Goel, 2000). Healing circles, such as the Hollow Water circles, are even more traditional variants of the circle paradigm, where non-indigenous judges do not sit in the circle with a veto. In Healing Circles the therapeutic goal is central and is aimed at the community as a whole.

Studies are overwhelmingly consistent in showing that RJ provides great benefits for victims in various measurements such as fairness, accountability, satisfaction, repentance and forgiveness, emotional wellbeing, and feelings of safety (Strang, 2002; Poulson, 2003; Latimer, Dowden & Muise, 2005). Summarizing numerous studies from Canada, the United States, Australia and New Zealand on victims' satisfaction, perception of fairness, participation and completion of restoration agreements, Immarigeon (1999) concludes that findings are significantly encouraging for victims. For instance, in the UK, victims who participated in direct mediation showed greater levels of satisfaction with the system; they regarded the apology, as well as the negotiation of restitution, crucial in the success of the process. Maxwell and Morris's (1993) conclusion regarding Family Group Conferencing showed that approximately 60 percent of participating victims found the FGC helpful. In general, the authors argue, victims felt better because they were included rather than excluded from the process. Importantly in the context of victims' wellbeing, Caroline Angel (2006) found that face-to-face RJ significantly reduced post-trauma symptoms among British burglary and robbery victims.

Notwithstanding important questions regarding the ability of RJ to reduce crime,[5] a TJ perspective suggests that as long as RJ does not *increase* crime, its significant contribution to victims' wellbeing and satisfaction provides strong justification to use it broadly. Considering the positive effects of RJ particularly on those who have been most affected by crime, it is suggested that it can be applied even in the more complex fields such as sexual assaults (Hudson, 2002) and domestic violence (Sherman, 2000). There are significant benefits in using RJ practices in severe crimes: RJ achieves denunciation of serious crimes through the presence of the abuser's family and friends; it takes crime very seriously by focusing on its consequences and searches for meaningful ways of holding offenders accountable (Morris, 2002b). The question that needs to be asked then is whether RJ poses similar benefits for child victims and what are the risks that should be considered.

5. In a nutshell, a systematic review of well-constructed experiments comparing RJ and court processes found that RJ did not increase recidivism (in all but one study), and in many cases in fact reduced recidivism rates. See Sherman and Strang 2007.

5. Restorative Justice and Child Victims: Concerns and Practical Solutions

Considering the anti-therapeutic effects of the criminal process on child victims on the one hand, and the evidence on the therapeutic benefits of RJ to crime victims in general on the other, TJ calls for the expansion of the use of RJ involving child victims. Restorative justice initiatives involving child victims appear in many countries including New Zealand, Australia and Canada and often show positive outcomes.[6] Although there are no studies specifically focused on the involvement of child victims in RJ (in comparison with or separately from adult victims), it is still worth noting that studies have consistently shown higher levels of satisfaction and better recovery signs for the majority of 'conferenced' victims, including children, compared to court victims (McCold & Wachtel, 1998; McGarrell, Olivares, Crawford & Kroovand, 2000; Strang, 2002; Poulson, 2003). Furthermore, the experience in some of the RJ programs that involved child victims demonstrated that where significant efforts are made to allow young victims to actively participate, their participation can be considerable and the outcome results better than those achieved by other practices.

However, along with the general success of different RJ programs, not all victims, young and adult, were satisfied, nor were they all healed from their victimization. To ensure that RJ can indeed become a therapeutic alternative to the formal legal process for child victims it is important to address the concerns that arise regarding their involvement in such direct encounters with their offenders. The following paragraphs discuss the main difficulties found in some of the unsuccessful restorative processes involving child victims as well as their identified causes and possible solutions.

a. Re-Victimization of Child Victims

Perhaps the most serious concern regarding the involvement of young victims in restorative processes is the fear of exposing them to a revictimizing and intimidating encounter with the offender and the offender's support group. Indeed, RJ processes are intensive, emotional encounters that can be either very positive or very negative for the participants. Cases of revictimization and intimidation were recorded for example, though at very low rates, in New

6. For a detailed discussion regarding these programs and their evaluation see Gal (2011), ch. 5.

Zealand (Maxwell & Morris, 1993) and in South Australia (Daly, 2001). However, it was possible to identify at least some of the reasons for these failures. These were mainly: inadequate preparation of victims; inadequate search for support persons; operational issues (such as an encounter with the offender's family in the waiting area); and, critically, facilitators who were either too dominating or too passive in the protection of victims' interests. Conversely, victims responded positively to conferences when they were adequately prepared for what would happen; were greeted and introduced in the beginning of the conference; understood what was happening; were treated with respect; were involved in the decision-making; and received what they saw as a genuine apology from the offender (Maxwell et al., 2004). Indeed, the training and personal skills of the facilitator are critical to the success of the conference (Fraser & Norton, 1996; Maxwell & Morris, 1996; Marsh & Crow, 1996), and an insensitive facilitator can cause harm to the victim even when all formal requirements are met. Additionally, a thorough, face to face preparation of the victim and equally important, the offender, prior to the process has been recognized as crucial from the victim's perspective (Pennell & Burford, 1995; Umbreit, 1998; Maxwell et al., 2004). The preparation phase allows the facilitator to evaluate the ability of the offender to take responsibility for the crime without blaming the victim. It provides the victim an opportunity to become familiar and develop trust with the facilitator, so that there is free exchange of information between them. Moreover, when during the preparation phase victims are given adequate information, they know what to expect from the process and what will be expected of them.

Naturally, when the victim is a child the individual preparation is doubly important. It is an opportunity to identify the specific needs—rights of the child and to provide him or her with the appropriate tools to overcome their weaker position due to age, lack of experience and past victimization. The preparation phase further provides an opportunity for the facilitator to exclude the child from the conference and decide on alternative participation methods, be it according to the child's own wishes or the facilitator's concerns about the child's wellbeing. For example, in some child protection FGCs in New Zealand, facilitators decided to exclude either the child or the alleged abuser from conferences, in light of fears of additional trauma for the child (Robertson, 1996). In South Australian juvenile justice conferences, when young victims were reluctant to participate, other options were suggested during the preparation phase, such as nominating a friend or a victim's advocate to represent them at the conference. Other methods were the use of a tape recorder, letters or photos, in which victims could provide their perspectives without the need of being present at the conference (Wundersitz & Hetzel, 1996).

In the Family Group Decision Making Project (FGDM) addressing family violence in Newfoundland and Labrador, children who did participate in conferences were, as a requirement, escorted by an adult support person of their choice. The role of the support person was to provide emotional support, to speak on behalf of the child as needed, and to leave the room with the child for a break when this was required (Pennell & Burford, 1995). Another lesson learned is the importance of practical details, such as having an extra room available for children who get bored or need a rest from an emotionally charged conference (Marsh & Crow, 1998). It seems, then, that the flexibility of the process allows for a wide array of arrangements that can significantly minimize the risk of re-victimization and harm of child victims.

b. Children Being Silenced by Adults

Therapeutic jurisprudence highlights the importance of empowering victims to speak up and assert some control over the restorative process. Being able to influence the outcomes and, more broadly, being heard and taken seriously by the other participants is the antidote to the disempowerment and loss of control victims feel through their victimization. Meaningful participation of young participants, however, is challenging, whether they are victims or offenders. Indeed concerns that have been raised with regard to young offenders and their ability to participate in an adult-dominated discourse (Haines, 1998; Umbreit, 1998) are relevant to young victims as well: child-adult imbalance; adults paying lip-service to giving the young person the opportunity to speak, but not really listening to them; and young participants being "pushed into things" in the decision-making phase.

Nevertheless many RJ programs have found ways to empower young victims to speak up even in front of adults. The following are some solutions that draw from practical experience and observations of successful processes. First, the inclusion of support circles for both sides that include youngsters and adults, men and women can ensure that those who are silenced would be encouraged to speak up and those who dominate would be silenced by the other participants (Braithwaite, 2002; Morris, 2002b). Second, individual preparation is very important for the young participant, as lack of preparation may result in insufficient understanding of the process and lack of meaningful participation (Umbreit, 1998). At the same time, care should be taken not to dominate young participants in the course of informing them of the process and the possible outcomes (Morris, Maxwell, Hudson & Galaway, 1996).

Procedural fairness may also be helpful in preventing (or minimizing) young participants from being overlooked; this can be achieved by a protocol requirement to ask for the young participant's opinion at every stage of the process. To ensure that victims' views are communicated effectively, victims' advocates should take part in the process (Hudson, 1998). The role of professionals and community members in supporting victims during restorative conferences should, however, be well defined, and caution should be taken not to mute the victim and other participants through the introduction of yet another professional in the room.

c. *Young Victims Being Pressured to Be Forgiving*

Some programs, especially in the earlier stages of restorative justice, have been perceived as offender oriented. This led to criticism regarding victim insensitivity and facilitators putting explicit or implicit pressure on victims to help rehabilitate offenders, and to grant forgiveness, thus enhancing victims' feelings of re-victimization (Umbreit, 1998). Victim's feelings of being coerced to agree with others may occur even in a more victim centered practice, if the conference is unbalanced and when facilitation is inadequate. Indeed, Braithwaite (2002) warns against asking or expecting victims to forgive. Forgiveness, the author claims, is a gift victims can give, and making it a duty would destroy its power.

d. *Child Abuse: A Special Case Warranting Special Consideration*

Even if there are ways to overcome the special vulnerabilities and weaker position of children and to include them in restorative justice processes, still there are additional challenges in child abuse and other intrafamilial cases that warrant further discussion. These include extreme power imbalance, the ongoing nature of the relationship and the safety of the child. These are particularly complex because most victims of child abuse are of young ages, typically under eight years old (Finkelhor, 2008, p. 40), and many live in a violent environment in which the mother is also a victim of abuse (Edleson, 1999).

Power imbalance is of particular concern in many cases of prolonged child abuse. In such cases, not only are there often age differences between victim and offender, there is usually a relationship of control and coercion, where the child is "trained" to obey the victimizer (Morris, 2002a). This extreme power imbalance, which is typical in domestic violence cases as well, presents a serious challenge to restorative justice (Busch, 2002; Stubbs, 2002).

To address the power imbalance, in both domestic violence and child abuse cases, restorative justice proponents suggest that victims must be especially empowered, and coordinators have to ensure that the victim's voice and interests are heard, not only with regard to the outcome, but also when discussing the harms. In child abuse cases, adequate child representation is crucial (Bazemore & Earle, 2002). Furthermore, the flexible nature of restorative justice permits the involvement of multiple supporters for the victim including extended family members and friends; other participants, such as the family doctor or a school teacher may also act as protectors against any controlling, manipulative or aggressive behavior (Braithwaite & Daly, 1994).

Another important way of addressing extreme power imbalances is the use of indirect contact between victims and offenders (Zehr, 1990). With indirect contact, child victims can still benefit from the therapeutic advantages of restorative justice while enjoying the safety of not meeting their offender. They are able to ask questions and receive answers; to express their own feelings and wishes, and to have an impact on the final resolution; they are also more likely to receive apology and material restoration than through a court process. Nevertheless, while there is evidence that crime victims who directly meet their offenders in restorative justice conferences benefit from improved emotional state (Angel, 2004) there is no evidence as of today that *indirect* restorative processes actually help victims. Nevertheless with very young or traumatized victims this is sometimes the preferred alternative.

A second concern typical to family violence is the continual nature of the violence, the prospects for the future relationship between the offender and the victim, and concerns for the victim's safety that are typically peripheral in most other crimes (Stubbs, 2002). Accordingly, perhaps victims of family violence (both children and women) have needs that differ from those that restorative justice can meet:

> *"... while restorative justice literature emphasizes participation, apology and reparation, victims of domestic violence have emphasized safety and external validation of their attempts to stop abuse, together with deterrence and rehabilitation, over other possible outcomes" (Stubbs, 2002, p. 51).*

It seems, however, that RJ can address these issues much better than the punitive justice approach because it creates safety mechanisms based on the victim's supportive community and emphasizes the victim's safety (Sherman, 2000). The Newfoundland and Labrador experience, where Family Group Decision Making was practiced, showed that the safety of abused children can be maintained during and after the conferences, and that these processes can prove effective in reducing future family violence (Burford and Pennell, 1998).

Restorative justice programs in South Australia (Doig & Wallace, 1999; Daly, 2002; Daly & Stubbs, 2006) also demonstrated that sexual offences can be dealt with effectively through restorative justice conferences, and that RJ works well when there is an existing relationship between the victim and the offender. Moreover, the use of FGC has been successful in multiple-problem and complex cases such as those involving child sexual abuse and domestic violence (Wolfe, 2001; Jones & Finnegan, 2003).

Moreover, RJ proponents claim that particularly in serious crimes, victims can benefit more from a restorative process, as the emotional restoration is much greater through such a response (Marshall, 1999; Strang, 2002). Indeed, RJ has a lot to offer to victims of violent crimes, including compensation as a right; putting the victim's story at the center; restoring the relationships between the parties involved, as well as the more rehabilitative, restorative alternatives to punishment (Pranis, 2002; Hudson, 2002). Child victims in particular, it is argued, have an interest in the restorative option instead of the criminal justice alternative, especially in cases of intra-familial abuse:

> *"Children tend to love their parents come what may, and want the behavior to stop rather than their father imprisoned; children may be afraid of the consequences of breaking up the family ..." (Hudson, 2002, p. 622).*

Nevertheless, these concerns pose real challenges and require special precautions. Whether or not one is optimistic about the ability of restorative processes to overcome these challenges, it is clear that if RJ is to be practiced in child abuse cases, it must be constructed differently than for other crimes against children, and perhaps in conjunction with domestic violence cases. This was the case in the Newfoundland and Labrador FGDM experience, where a 'feminist praxis' was used and intensive work was invested in securing the safety and empowerment of abused family members, both women and children (Pennell & Burford, 2002).

6. A Lenient Response?

Even if, from the therapeutic perspective, restorative justice may be an appealing alternative for child victims, including in child abuse cases, there might be other arguments against it, external to the child's wellbeing but nevertheless important. One of these concerns is the appropriateness of RJ as a response to serious crimes. Perhaps serious crimes such as physical and sexual violence against children should be left for the court to resolve because of the grave violation of communal norms. Perhaps RJ does not provide a sufficient response in such cases. The criminal process addresses the public call for condemnation in cases of severe crimes, an aspect that is missing in RJ practices (Hudson, 2002). Further, perhaps it is simply against basic perceptions of fairness to "let offenders go" without being punished in such severe cases. In addition, concerns exist with regard to perpetrators who are clearly dangerous to society or who are unwilling to repair the harm and refrain from future crime (Hudson, 1998).

On the other hand, it is stressed that in reality the criminal process does not punish or condemn most offenders and in fact, in most cases 'nothing happens' (Daly, Curtis-Fawley & Bouhours, 2003). This is particularly so in child abuse cases, in which reporting levels are very low and evidentiary difficulties are common (Finkelhor, 2008, p. 103). It is also argued that the public call for punishment and condemnation is not supported by findings about victims' wishes, which are typically about the fairness of the process rather than its outcomes, and about material and emotional reparation rather than punishment alone (Strang, 2002). Moreover, the expression of disapproval of the act may be generated through the open, equal and non-dominated nature of the RJ process, where 'weak' victims can speak freely, and the process encourages progressive views (Hudson, 1998). Conversely, some argue that RJ processes include retributive elements in their outcomes, even when this is not their purpose (Daly, 2002). Hence, punishment is not completely irreconcilable with restorative justice values (Strang, 2002), as long as it is not perceived as a goal for itself (Zehr, 1990). Finally, a flexible RJ scheme might allow for severe crimes to be dealt with restoratively *after* a court process has started, either pre- or post-sentencing. Such an approach allows for both punishment and restoration to occur, integrating the formal court process with restorative and therefore therapeutic, elements.

7. Conclusion

Child victims within the current criminal justice system are a particularly vulnerable population. Their involvement in the criminal justice process has often anti-therapeutic results even when considering recent reforms and their implementation in the system.

Even though recent reforms within criminal justice systems apply many therapeutic principles, in practice they may be in conflict with some of the core elements of the criminal justice process such as fact findings, guilt establishment and evidentiary rules. Bearing in mind a therapeutic jurisprudence model, this chapter discussed RJ as a way to promote child victims' wellbeing through processes in which young victims who desire to do so are empowered to participate in safe, supportive face-to-face encounters with their perpetrators.

Beyond a call for the development and expansion of child-centered RJ, this chapter suggests that even within the criminal justice system there is merit in implementing RJ principles in cases involving child victims. A restorative approach within the justice system means enabling children to participate in the process by letting them tell their stories on their own terms, have their harms acknowledged, receive an apology from the offender, and experience a sense of control and empowerment during the process. These can minimize the criminal justice system's anti-therapeutic effects and maximize its therapeutic impact on child victims. More satisfied and healed victims means more cooperative witnesses and greater reporting rates of further crimes. Treating young victims restoratively, then, is not only beneficial for their own wellbeing as this chapter suggests; it might also increase the effectiveness of the justice system in preventing further harm.

References

Andrews, D.A. and Bonta, J. (2003). *The Psychology of Criminal Conduct*, Anderson, Cincinnati.

Angel, C. (2004). "Crime Victims Meet Their Offenders: Testing the Impact of RJ Conferences on Victims' Post-Traumatic Stress Symptoms." Presented at the American Society of Criminology Annual Meeting, Nashville Convention Center and Renaissance Hotel (Nov. 17–20).

Basic Principles on the Use of Restorative Justice Programmes *in Criminal Matters*: 2002. Economic and Social Council Resolution 2002/12.

Bazemore, G. and Earle, T.H. (2002). Balance in the response to family violence: Challenging restorative principles, *in* H. Strang and J. Braithwaite (Eds.), *Restorative Justice and Family Violence*, Cambridge: Cambridge University Press, p. 153.

Bonta, J., Jesseman, R., Rugge, T., and Cormier, R. (2006). Restorative justice and recidivism: Promises made, promises kept?, *in* D. Sullivan and L. Tifft (Eds.), *Handbook of Restorative Justice: A Global Perspective*, Oxon: Routleldge, pp. 108–120.

Braithwaite, J. (1989). *Crime, Shame and Reintegration*, Cambridge: Cambridge University Press.

Braithwaite, J. (1999). Restorative justice: Assessing optimistic and pessimistic accounts, *Crime and Justice* 25, 1–127.

Braithwaite, J. (2002). *Restorative Justice and Responsive Regulation*, New York: Oxford University Press.

Braithwaite, J. (2003). Principles of restorative justice, *in* A. Von-Hirsch, J.V. Roberts and A. Bottoms (Eds.), *Restorative Justice and Criminal Justice: Competing or Reconcilable Paradigms?*, Portland, Oregon: Hart Publishing pp. 1–20.

Braithwaite, J. and Daly, K. (1994). Masculinities, violence and communitarian control, *in* N. Tim and B. Stanko (Eds.), *Just Boys Doing Business: Men, Masculinity and Crime*, London: Routledge, pp. 221–251.

Braithwaite, J. and Strang, H. (2001). Introduction: Restorative justice and civil society, *in* H. Strang and J. Braithwaite (Eds.), *Restorative Justice and Civil Society*, Cambridge: Cambridge University Press, pp. 1–13.

Burford, G. and Pennell, J. (1998). Family group decision-making project: Outcome report, *Technical Report 1*, Memorial University of Newfoundland.

Burton, M., Evans, R., and Sanders, A. (2006). Are special measures for vulnerable and intimidated witnesses working? Evidence from the criminal justice agencies, *Technical Report 01/06*, Home Office.

Busch, R. (2002). Domestic violence and restorative justice initiatives: Who pays if we get it wrong?, *in* H. Strang and J. Braithwaite (Eds.), *Restorative Justice and Family Violence*, Cambridge: Cambridge University Press, pp. 223–249.

Cashmore, J. (1995). The evidence of children, *Technical report*, Judicial Commission of New South Wales.

Cashmore, J. (2002). Innovative procedures for child witnesses, *in* H. L. Westcott, G. M. Davies and R. H. Bull (Eds.), *Children's Testimony: A Handbook of Psychological Research and Forensic Practice*, West Sussex: John Wiley and Sons, pp. 203–218.

Cashmore, J. and Trimboli, L. (2005). An evaluation of the NSW child sexual assault specialist jurisdiction pilot, *Technical report*, NSW Bureau of Crime Statistics and Research.

Christie, N. (1977). Conflicts as property, *British Journal of Criminology* 17, 1–15.

Daly, K. (2001). Conferencing in Australia and New Zealand: Variations, research findings, and prospects, *in* A. Morris and G. Maxwell (Eds.), *Restorative Jusice for Juveniles: Conferencing, Mediation and Circles*, Portland, Oregon: Hart Publishing, pp. 59–84.

Daly, K. (2002). Sexual assault and restorative justice, *in* H. Strang and J. Braithwaite (Eds.), *Restorative Justice and Domestic Violence*, Cambridge: Cambridge University Press, pp. 62–88.

Daly, K., Curtis-Fawley, S., and Bouhours, B. (2003). Sexual offence cases finalized in court, by conference, and by formal caution in South Australia for young offenders, 1995–2001, *Technical report*, School of Criminology and Criminal Justice, Griffith University, SA.

Daly, K. and Stubbs, J. (2006). Feminist engagement with restorative justice, *Theoretical Criminology* 10(1), 9–28.

Doig, M. and Wallace, B. (1999). Family conference team, youth court of South Australia, *Restoration for Victims of Crime Conference*, Australian Institute of Criminology in conjunction with Victims Referral and Assistance Service, Melbourne.

Eastwood, C. and Patton, W. (2002). The experiences of child complainants of sexual abuse in the criminal justice system, *Technical report*, Report to the Criminology Research Council. URL: http://www.aic.gov.au/crc/reports/eastwood.html.

Economic and Social Council (2005). *Guidelines on Justice in Matters Involving Child Victims and Witnesses of Crime*, UN (E/CN.15/2005/20).

Edleson, J.L. (1999). Children's witnessing of adult domestic violence, *Journal of Interpersonal Violence* 14, 839–870.

Erez, E., Roeger, L., and O'Connell, M. (1994). Victim impact statements in South Australia, *in* C. Sumner, M. Israel, M. O'Connell, and R. Sarre (Eds.), *International Victimology: Selected Papers from the 8th International Symposium*, Australian Institute of Criminology, Canberra, ACT, pp. 205–216.

Finkelhor, D. (2008). *Childhood victimization: violence, crime, and abuse in the lives of young people*, New York: Oxford University Press.

Finkelhor, D. and Kendall-Tackett, K. (1997). A developmental perspective on the childhood impact of crime, abuse, and violent victimization, *in* D. Cicchetti and S. L. Toth (Eds.), *Developmental Perspectives on Trauma: Theory, Research, and Intervention*, New York: University of Rochester Press, pp. 1–32.

Finkelhor, D., Ormrod, R., Turner, H., and Hamby, S.L. (2005). The victimization of children and youth: A comprehensive, national survey, *Child Maltreatment* 10 (1), 5–25.

Fortin, J. (2003). *Children's Rights and the Developing Law*, second ed., London: Butterworths.

Fraser, S. and Norton, J. (1996). Family group conferencing in New Zealand child protection work, *in* J. Hudson, A. Morris, G. Maxwell, and B. Galaway (Eds.), *Family Group Conferences: Perspectives on Policy and Practice*, Leichhardt, NSW, Australia: The Federation Press; Criminal Justice Press, pp. 37–48.

Gal, T. (2011). Child Victims and Restorative Justice: A Needs-Right Model, New York: Oxford University Press.

Ghetti, S., Weede, K.A., and Goodman, G.S. (2002). Legal involvement in child sexual abuse cases: Consequences and interventions, *International Journal of Law and Psychiatry* 25, 235–251.

Goel, R. (2000). No women at the center: The use of the Canadian sentencing circle in domestic violence cases, *Wisconsin Women's Law Journal* 15, 293–334.

Goldsmith, A., Israel, M., and Dally, K. (Eds.) (2003). *Crime and Justice: An Australian Text Book in Criminology*, 2nd ed., Lawbook Co.

Goodman, G.S., Tobey, A.E., Batterman-Faunce, J.M., Orcutt, H., Thomas, S., Shapiro, C., and Sachenmaier, T. (1998). Face-to-face confrontation: Effects of closed-circuit technology on children's eyewitness testimony and jurors' decisions, *Law and Human Behavior* 22, 165–203.

Groenhuijsen, M. (2004). Victims' rights and restorative justice: Piecemeal reform of the criminal justice system or a change of paradigm?, *in* K. Hendrik and M. Malsch (Eds.), *Crime, Victims and Justice: Essays on Principles and Practice*, Hampshire: Ashgate Publishing Limited, pp. 63–79.

Haines, K. (1998). Some principled objections to a restorative justice approach to working with juvenile offenders, *in* L. Walgrave (Ed.), *Restorative Justice for Juveniles: Potentialities, Risks and Problems for Research*, Leuven, Belgium: Leuven University Press pp. 93–114.

Herman, J.L. (1992). *Trauma and Recovery*, New York: BasicBooks.

Herman, J.L. (2003). The mental health of crime victims: Impact of legal intervention, *Journal of Traumatic Stress* 16(2), 159–166.

Hudson, B. (1998). Restorative justice: The challenge of sexual and racial violence, *Journal of Law and Society* 25, 237–256.

Hudson, B. (2002). Restorative justice and gendered violence, *British Journal of Criminology* 42, 616–634.

Hudson, B. (2003). *Justice in the Risk Society: Challenging and Re-Affirming 'Justice' in Late Modernity*, Lancashire, UK: Sage Publications.

Immarigeon, R. (1999). Restorative justice, juvenile offenders and crime victims: A review of the literature, *in* G. Bazemore and L. Walgrave (Eds.), *Restorative Juvenile Justice: Repairing the Harm of Youth Crime*, pp. 305–326.

Jones, L.P. and Finnegan, D. (2004). Family unity meetings: Decision making and placement outcomes, *Journal of Family Social Work* 7(4), 23–43.

King, M.S. (2008a). Therapeutic Jurisprudence, child complainants and the concept of a fair Trial, *Criminal Law Journal* 32, p. 303.

King, M.S. (2008b). Restorative justice, therapeutic jurisprudence and the rise of emotionally intelligent justice, *Melbourne University Law Review* 32, 1096.

Kurki, L. (2003). Evaluating restorative justice practices, *in* A. Von Hirsh, J. V. Roberts and A. Bottoms (Eds.), *Restorative Justice and Criminal Justice: Competing or Reconcilable Paradigms?*, Portland: Hart Publications, pp. 293–314.

Kreiger, S. (2002). The dangers of mediation in domestic violence cases, *Cardozo Women's Law Journal* 8, 235.

Latimer, J., Dowden, C., and Muise, D. (2005). The effectiveness of restorative justice practices: A meta-analysis, *The Prison Journal* 85(2), 127–144.

Malloy, L.C., Mitchell, E.B., Block, S.D., Quas, J.A., and Goodman, G.S. (2006). Children's eyewitness memory: Balancing children's needs and defendants' rights when seeking the truth. In M.P. Toglia, J.D. Read, D.F. Ross, and R.C.L. Lindsay, *Handbook of Eyewitness Psychology: Volume 1: Memory for Events* (pp. 545–574). Mahwah, NJ: Lawrence Erlbaum Associates, Inc.

Marsh, P. and Crow, G. (1996). Family group conferences in child welfare services in England and Wales, *in* J. Hudson, A. Morris, G. Maxwell, and B. Galaway (Eds.), *Family Group Conferences: Perspectives on Policy and Practice*, Leichhardt, NSW, Australia: The Federation Press; Criminal Justice Press, pp. 152–166.

Marsh, P. and Crow, G. (1998). *Family Group Conferences in Child Welfare*, Malden, MA: Blackwell Science.

Marshall, T.F. (1999). Restorative justice: An overview, *Technical report*, Home office, London.

Maxwell, G.M. and Morris, A. (1993). *Family, Victims and Culture: Youth Justice in New Zealand*, Social Policy Agency and Institute of Criminology, Wellington: Victoria University of Wellington.

Maxwell, G. and Morris, A. (1996). Research on family group conferences with young offenders in New Zealand, *in* J. Hudson, A. Morris, G. Maxwell, and B. Galaway (Eds.), *Family Group Conferences: Perspectives on Policy and Practice*, Leichhardt, NSW: The Federation Press; Criminal Justice Press, pp. 88–110.

Maxwell, G. and Morris, A. (2001). Putting restorative justice into practice for adult offenders, *The Howard Journal of Criminal Justice* 40(1), 55–69.

Maxwell, G., Kingi, V., Robertson, J., Morris, A., and Cunningham, C. (2004). *Achieving Effective Outcomes in Youth Justice: Final Report*, Ministry of Social Development, New Zealand.

McCold, P. and Wachtel, B. (1998). *Restorative Policing Experiment: The Bethlehem Pennsylvania Police Family Group Conferencing Project*, Community Service Foundation, Pipersville, PA.

McGarrell, E.F., Olivares, K., Crawford, K., and Kroovand, N. (2000). *Returning Justice to the Community: The Indianapolis Juvenile Restorative Justice Experiment*, Hudson Institute, Indianapolis, IN.

Merkel-Holguin, L. (2000). Diversions and departures in the implementation of family group conferencing in the United States, *in* G. Burford and J. Hudson (Eds.), *Family Group Conferencing: New Directions in Commu-*

nity-Centered Child and Family Practice, Aldine De Gruyter, New York, pp. 224–231.

Moore, D. and McDonald, J. (2000). *Transforming Conflict*, Transformative Justice Australia PTY LTD, Sydney.

Morgan, J. and Zedner, L. (1992). *Child Victims: Crime, Impact and Criminal Justice*, Oxford: Clarendon Press.

Morris, A., Maxwell, G., Hudson, J., and Galaway, B. (1996). Concluding thoughts, *in* J. Hudson, A. Morris, G. Maxwell and B. Galaway (Eds.), *Family Group Conferences: Perspectives on Policy and Practice*, Leichhardt, NSW: The Federation Press; Criminal Justice Press, pp. 221–234.

Morris, A. and Maxwell, G. (2001). Implementing restorative justice: What works?, *in* A. Morris and G. Maxwell (Eds.), *Restorative Justice for Juveniles: Conferencing, Mediation and Circles*, Portland, Oregon: Hart Publishing, pp. 268–281.

Morris, A. (2002a). Children and family violence: Restorative messages from New Zealand, *in* H. Strang and J. Braithwaite (Eds.), *Restorative Justice and Family Violence*, Cambridge, UK: Cambridge University Press, pp. 89–107.

Morris, A. (2002b). Critiquing the critics, *British Journal of Criminology* 42, 595–615.

Myers, J.E.B. (1994). Adjudication of child sexual abuse cases, *The Future of Children* 4(2), 84–101.

Pennell, J. and Burford, G. (1995). Family group decision-making: New roles for 'old' partners in resolving family violence: Implementation report, *Technical Report 1*, Memorial University of Newfoundland. http://social.chass.ncsu.edu/jpennell/fgdm/ImpReport/index.htm.

Pennell, J. and Burford, G. (2002). Feminist praxis: Making family group conferencing work, *in* H. Strang and J. Braithwaite (Eds.), *Restorative Justice and Family Violence*, Cambridge: Cambridge University Press, pp. 108–127.

Peters, J.M., Dinsmore, J., and Toth, P. (1989). Why prosecute child abuse?, *South Dakota Law Review* 34, 649–659.

Plotnikoff, J. and Woolfson, R. (2004). In their own words: The experiences of 50 young witnesses in criminal proceedings, *Technical report*, NSPCC/Victim Support, London.

Poulson, B. (2003). A third voice: A review of empirical research on the psychological outcomes of restorative justice, *Utah Law Review* 2003, 167–203.

Pranis, K. (2002). Restorative values and confronting family violence, *in* H. Strang and J. Braithwaite (Eds.), *Restorative Justice and Family Violence*, Cambridge: Cambridge University Press, pp. 23–41.

Robertson, J. (1996). Research on family group conferences in child welfare in New Zealand, *in* J. Hudson, A. Morris, G. Maxwell and B. Galaway (Eds.), *Family Group Conferences: Perspectives on Policy and Practice*, Leichhardt, NSW: The Federation Press; Criminal Justice Press, pp. 49–64.

Roche, D. (2003). *Accountability in Restorative Justice*, Clarandon Studies in Criminology, New York: Oxford University Press.

Scheppele, K.L. (1989). Telling stories, *Michigan Law Review* 87, 2073–2098.

Schiff, M. (2003). Models, challenges and the promise of restorative conferencing strategies, *in* J.V. Von Hirsch, A. Roberts, and A. Bottoms (Eds.), *Restorative Justice and Criminal Justice: Competing or Reconcilable Paradigms?*, Portland, Oregon: Hart Publications, pp. 315–338.

Shapland, J. (2003). Restorative justice and criminal justice: Just responses to crime?, *in* A. Von Hirsch, J.V. Roberts and A. Bottoms (Eds.), *Restorative Justice and Criminal Justice: Competing or Reconcilable Paradigms?*, Portland, Oregon: Hart Publications, pp. 195–218.

Shapland, J. (1984). Victims, the criminal justice system and compensation, *British Journal of Criminology* 24, 131–149.

Sherman, L.W. (2000). Domestic violence and restorative justice: Answering key questions, *Virginia Journal of Social Policy and the Law* 8, 263–289.

Sherman, L.W. (2003). Reason for Emotion: Reinventing Justice with Theories, Innovations, and Research: The American Society of Criminology 2002 Presidential Address. Criminology 41 (1), 1–38.

Sherman, L.W. (2003). Reason for Emotion: Reinventing Justice with Theories, Innovations, and Research—The American Society of Criminology 2002 Presidential Address, *Criminology* 41(1), 6.

Sherman, L.W. and Strang, H. (2007). *Restorative Justice: The Evidence*, The Smith Institute, London.

Smith, P., Goggin, C., and Gendreau, P. (2002). The effects of prison sentences and intermediate sanctions on recidivism: General effects and individual differences, *Technical Report 2002-01*, Solicitor General Canada.

Strang, H. (2002). *Repair or Revenge: Victims and Restorative Justice*, Oxford, UK: Clarandon Press.

Strang, H. and Sherman, L.W. (2003). Repairing the harm: Victims and restorative justice, *Utah Law Review* 2003, 15–42.

Stubbs, J. (2002). Domestic violence and women's safety: Feminist challenges to restorative justice, *in* H. Strang and J. Braithwaite (Eds.), *Restorative Justice and Family Violence*, Cambridge: Cambridge University Press, pp. 42–61.

Taylor, S.C. (2004). *Court Licensed Abuse: Patriarchal Lore and the Legal Response to Intrafamilial Sexual Abuse of Children*, New York: Peter Lang Publishing.

Tyler, T.R. (1990). *Why People Obey the Law*, New Haven, Conn.: Yale University Press.

UNICEF. (2002). No Peace Without Justice and UNICEF Innocenti Research Centre.

UNODC and UNICEF. (2009). *Justice in Matters involving Child Victims and Witnesses of Crime:Model Law and Related Commentary*. United Nations, New York. URL: http://www.unodc.org/documents/justice-and-prison-reform/UNODC_UNICEF_Model_Law_on_Children.pdf (Last accessed Sept. 26, 2009).

Umbreit, M. (1998). Family group conferencing: Implications for crime victims, *Technical report*, Center for Restorative Justice and Peacemaking, St. Paul, MN.

Umbreit, M. (1999). Avoiding marginalization and 'McDonaldization' of victim-offender mediation: A case study in moving toward the mainstream, *in* G. Bazemore and L. Walgrave (Eds.), *Restorative Juvenile Justice: Repairing the Harm of Youth Crime*, Monsey, New York: Criminal Justice Press, pp. 213–234.

Umbreit, M., Coats, R.B., and Voss, B. (2001). The impact of victim-offender mediation: Two decades of research, *Federal Probation* 65, 29–35.

Van Ness, D. and Strong, K.H. (1997). *Restoring Justice*, Cincinnati, OH: Anderson Publishing Co.

Wade, A. (2002). New measures and new challenges: Children's experiences of the court process, *in* H.L. Westcott, G.M. Davies and R.H. Bull (Eds.), *Children's Testimony: A Handbook of Psychological Research and Forensic Practice*, West Sussex: John Wiley and Sons, pp. 219–232.

Wemmers, J.-A. (2009). The meaning of justice for victims, *in* S.G. Shoham, P. Knepper and M. Kett (Eds.), *International Handbook of Victimology*, CRC Press, pp. 27–42.

Wexler, D.B. (1992). Putting mental health into mental health law: Therapeutic Jurisprudence, *Law and Human Behavior* 16(1), 27–38.

Whitcomb, D. (2003). Legal interventions for child victims, *Journal of Traumatic Stress* 16(2), 149–157.

Wolfe, D.A. and Jaffe, P.G. (2001). Prevention of domestic violence: Emerging initiatives, *in* S. Graham-Bermann and J.L. Edleson (Eds.), *Domestic Violence in the Lives of Children: The Future of Research, Intervention, and Social Policy*, APA, Washington, DC, pp. 283–298.

Wundersitz, J. and Hetzel, S. (1996). Family conferencing for young offenders: The South Australian experience, *in* J. Hudson, A. Morris, G. Maxwell and B. Galaway (Eds.), *Family Group Conferences: Perspectives on Policy and Practice*, Leichhardt, NSW: The Federation Press; Criminal Justice Press, pp. 111–139.

Zedner, L. (2004). *Criminal Justice*, Oxford: Oxford University Press.

Zehr, H. (1990). *Changing Lenses: A New Focus for Criminal Justice*, Scottdale, PA: Herald Press.

9

Therapeutic Jurisprudence, Apartheid's Victims, and the South African Truth and Reconciliation*

Fran Buntman

Abstract

South Africa created the Truth and Reconciliation Commission (TRC) in the 1990s to address gross human rights abuses under apartheid. This quasi-judicial body with legal and political mandates was intended to substantially contribute to healing victims, both individual and collective, from the wounds of apartheid and its accompanying violence. Without invoking the term therapeutic jurisprudence, the TRC sought to achieve healing through using the law for a "therapeutic investigation." Whether the TRC is judged to have been therapeutic for victims depends significantly on whom the victims are understood to be. Four categories of victims are identified: (i) victims who came forward to the TRC, (ii) victims as defined by the TRC's legislative authority but who did not come forward to the TRC, (iii) victims of apartheid who were not victims of gross violations of human rights, as defined by the law, and (iv) the nation as victim, that is, the conflict ridden, fractured, and torn South African society emerging from apartheid and into democracy. Although the evidence is often mixed and uneven, the evidence suggests the TRC's greatest success came at the national level; it played a significant role in facilitating a united nation based in the rule of law and built on human rights principles. A great limitation, if necessary constraint, of the Commission was its narrow

* In memory of Bheki Mlangeni who has not been remembered enough. Thanks to Adam Dale for his research assistance and Edna Erez for her loyalty and interest. An anonymous reviewer's comments were helpful and are appreciated.

definition of victims. For the best-known group of victims, those who actually came forward to the TRC, the record is mixed or unknown, with somewhat more negative than positive reports. Because healing and therapeutic effects of this legal and quasi legal process are inextricably tied to reconciliation, five implicit logics of reconciliation—pragmatism, Christian notions of grace and forgiveness, African communalism, positivism, and law—underlying the TRC, and how these have impacted upon victims, are also examined.

1. Introduction

A year into its existence, South Africa's first non-racial and democratic parliament created the Truth and Reconciliation Commission (TRC) to address gross human rights abuses under apartheid. The Promotion of National Unity and Reconciliation Act of July 1995 established the TRC as a quasi judicial body with both a legal and political mandate. It was intended to substantially contribute to healing South Africa from apartheid's wounds, particularly the illegality and violence employed in the unequal struggle between the dominant government forces and their anti-apartheid opponents. Without invoking the term therapeutic jurisprudence, the TRC sought to achieve a "therapeutic investigation," using the law to heal and promote pro-therapeutic effects and provide a "healing paradigm"[1] (Leebaw, 2003, p. 44) for individual victims of human rights abuses as well as the society. The Commission had other mandates, including granting perpetrators amnesty under certain conditions. But the TRC was explicit in emphasizing individual victims and social healing as a core purpose and practice: "The role of a Truth Commission is precisely that it represents the state, giving official sanction and status to the restoration of the victims' human and civic dignity through these proceedings" (Du Toit, 2005, p. 444).[2]

Deciding whether the TRC proved to be therapeutic depends significantly on how victims are defined. This chapter identifies four victim categories: (i) victims (as defined by the TRC's legislative authority) who came forward to the TRC, (ii) victims legally eligible to come forward to the TRC who did not do so, (iii) victims of apartheid but not victims of gross human rights violations (as defined by the law) who were not eligible for TRC consideration, and

1. Leebaw, B. 'Legitimation or Judgment? South Africa's Restorative Approach to Transitional Justice' (2003) 36(1), *Polity*, 23–51.

2. Du Toit, A. 'Experiments with Truth and Justice in South Africa: Stokenstrom, Gandhi and the TRC' (2005, June) 31(2), *Journal of Southern African Studies*, 419–448.

(iv) the South African nation as victim, torn, and fractured by apartheid and emerging into democracy. Because the healing power of the TRC was understood largely in terms of reconciliation, five internal or implicit logics of reconciliation—pragmatism, Christian notions of grace and forgiveness, African communalism, positivism, and law—underlying the TRC are examined to consider their impact on victims. The research reveals patterns indicating both the presence and absence of therapeutic effects for different sets of victims, despite uneven and often mixed evidence.

This chapter begins by providing background concerning apartheid and how it was shaped by both law and resistance. It then introduces the TRC, its legal and political framing, and the key issues concerning victims, perpetrators (in terms of victims and amnesty), and therapeutic jurisprudence. The heart of the study lies in the next sections which analyze the four victim categories in light of therapeutic jurisprudence and link five conceptualizations of reconciliation to their impact on victims.

2. Apartheid, Resistance, and Law

Apartheid was a comprehensive political, economic, social, and legal system whereby South Africa's white minority discriminated against and exploited the black majority over decades, entrenching, consolidating, and adapting racial rule to promote white privilege. For apartheid's architects and functionaries, led by the white Afrikaner nationalist National Party (NP) (1948–1994), the law was a key tool to advance their system of social control. That is, the racialized social, economic, and political goals of apartheid were realized in significant part through an extensive web of law. Laws defined racial groups and then regulated jobs, voting, property ownership, education, and sexual interaction based on race. Core civil liberties—habeas corpus, due process, and basic rights of speech, movement, and association—were severely limited for all, with a disproportionate burden for blacks.

Importantly, apartheid was resisted in multiple ways including by often sophisticated opposition groups and strategies, both legal and illegal. The government was determined to combat this resistance and retain control. Consequently, the very definition of apartheid increasingly involved ever greater efforts to clamp down on the individuals, organizations, and ideas which rejected white rule.

While the law authorized and facilitated most repressive functions (e.g., detention without trial), state efforts to prevent dissent increasingly violated the law. Government agents broke the law and violated human rights in order to repress "enemies of the state." Opponents of apartheid violated the law too, mostly in non-violent and peaceful ways by engaging in activities that would be protected in a democracy. But anti-apartheid organizations and their members also used violence and occasionally abused human rights; the latter were limited in both scale and time period, and neither came anywhere near the extent of state misconduct.

3. Truth, Justice, and the Mission of the TRC

The TRC is a product of the political process and compromise in which it was conceived. South Africa's shift from authoritarian apartheid to a non-racial democracy involved a classic elite settlement (Higley & Gunther, 1991)[3] between two major political forces, the NP and the dominant liberation movement, the African National Congress (ANC). (Various other interests, parties, and forces were also players but were less influential.) Following decades of uneven conflict, the state and the ANC finally acknowledged neither could win and began to negotiate a change in rules, power, and regime.

Activist opponents of apartheid and black people in general undoubtedly bore the brunt of apartheid. Until a negotiated transfer of power was realistic, the ANC and other anti-apartheid groupings had often called for Nuremberg-type criminal or war crimes trials for apartheid's architects and (worst) perpetrators (Asmal & Roberts, 1998; Boraine, 2000, p. 143).[4] They certainly opposed amnesty for apartheid's perpetrators (Leebaw, 2003, p. 35).[5] Indeed, Thabo Mbeki (then deputy president and later president) noted that ANC members had once sought to "catch the bastards and hang them" before realizing "that you could not simultaneously prepare for a peaceful transition while saying we want to catch and hang people.... Had there been a threat of Nuremberg-style trials over members of the apartheid security establishment we would never have undergone the peaceful change." Forgoing retributive justice was part of the "price for the transition" as Mbeki explained it, and a precondition for a mostly non-violent transition rather than continued violence, repression,

3. Higley, J. and Gunther, R. (Eds.), *Elites and democratic consolidation in Latin America and Southern Europe*, (New York, Cambridge University Press, 1991).

4. Asmal, K., and Roberts, R. S., *Reconciliation through truth: A reckoning of apartheid's criminal governance*, (New York, St. Martin's Press, 1998); Boraine, A., 'Truth and Reconciliation in South Africa: the third way' in R. I. Rotberg and D. Thompson, *Truth v. justice: The morality of truth commissions* (Princeton, Princeton University Press, 2000).

5. Leebaw, 'Legitimation or Judgment?'

and conflict (Mbeki cited by Magubane, 2000, p. 74).[6] The NP came from the opposite perspective, seeking a blanket amnesty without disclosure or responsibility taken by perpetrators, individual or collective. Accepting the TRC then was a pragmatic *realpolitik* compromise between prosecution and retribution on the one hand and impunity and legal amnesia or denial about the past; amnesty would be "a *quid pro quo* for full disclosure" (Simpson, 2002, p. 221).[7]

The TRC was established to investigate gross violations of human rights, defined in the Act as "the violation of human rights through ... killing, abduction, torture or severe ill-treatment of any person" or facilitating such abuses through "attempt, conspiracy, incitement, instigation, command or procurement to commit" one of these crimes.[8] Crucially, amnesty required the offender to have acted "with a political motive."[9] The Commission's focus on

---

6. Magubane, B., 'Race and democratization in South Africa' (2000) 9 *Macalester International*, 33–82.

7. Simpson, G., 'Tell No Lies, Claim No Easy Victories': A brief evaluation of South Africa's Truth and Reconciliation Commission' in G. Simpon and D. Posel (Eds.), *Commissioning the past: Understanding South Africa's Truth and Reconciliation Commission* (Johannesburg, Witwatersrand University Press, 2002) pp. 220–251.

8. Promotion of National Unity and Reconciliation Act, Act 95-34, 26 July 1995. Available at http://www.fas.org/irp/world/rsa/act95_034.htm.

Applications for amnesty had to concern acts between March 1, 1960 and May 1994, the latter based on a change to the original cut-off date. The first victim's hearing—which was also the first public act of the TRC—was in April 1996 (Tutu, 1999). Following numerous deadline extensions and changes in the allowed time frameworks, the following deadlines applied: May 1997 was the deadline for amnesty applications, the Human Rights Violation Committee completed its public hearings in March 1998, investigations continued until July 1998, the interim final *Report* was published in October 1998 following a three month writing and compilation period, the Amnesty Committee held public hearings until May 2001 and concluded with amnesty decisions in November 2001. "The Commission formally closed on 30 November [2001], with only the revised version of the final report to be completed by April 2002" (Pigou, 2002, pp. 41–42).

9. The complexity of determining human rights violations was exacerbated by at least two sets of factors. First, what acts were, or were not, "political," and therefore eligible for amnesty, was often a vexed question. Was illegal behavior criminally or politically motivated? (Posel and Simpson, 2002; Pigou, 2002; Simpson 2002). Is racism an expression of politics? The TRC usually answered no, thus excluding consideration of racism as a political motive, but inconsistently. Privileging political violence led to neglecting other factors that shaped violence such as race, gender, ethnicity, and economic tensions (Simpson, 2002, p. 244–245; see also Buur, 2002, pp. 70–71). Second, there was considerable violence among non-governmental and more or less ostensibly anti-apartheid groups. The most notable conflict was between supporters of the Azanian People's Organization (AZAPO) and the United Democratic Front (UDF), especially in the 1980s (Lodge in Lodge and Nasson, 1991;

human rights violations as "killing, abduction, torture or severe ill-treatment of any person" profoundly shaped and narrowed the scope of the TRC's work. Although apartheid had been declared 'a crime against humanity' by the United Nations (UN), 'ordinary' manifestations of white rule like forced removals or pass laws were not part of the TRC's mandate or purview.[10] Furthermore, the concessions also meant the actions of the ANC's own members would be subject to TRC jurisdiction and scrutiny.

Although the TRC was a compromise about dealing with the past, it was also intended to play a vital role in shaping the future. At stake was not only how to respond to the human rights abuses of apartheid (for the most part) and resistance to apartheid (as the lesser concern), but how to mould a united society and country. Even before becoming statutory law, the TRC was envisaged in the Interim Constitution that laid the basis for democratic rule, importantly and significantly under the heading "National Unity and Reconciliation." This foundational and constitutive document described itself as a

> historic bridge between the past of a deeply divided society characterized by strife, conflict, untold suffering and injustice, and a future founded on the recognition of human rights, democracy and peaceful co-existence and development opportunities for all South Africans, irrespective of color, race, class, belief or sex. (Interim Constitution, Chapter 15)[11]

"National unity" required "reconciliation between the people of South Africa" as well as "the reconstruction of society" (Interim Constitution, Chapter 15). The "gross violations of human rights [and] the transgression of humanitarian principles in violent conflicts" and related apartheid legacies required, according to the Interim Constitution, "a need for understanding but not for

---

Seekings, 2000) and the UDF and/or the ANC and Inkatha, later the Inkatha Freedom Party (IFP), in the 1980s and early 1990s (Bonner and Nieftagodien, 2002; Khumalo 2006; Seekings, 2000). But as Bonner and Nieftagodien point out, the causes of violence, especially in the decade preceding the transition to democracy, were often extremely complex and multi-faceted: apartheid writ large, economics, ethnicity, politics, space, criminality, and other factors informed violence, even if superficial readings emphasized one cause over another.

10. Indeed, as Leebaw (2003, p. 43) notes, the ANC's concession to limit the scope of the TRC to illegalities within apartheid rather than the illegitimacy of apartheid was a dramatic contrast to the UN's Economic and Social Council 1967 resolution which identified apartheid itself as involving "gross violations of human rights and fundamental freedoms." Leebaw, 'Legitimation or Judgment?'

11. http://www.constitutionalcourt.org.za/site/constitution/english-web/interim/ch15.html.

vengeance, a need for reparation but not for retaliation, a need for ubuntu but not for victimization." "Ubuntu" emphasizes that individuals are social and communal beings who have no meaning in isolation; in other words, the idea that a person is a person through other people.[12] Ubuntu is a central tenet of African communalism or humanism which is a key element to understanding the logic and practices of the TRC. Amnesty for "acts, omissions and offenses associated with political objectives" in the context of apartheid's "conflicts" would facilitate these lofty goals of national building through "reconciliation and reconstruction."

Reflecting its multiple missions, the TRC's work was divided among its three sub-committees; the Amnesty Committee, the Human Rights Violation Committee (HRVC), and the Reparations and Rehabilitation Committee (RRC). Each of these committees were relevant to victims, although in different ways and to different extents. The Amnesty Committee[13] considered a perpetrator's requests for legal reprieve for criminal acts. Applicants were required to fully disclosed their crime and show it was motivated by political beliefs on behalf of a bona fide organization or institution.[14] Perpetrators who did not cooperate with the TRC, or did so partially, faced the continuing threat of prosecution.[15] Amnesty aimed to elicit the truth about abuses, threaten perpetrators with consequences for continued deception and denial, and provide benefits for truth-telling, from freedom from prosecution to reintegration into the new nation.[16] In practice, there was considerable unevenness in the amnesty submissions, investigations, and decisions (Pigou, 2002, pp. 50, 58; see also Sarkin-Hughes, 2004).[17]

---

12. "*Ubuntu* is the mainspring of the African humanist world-view, and attitude of tolerance and empathy grounded in the interdependence of the individual and the collective." Simpson, G. " 'Tell No Lies, Claim No Easy Victories': A Brief Evaluation of South Africa's Truth and Reconciliation Commission" in Posel, D., and Simpson, G., *Commissioning the past: Understanding South Africa's Truth and Reconciliation Commission* (Johannesburg, Witwatersrand University Press, 2002), p. 248 fn. 3.

13. Posel and Simpson (2002, p. 4) point out that there were several Amnesty Committees.

14. Posel, D., and Simpson, G., *Commissioning the past: Understanding South Africa's Truth and Reconciliation Commission* (Johannesburg, Witwatersrand University Press, 2002)

15. Leebaw 'Legitimation or Judgement?', p. 25.

16. Wilson (2000, p. 79) argues that: "The amnesty hearings were a theatricalization of the power of the new state, which compelled key actors in the previous political conflict to confess ... [and] speak the new language of human rights and in so doing recognize the new government's power to admonish and punish."

17. Pigou, P. 'False promises and wasted opportunities? Inside South Africa's Truth and Reconciliation Commission' in G. Simpson and D. Posel (Eds.), '*Commissioning the past*'

Although the TRC's greatest legal power was to grant amnesty, the public face of the TRC for most South Africans, and perhaps its most lasting imprimatur on the newly democratic state, was the HRVC, the committee most directly focused on victims. It took and received statements from over 21,000 victims and heard public testimony from about 2,000 among those.

> Throughout 1996 and 1997, the Human Rights Violations Committee held 80 hearings in town halls, hospitals, and churches all around the country to which thousands of ordinary citizens came and testified about past abuses. This process received wide national media coverage and brought ordinary, mostly black, experiences of the apartheid system into the national public space in a powerful way. (Wilson, 2000, p. 79)[18]

In addition to gathering victims' accounts, the HRVC investigated the plausibility or accuracy of the accounts. Once HRVC had verified cases, these were passed on the RRC. The HRVC also compiled and categorized national data about gross human rights abuses (Posel & Simpson, 2002, p. 4; Wilson, 2000, p. 79).[19]

The RRC only had the power to recommend reparations, not provide these, and was therefore by far the weakest component of the TRC. Although the ANC government was subsequently to disappoint even the TRC's low expectations for reparations, the Commission warned victims not to expect much. Recommended reparations were to be both symbolic and financial (Wilson, 2000, p. 79).[20] Representational reparations like memorials underscored the TRC's broad mandate in nation building, but also anticipated even optimists expectations for financial recompense.

Du Toit (2005, p. 440) insightfully notes that the TRC's self-understanding was malleable and adjusted to changing emphases, primarily of the Commission, but also of the country.[21] First, in the TRC's planning and early stages, reconciliation was framed politically in terms of the nation building between previously warring sides. Second, once the TRC began victim hearings, the Commission's dominant emphasis was the therapeutic value of reconciliation given the awful truths being disclosed. Many commentators have correctly

18. Wilson, 'Reconciliation and Revenge.'

19. Posel and Simpson, 'Commissioning the Past'; Wilson, R. A. 'Reconciliation and Revenge in Post-Apartheid South Africa: Rethinking Legal Pluralism and Human Rights' 41(1) (2000) *Current Anthropology*, 75–95.

20. Ibid.

21. Du Toit, A., 'Experiments with Truth and Justice in South Africa: Stokenstrom, Gandhi and the TRC.' (June, 2005) *31*(2), *Journal of Southern African Studies*, 419–448.

noted the critical importance of Christian ideas of redemption, renewal, and forgiveness playing a key role in this regard, above all shaped by Archbishop Desmond Tutu who chaired the TRC (Du Toit, 2005, p. 440; Wilson, 2000, pp. 82–83).[22] This chapter argues, as discussed below, that Tutu melded his Christianity with African communalism or humanism and these intertwined ideas became key to the meaning of reconciliation. This period and its legacy were shaped through the emphasis on victims telling their own stories. Third, as the TRC's focus shifted later from the victim's accounts to the amnesty requests of the perpetrators, "the *quasi-judicial and adversarial procedures* of the amnesty hearings" (Du Toit, 2005, p. 440, emphasis in original) highlighted procedural rights, whether of those confessing or implicated by others' testimony.[23] Lawyers and perpetrators increasingly eclipsed victims as the central figures in the TRC drama. The TRC's publication of a legislatively mandated Report[24] underscored the compartmentalization of the victim's hearings and the TRC's broader focus on "making *victim and perpetrator findings*" based on "systematic data-processing and corroboration of statements" (Du Toit, 2005, p. 440, emphasis in original).[25]

The TRC "was inextricably intertwined with the law" (Posel & Simpson, 2002, p. 5);[26] it had some quasi judicial functions and processes without being

22. "During the early stages of the Commission's actual work, a pronounced *religious and therapeutic* sense of reconciliation through the disclosure of truth ... became more salient" (Du Toit, 2005, p. 440, emphasis in original). See also Wilson, 'Reconciliation or Revenge.'

23. Du Toit (2005, p. 440) argues that as more and more evidence of atrocities emerged through the TRC's processes, these "tended to reinforce a countervailing popular narrative demanding (retributive) 'justice' and punishment." Wilson (2000) also discussed retributive grass roots reactions and how they differed from the TRC's attempt to define a hegemonic response to the past.

24. The TRC submitted an interim report in 1998 and a final report in 2003. Sarkin-Hughes-Hughes (2004, p. 98) notes that "The first five volumes of the TRC Report were handed to President Mandela in October 1998. The last two volumes, held up by the Amnesty Committee's work in granting amnesty, as well as various court cases aiming to suppress findings, were only handed over in March 2003." The differences between the reports are not especially relevant for this chapter's focus. For example, the Interim Report calls for extensive reparations for victims, and in the Final Report Archbishop Tutu laments what he considers the government's failures with respect to reparations. This chapter notes the gap between the TRC's call and the state's response on the issue of reparations without needing to focus on the particularities of the two reports. Sarkin-Hughes, J. 'Carrots and sticks: the TRC and the South African amnesty process,' Intersentia, 2004.

25. Du Toit, 'Experiments with Truth and Justice in South Africa.'

26. Posel and Simpson, 'Commissioning the Past.'

a court.[27] It was empowered to subpoena witnesses and seize evidence in addition its enormous power to grant amnesty (Wilson, 2000, p. 80).[28] Amnesty hearings were sometimes contested and adversarial, though not often. Nevertheless, victims remained central to the TRC: "The hearings on human rights violations, which went on almost continuously, dominated the life of the Commission and the work of the researchers" (Cherry, Daniel & Fullard, 2002, p. 20).[29] Therapeutic jurisprudence's emphasis on "the law's impact on emotional life and psychological well-being" and "law in action," not only in theory (Wexler, 2008, p. 20),[30] underscores the relevance of therapeutic jurisprudence to understanding, interpreting, and critiquing the work of the TRC.

4. Victims: Testimony, Healing, Therapeutic and Restorative Justice

This centrality of victims was shaped by a commitment to restorative justice and healing through a pro-therapeutic use of the law for direct victims and the nation. Although the Commission did not use the term therapeutic jurisprudence, the TRC intended the process to be salutary, restoring dignity to victims and contributing to healing the nation.

> ... By foregrounding the interests of victims, the TRC would attempt to restore the moral balance to an amnesty agreement born of political compromise. This fusion of amnesty with truth recovery and reparation was without precedent ... [T]ruth recovery was viewed ... as an alternative restorative (rather than punitive) approach to justice ...
>
> ... [S]ome argue that the focus on the interests of the victims was the TRC's main accomplishment. (Simpson, 2002, p. 223)[31]

---

27. This quasi-judicial model is consistent with the "specialized courts" like drug, family, or mental health courts (Rottman, 2000). Although in many ways different from these specialized courts, the TRC shares in common many of their features or attributes.

28. Wilson, 'Reconciliation and Revenge.'

29. Cherry, J., Daniel, J., and Fullard, M., 'Researching the 'truth': A view from inside the Truth and Reconciliation Commission' in G. Simpson and D. Posel (Eds.), *Commissioning the Past.*

30. Wexler, 'Two Decades of Therapeutic Jurisprudence.'

31. Simpson, G. 'Tell No Lies, Claim No Easy Victories': A brief evaluation of South Africa's Truth and Reconciliation Commission' in G. Simpon and D. Posel (Eds.), *Commissioning the Past* (Johannesburg, Witwatersrand University Press (pp. 220–251). Johannesburg: Witwatersrand University Press, 2002).

Therapeutic jurisprudence and the TRC share emphases on balancing rights and care, as well as integrating humanism (Wexler, 2008, p. 22), restorative, and community justice[32] (Rottman & Casey, 1999, p. 13). This restorative dimension links individual and collective healing. As Leebaw (2003, pp. 25–26) notes, while restorative justice typically assumes shared community norms,[33] in South Africa the TRC intended its brand of therapeutic law and healing justice as a foundation for "future political community." Whether or not these restorative goals and attributes were achieved, for whom, and to what extent, is core to evaluating the TRC, especially given the Commission's self-conscious emphasis on victims.

The TRC assumed that victim testimony about abuses they suffered would be cathartic and healing, as well as prevent retributive violence. This former assumption is wide-spread, often in the realm of 'taken for-granted "truths"' and "common sense," both with respect to transitional justice[34] and ordinary criminal justice. The idea that victim testimony provides positive "psychological and emotional effects—creating a sense of justice for victims, healing emotional and psychological trauma" (Mendeloff, 2009, p. 593),[35] in addition to valuable social or collective effects through individual and structural means[36] (see also Minow, 1999; Leebaw, 2003), is widespread in transitional justice contexts.

In contrast, the evidence about the value of victim's sharing their experiences is at best mixed and remains sparse. Some victims are helped; others are hurt:

> There are too few rigorous and systematic studies to conclude that truth-telling has the psychological benefits claimed by proponents, or the harms charged by the critics. Though the available data ... is lim-

---

32. Rottman, D., and Casey, P., 'Therapeutic Jurisprudence and the Emergence of Problem-Solving Courts' (1999) *National Institute of Justice Journal*, 12–19.

33. Leebaw 'Legitimation or Judgement?'

34. Transitional justice refers to the means and approaches countries adopt to deal with violence and human rights abuses of the past as they transitioning to democracy from authoritarian rule, civil war, and related forms of conflict and violence. A truth commission is but one means of transitional justice, and even then the particular forms of truth commission that have been or could be used vary widely. See, for example, Hayner 1994, 1996, and 2000; http://ictj.org/en/tj/.

35. Mendeloff, D., 'Trauma and Vengeance: Assessing the Psychological and Emotional Effects of Post-Conflict Justice' (2009) 31 *Human Rights Quarterly*, 592–623.

36. Much of the discussion about the relative merits or demerits of testimony in truth commissions compares these investigative bodies with trials. This topic is, however, beyond the scope of the paper. Mendeloff (2009, p. 602) further notes that "[W]e rarely see victims satisfaction with Western criminal justice systems, then we would rightly question the assumption that a war crimes trial [or trials responding to other state sponsored human rights abuses] is better able to satisfy victims of wartime atrocity."

> ited, the very best studies, while they do not entirely confirm critics' most pessimistic assessments, raise doubts about proponents more optimistic claims. (Mendeloff, 2009, p. 596)[37]

Irrespective of the emotional or empirical outcomes, the common pattern for societies undergoing transitional justice is that "victims and survivors have strong preferences for justice and accountability through truth-telling" (Mendeloff, 2009, p. 594).[38] The mixed impact of testimony for victims who came to the TRC is further discussed below.

5. Amnesty, Perpetrators, and Implications for Victims

Victims came to seek as well as share truths and the country looked to the perpetrators for information, as abuses were typically hidden, denied, and distorted. Truth commissions, transitional justice, and the TRC in particular want to find out 'what happened' as well as make previously denied truths part of the official record. For decades, and especially in the 1980s, the apartheid state had claimed to work within the law (albeit its law), denying illegality from routine torture to the operation of death squads. With some notable exceptions (see, for example, Gobodo-Madikizela, 2003; Harris, 2008), the ANC and other anti-apartheid forces did not have the evidence to launch successful criminal prosecutions of those who orchestrated or implemented the gross human rights abuses about which victims were testifying. In criminal trials, perpetrators typically benefit by minimizing or denying guilt and responsibility, and indeed, a number of prosecutions of apartheid perpetrators were unsuccessful. In contrast, most perpetrators who testified to the TRC and fulfilled the legal requirements (disclosure, political motive, and organization) received amnesty. This fact-finding imperative was a calculated gamble shaping the transition to democracy in South Africa. This bet achieved more in preventing political violence, however, than in revealing and confirming the truth.[39]

In the end, relatively few of the over 7,000 people who applied for amnesty were legitimate cases (most were ordinary criminals), and even fewer of the

---

37. Mendeloff, 'Trauma and Vengeance.'

38. Ibid.

39. Pigou (2002, pp. 40, 60) attributes some of the failure of TRC to learn more about the truth of human rights violations to the lack of appropriate interaction between the HRVC and the Amnesty Committee, and the insufficient use of the TRC's legal powers.

1,146 who received amnesty held senior positions (Philips, 2008; see also Du Bois-Pedain, 2007 and Mallinder, 2009). Most perpetrators calculated their secrets were safe, and assumption that has so far been correct for the majority of those who created apartheid's violence, repression, and illegality. The democratic government has done little to investigate or prosecute apartheid perpetrators, and some of the few attempts they did make were unsuccessful—arguably reinforcing the utility of the amnesty approach, but also its limits.[40] Victims still seek answers; surely few victims experienced perpetrators' amnesty as pro-therapeutic, even if they accepted the necessity of the amnesty trade-off.

6. Therapeutic Jurisprudence and Victims: Four Categories of Victimhood

Although 'victims' and 'perpetrators' are discussed as discreet and readily identifiable groups, the reality is inevitably more complex, from internal diversity within the categories to problems with classifications.[41] First, the TRC's definition of victims always included family members, especially when loved ones were killed in gross human rights violations. Second, the labels hide internal diversity within groups. "Perpetrators" included people as diverse as Dirk Coetzee, a multiple murderer who ran the covert hit squad Vlakplaas, and Tom Wiltshire Robbins, a conscientious objector who applied for amnesty to remove his criminal conviction for refusing to serve in the South African Defense Force, a key institution upholding apartheid (Borer, 2003, pp. 1097–1098).[42] Victims who testified were disproportionately female, black, and poor. Most of these people were, however, speaking on behalf of male family members, and in fact the TRC did not get an adequate picture of the suffering of women (and girls) as victims, nor the full implications of the gendered nature of the violence and abuses.[43] Third, many people who were victims

---

40. Carter's (2006) newspaper article "Is the TRC threatening to become a cold case?" reflects on those behind the worst repression ten years after the TRC began. It is a sobering reminder of the limits of any justice for some of the worst perpetrators.

41. See Backer, 2004, p. 134 for an overall profile of victims.

42. Borer, T. A., 'A Taxonomy of Victims and Perpetrators: Human Rights and Reconciliation in South Africa' (November, 2003) 25(4) *Human Rights Quarterly*, 1088–1116.

43. See, for example, Byrne, 2004; Jolly, 2004; Goldblatt & Meintjes, 1996, 1998. Posel (2002, p. 166) notes that the *Report* briefly alluded to gender as a significant factor in explaining violence.

under the TRC's legal mandate did not identify as victims. Fourth, the TRC defined victims and perpetrators in terms of gross human rights abuses and *not* apartheid, so acts of both anti-government and government forces were included.[44] Fifth, definitions could be blurred, changing, or multiple. Winnie Mandela is emblematic as both a victim and a perpetrator of torture and violence (Borer, 2003, p. 1099).[45] What were political, as opposed to criminal acts, were often confused or distorted (Borer, 2003, p. 1095; Simpson, 2002, p. 224).[46] Finally, arguably South African society, particularly the black majority, needs to be understood as victims of apartheid, in contrast to parliament's definition for the TRC's legislation.

Both in spite and because of these complexities, this chapter discerns four categories of victims and assesses whether, how, or to what extent, the TRC provided these victim groups with therapeutic jurisprudence. These four groups are: victims who identified themselves as such to the TRC; people who were eligible to go to the TRC as victims but did not do so; those who were victims of apartheid but not gross violations of human rights; and the South African nation itself. Therapeutic jurisprudence involves the use of the law to serve pro-therapeutic ends (while not undermining other legal goals, like due process), in this case to address the needs of victims of South Africa's pre-democratic past.

6.1 Victims Who Came Forward to the TRC

The TRC received 21,519 victim statements which referred to 30,884 gross human rights abuses, based on the legal definition (Carter, 2006).[47] Of those people, about 2,000 testified in 140 hearings. In addition to the people who the TRC classified as victims, others came forward to the TRC but were not defined as victims based on the TRC staff's interpretation, a sometimes arbitrary process.[48]

---

44. The ANC rejected the idea that military or guerilla violence on behalf of liberation from apartheid involved gross human rights abuses, but the TRC did not do the same if civilian deaths resulted.

45. Borer, 'A Taxonomy of Victims and Perpetrators.'

46. Ibid.; Simpson, 'Tell no Lies.'

47. Carter, 'News—South Africa.'

48. Pigou (2002), for example, provides a detailed account of a man who was shot by police suppressing protest. The TRC, however, classified the shooting as an accident, not a consequence of the highly politicized riot police's "crowd control." The case therefore became "out of mandate" and this man was not included as a victim, for purposes of TRC data or reparations. In another example, Byrne (2004, p. 247) interviewed a victim who said

The evidence is mixed regarding how victims fared in, or felt after, their interaction with the TRC. Most public broadcasts highlighted victims who were relieved and less burdened by having testified. Archbishop Tutu (1999, p. 118) emphasized the "extraordinary magnanimity" of testifying victims.[49] The TRC's Report asserts that "the process of giving testimony served a therapeutic function" (Kaminer et al., 2001, p. 373).[50]

Social science findings about the effect on victims are more complex; scholars have discerned both positive and negative effects of the TRC on victims.[51] Based on "lengthy semistructured interviews" with 30 black people who submitted their experiences to the TRC, Byrne's (2004) respondents voiced both positive and negative experiences of the TRC, some people voicing both.[52] Despite the small sample of respondents, reactions were extremely diverse. Nevertheless, criticisms and unmet expectations prevailed among her interviewees.

> Although a number of victims felt fortunate to tell their story publicly or said they gained important information, many other survivors talked about the disappointment, challenges, and struggles they faced when engaging with the TRC process: emotional strain, feeling lied to, or not hearing the truth, not sensing a show of perpetrator remorse, problems with TRC informational clarity, and so on. (Byrne, 2004, p. 250)[53]

Backer's (2004) research is the most comprehensive study of victims of gross human rights abuses and their perspective of the TRC. Using various methods, he studied 404 victims, most of whom had not testified to the TRC (p. 181).[54]

---

she was raped by the police and her nephew was killed but she was still not classified as a victim by the TRC.

49. Tutu, D., *No future without forgiveness*, (New York, Doubleday, 1999).

50. Kaminer, D., Stein, D. J., Mbanga, I., and Zungu-Dirwayi, N. 'The Truth and Reconciliation Commission in South Africa: relation to psychiatric status and forgiveness among survivors of human rights abuses' (2001) *British Journal of Psychiatry*, 373–377.

51. In addition to my identification of some of the key studies and literature, Mendeloff (2009, pp. 604–607) provides a comprehensive summary of the research regarding victims' responses to the TRC.

52. Byrne, C. C., 'Benefit or Burden: Victims' Reflections on TRC Participation' (2004) 10(3) *Peace and Conflict: Journal of Peace Psychology*, 237–256.

53. Ibid.

54. Backer, D. *The human face of justice: Victims' responses to South Africa's Truth and Reconciliation Commission process* (Unpublished doctoral dissertation), 2004 (University of Michigan, United States). Because Backer examines both people who did and did not offer testimony to the TRC, his study is pertinent not only to this sub-section.

His subjects offered complex opinions and experiences; even people who were critical of the TRC's treatment of victims considered the TRC's role an important one (2004, p. 179).[55] They variously praised and rejected aspects of the TRC, from the structure and mandate to its practical workings. Victim criticism was especially vocal regarding reparations and the punishment of perpetrators (p. 181).[56] (Importantly, however, these were factors beyond the TRC's control.)

Victims widely shared criticisms of the government's reparations policy.[57] Although the TRC's HRVC hearings ended in early 1998 and the Commission's Interim Report came out late that year, only in 2003 did the government announce it would give the approximately 20,000 TRC approved victims each a one-time grant of R30,000 (about US $4,000) (Sebelebele, 2003).[58] By March 2006, 15,330 beneficiaries had received this support, and at least 350 people died before they could receive this modest reparation (comment by Mochubela Seekoe in Villa-Vicencio & Du Toit, 2006, p. 39). Indicative of most victims, members of Khulamani, a victim's rights organization and support group, argued that the reparations were "too little too late" (Villa-Vicencio & Du Toit, 2006, p. 47).[59]

Given the TRC's emphasis on healing victims, one perhaps surprising weakness of the TRC was psychological support of victims. The TRC did have

---

55. Ibid.

56. Ibid.

57. Many victims who submitted statements to the TRC and were angry about reparations did not understand that the power to give reparations lay with the government, not the Commission. Archbishop Tutu has been very critical of the delays, the paucity, and the conceptualization of reparations. (See for example Tutu cited in Villa-Vicencio & Du Toit, 2006 pp. 14–15.) In addition to the financial reparations, there were symbolic reparations such as monuments (Minty, 2006 p. 423, 438; Marschall, 2004).

58. Sebelebele, M. (2003, April 16). Grants for apartheid victims. *SouthAfrica.info.* Previously R50 million (about US $6 million) was paid as an interim measure to address victims' immediate needs.

59. Khulumani's origin were in trauma counseling provided by the Centre for the Study of Violence and Reconciliation "for victims of apartheid-era abuses. In 1995, this framework was converted into a formal association, in part to represent victims' interests before the TRC. Khulumani has since expanded to all nine provinces and now has more than 20,000 members. In addition to activities at a community level, it assumed an active role in policy debates, spearheading demands for the South African government to deliver upon its promises of reparations. Khulumani's frustrations in the latter regard induced the organization to become a plaintiff in one of the reparations lawsuits. The government has since initiated the payment of final compensation—albeit considerably less than the R17,000–23,000 annual payments over six years recommended by the TRC—to individuals who were officially recognized as victims." (Backer, 2005).

"briefers," colloquially known as "cry people" as they were often seen comforting distressed witnesses. They were, however, laypeople, not psychologists or social workers although "most had some basic psychological training or counseling skills" (Hamber, 1998, p. 20).[60] Overall, the briefers were well received, although there were exceptions.[61] The lack of psychological support can only partially be explained by South Africa's uneven mental health system, especially the very limited mental health services for the poor and in rural areas. Psychological support services and groups did exist. Especially in urban areas, the developed civil society sector and a range of well-trained people in psychological services meant victims could and should have received greater mental health support than they did (Lodge, 2002, p. 189). The TRC did not, however, always share service information with victims making statements. TRC briefers were explicitly told that they were not "an implementing or service-providing body" (Wildschut & Haupt, p. 14).[62] The lack of resources was worse when victims made private statements rather than gave public testimony (Wildschut & Haupt, 2004, p. 14).[63]

The complex needs should not be understated. Hamber makes the essential point that most victims who came forward to the TRC lived extremely hard lives with many sources of stress (often including violence). It is therefore hard to separate out traumas and their causes and consequences: "Uncomplicated post-traumatic stress" was uncommon "because, in most cases, individual past traumas (e.g., being tortured, abuses by the police, etc.) have been overshadowed by present psychological and social problems" (Hamber, 1998, pp. 12–13).[64] Likewise, Kaminer et al. (2001, p. 375) note that "short-term relief associated with giving testimony is unlikely to be sustained in the face of chronically high levels of community trauma."[65]

---

60. Hamber, B. 'The Burdens of Truth: An Evaluation of the Psychological Support Services and Initiatives Undertaken by the South African Truth and Reconciliation Commission' (1998) 55(1) *American Imago*, 9–28.

61. In a particularly extreme instance, an insensitive debriefer (the terms 'briefer' and 'debriefer' are both used) was nearly beaten up by victims (Posel and Simpson, 2002, p. 128).

62. Wildschut and Haupt, *I'll Walk Beside You: Providing emotional support for testifiers at the South African Truth & Reconciliation Commission.*

63. Wildschut, G. and Haupt, P. (2004). *I'll Walk Beside You: Providing emotional support for testifiers at the South African Truth & Reconciliation Commission* (Rep.). Retrieved October 10, 2009, from New Tactics in Human Rights Project, The Center for Victims of Torture website: http://www.newtactics.org/IllWalkBesideYou.

64. Hamber, 'The Burdens of Truth.'

65. Kaminer, 'The Truth and Reconciliation Commission.'

There is no simple answer to the question of whether victims who submitted testimony to the TRC achieved a net benefit from participatin. Summarizing key findings, Backer (2005) underscores the diversity of his responses and the fact that "most victims are ambivalent, if not deeply conflicted, and their views fluctuate over time as a function of their exposures to different stages of the TRC process." Optimism prevailed along with doubt, but—importantly—very few victims believe they "received justice" for the wrongs committed against them.[66]

> Their misgivings emphasize substantive considerations (punishment, reparation, etc.) more so than procedural dimensions. There are also frequent demands for the alleviation of social, political and economic inequalities. In that sense, the TRC pays the price for the lack of transformation as well as the paltry reparations program. Thus, even if this exercise has been constructive for the nation as a whole, the cohort of victims remains largely unfulfilled. (Backer, 2005)[67]

Nor is South Africa unique in this regard. In the significant and growing number of truth commissions in many countries, the impact of testimony for victims is diverse; *both* pro-therapeutic and anti-therapeutic effects[68] abound, as Mendeloff underscores in his survey of both criminal and transitional justice mechanisms:

> Victims' responses to truth-telling are highly individualized and idiosyncratic. Truth-telling's psychological impact is occasionally positive, but is often negative.... [I]t is quite possible that truth-telling has no significant impact, either positive or negative, on victims' sense of justice, their demands for revenge and violent retribution, or the amelioration of their psychological trauma. (Mendeloff, 2009, pp. 615–616)[69]

---

66. Backer, D., 'Evaluating Transitional Justice in South Africa From a Victim's Perspective' (2005) 12(2) *The Journal of the International Institute.*

67. Ibid.

68. Pigou (2002; 2002b), for example, provides particularly disturbing case studies of people whose trauma was exacerbated by participation in the TRC, including because they felt the TRC was geared to perpetrators, not victims (2002, p. 106), a not unusual complaint.

69. Mendeloff, 'Trauma and Vengeance.' Laplanta and Theidon (2007) have similar findings for Peru.

6.2 *Victims According to the TRC's Legislative Authority but Who Did Not Come Forward to the TRC*

Even based on the narrow definition of victim used for the TRC, the 20,000 or so people who came forward to the Commission were a small proportion of the number of people who suffered gross human right violations under apartheid. Buur (2002, p. 78) notes, for example, that 35,000 people (including over 10,000 children) alone were detained between 1984 and 1986; many and probably most detainees were physically abused or tortured.[70] Over the more than three decades the TRC covered, thousands of people—probably tens of thousands—were killed by police and military personnel, from the Sharpeville massacre of 1960 to the student uprising of 1976 to the mass mobilization of the 1980s, especially in the mid-1980s.[71] Political violence orchestrated by or benefiting the state claimed the lives of thousands of people but is often excluded from counts which distort conflicts as 'black on black' or inter-ethnic violence (see, for example, Simpson, Mokwena & Segal, 1992; ANC, 1996; Coleman, 1998). Some of the worst violence occurred in the 1990 to 1994 transitional period which saw fewer victims coming forward to the TRC. The toll on the countries' neighboring South Africa and the South African exiles within them is almost certainly understated: Cherry, Daniel & Fullard (2002, p. 32) note that state violence under apartheid killed more people outside than within South Africa, a number they put in the "hundreds of thousands of direct and indirect victims of destabilization outside South Africa."[72]

The number of people who qualified to go to the commission but did not come forward was larger than those who did go to the TRC. We will never know all the reasons people in this category had, but a number of explanations help explain their motivations and perspectives. For a start, many people saw themselves not as victims but as resisters, activists, survivors (Borer, 2003,

70. Buur, L. 'Monumental historical memory: Managing truth in everyday work of the South African Truth and Reconciliation Commission' in G. Simpson and D. Posel (Eds.), *Commissioning the past: Understanding South Africa's Truth and Reconciliation Commission* (pp. 66–96) (Johannesburg, Witwatersrand University Press, 2002).

71. Freeman and Hayner (n.d., p. 144) put the number of people killed and disappeared at about 25,000. Freeman, M., and Hayner, P. (n.d.). The Truth Commissions of South Africa and Guatemala (pp. 141–144). Retrieved October 23, 2009, from http://www.idea.int/.

72. Cherry, 'Researching the Truth'. As Cherry, Daniel, and Fullard (2002) note, although the scale of violence beyond South Africa's borders was significant, the TRC relied on secondary sources rather than direct victim testimony for these evaluations and victims were therefore excluded from both the counts and the reparations.

p. 1094, 1097).[73] People within this grouping are more likely to have been members of political organizations. Moreover, based on the respondents in Backer's study, 76 percent of the respondents did not submit statements to the TRC because they did not know when or where to do so; a little over a third "did not want to relive the traumatic experience," and almost a third were skeptical that anything would be accomplished by their testimony (Backer, 2004, p. 182, table 7.1). Reasons like opposition from local community leaders were minimal, and fears about safety or that the abuse did not fall into the TRC's mandate explained about 20 percent.[74] Disagreement with one or more premise of the TRC was a factor: at least in the Vaal townships that Wilson studied but no doubt beyond, "there was profound disdain for the TRC among local political actors"[75] (Wilson, 2000, p. 84). (People from these communities believed TRC practices violated their own notions of justice, from the lack of punishment for perpetrators to the insufficient reparations to victims.) The Zulu-nationalist Inkatha Freedom Party boycotted the TRC, and its members contributed significantly to the number of both victims and perpetrators in the late 1980s and early 1990s. There were likely also factors of cultural appropriateness, or even shame, especially concerning sexual violence.

6.3 Victims of Apartheid Who Were Not Victims of Gross Violations of Human Rights, as Defined by Law

To restate an important point: the TRC only dealt with victims of gross human rights abuses under apartheid, not with the victims of apartheid as a human rights violation. This narrow focus was widely understood to be based on the legislation which created the TRC. Furthermore, while lamentable, this constricted approach was also more manageable. Had the TRC attempted to consider apartheid as a gross human rights abuse, its task—already daunting—would have been overwhelming. This tension between broad and nar-

73. Numerous contributors consider the difficulty of the term "victims." Most point out that they were following the TRC's lead, which in terms accepted the frames of reference of the enabling legislation. In Byrne's case, furthermore, victim "is the term chosen by the support group from which the interviewees were drawn." She adds: The "victims interviewed are indeed survivors who show remarkable resistance and resilience with regard to what they have had to endure" (Byrne, 2004, p. 238).

74. One may reasonably hypothesize that the lack of knowledge, fear, or political interference by local leadership would have been greater in more rural communities.

75. Wilson, 'Reconciliation and Revenge.'

row definitions of human rights abuses in transitional justice is ubiquitous: "defining the field of transitional justice too narrowly will limit possible achievements, while overburdening transitional justice mechanisms by trying to address everything might undermine the entire project of transitional justice" (Sirleaf, 2008, p. 31).[76]

Nevertheless, even from the most sympathetic perspective, given that the TRC was tasked with exposing the *truth* of apartheid to enable reconciliation, there is something absurd and offensive about separating out the legal depravity of apartheid from its illegal repressive consequences. Pass law violations; forcibly broken families through Bantustans and the Group Areas Act; denials of education and jobs through a myriad of laws, and beyond: these realities were apartheid. Looking at apartheid's human rights victims in this way makes all black South Africans victims, differing only in their degree of devastation.

Rejecting the interpretation that the TRC was required to limit its focus to victims of gross human rights abuses, Mamdani argued that the Commission chose to interpret the legislation too narrowly. He criticized the TRC for *individualizing* apartheid's victims. Mamdani noted, for instance, that in the forced removed of about 3.5 million people to create black, ethnically defined, homelands, the TRC recognized that the process involved "collective expulsions, forced migration, bulldozing, gutting or seizure of homes, the mandatory carrying of passes, forced removals into rural ghettos and increased poverty and desperation," all ingredients of gross human rights abuses based on political purpose. This violation should have fallen within the Commission's purview, he asserted, because "[f]orced removals violated both person and property of those targeted," communities and individuals. These violations were the "political project" of apartheid, and the TRC defined political motivation as a feature of gross human rights abuses (Mandani, 2002, pp. 45–46).[77]

Despite the TRC's circumscribed focus and the low numbers of perpetrators who came forward, the Commission nevertheless exposed abuses that, in number and degree, shocked even opponents of apartheid who thought they knew how repressive the regime was. The Commission learned, for example, of systematic murders of activists, of gang rapes of women activists by police, and of police officers who enjoyed a barbeque ("braai") as they burned their

76. Sirleaf, M., *Report on the JICA and ICTJ Workshop on "Transitional Justice and Development in Africa": Enhancing Socio-Economic Justice in Societies in Transition: Case Studies on the African Continent* (Rep.). (International Center for Transitional Justice, 2008).

77. Mamdani, M., 'Amnesty or Impunity? A Preliminary Critique of the Report of the Truth and Reconciliation Commission of South Africa (TRC)' (2002) 32(3–4) *Diacritics*, 33–59.

victim. As Cole (2007, p. 185) notes, "While South Africa's Truth and Reconciliation Commission was designed to contain and make manageable the effects of atrocity, the magnitude of atrocity constantly exceeded its bounds."[78]

Posel (2002) points out that the TRC was well aware of and uncomfortable with the constricted approach to rights abuses. In the Report, it recognized the problem of excluding 'ordinary' human rights abuses from the Commission's work and emphasized the need to see apartheid in its entirety as a violation of human rights. Nevertheless, there was no systematic articulation of apartheid's history or reality into the Report which continued to emphasize the narrower mandate of the Commission (Posel, 2002, p. 163).[79]

6.4 The Conflict Ridden, Divided, and Torn South African Society as Victim

The TRC was mandated to help reconcile a deeply divided nation. Divisions and hostility within South Africa were (and are) complex and over-determined, shaped by ideology, race, economic inequality, gender, among others, and awash in violence. The country writ large was therefore very much a victim. Has the therapeutic jurisprudence and restorative justice approach of the Commission provided any salve or healing? Not surprisingly, there is no definitive answer to this question either, and evidence is often contradictory or ambivalent. Nevertheless, there is notable evidence suggesting that the TRC made a substantial contribution to national healing.

Perhaps the TRC's most decisive achievements were its role in facilitating and legitimating as official the shared history of abuses, in affirming law and human rights, articulating healing as a national imperative, and offering its particular brand of 'therapy' to a wounded nation. The TRC greatly impacted upon the South African population in the earliest years of democratic transition. "Any South African," Hamber (1998, p. 12) points out, "will hotly debate the merits, and faults, of the process."[80] The TRC in general and the HRVC in particular were highly visible in the mass media over years. From individual testimony to the Report, the influence was complex and sustained over a few years. The TRC reshaped fundamental knowledge and therefore understanding in South Africa, making it generalized and shared. The Commission

78. Cole, C. M. (2007). Performance, Transitional Justice, and the Law: South Africa's Truth and Reconciliation Commission. *Theatre Journal, 59*(1), 167–187.

79. Posel, 'Commissioning the Past.'

80. Hamber, 'Forgiveness and Reconciliation.'

cast "light on political violence at the immediate, experiential level. It records the diverse experiences of absolutely ordinary South Africans [who ...] had tales to tell of a kind that had barely been acknowledged or examined in the apartheid era. They spoke ... 'to a nation whose time it was to listen'"[81] (Cherry, Daniel & Fullard, 2002, p. 25).[82]

Gibson's rigorous research aimed to systematically assess the legacy of the TRC on public understanding and perception in South Africa; how did the quest for "truth" in the TRC contribute to the pursuit of reconciliation? Identifying four meanings of reconciliation—interracial reconciliation, political tolerance, support for human rights principles, and legitimacy of a democratic South African state—he found the TRC's truth seeking to improve some racial attitudes without "harm[ing] race relations in South Africa,"[83] (Gibson, 2004, p. 166). Divergent findings were largely based on respondents' race. White, coloreds, and Indians improved their regard to other racial groups because of the truth the TRC exposed.

Although Gibson (2004, p. 166) found "truth seemed to contribute little to reconciliation"[84] for black South Africans, Lodge (2002, p. 199) argued that "black South Africans seem to have been more favourably [sic] disposed to the TRC than whites."[85] Moreover, as Gibson notes, fears that official acknowledgement about apartheid abuses would harden black attitudes to whites did *not* transpire. Given the immediate historical background to the democratic transition and the TRC, Gibson suggests his surveys uncovered "remarkable" levels of racial reconciliation. Despite important limits to the TRC's positive influence, Gibson concluded that the Commission measurably contributed to key elements of reconciliation: a shared recognition of past abuses, the need for racial reconciliation, and an expanded understanding of and commitment to human rights and democracy.

Consistent with the frequent disappointment of victims, especially those who gave statements to the TRC, victims were often more disillusioned than the general public. Even victims, however, sometimes saw a more positive impact of the TRC beyond their own direct experiences as they often believed

---

81. Cherry, 'Researching the Truth.'

82. But see van der Merwe (2002, p. 215) for a contrasting view, at least regarding his case study of Duduza. Lodge (2002, p. 197) and Wilson (2000) also offer quite different assessments of black support for amnesty.

83. Gibson, J. L., *Overcoming Apartheid: Can Truth Reconcile a Divided Nation?* (New York, Russell Sage Foundation, 2004).

84. Ibid.

85. Lodge, 'Politics in South Africa.'

that the TRC had done good work in other parts of the country, or for high profile victims, but not for their own communities (Hamber et al., 1998).[86] In contrast, some victims believed the TRC process had sometimes aggravated violence and tensions. Nevertheless, despite extensive criticisms and reservations, the consensus of over 500 Khulumani members was that the TRC had probably begun reconciliation, although not achieved it (Hamber et al., 1998). This tentative and partial victim endorsement of the TRC is consistent with Hamber's (2007, p. 121) recognition that "the process of reconciliation also contains paradoxes and even contradictions; it is neither neat nor easy and in itself can seem incongruous."[87]

7. Reconciliation: A Double-Edged Sword for Victims

The array of perspectives regarding the therapeutic value of the TRC for victims, variously defined, reflects many of the inherent tensions within the TRC. The TRC was supposed to benefit victims but actually often put the greatest pressure on this most vulnerable and damaged group. This paradox is all the more ironic because it was not only structural, in terms of being rooted in the Commission, but in part it was a result of the value system of Archbishop Tutu in particular, a man deeply devoted to victims as well as the broader principle of reconciliation.

At least five, often linked and potentially contradictory, assumptions were made about how reconciliation was be achieved through the TRC process, all of which have implications for victims. The first assumption, a pragmatic *Realpolitik* understanding, asserted that the post-apartheid government required consent (if not support) from whites, including apartheid's ideologues and security-force torturers and murderers. In 1981 Tutu promised at the funeral of assassinated anti-apartheid lawyer Griffiths Mxenge that "justice will be done"[88] (Rosenberg, 1996, p. 88). As TRC chair in 1996, however, he argued that "if justice is your last word, you've had it"[89] (Gevisser, 1996, p.12). If true justice was sought, it would only come "with ashes." Victims would have to accept this pragmatic calculation in order to make the future possible.

---

86. Hamber, 'Forgiveness and Reconciliation.'

87. Ibid.

88. Rosenberg, T., 'Recovering from Apartheid' (December 18, 1996) *The New Yorker*, 86–95.

89. Gevisser, M., 'The Ultimate Test of Faith. (April, 12, 1996) *Mail and Guardian*, 12.

A second rationale for reconciliation emphasized religious, especially Christian, theology.[90] Although Tutu was the most important Christian influence, he was not alone. Churches were the most significant civil society sector involved with the TRC (Wilson, 2000).[91] In particular, Tutu argued for "a faith of grace" (Gevisser, 1996, p. 12)[92] where grace involves righteousness and compassion by the aggrieved towards the—usually repentant—transgressor. Ideally, grace involves both the remorseful wrong doer and the wronged person who accepts the apology and forgives (Campbell/"Grace" in Metzger & Coogan, 1993, p. 259).[93] But sometimes grace comes only from one party, as might occur in the TRC with perpetrators whose amnesty admission was merely to protect themselves from criminal prosecution or punishment, not to repent.

Although this invocation of grace puts the burden of responsibility on victims, it inverted racist logics of apartheid by making apartheid's mainly black victims the superior moral force, endowed with God-like capacities to forgive the evil and sacrilegious (mainly) white perpetrators of apartheid. As Jesus accepted the burdens of Christian sin to facilitate future redemption, so victims'

---

90. In contrast to my emphasis on ubuntu and related concepts of humanity and human rights in an African (and Christian) context, Wilson (2000, p. 80) argues that the TRC's interpretation of reconciliation melded "transnational human rights values and a Christian ethic of forgiveness and redemption." Although universalist notions of human rights and international law were (and are) key in opposing apartheid and developing a democratic South Africa, including in the TRC, I argue that the international dimension was far less conspicuous than a national South African/African ethos in articulating the meaning of reconciliation and the point and role of the TRC. In her critique of Wilson, Merry (comment on Wilson, 2000, p. 91) makes a similar point: The TRC's use of human rights law "is also distinctive to South Africa, more influenced by Christian values of reconciliation and forgiveness than human rights law in general." "The appointment of Archbishop Tutu as Chairperson, along with a number of religious leaders and others from the counseling professions as Commissioners, lead to the increasing prominence of a religious and therapeutic discourse and a pronounced symbolism of 'healing' and 'reconciliation'." Du Toit, 2005, p. 440; see also p. 441.

91. Wilson, 'Reconciliation and Revenge.' Note that South Africa has a secular constitution and formal separation of religion and state with strong religious freedom. At the same time, it is a majority Christian country that tends to see religion in general and Christianity in particular as normative. The preamble to the Constitution, for instance, invokes God ("In humble submission to Almighty God") as does the national anthem and the closing words of the Constitution. Nkosi sikelel' iAfrika// God seën Suid-Afrika// Morena boloka sechaba sa heso// May God bless our country// Mudzimu fhatutshedza Afrika// Hosi katekisa Afrika.

92. Gevisser 'The Ultimate Test of Faith.'

93. Campbell, E.F. (1993). Grace. In B. M. Metzger and M. D. Coogan (Eds.), *The Oxford companion to the Bible* (p. 259). New York: Oxford University Press.

grace could pave the path to a peaceful South Africa. Indeed, Tutu reminded critics of Jesus' words on the cross: "Forgive them, for they do not know what they do."

Against this notion of grace, Claudia Braude (1996, p. 11) employs Primo Levi's *The Drowned and the Saved* to argue that it was unrealistic and cruel to ask victims to forgive perpetrators:

> Levi would ... have been outraged by survivors bearing the costs of their oppressor's amnesty: "It is the oppressor, and he alone, who has prepared [the trap in which both live] and activate it, and if he suffers from this, it is right that he should suffer; and it is iniquitous that the victim should suffer from it as indeed he does suffer from it, even at the distance of decades."[94]

Wilson (2000, p. 81) also criticizes the emphasis on forgiveness and argues the TRC superimposed a "redemptive template" over individual victims' testimony; all suffering was equalized, and people were denied space for their own feelings or perspectives if they did not accord with the world-view of the TRC. "The hearings were structured in such a way that any expression of a desire for revenge would seem out of place. Virtues of forgiveness and reconciliation were so roundly applauded that emotions of vengeance, hatred, and bitterness were rendered unacceptable, an ugly intrusion on a peaceful, healing process" (Wilson, 2000, p. 81).[95]

Research suggests, however, that forgiveness often helps victims (Allan et al., 2006, pp. 87–88).[96] Allan and his colleagues studied the TRC as natural experiment concerning the relationship of apology, or lack thereof, to victims and their feelings concerning forgiveness. They found being able to forgive is likely beneficial to society and the perpetrator, but also to the victim. Receiving apologies greatly advances the likelihood victims will forgive those that have wronged them (Allan et al., 2006). "[V]ictims of serious human rights violations are more forgiving if they believe the wrongdoer is truly sorry" (Allan

94. Braude, C., 'S.A.'s hearings are not Nuremberg, but expediency must not fudge the truth' (May 26, 1996) *The Sunday Independent*, p. 11.

95. Wilson, 'Reconciliation and Revenge' In contrast Hamber (2007, p. 18) pointed to research which claimed that the TRC did not in fact encourage or focus on forgiveness in victim testimony. Victims were often angry, including at the TRC, and expressed that. But he notes some victims "complained of 'false reconciliation': that is, the felt forced to reconcile or that they were expected to forgive the perpetrators" (p. 119).

96. Allan et al., 'Exploration of the association between apology and forgiveness amongst victims of human rights violations,' pp. 87–88.

et al., 2006, p. 99).[97] Interestingly, many Khulamani victims complained that they had wanted to meet with the perpetrators and criticized the TRC for not having a comprehensive victim/offender mediation program (Hamber et al., 1998, p. 5).[98]

The Christian emphasis interacted strongly with another ideology, African communalism or African humanism, mostly succinctly expressed in the notion of ubuntu. This third rationale of reconciliation, African communalism, mockingly undermined apartheid faith. In apartheid ideology, the salvation of whites (and other "racial groups") lay in separateness and hierarchy, primarily on racial lines but also on other bases such as language. The safety of the body politic lay in its exclusivity and rank. By contrast, African communalism assumed ubuntu, inclusion, and an equal humanity as the means to the health of the polity and the community.[99]

Like the Christian requirement of grace, African communalism both elevated and burdened victims. In this case, however, the obligation was less on the narrowly defined victim group who submitted statements to the TRC and more on the collective victims of apartheid, black South Africans and those (of all races) who struggled against apartheid and supported democracy. Apartheid sinners were saved by the nonracial national body. More specifically, the TRC was a means of reuniting the nation, incorporating racist and repressive elements of the apartheid state, as well the liberation movements and ordinary South Africans. Emblematic of the remaking of the polity was the request of former political prisoner, Wilton Mkwayi, who was imprisoned in the Robben Island prison for 25 years.[100] Mkwayi asked that, when he died, his ashes be scattered in the seas around his former prison home. He wanted his spirit to rest where he had spent the longest period in his life, but he also

97. In the sample of 134 victims of gross human rights abuses, "80% of the participants had not forgiven the wrongdoers, though more than half of them believed they had commenced the forgiving process" (Allan et al., pp. 93–94).

98. Hamber et al., 'Submission to the Truth and Reconciliation Commission: Survivors' Perceptions,' p. 5.

99. Tutu's African communalism and notion of the "rainbow nation" resonates with the ANC's nonracialism, especially the Freedom Charter's promise that "the land belongs to all who live in it, black and white," though perhaps with less emphasis on nationalism and more on African communalism and Christianity, as captured in his book title, *The Rainbow people of God* (1996). http://www.anc.org.za/ancdocs/history/charter.html and 0385483740 or 978-0385483742.

100. See Buntman, F. L., *Robben Island and Prisoner Resistance to Apartheid.* (New York, Cambridge University Press, 2003), on the role of these prisoners in opposing apartheid and influencing democracy.

wanted fish to "swallow his ashes [so that] maybe, once racists eat those fish, they will forgo discrimination"[101] (Smith, 1997, p. 15).

The fourth rationale of reconciliation was the TRC's positivist faith in the healing power of truth and knowledge; the Commission's web-site proclaimed "Truth: The Road to Reconciliation."[102] A premise of the TRC was that victims, especially surviving family members, would learn the truth about repression from amnesty applications. Those who had lost loved ones yearned to know "what really happened" to "disappeared" or killed friends, comrades, or family members. Denials of abuses that had occurred, criminalization of political acts, or denigration of activists, could be somewhat repaired with corrective truth. Many who spoke before the TRC emphasized their need to know, for instance, where a person's remains were buried to allow appropriate religious or family rites. The problem, however, was that the promised and hoped for information was often not forthcoming. "The TRC's capacity to verify the evidence and information placed before it was severely impaired. This significantly compromised the quality of the empirical data necessary to sustain the sorts of positivist outcomes anticipated in the TRC's legislative and political mandate"[103] (Posel and Simpson, 2002, p. 5; see also Buur, 2002).

Law was the fifth rationale facilitating reconciliation. The TRC was enabled by both constitutional and statutory law and its goal was to use the law to combat the lawlessness of gross human rights abuses. Legal processes to create a society where human rights abuses could not occur again was one means of reconciliation. Amnesty was, of course, a lawful means to circumvent a more traditional legal approach to criminal wrongs, but it wove notions of restorative justice and therapeutic jurisprudence into the law, as well as associated ideas of redemption and redefinition through African communalism and Christian forgiveness. As Tutu (cited in Rosenberg, 1996, p. 90) argued, "The African notion [of justice] is far more restorative [than Western notions of justice-as-retribution]—not so much to punish as to redress or restore a balance that has been knocked askew.... You are not saved as an individual, but through incorporation into a body."[104] This notion of bodily incorporation is implicit in

101. Smith, C. 'Prison bars were no match for the love between Wilton and Ireen' (October 5, 1997) *The Sunday Independent*, p. 15.

102. In fact, as Posel (2002, 154) explains, the TRC identified four kinds of truth: "factual or forensic truth; personal or narrative truth; social or 'dialogue' truth ... and healing and restorative truth." (TRC Report 1998, vol. 1, cj/ 5., para 29 cited by Posel, 2002, 154).

103. Posel and Simpson, 'The Power of Truth'; Buur, "Monumental Historical Memory.'

104. Rosenberg, 'Recovering from Apartheid.'

both Mkwayi's quest to have the racists eat his ashes and Christian notions of taking the body of Christ at communion. But neglecting that social and political body continues to hurt victims of past abuses (and the nation): Khulamani victims reported that police officers who violated others' rights under apartheid retained their jobs and power in the democratic order (Hamber et al., 1998).[105]

8. Conclusion

This chapter suggests that, with important caveats, in terms of promoting therapeutic jurisprudence's restorative, healing, and salutary goals, the TRC's greatest success came at the national level; it played a significant role in facilitating a united nation based in the rule of law and built on human rights principles. Moreover, this influence is likely to continue into the future.[106] A great limitation of the TRC, or, more correctly, its legal and political foundations, was the narrow definition of victims the TRC was required to use. For the best known group of victims, those who actually came forward to the TRC, the record is mixed or unknown, with somewhat more negative than positive reports. Perhaps the greatest mystery concerns those who were eligible to be defined as victims by the TRC but did not come forward.

Five rationales underscoring reconciliation point to inherent tensions within the TRC and their impact on victims. As Backer (2004, p. 3) notes, "truth commissions are controversial precisely because they impose an implicit cost on victims."[107] Although the TRC sought to—and in many senses succeeded —in centering victims and giving them their due in previously unprecedented terms, victims also bore the brunt of many of the Commission's assumptions. The pragmatic *realpolitik* that privileged white and old-guard cooperation arguably made the TRC possible, but also limited it. Similarly, law both expanded victims' and perpetrators' rights; amnesty was at the expense of the victims of the past. The promise of truth seemed to offer the most tangible therapeutic benefit to victims who believed some healing would come with knowledge, but information did not transpire to the extent people hoped, although many

105. Hamber, 'The Burdens of Truth.'

106. The societal benefits have disproportionately benefited whites, unfairly and ironically, but this paradox raises another set of issues, beyond the scope of this paper. Another issue beyond the scope of this work is the irony of TRC masking social conflicts that bred criminal violence therefore exacerbating a new generation of victims in South Africa.

107. Backer, 'The Human Face of Injustice.'

victims obtained facts and recognition that had previously been denied. Emphases on grace and forgiveness as well as the expansive communalism of ubuntu intended to give victims tools for coping and reintegration, but also burdened those who suffered most in the quest for national healing. Simultaneously responding to individual victims and national traumas was a difficult reality.

It is easy to condemn the multiple limitations of the TRC, but arguably its virtues profoundly outweigh its faults and flaws. Du Toit (p. 448) argues that the TRC sought "the politically impossible," and in so doing, "extend[ed] the boundaries of what was politically possible." Compared to truth commissions in other countries,

> the South African TRC was much more ambitious in its range of objectives, although its critics tended to insist that it should have been even more ambitious, taking on the whole of the apartheid past, not just a limited range of gross human rights violations. To a considerable extent, this accounts for both its substantial achievements and its specific failures. (Du Toit, 2005, p. 448)[108]

With the exception of people who were opposed to the TRC from the political right, most TRC critics, including victims broadly and narrowly defined, would have had the TRC do more—more justice, more reparations, more investigating, a broader scope, and so on. In its own way, this is a vote of confidence in Commission, albeit a limited one.

References

Allan, A., Allan, M., Kaminer, D., and Stein, D. (2006). Exploration of the association between apology and forgiveness amongst victims of human rights violations. *Behavioral Sciences & the Law, 24*(1), 87–102. doi: 10.1002/bsl.689.

African National Congress (ANC). (1996). *ANC Submission to the Truth and Reconciliation Commission* (Rep.). Retrieved October 21, 2009, from http://www.anc.org.za/ancdocs/misc/trcsum.html.

Asmal, K. (1996). *Reconciliation through truth a reckoning of apartheid's criminal governance.* Cape Town: David Philip, in association with Mayibue Books, University of the Western Cape.

108. Du Toit, 'Experiments with Truth and Justice.'

Asmal, K. and Roberts, R.S. (1998). *Reconciliation through truth: A reckoning of apartheid's criminal governance.* New York: St. Martin's P.

Backer, D. (2004). *The human face of justice: Victims' responses to South Africa's Truth and Reconciliation Commission process* (Unpublished doctoral dissertation). University of Michigan, United States. Retrieved October 2, 2009, from ProQuest: Dissertations & Theses: Full Text.(Publication No. AAT 3150153).

Backer, D. (2005). Evaluating Transitional Justice in South Africa From a Victim's Perspective. *The Journal of the International Institute, 12*(2). Retrieved October 18, 2009, from http://quod.lib.umich.edu/cgi/t/text/text-idx?c=jii;cc=jii;sid=3ab9098367a9ef64dc87eb6af29f60b8;rgn=main;view=text;idno=4750978.0012.207.

Bonner, P. and Nieftagodien, N. (2002). The Truth and Reconciliation Commission and the pursuit of 'social truth': The case of Kathorus. In *Commissioning the past: Understanding South Africa's Truth and Reconciliation Commission* (pp. 173–203). Johannesburg: Witwatersrand UP, Distributed by Thorold's Africana Books.

Boraine, A. (2000). Truth and Reconciliation in South Africa: the third way. In R.I. Rotberg and D. Thompson (Authors), *Truth v. justice: The morality of truth commissions.* Princeton, N.J: Princeton UP.

Borer, T.A. (2003, November). A Taxonomy of Victims and Perpetrators: Human Rights and Reconciliation in South Africa. *Human Rights Quarterly, 25*(4), 1088–1116.

Braude, C. (1996, May 26). S.A.'s hearings are not Nuremberg, but expediency must not fudge the truth. *The Sunday Independent*, p. 11.

Brounéus, K. (2008, February). Truth-Telling as a Talking Cure? Insecurity and Retraumatization in the Rwandan Gacaca Courts. *Security Dialogue, 39*(1), 55–76.

Buntman, F.L. (2003). *Robben Island and Prisoner Resistance to Apartheid.* New York: Cambridge UP.

Buur, L. (2002). Monumental historical memory: Managing truth in everyday work of the South African Truth and Reconciliation Commission. In G. Simpson and D. Posel (Eds.), *Commissioning the past: Understanding South Africa's Truth and Reconciliation Commission* (pp. 66–96). Johannesburg: Witwatersrand UP, Distributed by Thorold's Africana Books.

Byrne, C.C. (2004). Benefit or Burden: Victims' Reflections on TRC Participation. *Peace and Conflict: Journal of Peace Psychology, 10*(3), 237–256.

Campbell, E.F. (1993). Grace. In B.M. Metzger and M.D. Coogan (Eds.), *The Oxford companion to the Bible* (p. 259). New York: Oxford University Press.

Carter, C. (2006, April 8). News—South Africa: Is the TRC threatening to become a cold case? Retrieved October 16, 2009, from http://www.iol.co.za/index.php?set_id=1&click_id=13&art_id=vn20060408100132911C850371.

Cherry, J., Daniel, J., and Fullard, M. (2002). Researching the 'truth': A view from inside the Truth and Reconciliation Commission. In G. Simpson and D. Posel (Eds.), *Commissioning the past: Understanding South Africa's Truth and Reconciliation Commission* (pp. 17–36). Johannesburg: Witwatersrand UP, Distributed by Thorold's Africana Books.

Cole, C.M. (2007). Performance, Transitional Justice, and the Law: South Africa's Truth and Reconciliation Commission. *Theatre Journal, 59*(1), 167–187.

Coleman, M. (Ed.). (1998). *Crime against humanity: Analysing the repression of the Apartheid State.* Johannesburg: Human Rights Committee, Mayibuye Books, University of the Western Cape, David Philip Pub.

Daley, S. (1997, November 9). Apartheid torturer testifies, as evil shows its banal face. *The New York Times*, p. 1.

Du Bois-Pedain, A. (2007). *Transitional amnesty in South Africa.* New York/Cambridge: Cambridge UP.

Du Toit, A. (2005, June). Experiments with Truth and Justice in South Africa: Stokenstrom, Gandhi and the TRC. *Journal of Southern African Studies, 31*(2), 419–448.

Dube, P.S. and Posel, D. (2002). The story of Thandi Shezi. In G. Simpson (Ed.), *Commissioning the past: Understanding South Africa's Truth and Reconciliation Commission* (pp. 117–130). Johannesburg: Witwatersrand UP, Distributed by Thorold's Africana Books.

Ex-General admits executing anti-apartheid activist. (1997, September 24). *South African Press Association.* Retrieved September 25, 2009, from http://www.truth.org.za.sapa9709/s970924b.html.

Freeman, M. and Hayner, P. (n.d.). The Truth Commissions of South Africa and Guatemala. In (pp. 141–144). Retrieved October 23, 2009, from http://www.idea.int/.

Generals describe how they murdered. (1997, September 26). *South African Report*, p. 5.

Gevisser, M. (1996, April 12). The ultimate test of faith. *Mail and Guardian*, 12.

Gibson, J.L. (2004). *Overcoming apartheid: can truth reconcile a divided nation?* New York: Russell Sage Foundation.

Gobodo-Madikizela, P. (2003). *A human being died that night: A story of forgiveness.* Claremont, Cape Town: David Philip.

Goldblatt, B. and Meintjes, S. (1996). Gender and The Truth and Reconciliation Commission. *Indicator: Crime and Development Studies.*

Goldblatt, B. and Meintjes, S. (1998). Dealing with the aftermath—Sexual Violence and the Truth and Reconciliation Commission. *Agenda, 36.*

Hamber, B. (1998). The Burdens of Truth: An Evaluation of the Psychological Support Services and Initiatives Undertaken by the South African Truth and Reconciliation Commission. *American Imago*, *55*(1), 9–28.

Hamber, B. (2007). Forgiveness and Reconciliation: Paradise Lost or Pragmatism? *Peace and Conflict: Journal of Peace Psychology*, *13*(1), 115–125.

Hamber, B., Maepa, T., Mofokeng, T., and Van der Merwe, H. (1998?). *Submission to the Truth and Reconciliation Commission: Survivors' Perceptions* (Rep.). The Centre for the Study of Violence and Reconciliation and the Khulumani Support Group. http://www.csvr.org.za/index.php?option=com_content&task=view&id=728&Itemid=200.

Harris, P. (2008). *In a different time: The inside story of the Delmas four*. Roggebaai: Umuzi.

Hayner, P. (1994). Fifteen truth commissions—1974 to 1994: A comparative study. *Human Rights Quarterly*, 598–655.

Hayner, P. (2000). *Unspeakable Truths Confronting State Terror and Atrocity*. New York: Routledge.

Hayner, P.B. (1996). Commissioning the truth: Further research questions. *Third World Quarterly*, *17*(1), 19–30. doi: 01436599650035752.

Higley, J. (1991). *Elites and democratic consolidation in Latin America and Southern Europe* (J. Higley and R. Gunther, Eds.). New York: Cambridge UP.

International Center for Transitional Justice. (n.d.). What is Transitional Justice? Retrieved October 23, 2009, from http://ictj.org/en/tj/.

Jolly, R. (2004). Spectral Presences: Narrating Women in the Context of South Africa's Truth and Reconciliation Commission. *Canadian Journal of African Studies*, *38*(3), 622–637.

Kaminer, D., Stein, D.J., Mbanga, I., and Zungu-Dirwayi, N. (2001). The Truth and Reconciliation Commission in South Africa: relation to psychiatric status and forgiveness among survivors of human rights abuses. *British Journal of Psychiatry*, 373–377.

Khumalo, F. (2006). *Touch My Blood: The Early Years*. South Africa: Umuzi.

Leebaw, B. (2003). Legitimation or Judgement? South Africa's Restorative Approach to Transitional Justice. [sic]. *Polity*, *36*(1), 23–51.

Lodge, T. (2003). *Politics in South Africa: From Mandela to Mbeki*. Bloomington: Indiana UP.

Lodge, T. and Nasson, B. (1991). *All, here, and now Black politics in South Africa in the 1980s*. [New York, N.Y.]: Ford Foundation, Foreign Policy Association.

Magubane, B. (2000). Race and democratization in South Africa. *Macalester International*, *9*, 33–82.

Mallinder, L. (2009, June 22). Amnesties, the TRC and the False Promise of Prosecutions in South Africa. In *Amnesties, Immunities and Prosecutions Conference.* Retrieved October 23, 2009, from http://www.law.qub.ac.uk/schools/SchoolofLaw/Research/InstituteofCriminologyandCriminalJustice/Research/BeyondLegalism/Conference/.

Mamdani, M. (2002, fall–winter). Amnesty or Impunity? A Preliminary Critique of the Report of the Truth and Reconciliation Commission of South Africa (TRC). *Diacritics, 32*(3–4), 33–59. doi: DOI: 10.1353/dia.2005.0005.

Marschall, S. (2004). Gestures of compensation: post-apartheid monuments and memorials. *Transformation, 55*, 78–95.

Matshoba, M., Simpson, G., and Posel, D. (2002). Nothing but the truth: The ordeal of Duma Khumalo. In *Commissioning the past: Understanding South Africa's Truth and Reconciliation Commission* (pp. 131–146). Johannesburg: Witwatersrand UP, Distributed by Thorold's Africana Books.

Mbhele, W. (2997, October 17). The semantic battles of Adriaan Vlok. http://wn.apc.org/wmail/issues/971017/NEWS11.html. Retrieved September 25, 2009.

Mendeloff, D. (2009). Trauma and Bengeance: Assessing the Psychological and Emotional Effects of Post-Conflict Justice. *Human Rights Quarterly, 31*, 592–623.

Minow, M. (1999). *Between Vengeance and Forgiveness Facing History after Genocide and Mass Violence.* New York: Beacon P.

Minty, Z. (2006). Post-apartheid Public Art in Cape Town: Symbolic Reparations and Public Space. *Urban Studies Journal, 43*(2), 421–440.

NO. 34 OF 1995: PROMOTION OF NATIONAL UNITY AND RECONCILIATION ACT, 1995, Pub. L. No. Assented to 19 July 1995-1111, South African Parlaiment (1995).

Philips, D. (2008?). South Africa—The Truth and Reconciliation Commission (Part 1): a reassessment. *London Grip.* Retrieved October 23, 2009, from http://www.londongrip.com/LondonGrip/SouthAfrica_TRC(1)_by_David_Philips.html.

Pigou, P. (2002). False promises and wasted opportunities? Inside South Africa's Truth and Reconciliation Commission. In G. Simpson and D. Posel (Eds.), *Commissioning the past: Understanding South Africa's Truth and Reconciliation Commission* (pp. 37–65). Johannesburg: Witwatersrand UP, Distributed by Thorold's Africana Books.

Pigou, P., and Posel, D. (2002). The murder of Sicelo Dlomo. In G. Simpson (Ed.), *Commissioning the past: Understanding South Africa's Truth and Reconciliation Commission* (pp. 97–116). Johannesburg: Witwatersrand UP, Distributed by Thorold's Africana Books.

Posel, D. and Simpson, G. (2002). The TRC Report: What kind of history. In D. Posel (Ed.), *Commissioning the past: Understanding South Africa's Truth and Reconciliation Commission* (pp. 147–172). Johannesburg: Witwatersrand UP, Distributed by Thorold's Africana Books.

Posel, D., Posel, D., and Simpson, G. (2002). The power of truth: South Africa's Truth and Reconciliation Commission in Context. In G. Simpson (Ed.), *Commissioning the past understanding South Africa's Truth and Reconciliation Commission* (pp. 1–16). Johannesburg: Witwatersrand UP, Distributed by Thorold's Africana Books.

Rosenberg, T. (1996, December 18). Recovering from Apartheid. *The New Yorker*, 86–95.

Rottman, D. and Casey, P. (1999). Therapeutic Jurisprudence and the Emergence of Problem-Solving Courts. *National Institute of Justice Journal*, 12–19.

Sarkin-Hughes, J. *Carrots and sticks: the TRC and the South African amnesty process.* (Intersentia, 2004)

Sebelebele, M. (2003, April 16). Grants for apartheid victims. *SouthAfrica.info*. Retrieved October 2, 2009, from http://www.southafrica.info/services/rights/trc-reparations.htm.

Seekings, J. (2000). *The UDF: History of the United Democratic Front in South Africa 1983–1991*. Cape Town: David Philip.

Seremane, J. (1993, November 19). Send my brother's bones home to rest. *Weekly Mail and Guardian: Letters Page.*

Simpson, G. (2002). 'Tell No Lies, Claim No Easy Victories': A brief evaluation of South Africa's Truth and Reconciliation Commission. In G. Simpon and D. Posel (Eds.), *Commissioning the past: Understanding South Africa's Truth and Reconciliation Commission* (pp. 220–251). Johannesburg: Witwatersrand UP, Distributed by Thorold's Africana Books.

Simpson, G., Mokwena, S., and Segal, L. (1992). Political Violence: 1990. In M. Robertson and A. Rycroft (Eds.), *Human Rights and Labour Law Yearbook 1991* (Vol. 2). Retrieved October 21, 2009, from http://www.csvr.org.za/index.php?option=com_content&task=view&id=708&Itemid=188, pp. 193–219. Cape Town: Oxford University P., 1992.

Sirleaf, M. (2008). *Report on the JICA and ICTJ Workshop on "Transitional Justicea nd Development in Africa": Enhancing Socio-Economic Justice in Societies in Transition: Case Studies on the African Continent* (Rep.). International Center for Transitional Justice. Retrieved October 2, 2009, from Japan International Cooperation Agency (JICA) website: http://ictj.org/static/Publications/ICTJ-JICA_TJandDevelopment_rp2008.pdf.

Smith, C. (1997, October 5). Prison bars were no match for the love between Wilton and Ireen. *The Sunday Independent*, p. 15.

South Africa. (1993). *Interim Constitution.* Retrieved September 15, 2009, from http://www.servat.unibe.ch/icl/sf10000_.html.

South Africa, Congress of the People, Kliptown. (1955). *The Freedom Charter.*

Teitel, R.G. (2000). *Transitional Justice.* New York: Oxford UP, USA.

Truth & reconciliation in South Africa 10 years on. (2006). Claremont, South Africa: David Philip.

Tutu, D. (1996, December 4). Letter to the Sunday Times (of South Africa). *The Sunday Times.*

Tutu, D. (1999). *No future without forgiveness.* New York: Doubleday.

Van der Merwe, H. (2002). National Narrative versus Local Truths: The Truth and Reconciliation Commission's engagement with Duduza. In D. Posel and G. Simpson (Eds.), *Commissioning the past: Understanding South Africa's Truth and Reconciliation Commission* (pp. 204–219). Johannesburg: Witwatersrand UP, Distributed by Thorold's Africana Books.

Villa-Vicencio, C. and Du Toit, F. (Eds.). (2006). *Truth & reconciliation in South Africa: 10 years on.* Claremont, South Africa: David Philip.

Wexler, D.B. (2008). Two Decades of Therapeutic Jurisprudence. *Touro Law Review, 24,* 17–29.

Wildschut, G. and Haupt, P. (2004). *I'll Walk Beside You: Providing emotional support for testifiers at the South African Truth & Reconciliation Commission* (Rep.). Retrieved October 10, 2009, from New Tactics in Human Rights Project, The Center for Victims of Torture website: http://www.newtactics.org/IllWalkBesideYou.

Wilson, R.A. (2000). Reconciliation and Revenge in Post-Apartheid South Africa: Rethinking Legal Pluralism and Human Rights. *Current Anthropology, 41*(1), 75–95. 1.1 (2000): 75–95.

Section 4: Controversies and Limits

10

Victims' Needs, Well-Being and 'Closure': Is Revenge Therapeutic?

Bas van Stokkom

Abstract

Considerable political pressure is currently being brought to impose severe punishments, and it is frequently suggested that these punishments would enhance the well-being of victims and achieve 'closure.' Populist images, such as 'victims have a right to revenge' have gained great influence. To what extent would therapeutic professionals have to support victims' needs that are shaped within such punitive contexts? When victims' needs take centre-stage in therapeutic jurisprudence, how does one deal with such emotions as anger and resentment? Would feelings of revenge also have therapeutic value? If so, would defenders of therapeutic justice be compelled to support that 'ideal'? This paper deals with problems related to therapeutic jurisprudence and the victim-oriented 'therapeutization' of restorative justice and asks: is revenge therapeutic? It is concluded that revenge may bring temporary relief, but anger rumination precludes healing.

1. Introduction

Criminal justice practices may be associated with many adverse effects, both for offenders and victims as well as their respective circles of friends and relatives: loss of reputation, feeling one has been deceived, affected integrity, worsened social relationships, the regeneration of hostility through conflicting interpretations of facts, etc. Many initiatives have been undertaken in the past to combat these adverse effects, such as protecting children, rehabilitation, recognition of victim rights, offers of compensation, etc. In this light, therapeutic jurisprudence can be viewed as one of the youngest members of this reformist family within the legal system.

The proponents of the therapeutic justice movement stress that there is no real limit on who could benefit from therapeutic applications, so victims too may benefit. It is also necessary to add victims to the application domain, if only to avoid the reproach that only the rehabilitation of offenders is important.

When victims' needs take centre-stage in therapeutic jurisprudence, how does one deal with such emotions as anger and resentment, which are ascribed healing functions? Would feelings of revenge also have therapeutic value? If so, would defenders of therapeutic justice be compelled to support that 'ideal'? Considerable political pressure is currently being brought to impose severe punishments, and it is frequently suggested that these punishments would enhance the wellbeing of victims and achieve 'closure.' Populist images, such as 'victims have a right to revenge' have gained great influence. To what extent would therapeutic professionals have to support victims' needs that are shaped within such punitive contexts?

In this paper I deal first with some problems related to therapeutic jurisprudence. In which respects do therapeutic aims fit in with criminal justice? Is it easier to align these aims with mediation and restorative justice? At the same time some critical remarks are made about the victim-oriented 'therapeutization' of restorative justice. Subsequent sections discuss the relationship between victims' needs and revenge. It is stressed, first, that revenge embraces ambivalent meanings. Although avengers are lauded in the popular imagination, feelings of revenge are still viewed as ethically unacceptable. In recent decades, however, a penal populism has been gaining ground as a result of which revenge was stripped of its pejorative associations. In a punitive climate it is believed that victims would demand harsher penalties and that such penalties would promote closure and peace. The final sections deal with the core question: is revenge therapeutic? Some social psychological research findings on revenge motives and revenge satisfaction are presented. It is also explained that revenge is partly a personality trait; vengeful victims rapidly attribute blame to others and are not really willing to judge offenders with charity. It is concluded that revenge may bring temporary relief, but anger rumination precludes healing.

2. Therapeutic Jurisprudence: Some Critical Remarks

'Therapeutic jurisprudence' is defined as 'the study of the role of the law as a therapeutic agent' (Wexler & Winick, 1996: xvii). The study concerns 'the extent to which a legal rule or practice promotes the psychological or physical well being of the people it affects'. Legal rules, procedures, and actors are seen as 'social forces that, whether intended or not, often produce therapeutic or anti-therapeutic consequences' (see also Wemmers & Cyr, 2005). Therapeutic jurisprudence also has higher ambitions, though: it suggests that 'legal professionals examine and adjust the roles they play so that they serve clients in a manner that is "therapeutically beneficial."' According to Wexler and Winick, therapeutic jurisprudence wants to 'ascertain whether the law's anti-therapeutic effects can be reduced, while enhancing its therapeutic effects, without subordinating due process and other justice values' (Wexler & Winick, 1996). Although therapeutic jurisprudence had its origin in the field of mental health law and focuses chiefly on offenders, they stress that the approach is equally relevant to crime victims (see also Wemmers & Cyr, 2005).

Therapeutic jurisprudence relies on the law as a therapeutic agent, promoting the interests of all parties, but it is difficult to see how law practices can function therapeutically. Many critics stress that existing legal systems are inherently anti-therapeutic (Arrigo, 2004; Roderick & Krumholz, 2006). In criminal justice practices concerns about the furtherance of well-being are deemphasized and ignored, although recent years have seen more concern for wellbeing in the sense of treating the participants with respect and giving them an opportunity to tell their story (the principles of procedural justice). These 'voice'-opportunities are generally minimal and not geared to letting the parties participate in solutions, in contrast to mediation.

Therapeutic jurisprudence thus finds no application in situations where judges function as fact-finders in evidentiary hearings. Of course, possible therapeutic impacts might be relevant when determining which types of treatment for offenders may be fruitful, but in my view the concept is still controversial when associated with statements to the effect that the law and legal procedures should stimulate healing per se. The whole idea of retributive justice, one of the chief pillars of criminal justice practices, seems to be irreconcilable with this approach. In my view, the criminal justice procedure should be organized primarily so that respect and recognition are guaranteed; any effects that are helpful to the wellbeing of the participants are only derivative.

The meaning of the statement that 'fair procedures are therapeutic' is that fair treatment may help victims to recover from their victimization. Although these effects certainly do occur, fair treatment is not intended to heal; rather, it aims to guarantee the dignity and respect of the participants. It is this quality of fair treatment that is decisive, not such instrumental benefits as recovery or regaining self-esteem.

'Therapeutic jurisprudence' suggests that formal reactions to crime should ideally comply with therapeutic victims' needs. In this way criminal justice procedures—as well as mediation and restorative justice conferences—seem to be charged with new tasks, such as pursuing lower scores on post-traumatic stress symptoms. Besides the classic aim that the criminal procedure should prevent secondary victimization, it is seductive to add a new aim: the procedure should serve to lessen the psychological consequences of primary victimization (Daems, 2007).

Introducing 'therapeutic discourses' into the criminal procedure (or into mediation in penal matters) may be risky when concepts such as 'healing', 'personal growth', 'closure' and 'reconciliation' gain the upper hand and start to outstrip discussions on the crime and its aftermath. I think that giving victims the opportunity to express their views has a proper and independent meaning, unconnected with therapeutic aims. The 'victim's voice' would seem to be decisive when it is constitutive to regaining trust and self-respect as a citizen, someone who deserves to be treated worthily, having equal rights, and who is owed a public censure of the unlawful behavior of the offender.

We should distinguish carefully between the question of what victims need and the question of what the legal system ought to provide. Judges are obliged to reach a fixed, categorical judgment; they are obliged to weigh a host of other factors against the victim's needs, including the rights of the defendant (Bandes, 2001). Moreover, the law has obligations to the public at large, which places constraints on how flexible the legal system can be in its attempt to pursue therapeutic goals. The closure that a legal system demands—which incorporates notions of fairness and due process—may not be linked with the therapeutic closure that victims seek. This closure can probably be far better provided by psychological, social and religious support systems.[1]

Therapeutic aims also seem to be incompatible with such core values of restorative justice as active participation and reciprocal communication. The primary aim of mediation is to offer a safe dialogue wherein the participants can express their personal experiences of the conflict. Both restorative justice and victim support/healing have their own goals and working methods. Of course, victim-offender dialogues can have unintended positive psychological effects. These dialogues can be transformative, because victims learn that the crime did not occur because of something they did (Strang, Sherman et al., 2006). Unexpected therapeutic effects constitute a 'bonus'. If one were to ex-

1. In terms of Pemberton et al. 2007: the law-related aspects of victimology are more fundamental than the psychology related aspects.

pect therapeutic effects, unnecessary extra pressure would come to bear on all participants. The mediator, however, would not have to accept a burden of proof to stimulate 'healing'. Besides that, in moral terms the victim-offender dialogue is not primarily a case of coping with suffering, but rather of accepting responsibility. For the victim this means telling his/her story, pursuing integrity and regaining control (Van Stokkom, 2008).

It is important to keep these two logics apart; the more so because there is considerable pressure to embrace therapeutic language in restorative justice (Richards, 2005). We are facing a new generation of evaluation research in which the measurement of positive victim effects has gained a prominent place. Many new terms are introduced in this research: healing, closure, emotional restoration, reducing the sense of alienation. A 'therapeutic logic' seems to dominate research issues. To give but one example, Lawrence Sherman and Heather Strang formulate the aims of the Jerry Lee Program on Restorative Justice in the following way: 'to learn whether a kind of justice can change people's lives for the better, with long-term effects'. This program focuses on many victim effects. The first research question addressed is: 'Can it [restorative justice] cure the post-traumatic stress symptoms and improve health of crime victims?' More and more evaluation research is coming to focus on the psychological needs of victims, aiming to measure positive 'victim effects' of restorative interventions (Strang, 2002; Strang, Sherman et al., 2006; Wemmers & Cyr, 2005).

This focus on 'victim effects' may have some strategic advantages for a reform movement such as restorative justice because it may increase its social and political appeal in a victim-sensitive context and, in addition, it may lead to larger numbers of victims willing to participate in restorative programs (Daems, 2007). Yet the particular focus on 'therapeutic effects' may have adverse consequences. For instance, one might be seduced into promoting strategies to enhance positive outcomes, for instance by encouraging offenders to offer an apology or, conversely, encouraging victims to take the offenders' handicaps into account. This could easily undermine the victim's dignity.

This, of course, is not to say that therapy and the fount of its knowledge, positive psychology, are irrelevant. On the contrary, positive psychology is very helpful in understanding such victim motivations as recognition, self-respect, revenge and forgiveness. This will become clear when we try to answer the questions in the next sections. Positive psychology also gives more insight into reasons why helpful or harmful effects may occur during criminal procedures and mediation (Pemberton et al., 2007).

In the following sections I want to deal with the problem that positive concepts like 'healing' and 'closure' are made to depend on the satisfaction of negative emotions like revenge. The question is whether vindictive and punitive feelings are appropriate tools for achieving well-being.

3. Ambivalent Views on Revenge

In Western cultures people are ambivalent about revenge: although we may feel that taking revenge is justified under certain circumstances, we also often find it petty and unethical. Revenge has been discredited as crazed, uncontrolled, subjective, and missing any rule of limitation. Western legal systems have sought to weed out and silence revenge in the search for more rational forms of justice. In literature and the cinema, though, we celebrate as heroes those who do not allow themselves to be walked over when harm is done to them. We even consider them more heroic according to the degree to which they are less mindful of the risks they incur in doing so (French, 2001). People delight in revenge fantasies and the revenge theme has a powerful appeal in mass entertainment. While few people will admit they approve of revenge, they clearly enjoy watching and hearing revenge stories. Nevertheless, in public we pretend that justice and vengeance have nothing to do with each other.

In fact, revenge and retribution do share many social and psychological mechanisms. Retributive punishment might be called 'cold' and vengeance 'warm' (French, 2001). Nevertheless, there are important differences (Nozick, 1981: 366–68). Retribution is committed to general principles and sets internal limits on the amount of punishment. The agent of retribution does not have a special or personal tie to the victim of the wrong. On the other hand, revenge is personal and depends on how one feels at the time about meting out appropriate injuries. Moreover, revenge involves pleasure in the suffering of another, while retribution involves no emotional tone, or involves only the pleasure attached to justice being done. Therefore, someone who pursues revenge will often want to experience the infliction of suffering.[2]

Many consider revenge the opposite of justice: the antithesis of detached, impersonal, proportionate and rule-bound. But according to the philosopher Solomon there is an irreducible connection between the emotional dimensions of revenge and punishment (1990: 40–41): '... to seek vengeance for a grievous wrong, to revenge oneself against evil: that seems to lie at the very foundation of our sense of justice, indeed, at the heart of ourselves, our dignity

2. For a critique, see Zaibert 2004 (arguing that retribution and revenge are not at all easy to distinguish; both the avenger and the retributive punisher feel indignation and outrage).

and our sense of right and wrong ... Vengeance is the "undoing of evil", "getting even" for wrong.' The victim's desire for revenge should be respected and acknowledged (see also Murphy, 2003). Vengeance may be primitive, but it is still the conceptual core of justice. We have an almost instinctive sense that we should not be violated, and when we are violated we naturally feel a desire to 'get even'. It seems that revenge does indeed have some morally worthy effects. Victims stand up and assert power; they act out anger and demonstrate their own conviction of self-respect.

Nevertheless, most people regard vengefulness as neither attractive nor sympathetic. The mere mention of the word 'vengeance' is still capable of frightening most people. Philosopher Trudy Govier says: 'One reason for doubts about the merits of revenge is that people often become obsessed with thoughts of revenge and may bring great harm to themselves and others in their quest for it. Another is that campaigns for revenge often escalate' (Govier, 2002: 8). Revenge behavior is indeed poorly modulated and can easily lapse into excessive mutual retaliation, partly due to such things as an exaggerated evaluation of the self and the harm done to that self (Newberg et al., 2000). Thus, avengers may make mistakes about the identity and motives of perceived offenders, direct their anger at innocent third parties, or fail to understand injuries to themselves in context. Individual acts of revenge may encourage others to imitate that behavior. Revenge often escalates conflicts and damages relationships (Tripp & Bies, 1997).

Is there anything wrong with the desire for revenge as such, considered apart from its consequences? According to philosopher Trudy Govier revenge is morally objectionable because it consists of a deliberate effort to damage and diminish another person. The offender is made to suffer in order that the victim may take satisfaction in that result. Using the suffering of others to satisfy oneself means that wrongdoers are treated as a means only, failing to respect their human worth and dignity. The argument in favor of restoring a kind of moral balance cannot change that: the victim puts herself on the same level as the offender, making him an instrument for her own satisfaction. Govier concludes that since morality is based on obligations to respect other persons and to limit human suffering, the quest for revenge is fundamentally immoral. What is wrong with revenge is that 'to act as agents of revenge, we have to indulge and cultivate something evil in ourselves' (Govier, 2002: 12). Respectable persons should not feel joy in the fact that we have caused another person to suffer.

In spite of this ethical interpretation, Govier and many other philosophers acknowledge that feelings of revenge cannot be eliminated from human behavior. No matter how upsetting, they are a vital part of our emotional life. The harm caused by those who break basic rules arouses moral indignation, anger and revenge. It is for that reason that the expression of 'punitive symbols' is so important in serious criminal justice cases: the condemnation of offenders is needed to tone down public rage. Censuring redirects destructive emotions in possibly morally acceptable and social constructive ways (Van Stokkom, 2007). Moreover, the task of retributive justice is to 'tame' vengeance and canalize vengeful desires in a legal framework of just desserts and proportionality. In the words of Susan Jacoby (1983: 152), retribution may serve as the domestication of the otherwise unbridled lust for revenge. Thus, the public's passion for vengeance is an extraordinarily powerful force and it often plays a major role in severe criminal cases. Durkheim (1984) suggested that this passion is 'the soul of punishment' and remains the primary motivation underlying penal practices.

Nowadays, there seems to be considerable political and cultural pressure to reassess the revenge feelings of victims. So much so that one may question whether revenge has acquired too much credit in modern society.

4. The Re-Evaluation of Revenge: Victim-Centered Discourse and Penal Populism

In a classic study on vengeance published in 1983, Susan Jacoby could still claim that revenge has been made a taboo in Western culture. 'We prefer to avert our eyes from those who persist reminding us of the wrongs they have suffered [...] Such people are disturbers of the peace; we wish they would take their memories away to church, a cemetery, psychotherapist's office ...' (Jacoby, 1983: 2–3). Nowadays the revenge taboo has been considerably weakened. Since the 'nineties there have been several noteworthy efforts to rehabilitate vengeance by stripping it of its usual pejorative connotations. We are witnessing a striking revival of revenge feelings, not only in masculine mass amusement products and sports, but also in political oratory, corporate takeovers and the legal professions. Anger, rancor and vindictiveness seem to have been awakened from their dormant state, they are praised and—like any other emotion—commercially exploited.

Victims are no longer strangers, anonymous, without a face. In newspaper and television reports their voice is heard louder then ever. In a 'world of lies' victim stories seem to represent the truth. In line with 'therapeutization' trends, all troubled feelings should be expressed; silence is suspect. Victims are often presented as martyred and avenging angels; they are not people so much as banners to galvanize public retribution (Meyer, 2005). Public support for penalties is sought in their name. Many populist politicians, lawyers and victim supporters claim that—in case of serious offences—one function of punishment is to offer psychological redress. Punishment should help victims to cope with their injuries. Many crime fighters and victim advocates argue that only tough penalties will show victims that they are being taken seriously by the criminal justice system (Elias, 1996). The failure to sentence a particular offender to a long prison term is often experienced as a devaluation of the worth of the victim's life and an infliction of pain on the victim's family.

A victim-centered discourse that refers to the public's preferred images of 'harmless' victims (hiding 'ugly' victims like drug runners or prostitutes) may have considerable social costs: it takes the focus off blameworthiness and individuation of the offender, and centers on the victim's troubles and painful emotions (Kanwar, 2004). Invited to talk about horrible sufferings, victims and the public may mobilize rage feelings and powerful punitive desires. They may work themselves into disappointment when offenders turn out to be humane and victimized themselves. 'Emotional conviction' is often the only weapon victims have available to fight back, but this engenders a reluctance to engage with them in debate and it can be a serious impediment to moderating victims' demands (Strang, 2002: 31). Putting their misery into perspective or offering objections often arouses severe indignation and any departure from the harshest penalty may be taken as a personal insult.

In the United States this tendency seems to be more manifest than in Europe. In the early 'nineties many victim groups—and the media—began to embrace the therapeutic discourse of 'closure' and 'healing.' 'Closure' has become the buzzword of the victims' rights movement and has even become an independent justification for harsh penalties. Groups such as Mothers Against Drunk Driving (MADD) show a missionary zeal for severe punishments. Since the 'nineties the opinion that harsh punishment does help victims find closure has come to play a dominant role in the discussion on capital punishment. The death penalty is regarded as a policy intended to serve the interests of the victims and those who love them, 'an undertaking to serve the needs of individual citizens for justice and psychological healing' (Zimring, 2003: 49). According to Franklin Zimring, the symbolism of 'closure' transforms the horrifying process of execution into a victim-service program. It gives the execution of a human being a positive impact with which many citizens can identify. 'It is assumed that there is a "zero-sum" relationship between the welfare of the victim's relative and that of the offender: the greater the suffering to be inflicted on the offender, the better the victim's loved ones should feel' (Zimring, 2003: 55).

Judith Kay points out that since the 1980s the public in the United States has come to believe that capital punishment is performed as a sort of therapy for survivors. Dominant scripts like 'revenge is natural,' 'the more he loved the deceased, the angrier he should be,' and 'a harsh punishment will make him feel better' are taken as truths, not presuppositions or delusions. These misunderstandings set up expectations, such as that 'people should feel vengeful' and 'relatives who oppose the death penalty, do not love the deceased' (Kay, 2007: 242).

On the other hand, many parents and relatives of murdered victims feel troubled by the rhetoric of revenge. They believe that capital punishment is not going to bring peace of mind. Many victims' families claim that the death penalty actually prolongs their grief and speak out against what many have dubbed 'the closure myth'. They assert that the anticlimax involved in an execution only adds to their pain, preventing them from moving forward with their lives.

Many researchers stress that 'revenge policies' do victims a disservice. Elias (1996: 22) comments: 'Despite the enormous pressures encouraging victims to "want" revenge, it is remarkable that many victims, nevertheless, do not seek revenge in practice, and are far less punitive than we might imagine.' Indeed, many research findings point out that the experience of victimization does not automatically increase support for punitive answers. Intuitive beliefs that victims are most likely to seek retributive or harsh consequences for offenders, are obviously inaccurate (Maruna & King, 2004). This is noteworthy since hard-line criminal justice policies are often justified with the claim that victims are the main proponents of a 'tougher' approach to sentencing.

In a recent study Vanessa Barker concludes that victims and victim advocacy have not been inevitable or uniform sources of punitiveness. Some victim movements have led to retributive approaches to crime, while others have led to more restorative approaches to victimization. The Californian movement to pass Proposition 8 (limiting the rights and liberties of defendants) encouraged a zero-sum logic in which the worthiness of victims and the victimized public is counterpoised against dehumanized criminal offenders. In this populist context, victims' rights were equated with offender-sanctioning. However, the Washington case study suggests that the link between victims and vengeance is much looser and much more variable than might be expected (Barker, 2007: 654).

Many victims do indeed seem to want revenge, but revenge certainly is not the only response of people who have been victimized. Many victims prefer to deal with their experience and move on; joining a punitive single-issue organization does not strike them as a particularly productive way to do so. Apparently, victims are not a monolithic group with similar preferences and needs.[3] Victims' responses about how to achieve closure and deal with grief vary widely.

Nevertheless, in a populist era, punishment has become more or less a victim service gesture. The government is frequently the servant of public desires. Moreover, it is assumed—see the zero-sum relationship that Zimring mentioned—that the well-being of the victim depends on inflicting pain on the offender. In sum, revenge feelings would have therapeutic benefits.

5. Is Revenge Helpful (Therapeutic)?

Do revenge feelings give psychological satisfaction? Does a vengeful act augment self-esteem? Let me first discuss some moral functions of revenge. Retaliation represents a form of self-defense, seen as necessary to preserve one's image and honor. It serves to restore the victim's self-image. 'The failure to respond to a perceived injustice can actually further diminish the victim, both in his or her own eyes, as the eyes of others' (Miller, 2001). In a similar way Trudy Govier (2002) defines revenge as a way to reassert ourselves, to attempt to get relief from the hurt and humiliation of being wronged. It is a desire to 'get even' and seek (anticipatory) satisfaction in attempting to harm the transgressor or offender. We expect to feel better if we can somehow express our negative feelings in actions intended to 'get back' at those who harmed us.

Three moral goals are often mentioned that may potentially underlie revenge motivations (Tripp and Bies, 1997; Orth, 2004; Miller, 2001; McCullough et al., 2001). First, revenge is the desire to 'get even,' or 'balance the scales.' Revenge is intended to re-equilibrate gains and losses caused by the assault, or to re-equilibrate power. It is linked to the norm of reciprocity expressed by the *lex talionis*. Thus, in the eyes of the vengeful person vengeance might be understood as truly moral. Second, revenge is intended to restore the victim's self-esteem; through revenge one can present oneself as a strong person who does not tolerate unjust treatment by others. Revenge is 'saving face': an attempt to change the belief of the offender and others that the victim is not worthy of better treatment. Third, revenge can have an educative

3. As it is often stressed: the connection between impact of crime and needs is problematic. 'Those suffering the worst harm or loss do not necessarily have correspondingly high needs. They may enjoy a supportive environment, be innately resilient, or otherwise able to overcome the effects of victimization. Victims suffering objectively less serious crimes may require greater support if they are vulnerable or isolated.' (Zedner 431)

mission: the desire to teach the offender a lesson. Vengeance in this way is moral instruction, designed to convince the offender that his behavior will not be tolerated or go unpunished. This preventive motivation may also have a purely instrumental aim: deterrence.

In a therapeutic context, the second motivation is important. Is the victim regaining status or gaining relief by an action intended to harm the offender? The view of the psychologist Nico Frijda (1994) is of special interest because one of his explanations would meet the zero-sum expectations within the logic of penal populism (put simply: 'his suffering is my healing'). According to Frijda the major social functions of vengeance are 'power equalization' and 'deterrence' (1994: 270). Restoration of the balance of power may also strengthen self-worth. Besides these (more or less) social functions Frijda also distinguishes an important personal function, which he calls 'the restoration of the balance of suffering.' This means that hurting someone who has hurt us could diminish our own suffering. If this is true, revenge would indeed have therapeutic value. What reasons does Frijda offer to substantiate these suppositions? One explanation is that emotions operate according to an 'additive theory of affect,' which states that pleasure and pain can be added to and subtracted from one another. 'If the pain inflicted on a wrongdoer may be subtracted from the pain he has caused me and if the two are commensurate, then indeed a restoration of the balance of suffering might be achieved' (quoted in Crombag, 2003: 334). Frijda is not satisfied with this interpretation, which is no more than a metaphor for Justice's scales. His alternative explanation is his Law of Comparative Feeling. Our feelings, he states, 'depend on how one's fortunes or misfortunes compare with one's fortunes or misfortunes at earlier times, or with those that were possible, or those of others' (Frijda, 1994: 274). It is the contrast between happiness and sorrow that matters: he is happy and I am suffering. This contrast is what vengeance is meant to remedy.

Are these suppositions convincing? There has not as yet been much empirical research into what moves people to take revenge and how they experience it. I shall discuss some research findings, especially those of Hans Crombag, a Dutch legal psychologist who has examined Frijda's theory. Crombag criticizes his alternative theory of balancing the suffering: it has implications that are 'at least counterintuitive, if not counterfactual'. One of the suppositions is that our happiness must increase as the number of unhappy people surrounding us rises. That is obviously not the case; the opposite is more likely. Moreover, Frijda's theory does not explain why in taking revenge our target is almost exclusively the person who has hurt us and not somebody else whose suffering might equally serve as a contrast to our relative happiness.

Nevertheless, does the infliction of harm on someone who has hurt us diminish our own suffering? Let us concentrate on Crombag's findings. In his study, a large group of respondents (students) were asked to think of a particular recent incident that made them feel vengeful, and to report whether they had acted on it or not, what their purpose had been in doing so, and how they felt afterwards. First it turned out that most respondents who have suffered from injustice do not actually retaliate, but restrict themselves to brooding about it, eventually to find a relatively peaceful way of dealing with it. The major reasons that elicited revenge feelings include 'false accusations' and 'violation of trust.'[4] Of the respondents who actually had acted to get even (do the same in return; end relationship; tell the truth loud and clear; etc.), 74 percent recalled that their action appeared to have served a purpose in that they had felt good about it.

When asked about their reason for taking revenge, the most common answer (54%) was: 'I wanted to make it clear to the perpetrator that I will not allow anybody to walk over me' (Crombag, 2003: 340). This answer comes close to the 'equalization of power' motive mentioned by Frijda. The second most frequent answer for taking revenge turned out to be the wish to restore the damaged feeling of self-worth (16%). Only few respondents chose the motives 'deterrence' (10%) and 'restoration of the balance of suffering' (11%) (inflicting an equal amount of pain; expectation that taking revenge would ease pain). These results do not bear out Frijda's supposition that restoration of the balance of suffering is an important motive for taking revenge, either in the form of the 'additive theory of affect' or in the form of his 'law of comparative suffering'.

When the two groups of respondents—those who did retaliate and those who did not—were asked whether the urge for revenge had since subsided, it turned out there was no significant difference in residual feelings of revenge. 'In both groups about two-thirds of the respondents indicated that their urge for revenge had entirely or at least partially subsided' (Crombag, 2003: 341). These data are surprising because earlier it turned out that 74% of those who had actually taken revenge indicated remembering that afterwards they felt satisfied or even triumphant. Crombag concludes that those satisfying feelings must have been very temporary, and that they do not appear to have contributed to peace of mind in the long run. In sum, actually taking revenge may give some instantaneous satisfaction, but in the end may not significantly speed up the process of leaving vindictive feelings behind.

---

4. These findings are also reported in Bies and Tripp (1996): most respondents do not appear to have retaliated, restricting themselves to brooding and revenge fantasies. In this research, too, the most frequent answer to the question why respondents decided to take revenge is 'violations of trust.'

In case of minor incidents—Crombag's young respondents generally reflected on everyday incidents—the passage of time appears to heal many wounds. But in case of grave intrusions, vindictive feelings do not wither easily. Many researchers point out that the motivations for seeking revenge frequently result from ruminative thinking about the injustice done to us and about possible ways to get even, although some acts of vengeance might be spontaneous and impulsive (McCullough et al., 2001). Rumination maintains or increases angry moods. Orth and colleagues (2006) found that feelings of revenge are significantly linked to post-traumatic stress reactions in crime victims. It is not the retaliation motive implied in feelings of revenge that explains this connection, though; most likely it is the ruminative nature of feelings of revenge. The authors conclude that revenge must presumably be regarded as a maladaptive coping reaction to experienced injustice, but not in the first period after victimization. This confirms Crombag's findings. In another study Orth (2004) found that punishment does satisfy feelings of revenge among victims of violent crimes, but only partially, and moreover only transitorily, and that in the long run feelings of revenge are not influenced by severity of punishment. Length of time since victimization (in Orth's study: four years) had no influence on the intensity of feelings of revenge. In this study anger rumination is again considered to be the crucial factor.

Ideally one may reason that punishing an offender eliminates the imbalance: justice is served. It is supposed that the victim should feel a sense of justice and then let go of the negative emotions (Tripp et al., 2007). As long as rumination continues, though, offering justice—the infliction of pain—is not enough. Besides, persons preoccupied by ruminative revenge feelings do not seem to be susceptible to mitigating factors (such as convincing excuses, sincere apologies or compensation) (for these factors see Miller, 2001).

6. Revenge as a Personal Disposition

Many psychologists stress that vengeance is a personal disposition (McCullough et al., 2001; Worthington, 2006). Some people might simply be more vengeful than others and thus less likely to be sympathetic, lenient or forgiving in the aftermath of transgressions. As stated, the motivations for seeking revenge frequently result from ruminative thinking about the offence, although some acts of vengeance might be spontaneous and impulsive. The irony of vengeance is that rumination may actually perpetuate the emotional distress that vengeance is intended to dissipate.

Indeed, McCullough and his colleagues (2001) found that some people are more amenable to 'anger rumination' and also maintain their motivation to seek revenge over time. They also tend to experience greater levels of negative affect and lower levels of life satisfaction. When victims have a strong desire to 'save face' they are more likely to seek revenge and respond in angry ways. Rather than proceeding with their own life and projects, and enjoying relationships for their own sake, they concentrate their energies on past grievances, rage, hatred of the offender, and destructive plots. These findings are not new. Psychoanalysts distinguish non-psychotic elaborations of mourning, in which the pain of mourning can be endured with the confidence that it can eventually be overcome, from psychotic elaborations of mourning which are based on the projection of blame onto the enemy. If victims avoid mourning over loss or humiliation and if they do not acknowledge their potential destructiveness, they are tempted to displace it by engaging in hostility (Mitscherlich & Mitscherlich, 1967). Victims who project blame often deal with unacknowledged feelings of guilt or shame (Scheff, 1994).

Nevertheless, McCullough says, it is possible that 'vengeful people' do maintain their desire for revenge rather out of principled moral reasoning that convinces them that seeking revenge is a morally justifiable response to having been injured (2001: 609). Victims who are more oriented toward concerns for justice (e.g., rules, fairness) than relational concerns (e.g., harmony, empathy, mercy) are likely to resist expressions of forgiveness if they are not satisfied that justice has been served (Exline & Baumeister, 2000; Pemberton et al., 2007). If justice standards are retributive ('guilty persons deserve to suffer'), forgiveness and other empathic options (pardon, mercy) are generally obstructed. Pardoning an offender's debt (forgiveness) and judging offenders with (some) charity often imply a willingness to bypass immediate self-interest and loosen justice-oriented rules in favor of mercy. In other words: when victims rely on standards of justice that dictate a reciprocity-based approach (be it retributive or restitutional), they tend to be reluctant to release a perpetrator without demanding punishment or repayment. In this context expressions of forgiveness might even be viewed as morally defective.

In an overview, Vidmar (2000: 24–26) also mentions that there is some evidence that a greater commitment to rules and obligations causes greater punitive responses to offenders. The same is true for persons scoring high on measures of authoritarianism. These 'high authoritarians' tend to view offenders as personally responsible for their actions, whereas low authoritarians stress environmental factors as a cause of criminal behavior (Vidmar, 2000; see also Gaubatz, 1995). They are more likely to perceive minor infractions as intentional and deliberate actions (attributing blame). People who easily blame offenders, even if they themselves partially initiated the sequence of events, are more likely to contemplate revenge and to enact revenge behaviors (Bradfield & Aquino, 1999; Stuckless & Goranson, 1992; Hennesy & Wiesenthal, 2005).[5] A host of research shows that individuals with 'high trait hostility' display biased social information processing (i.e., over-attribute a bad character to offenders) and are more likely to respond with aggression.

Thus it is seems important to help 'vengeful persons' to re-examine the accuracy of their attributions. If possible they should take notice of the context and details of the criminal act, including the motives of the perpetrator. However, it seems senseless to appeal directly to the moral standards of forgiveness and mercy. In order to challenge revenge justifications it might be more fruitful to appeal to the register of desert and reciprocity-related moral feelings: encouraging reflections about one's own real or potential culpability, and remissions after one's own transgressions (Berry et al., 2005).

7. Conclusions

The research findings discussed in this paper show that the major motives for revenge feelings are related to equalizing power and restoring self-respect ('telling the opponent the truth'; 'not letting oneself be walked over'). The expectation that revenge would ease pain ('balancing the suffering') plays only a marginal role in the views of Crombag's respondents. Punishment or other forms of 'dragging down' the offender may provide temporary satisfaction or relief, but punishment does not seem to change victims' long-term ability to deal with loss. These findings lead to two paradoxical conclusions. First, the victims' feelings of revenge should be considered as a comprehensible emotional reaction to the injustice suffered. In terms of coping with pain and developing nuanced judgments, victims must have experienced feelings of infuriation. Denial of these feelings may even initiate a process of anger-rumination. Second, when long-term rumination is concerned, it is plausible to view revenge as irrational: by brooding and impatiently waiting for our chance, we deprive ourselves of more rewarding and productive activities (Elster, 1990).

In a way victims of crime do have a 'natural' right to be enraged (Van Dijk, 2006). They want to express their anger and draw attention to the consequences of the crime. Withholding them these opportunities is experienced as an in-

---

5. Studies that have developed a Vengeance Scale (Stuckless and Goranson 1992; Vidmar 2000; Hennesy and Wiesenthal 2005) indicate that women consistently score lower than men. These studies also show that vengeance is a motivational factor that is implicated in a wide variety of antisocial and illicit acts including theft, vandalism, assault and rape.

fringement of their sense of justice, and even as additional punishment (Shapland et al., 1985; Pemberton, 2005). For these reasons, the criminal justice system should take the 'victim's voice' seriously and try to absorb it in its proceedings. Some reformers plead for a full right for victims to state their view, including tough opinions about the harm the offender caused and putting the blame on him (Van Dijk, 2008: 162–65). If this were to be allowed right at the end of the proceedings it would not interfere with the determination of punishment. Victims should also have the opportunity to obtain financial redress. According to Orth (2004), financial compensation for damages and suffering might have a greater mitigating impact on feelings of revenge than punishment.

Outside court we might encourage restorative justice conferences, which can be interpreted as a 'communicative form of revenge,' although victims are not allowed to articulate their case in violent ways and must be open towards the offender (Kool, 2005). We might even reinstate the 'civilized confrontation' in everyday life, in which citizens tell each other the truth, loud and clear. Too often unarticulated conflicts survive and the parties are tied down to rancorous feelings. To be sure, these 'vengeful acts' need modeling as well: ideally they should be proportional, subsidiary and directed at conflict resolution. Acting promptly and foregoing violence are other important conditions (Denkers, 2000).

One may wonder whether these disciplined acts of confrontation might be called 'vengeful.' The conditions mentioned illustrate that revenge is rather problematic from a moral perspective. Vengeful actions are typically more severe than the precipitating action in an attempt to exert power and control over the perceived violator and to produce an explicit conclusion to the dispute (Stuckless & Goranson, 1992; Elster, 1990). It may be concluded that revenge is not so much linked with justice, but is more connected with reclaiming honor and prestige, and exerting superiority (Meyer, 2005).

Not all victims' needs are legitimate or deserve support. As stated, some types of victims tend to maintain and even cherish anger rumination. For that reason the following statement from Winick merits a degree of criticism: 'the thrust of much of the existing therapeutic jurisprudence work is that the individual's own views concerning his or her health and how best to achieve it should generally be honored' (cited in Arrigo, 2004: 25). Of course, paternalism should be eschewed if possible, but, for instance, it would be unacceptable to support victims in their belief that harsh penalties would contribute to their healing.

The populist plea that harsh punishments would lead to closure is a fantasy. Obviously most victims have revenge feelings, but they do not think that the infliction of suffering might help them. They want justice to be done. Maybe we should keep in mind the words of Nietzsche in *The Gay Science*: let's not make ourselves uglier than we are, by punishing others and subsequently feeling disappointed. It is a tragedy that punishment cannot chase away the feelings of hate, bitterness, pain or grief.

References

Arrigo, B.A. (2004). The Ethics of Therapeutic Jurisprudence: A Critical and Theoretical Inquiry of Law, Psychology and Crime, *Psychiatry, Psychology and Law*, 11 (1): 23–43.

Bandes, S. (2001). *When Victims Seek Closure: Forgiveness, Vengeance, and the Role of Government*, http://papers.ssrn.com/paper.taf?abstract_id=223590.

Barker, V. (2007). The Politics of Pain: A Political Institutionalist Analyses of Crime Victims' Moral Protests, *Law & Society Review*, 41 (3): 619–663.

Berry, J.W. et al. (2005). Forgivingness, Vengeful Rumination, and Affective Traits, *Journal of Personality*, 73, 1, 183–222.

Bies, R.J. and Tripp, T.M. (1996). Beyond distrust: 'Getting even' and the need for revenge, in R.M. Karmer and T.R. Tyler (Eds.), *Trust in Organizations: Frontiers of Theory and Research*, Thousand Oakes: Sage, 246–260.

Bradfield, M. and Aquino, K. (1999). The Effects of Blame Attributions and Offender Likableness on Forgiveness and Revenge in the Workplace, *Journal of Management* 25 (5): 607–631.

Crombag, H. et al. (2003). On Vengeance, *Psychology, Crime & Law*, 9 (4): 333–344.

Daems, T. (2007). De slachtofferdimensie van herstelrechtelijke interventies. Een sluimerende therapeutisering? *Tijdschrift voor Herstelrecht*, 7(1), 7–21.

Denkers, F. (2000). 'De kunst van de vergevende wraak. Gestileerde wraak bij Abel Herzberg en bij Elia' In: P. van Tongeren (red.), *Is vergeving mogelijk? Over de mogelijkheid en moeilijkheid van vergeving, vooral in verband met oorlogsmisdaden*. Best: Damon 2000.

Durkheim, E. (1984) (1893), *The Division of Labour in Society*, New York: Free Press.

Elias, R. (1996). Paradigms and paradoxes of victimology, in: Chris Sumner, Mark Israel, Michael O'Connell and Rick Sarre (Eds.) *International victimology: selected papers from the 8th International Symposium*, Canberra: Australian Institute of Criminology. http://aic.gov.au/publications/proceedings/27/elias.html.

Elster, J. (1990). Norms of revenge, *Ethics*, 100: 862–885.

Exline, J.J. and Baumeister, R.F. (2000). Expressing Forgiveness and Repentance, in: M.E. McCullough et al. (Eds.), *Forgiveness. Theory, Research, and Practice*, New York and London: The Guilford Press, 133–155.

French, P. (2001). *The Virtues of Vengeance*, Kansas: University of Kansas Press.

Frijda, N.H. (1994). On Vengeance, In: S.H.M. van Goozen et al. (Eds.), *Emotions: Essays on Emotion Theory*, Hillsdale NJ: Erlbaum, 263–289.

Gaubatz, K. (1995). *Crime in the Public Mind*, Ann Arbor: The University of Michigan Press.

Govier, T. (2002). *Forgiveness and Revenge*, London and New York: Routledge.

Hennesy, D.A. and Wiesenthal, D.L. (2005). Driving Vengeance and Wilful Violations: Clustering of Problem Driving Attitudes, *Journal of Applied Social Psychology*, 35 (1): 61–79.

Jacoby, S. (1983). *Wild Justice. The Evolution of Revenge*, New York: Harper & Row.

Kanwar, V. (2001). Capital Punishment as "Closure": The Limits of a Victim-Centred Jurisprudence, *New York University Review of Law and Social Change*, 27, 215–255.

Kay, J.W. (2007). Murder victims' families for reconciliation, in D. Sullivan and L. Tift, *Handbook of restorative justice: a global perspective*, London: Routledge, 230–245.

Kool, R. (2005). Herstel: een communicatieve vorm van wraak, *Tijdschrift voor Herstelrecht*, 5 (3): 24–33.

McCullough, M.E. et al. (2001). Vengefulness: Relationships with forgiveness, rumination, well being, and the big five. *Personality and Social Psychology Bulletin*, 27, 601–610.

Maruna, S. and King, A. (2004). 'Public Opinion and Community Penalties', in A.E. Bottoms, S.A. Rex and G. Robinson (Eds.), *Alternatives to Prisons*, Cullompton: Willan, 83–112.

Meyer, L.R. (2005). *The New Revenge and the Old Retribution: Insights from Monte Cristo*, http://webspace.quinnipiac.edu/meyer/revenge.pdf.

Miller, D.T. (2001). Disrespect and the Experience of Injustice, *Annual Review of Psychology*, 52, 52–553.

Mitscherlich, A. and Mitscherlich, M. (1967). *The inability to mourn: Principles of collective behavior*, New York: Grove Press.

Murphy, J. (2003). *Getting Even: Forgiveness and its Limits*, New York: Oxford University Press.

Newberg, A. et al. (2000). The Neurological Correlates of Forgiveness, in: M.E. McCullough et al. (Eds.), *Forgiveness. Theory, Research, and Practice*, New York and London: The Guilford Press, 91–110.

Nozick, R. (1981). *Philosophical Explanations*, Oxford: Oxford University Press.

Orth, U. (2004). Does Perpetrator Punishment Satisfy Victims' Feelings of Revenge?, *Aggressive Behavior*, 30, 62–70.

Orth, U. et al. (2006). Feelings of Revenge, Retaliation Motive, and Posttraumatic Stress Reactions in Crime Victims, *Journal of Interpersonal Violence*, 2 (2): 229–243.

Pemberton, A. (2005). Het spreekrecht: vergelding of herstel? *Tijdschrift voor Herstelrecht*, 5 (3): 34–44.

Pemberton, A., Winkel, F.W. and Groenhuijsen, M.S. (2007). Taking victims seriously in restorative justice, *International Perspectives in Victimology* 3 (1): 4–13.

Richards, K.M. (2005). Unlikely Friends? Oprah Winfrey and Restorative Justice. *Australian and New Zealand Journal of Criminology*, 38(3), 381–399.

Roderick, D. and Krumholz, S.T. (2006). *Much Ado about Nothing? A Critical Examination of Therapeutic Jurisprudence*, www.snesl.edu/pub_ images/42e245c3614c419c8fe0fc6a51cf5fa7.pdf.

Sarat, A. (1997). Vengeance, Victims and the Identities of Law. *Social and Legal Studies*, 6(2), 163–190.

Scheff, T.J. (1994). *Bloody Revenge; Emotions, Nationalism and War*, Boulder Ca: Westview Press.

Shapland, J., Wilmore J. and Duff, P. (1985). *Victims in the criminal justice system*, Cambridge: Gower.

Solomon, R. (1990). *A Passion for Justice: Emotions and the Origins of the Social Contract*, New York: Addison-Wesley.

Strang, H. (2002). *Repair or Revenge: Victims and Restorative Justice.* Oxford: Oxford University Press.

Strang, H., Sherman, L., et al. (2006). Victim Evaluations of Face-to-Face Restorative Justice Conferences: A Quasi-Experimental Analysis, *Journal of Social Issues.* 62(2), 281–306.

Stuckless, N. and Goranson, R. (1992). The Vengeance Scale: development of a measure of attitudes toward revenge, *Journal of Social Behavior and Personality*, 7, 25–42.

Tripp, T.M. et al. (2007). A Vigilante Model of Justice: Revenge, Reconciliation, Forgiveness, and Avoidance, *Social Justice Research* 20 (1): 10–34.

Tripp, T.M. and Bies, R.J. Whats good about revenge? In: R.J. Lewicki et al. (Eds.), *Research on negotiation in organizations*, vol. 6, Greenwich CT: JAI Press, 145–160.

Van Dijk, J.J.M. (2006). *The Mark of Abel. Reflections on the Social Labelling of Victims of Crime*, inaugural lecture, Tilburg University. www.intervict.nl.

Van Dijk, J.J.M. (2008). *Slachtoffers als zondebokken*, Apeldoorn-Antwerpen: Maklu.

Van Stokkom, B. (2007). The expressive function of restorative punishment. A public interest perspective, in R. Mackay et al. (Eds.), *Images of Restorative Justice Theory*, Frankfurt am Main, Verlag für Polizei und Wissenschaft, 151–167.

Van Stokkom, B. (2008). Forgiveness and reconciliation in restorative justice conferences, *Ethical Perspectives*, vol. 15, nr. 3, 2008, pp. 399–418.

Vidmar, N. (2000). *Retribution and Revenge*, Duke Law School Working Paper SSRN. http://papers.ssrn.com/sol3/papers.cfm?abstract_id=875449.

Wemmers, J. and Cyr, K. (2005). Can Mediation Be Therapeutic for Crime Victims? An Evaluation of Victims' Experiences in Mediation with Young Offenders, *Canadian Journal of Criminology and Criminal Justice*, 47, July, 527–544.

Wexler, D. and Winick, B. (Eds.). (1996). *Law in a Therapeutic Key: Developments in Therapeutic Jurisprudence*, Carolina Academic Press.

Worthington, E. (2006). *Forgiveness and Reconciliation: Theory and Application*, New York: Routledge.

Zedner, L. (2002). Victims, in: M. Maguire et al. (Eds.), *The Oxford Handbook of Criminology*, Oxford University Press, 419–456.

Zimring, F.E. (2003). *The Contradictions of American Capital Punishment*. Oxford: Oxford University Press.

11

The Controversial Nature of Victim Participation: Therapeutic Benefits in Victim Impact Statements

Antony Pemberton & Sandra Reynaers

Abstract

Over the past thirty years the position of victims of crime in the criminal justice system has shown vast improvement. Many victims' rights are relatively uncontroversial. Generally recognized rights include that victims should be treated with respect and recognition, that they should receive comprehensible information, be able to receive support and assistance and be reimbursed for their expenses as well as be compensated for their damages. Participation in the criminal justice system is a more complicated matter. The topic of this paper, the victim impact statements, is criticized on the grounds of the pressure it may place on the rights of suspects and the impartial nature of the trial. Moreover, it is argued that the therapeutic focus of these reforms is in essence alien to the criminal justice process. Finally, the effectiveness of victim impact statements is called into question. In this paper it will be argued that specifying therapeutic benefits and closer inspection of the therapeutic literature will simultaneously reduce the tension with established criminal justice principles and provide a more fruitful base for conducting research into the effectiveness of victim impact statements.

1. Introduction

The position of victims of crime has shown vast improvement since the 1970s. Thirty years ago it was correct to assert that the victim was the forgotten party of the criminal justice process, while today this would be at odds with the actual situation of victims (e.g., Groenhuijsen & Letschert, 2008). International legal instruments, like the UN Declaration of Basic Principles for Victims of Crime and Abuse of Power, the Council of Europe Recommendations (85)11 and (2006)8 and the EU Framework Decision on the standing of victims in criminal proceedings as well as national legislation in a large number of countries illustrate that the following rights for victims are increasingly recognized (e.g., Groenhuijsen & Pemberton, 2009):

- A right to respect and recognition at all stages of the criminal proceedings;
- A right to receive information and information about the progress of the case;
- A right to provide information to officials responsible for decisions relating to the offender;
- A right to have legal advice available, regardless of the victim's means;
- A right to protection, of victims' privacy and their physical safety;
- A right to compensation, from the offender and the State;
- A right to receive victim support;
- The duty for governments to promote mediation in criminal cases for offences which it considers appropriate for this sort of measure;
- The duty for the State to foster, develop and improve cooperation with foreign States in cases of cross border victimization in order to facilitate more effective protection of victims' interests in criminal proceedings.

A number of these rights are relatively uncontroversial. The notions that victims should be treated with respect and recognition, receive support in coping with crime and information concerning the criminal justice procedure, adequate protection and compensation are widely shared and not often debated with any intensity.

The same cannot be said for victims' rights which, depending on the way that they are interpreted, imply a stronger procedural position for victims of crime. This is clearly evident in the right to mediation. The debate concerning victim-offender mediation and the related concept of restorative justice, has led to a vast literature containing the arguments for and against (e.g., Christie, 1977; Ashworth, 2002; Braithwaite, 2002; Strang, 2002; Daly 2002; Groenhuijsen, 2000), not in the least part, due to the fact that many restorative justice advocates argue the necessity of a full-fledged overhaul of the criminal justice system (see recently Walgrave, 2008).

However, less far-reaching instruments which offer victims the right to be heard in the criminal justice procedure are also controversial. The case in point, discussed in this paper, is the class of measures referred to as victim impact statements. The precise form of victim impact statements can vary, from a written statement that primarily serves a function in awarding compensation to an oral statement that may influence the sentence given to the offender (also referred to as a victim statement of opinion). All have in common that they allow victims the right to express the harm they have experienced as a part of the court proceedings (Erez, 2004).

In this paper we will outline two central debates concerning victim impact statements. First there is discussion of the pressure victim impact statements exert on the rights of the offenders and other central criminal justice norms like proportionality and due process. The tension between the therapeutic rationale underlying victim impact statements and criminal justice principles has led opponents of these instruments to dismiss striving for therapeutic benefits for victims as a paradigm, alien to the criminal justice system. Although we agree with many of the arguments put forward against the introduction of concepts like 'healing' or 'closure,' we find that other therapeutic constructs do not suffer from the same problems.

Second there is controversy concerning the effectiveness of victim impact statements. Do they in fact enhance victims' well-being? Or are they ineffective or even counter-productive in the sense that they entail victims risking secondary victimization?

In both debates the therapeutic perspective is relatively amorphous. Therapeutic jurisprudence is a container-term and can incorporate any construct that is related to victims' mental welfare (e.g., Winick, 2008). The central argument of this paper is that the tension between established criminal justice principles and therapeutic benefits for victims can be reduced by clearly specifying *what* therapeutic constructs are invoked. In addition, we will underline the difference between therapeutic sounding language and constructs and mechanisms that actually reflect the current psychological literature concerning victims of crime. This has implications for the way that effectiveness of victim impact statements should be studied.

2. Balancing Victim Participation and Criminal Justice Concerns: Gauging Criminal Justice Correspondence

2.1 Central Issues in the Debate Concerning Victim Impact Statements

Erez (2004) shows that the introduction of victim impact statements has been argued on a variety of grounds. First the victim's expression of harm may be used as a tool for the courts to grant compensation to victims. This is particularly relevant to common law jurisdictions, who unlike their civil law counterparts, do not allow victims the opportunity to file for compensation in the capacity of an injured party (e.g., Brienen & Hoegen, 2000). Compensation is the least controversial function. In most civil law jurisdictions, instruments with a similar focus have been in place for a long time. The scholars critical of enlarging the position of the victim within the criminal justice system concur that, as Ashworth (2002) states, 'the victim's legitimate interest is in compensation and reparation.' In essence, regarding this purpose, the victim impact statements fulfill a tort law, rather than a criminal law function. The harm caused is therefore a natural and necessary component of the justice procedure (e.g., Duff, 2003).

Second there is the reduction of secondary victimization. The lack of a role in the criminal proceedings has been shown to be a primary source of victims' dissatisfaction (Shapland et al., 1985). Social acknowledgement of the harm done to victims is a protective factor in the development of traumatic complaints (Maercker & Muller, 2004) and recent research has shown acknowledgement to be an important criterion for victims' assessment of sentencing outcomes (Orth, 2003). Third and related is the opportunity that victim impact statements allow for 'voice.' The body of research into procedural justice demonstrates that offering participants a role in the proceedings enhances its legitimacy and the acceptance of its outcome (e.g., Röhl, 1997; Tyler, 1990; Tyler & Huo, 2002) and this also applies to victims of crime (Wemmers, 1996). Erez finds this function to be central to victim impact statements (see Erez, 2004; Roberts & Erez, 2004). It is not the influence on the sentence that is important, but rather the mere fact that the victim is given a role in the proceedings.

Finally the victim impact statements (VIS) are promoted as a means for victims to influence the sentence of the offender. This is particularly relevant to the class of VIS known as the victim statements of opinion. With these instruments the victim is explicitly invited to express a preference concerning the sentence. These are the most controversial form of victim impact statements, in particular as they are also admissible in capital cases in the United States.

The discussion concerning the victim statements of opinion brings the two central concerns concerning victim impact statements to the fore. First of all it is argued that victim statements of opinion will lead to harsher, disproportionate and inconsistent sentences, which is of particular concern in death penalty cases (as discussed in Erez, 2004). Second it is argued that the motivation for these measures introduces an alien, therapeutic, victim-focused paradigm into the criminal justice procedure (Van Stokkom, this volume). We will discuss these objections in turn.

2.2 Victim Impact Statements and the Effects on Sentences

The debate concerning the effects on sentencing revolves around two separate questions. The main initial concern was that allowing victim impact evidence to influence sentencing would lead to harsher sentences. As Erez (2004) notes, victims were also portrayed as vindictive, punitive, and motivated by a desire to maximize sentence severity. This portrayal is, as Erez shows, at odds with most research findings, consistently showing victims to be no more or less punitive than non-victims (e.g., Maruna & King, 2004) and with research showing many victims to prefer restorative options (Strang, 2002). Nevertheless there is some room for concern. It is still quite possible that victims are more punitive than magistrates (e.g., De Keijser et al., 2007). Moreover the research showing the relatively lenient position of victims is based on large-scale population surveys. Most victims in these surveys have suffered relatively minor crimes. Pemberton (2008) hypothesizes that the perspective of victims of severe crimes, like co-victims of homicide, does not have to follow this more general pattern. He notes that both the available research into these groups (e.g., Rock, 1998) and the actions of organizations representing their particular interests (see for a description, Goodey, 2005) suggests a higher level of punitiveness. As victim impact statements are often solely on offer for victims of severe crimes, caution is necessary in applying the image of the non-punitive victim.

Concerning consistency, Ashworth (2002) points out that offenders may benefit or be disadvantaged due to differences between 'their' victims. A victim's opinion of the desired sentence is likely to be influenced by many other factors than the culpability of the offender, which is the issue at stake in the trial.

Instead of viewing the outcome of the trial in terms of the wrong committed, victims will be likely to use the harm caused as their primary criterion, which will lead to inconsistency (see Buruma, 2004; Pemberton, 2007). The disparity this causes is partly, but not completely cushioned by the fact that harms and wrongs are correlated in criminal justice (Duff, 2003). Differences in personality characteristics, like trait vengefulness and forgiveness (e.g., McCullough et al., 2001), will also play a role. People vary in the extent they are vengeful and this general notion applies to victims as well. It is clear that if the victim's opinion were directly translated into the sentence the principle of consistency would be threatened.

Notwithstanding the merit of these principled objections, however, research has yet to show that victim impact statements in fact lead to more severe sentences or to inconsistency in sentencing (Erez, 1999). It appears that the mitigating influence of the judge or jury presiding over the case largely reduces the effects of victim impact statements on sentencing. Even concerning the victim statements of opinion, evidence of victim impact on sentencing has yet to be shown.

Moreover, it is questionable whether victims desire a direct influence over the sentence. Research suggests that most victims prefer their opinion to be heard, rather than decision control over the sentence (Wemmers & Cyr, 2004). In fact, victims may consider more far-reaching forms of control over the outcome of the process to be an unwanted burden (e.g., Reeves & Mulley, 2000).

Nevertheless, for some victims influencing the sentence of the offender is the main reason for participation. Sanders et al.'s (2001) results showed about half of the participating victims mentioning this motive (although nearly two thirds did so for 'therapeutic' reasons). Pemberton (2005) reports that 59% of Dutch victims would welcome the opportunity to submit a victim impact statement, even if it did not have any impact on the sentence. However, if it would have an influence, this percentage increased to 84%.

2.3 Therapeutic Notions in Criminal Justice

In Van Stokkom's contribution to this volume he criticizes the notion of victim-centered therapeutic jurisprudence (Van Stokkom, 2011). Van Stokkom views striving for therapeutic benefit as a component of a separate paradigm, alien to the criminal justice process. It may be risky where concepts as 'harmony,' 'healing,' 'personal growth,' 'closure' and 'reconciliation' get the upper hand and are outstripping discussions on the crime and its aftermath. And this risk has become a reality in the case of the victim statements of opinion. As Daems (2007) shows the concept of victim 'closure' was regularly invoked in the rhetoric surrounding victim statements of opinion in death penalty cases. Furedi comments that surrounding the trial of Timothy McVeigh, 'closure' was the most frequently used word (Furedi, 2004). Allowing victim statements of opinion in death penalty cases is supposed to help victims achieve closure, so they can 'move on with their lives' and is one of the main drivers for their implementation (see for a critical discussion Sarat, 1997). This leads to the situation that key criminal justice principles, like proportionality, are in danger of being sacrificed or compromised in the name of achieving closure.

There are a number of different reasons to share Van Stokkom's reservations. First of all, the 'therapeutic' notions that he mentions have in common that they are vague, underspecified and are in fact not often used in recent psychological literature concerning therapeutic approaches to victims of crime (see Winkel, 2007). A search of the contents of the *Journal of Traumatic Stress,* the leading scientific journal on stress reactions to victimization, reveals that not one article in the past 20 years included the words 'healing' or 'closure' in its title. Moreover 'closure' only appeared twice in the text bodies of the articles in this journal.

As these constructs are not normally used in scientific research, it should not be surprising that there is no reliable evidence for or against the notion that victim impact statements lead to healing or closure. Evidence is either anecdotal or derived from research with other constructs, for instance satisfaction.[1] This leads to a strong emphasis on individual cases and paves the way for hijacking of the victim's plight by populists. This is particularly problematic in the case of closure due to victim statements of opinion. The criminal justice process is neither equipped nor intended to reach this goal. The impact of sudden bereavement, in particular due to violent causes, cannot be overstressed (e.g., Kaltmann & Bonanno, 2003). Coming to terms with this impact is often a long and arduous process, which will not be magically achieved through the outcome of a justice procedure (Pemberton, 2008b). Moreover the process leading to capital punishment prolongs victims' suffering, with research showing that the process is an equal burden for the families of the victim and the offender alike (King, 2004).

In sum: Van Stokkom is quite right to be concerned about the influx of therapeutic sounding language in the discourse concerning victims' rights in criminal justice. But does this lead to the conclusion that striving for therapeutic benefits for victims is necessarily alien to the criminal justice system, as Van

1. See Erez, 2004 for examples of the confusing use of measures of satisfaction.

Stokkom suggests? The fact that the application of some therapeutic constructs within criminal justice is problematic, does not rule out the possibility that others may be more easily aligned with the criminal justice procedure.

Instead, the previous discussion can provide two central principles to assess the match between therapeutic jurisprudence and the criminal justice system. First, the goal of achieving 'closure' through victim statements of opinion in capital cases is unrealistic; in the sense that it is not supported by evidence and it is not reasonable to expect a justice procedure to reach this goal. This suggests that proposed therapeutic benefits need to be realistic and evidence-based. Moreover, where therapeutic constructs are used or therapeutic analogies invoked, they need to accurately and fully reflect current victimological and psychological knowledge. It makes obvious sense to use therapeutic constructs that are actually employed in current therapeutic approaches to psychological suffering after criminal victimization. Together this is what we call '*therapeutic coherence.*' Second, Van Stokkom's objections show that closure in death penalty cases introduces a therapeutic construct that may conflict and even 'get the upper hand' over criminal justice principles. To prevent this we propose that striving for therapeutic benefit for victims should be restricted by the limits placed by established criminal justice principles (see also Winick, 2008). In addition, therapeutic benefits should be aligned with criminal justice goals, implying that therapeutic perspectives should correspond with the purpose of the criminal justice system for victims. This is what we call '*criminal justice correspondence.*' We will expand the latter point in the remainder of this section. Therapeutic coherence will be discussed in the following section.

2.4 Matching Therapeutic Jurisprudence and Criminal Justice: Reduction of Anger and Anxiety

To assess the match between therapeutic benefits for victims and the criminal justice system we need to reflect briefly on the purpose of the criminal justice system for victims. In terms of the ultimate outcome of the criminal justice system, the punishment of the wrongdoer, the two most pronounced motives are retribution (as implied by 'just deserts' theory) or behavior control (as implied by utilitarian theories of punishment) (see Vidmar, 2000). Most social-psychological research suggests that the first motive is predominant in lay-people's judgments (see Carlsmith, Darley & Pittman, 2002; Carlsmith, 2006).

Orth (2003) connects these general perspectives on punishment to victims' punishment goals. He notes that victims may want to see offenders punished due to their feelings of anger at the injustice suffered and the associated desire for revenge (see also Fitzgibbons, 1986) and/or their need to protect themselves and reduce their fear of repeat victimization by the offender. The former goal is related to retribution, the latter to behavior control. The punishment goals map onto the two most important emotional reactions to victimization, namely anger and anxiety (Winkel, 2007).[2]

Reduction of anger and anxiety are not only goals that are directly related to the central functions of the criminal justice procedure, but also lie at the core of therapeutic approaches to aid victims of crime. The approaches relating to anxiety are well known with post-traumatic stress disorder being classified as an anxiety disorder (see NICE, 2005 for an overview of techniques), but reduction of anger is a therapeutic goal as well. This is most evident in the various forms of forgiveness therapy (Wade et al., 2005), but also in anger management (Howells & Day, 2002) and cognitive behavioral therapy for domestic violence perpetrators (Dutton, 2006). Moreover recent research shows successful techniques for reducing or resolving PTSD simultaneously reduce anger (Renssen, 2002; Winkel, 2007).[3]

In our opinion, specifying the therapeutic benefit of the criminal justice procedure in terms of reduction of anger and anxiety reduces the tension between the therapeutic and justice paradigms. Unlike constructs like 'closure' or 'healing,' reduction of anger and anxiety are well specified in the relevant psychological literature and are the focus of recent academic work into therapeutic approaches for victims of crime. Moreover reduction of anger and anxiety is closely connected to the central functions of the criminal justice procedure, retribution and behavior control. Finally, as we will show in the following section, reducing anxiety and anger reduction does not necessarily imply pressure on other criminal justice principles.

3. Therapeutic Mechanisms in Criminal Justice: Reviewing Therapeutic Coherence

The second debate concerning the victim impact statements relates to their effectiveness. According to one often cited evaluation of the victim impact statements, they 'don't work, can't work' (Sanders et al., 2001: 447), while others find exactly the opposite (Chalmers et al., 2007).

---

2. Winkel (2007) shows conclusively that, in emotional terms, anger is an equally prominent reaction to criminal victimization as anxiety, although the latter receives far more attention in policy and research (see also Ditton et al., 1999).

3. In fact, according to Winkel (2007), PTSD could be seen as an anger disorder as well as an anxiety disorder.

This discussion is hampered by a lack of research evidence concerning the therapeutic effects of victim impact statements. First of all the outcome measure employed is invariably the victim's satisfaction or a similar construct. However, neither satisfaction nor dissatisfaction can be directly translated into therapeutic and anti-therapeutic effects. Second, where therapeutic analogies are invoked to explain the mechanism by which victim impact statements could lead to positive or negative effects, the literature is not adequately reflected. Finally the debate neglects the possibility that individual differences in victims' personal characteristics or the crime suffered mediate or moderate the effects and the usefulness of participating in victim impact statements. There is marked lack of use of relevant research findings and theory from the psychological study of victims in the on-going debate with respect to all three of these issues.[4]

3.1 Victims' Satisfaction and Dissatisfaction

Surveys of victims' experiences in the criminal justice system tend to employ victims' satisfaction as an outcome measure (e.g., Winkel, 2002; Pemberton, Winkel & Groenhuijsen, 2007). The use of satisfaction is problematic for two reasons. The first is a general one. The construct validity of satisfaction is questionable (Bouckaert & van de Walle, 2003). Satisfaction measures many other things than the quality of service. Expectations and intrinsic aspects of the service are also known to influence satisfaction (with fire-fighters generally being the most valued public service, irrespective of their performance (Bouckaert & Van de Walle, 2003)). Moreover, satisfaction is influenced by the frequency of use of the service, the knowledge of the service, the homogeneity of service and the directness of contact (Dinsdale & Marson, 1999), regardless of the quality of service. Second, and more specific for victimology, satisfaction has shown to be a poor measure of therapeutic benefit. Various studies (McNally, Bryant, & Ehlers, 2003; Zech & Rime, 2005) have documented that satisfaction is *not* a reliable indicator of therapeutic performance. Psychological debriefing, for example, is a widely used method to mitigate psychological distress and to prevent the emergence of PTSD. The majority of debriefed victims describes it as helpful, and report high levels of satisfaction with the intervention. However, there is no convincing evidence that debriefing reduces the incidence of PTSD, and some controlled studies suggest that it may impede

4. In this respect it represents an example of what we call the 'two faces of victimology' (Winkel, 2002; Pemberton, Winkel and Groenhuijsen, 2007), which denotes the divide between the 'law-related' disciplines in victimology and the 'psychology-related' disciplines.

natural recovery (Van Emmerik et al., 2002). McNally et al. (2003:65) concluded: "we believe that consumers' satisfaction ratings apparently reflect polite expressions of gratitude, rather than intervention efficacy."

The evaluation studies of victim impact statements have also used satisfaction as an outcome measure and therefore suffer from the same shortcomings (for an overview of studies, see Erez, 2004 and Roberts and Erez, 2004). Both supporters and opponents of the measures have exhibited a tendency to extrapolate from satisfaction (or dissatisfaction) to other consequences.[5] That input at sentencing leads to satisfied victims may well be true (see Wemmers, 2002), however, whether it reduces trauma to any significant extent remains to be seen (e.g., Orth & Maercker, 2004). Similarly it may well be true that failing to meet victims' raised expectations may lead to (some) dissatisfaction, as Ashworth (2000), Edwards (2001) and Sanders et al. (2001) suggest. But disappointment is not synonymous with secondary victimization (see Orth, 2002 for the most convincing development of the latter construct) and we fail to see why preventing the *possibility* of victims being disappointed should be used as an argument against measures purporting to serve victims' interests.

3.2 Reduction of Anger and Anxiety through Victim Impact Statements: The Importance of Voice

In the previous section we have already stated that the victim's primary interest in the use of victim impact statements is 'voice,' i.e., the opportunity to be heard in their own case. The fact that the victim's own expression is taken to be the primary mechanism for therapeutic benefits has led some authors to assume a correspondence with the importance of expression in a therapeutic setting. Erez (2004) for example cites the well-known book *Opening Up: The Healing Power of Confiding in Others* by James Pennebaker (1990) in this respect. In the debate surrounding the Dutch oral victim impact statement, similar arguments were used against the new instrument (e.g., De Keijser & Malsch, 2002). The gist of these arguments is that the courtroom is not a suitable setting for allowing the sort of therapeutic catharsis intended by Pennebaker. A

5. In addition, the interpretation of the results is sometimes questionable. The Sanders et al. (2001) conclusion of 'Don't Work, Can't Work' is based on a survey in which 77% of participating victims found the VIS to be helpful directly after submission of a written victim impact statement and 59% at the end of the process, which does not seem to support the rather flippant title of their article.

therapeutic environment is one of confidence and safety, which qualities are notoriously absent in most courtrooms (see also Herman, 2003).

In addition, the oral versions of the victim impact statements lack most of the necessary ingredients of therapeutic techniques for victims of crime. There is no evidence for the efficacy of 'one-shot' forms of expression in the reduction/prevention of trauma (see Van Emmerik et al., 2002; Winkel, 2007). This would imply that making a victim impact statement, oral or not, will not lead to therapeutic benefits for victims merely through the act of expression.

However, this does not imply that victim impact statements will not have therapeutic benefits. On the contrary, there are various avenues through which this could be the case. It is not the mere act of expression that leads to the supposed benefit, but the significance of expression during a court case.

First of all, there is the assessment of procedural justice. As has been repeatedly shown, allowing victims the possibility of participating in their own case leads to a higher sense of procedural justice. Relevant is that enhancing procedural justice will diminish anger and retributive tendencies (see Karremans en Van Lange, 2005; Tripp et al., 2007). This is also evidenced by evaluations of restorative justice programs in which high levels of perceived justice coincide with stark reductions of anger (Strang, 2002). This reduction of anger, which may also be seen as a process of forgiveness (Worthington & Scherer, 2004) is also shown to have a beneficial effect on victims' mental health (Karremans et al., 2003).

Second, the choice to participate in a VIS-program can be viewed as a method of giving victims control over their own recovery and an avenue for action (see Pemberton, 2008b). Both of these features of victim impact statements can be linked to theories of recovery after post-traumatic stress. Frazier (2003) shows that victims who have a strong sense of control over their own recovery and are focused on avenues for action in the present, have a low risk of developing post-traumatic stress disorder. Similarly, recent research into the concept of post-traumatic growth (Tedeschi & Calhoun, 1996) has shown that avenues for action are important in making sense of extreme negative experiences (Hobfoll et al., 2007). Participating in one's own court case, could be such an avenue (Pemberton, 2007).

On theoretical grounds, therefore, there is reason to believe that victim impact statements may reduce victims' anxiety and anger. We should note that in both instances this reduction of anger and anxiety may be achieved without placing undue pressure on other criminal justice principles, as neither achieving a sense of procedural justice and/or a perception of control necessitates victim control over sentencing.

3.3 Individual Differences

Debates concerning victim instruments tend to suffer from the application of a single stereotype of victims. This leads to general statements concerning the effects of criminal justice measures on victims, which disregard the variety in victims' relevant psychological characteristics, the differences in their experiences and the context of their victimization.[6] In many instances the debate centers on the question whether an instrument 'works' for victims *in general,* rather than the question for *which* victims an instrument works or under *which conditions* this is the case.[7] However, in therapeutic approaches to victimization the latter question is the more important one. Approaches to mass victimization stress the importance of matching treatment to the individual circumstances of victims, rather than applying certain methods across the board (see for example Foa et al., 2005; Pemberton, 2009). There are a number of reasons to apply this conditional approach to the study of victim impact statements.

First of all there is the correlation between victims' experiences with crime and their perspective on justice. The importance of retributive justice and thereby punishment of the offender increases with the severity of crime (see Gromet & Darley, 2006). In addition, both the age of the offender and the question whether the offender and the victim belong to the same community play a role. Wenzel, Okimoto, Feather and Platow (2008) show retribution to be less important in cases with young offenders and more important in cases where victims and offenders do not belong to the same community or group.

These differences in perspectives on justice are likely to impact victims' perspectives on the function of victim impact statements. As we have already noted, where most victims primarily use victim impact statements for their expressive function ('voice'), a sizable minority sees them as a means to influence sentencing (see Sanders et al., 2001; Pemberton, 2005). This use of a justice instrument for different purposes is also clearly visible in victim participation in restorative justice procedures (see Strang, 2002; Daly, 2003). The perspectives on the purpose of an instrument are likely to have an effect on victims' evaluation of these instruments.

Finally recent research suggests that extreme anger and anxiety may form barriers for the experience of procedural justice. Murphy (2008) shows that fair procedures do not affect the experience of justice of people who have high in-

6. See Pemberton, Winkel and Groenhuijsen, 2008 for a more extensive discussion of this point.

7. See case Pemberton, 2008 for an application of this notion to restorative justice.

tensity anger. Winkel (2007) shows that the benefits of participating in restorative justice conferences only apply to victims who do not suffer from post-traumatic stress disorder (see also Cheon & Regehr, 2006).

4. Conclusion

The introduction of victim participation in the criminal justice procedure is controversial, particularly when motivated by therapeutic concerns. However, by clearly specifying the nature of the therapeutic constructs and reviewing how these constructs relate to the fundamental goals of the criminal justice process this apparent tension can be reduced. This review is what we have called *criminal justice correspondence.* Retribution and behavior control are the most important purposes of the criminal justice system. These general perspectives may be connected to victims' punishment goals. Their perspective on punishment is related to their anger at the offender and/or their fear of being revictimized by the offender. This implies that striving to reduce anger and anxiety, the most important therapeutic goal for victims of crime, is not at odds *a priori* with established criminal justice principles.

We have argued for the correct application of relevant therapeutic knowledge to criminal justice instruments. Correct use of therapeutic constructs is what we have dubbed *therapeutic coherence.* The literature reviewed in this article suggests the use of outcome measures relating to anger and anxiety, rather than satisfaction; shows the effects of these instruments to be explained through the concept of voice, rather than through an analogy to expression in therapeutic settings; and stresses the need for an individual differences perspective, rather than viewing victims as a sociological class.

References

Ashworth, A. (2000). Victims' rights, defendants' rights and criminal procedure. In A. Crawford, A. and Goodey, J. (Eds.). *Integrating a victim perspective within criminal justice.* Aldershot: Dartmouth Publishing.

Ashworth, A. (2002). Responsibilities, rights and restorative justice. *British Journal of Criminology*, 42, 578–595.

Bouckaert, G. and Van de Walle, S. (2003). Comparing Measures of Citizen Trust and User Satisfaction as Indicators of "Good Governance": Difficulties in Linking Trust and Satisfaction Indicators. *International Review of Administrative* Sciences, 69(3), 329–343.

Braithwaite, J. (2002). *Restorative justice and responsive regulation.* Oxford: Oxford University Press.

Brienen, M.E.I. and Hoegen, E.H. (2000). *Victims of crime in 22 European criminal justice systems.* Nijmegen: Wolf Legal Publishers.

Buruma, Y. (2004). Doubts on the Upsurge of the Victim's role in Criminal Law. In: Kaptein, H. and Malsch, M. (Eds.). *Crime, Victims and Justice. Essays on Principles and Practice.* Aldershot UK: Ashgate.

Carlsmith, K.M. (2006). The roles of retribution and utility in determining punishment. *Journal of Experimental Social Psychology,* 42, 437–451.

Carlsmith, K.M., Darley, J.M., and Robinson, P.H. (2002). Why do we punish? Deterrence and just deserts as motives for punishment. *Journal of Personality and Social Psychology,* 83, 1–16.

Chalmers, J., Duff, P., and Leverick, F. (2007). Victim impact statements: Can work, do work (for those who bother to make them). *Criminal Law Review,* May, 360–379.

Cheon, A. and Regehr C. (2006). Restorative justice models in cases of intimate partner violence: Reviewing the Evidence. *Victims and Offenders,* 1(4), 369–394.

Christie, N. (1977). Conflicts as property. *British Journal of Criminology,* 17(1), 1–17.

Daems, T. (2007) De slachtofferdimensie van herstelgerichte interventies. Een sluimerende therapeutisering? *Tijdschrift voor Herstelrecht,* 7(1), 7–21. (In Dutch: with an English summary).

Daly, K. (2002). Restorative justice: the real story. *Punishment & Society,* 4 (1), 55–79.

Daly, K. (2003). Mind the gap: Restorative Justice in Theory and Practice. In: Von Hirsch, A., Roberts, J.V., Bottoms, A., Roach, K. and Schiff, M. (Eds.) *Restorative and criminal justice: competing or reconcilable paradigms.* Oxford, UK: Hart Publishing.

De Keijser, J.W. and Malsch, M. (2002). Is spreken zilver en zwijgen goud? Spreekrecht en het ontstemde slachtoffer. *Delikt en Delinkwent,* 32(1), 5–20.

De Keijser, J.W., Van Koppen, P.J., and Elffers, H. (2007). Bridging the gap between judges and the public. A multi-method study. *Journal of Experimental criminology,* 2007(3), 131–161.

Dinsdale, G. and Marson, B.D. (1999) Citizen/Client Surveys: Dispelling Myths and Redrawing Maps. Ottawa: Canadian Centre for Management Development.

Duff, R.A. (2003). Restoration and retribution. In: Von Hirsch, A., Roberts, J.V., Bottoms, A., Roach, K. and Schiff, M. (Eds.) *Restorative and crimi-*

nal justice: competing or reconcilable paradigms. Oxford, UK: Hart Publishing.

Dutton, D.A. (2006). *Rethinking domestic violence.* Toronto: UBC Press.

Edwards, I. (2001). *Victim participation in sentencing. The problem of incoherence.* The Howard Journal, 40(1), 39–54.

Edwards, I. (2004). An ambiguous participant: The Crime Victim and Criminal Justice Decision-Making, *British Journal of Criminology*, 44(6), 967–982.

Emmerik, Van, A.A.P., Kamphuis, J.H., Hulsbosch, A.M., and Emmelkamp, P.M.G. (2002). Single session debriefing after psychological trauma: A meta-analysis. *Lancet*, 360, 766–771.

Erez, E. and Laster, K. (1999). Neutralizing victim reform: Legal Professionals' perspectives on victims and impact statements. *Crime and delinquency*, 45(4), 530–553.

Erez, E. (2004). Integrating restorative justice principles in adversarial proceedings through victim impact statements. In: Cape, E. (Ed.). *Reconcilable rights? Analysing the tension between victims and defendants.* London: Legal Action Group.

Foa, E.B., Cahill, S.P., Boscarino, J.A. et al. (2005). Social, Psychological, and Psychiatric Interventions Following Terrorist Attacks: Recommendations for Practice and Research. *Neuropsychopharmacology*, 30, 1806–1817.

Frazier, P.A. (2003). Perceived Control and Distress Following Sexual Assault: A Longitudinal Test of a New Model. *Journal of Personality and Social Psychology*, 84, 1257–1269.

Furedi, F. (2004). *Therapy Culture.* London. Routledge.

Goodey, J. (2005). *Victims and victimology. Research, policy, practice.* Harlow, UK. Pearson.

Groenhuijsen, M.S. and Letschert, R.M. (2008). Reflections on the development and Legal Status of Victims' rights instruments. in: Groenhuijsen, M.S. and Letschert, R.M. (Eds.) *Compilation of International Victims' rights Instruments (2nd edition)*, Nijmegen, Wolf Legal Publishers.

Groenhuijsen, M.S. and Pemberton, A. (2009) The EU Framework Decision on Victims. Does hard law make a difference? *European Journal on Crime, Criminal Law and Criminal Justice*, 17, 43–59.

Groenhuijsen, M.S. (2000). Victim-offender mediation: legal and procedural safeguards. Experiments and legislation in some European jurisdictions." In The European Forum for Victim-Offender Mediation and Restorative Justice (Ed.). *Victim-Offender Mediation in Europe. Making Restorative Justice Work.* Leuven, Belgium. Leuven University Press.

Gromet, D.M. and Darley, J.M. (2006). Restoration and Retribution: How Including Retributive Components Affects the Acceptability of Restorative Justice Procedures. *Social Justice Research*, 19(4), 395–432.

Herman, J.L. (2003). The Mental Health of Crime Victims: Impact of Legal Intervention. *Journal of Traumatic Stress*, 16(2), 59–166.

Howells, K. and Day, A. (2002). Readiness for anger management. Clinical and theoretical issues. *Clinical Psychology Review*, 23, 319–337.

Kaltman, S., and Bonanno, G.A. (2003). Trauma and bereavement: Examining the impact of sudden and violent deaths. *Journal of Anxiety Disorders*, 17, 131–147.

Karremans, J.C., Van Lange, P.A.M., Ouwerkerk, J.W., and Kluwer, E.S. (2003). When forgiving enhances psychological well being: The role of interpersonal commitment. *Journal of Personality and Social Psychology*, 84, 1011–1026.

Karremans, J.C. and Van Lange, P.A.M. (2005). Does activating justice help or hurt in promoting forgiveness? *Journal of Experimental Social Psychology*, 41: 290–297.

King, K. (2004). It hurts so bad. Comparing Grieving Patterns of the Families of Murder Victims with Those of Families of Death Row Inmates. *Criminal Justice Policy Review*, 15(2), 193–211.

Lens, K.M.E., Pemberton, A. and Groenhuijsen, M.S. (2010). *Het spreekrecht in Nederland: Een bijdrage aan het emotioneel herstel van slachtoffers?* Tilburg: Intervict (in Dutch: with an English summary).

Maercker, A. and Muller, J. (2004). Social Acknowledgment as a Victim or Survivor: A Scale to Measure a Recovery Factor of PTSD, *Journal of Traumatic Stress*, 17(4).

Maruna, S. and King, A. (2004). Public opinion and community penalties. In Bottoms A.E., Rex, S.A. and Robinson, G. (Eds.). *Alternatives to Prisons*. Cullompton, Devon, UK. Willan.

McCullough, M.E., Bellah, C.G., Kilpatrick, S.D., and Johnson, J.L. (2001). Vengefulness: Relationships with forgiveness, rumination, well-being, and the big five. *Personality and Social Psychology Bulletin*, 27, 601–610.

McNally, R.J., Bryant, R.A., and Ehlers, A. (2003). Does early psychological intervention promote recovery from posttraumatic stress? *Psychological Science in the Public Interest*, 4, 2, 45–79.

Murphy, K. (2008). Procedural justice and affect intensity: understanding reactions to regulatory authorities. *Social Justice Research*, 22, 1–30.

NICE: National Institute for Clinical Excellence. (2005). *Posttraumatic stress disorder. The management of PTSD in adults and children in primary and secondary care.* Gaskell and the British Psychological Society. Downloaded from: http://guidance.nice.org.uk/CG26/guidance/pdf/English/?template =download.aspx.

Orth, U., and Maercker, A. (2004). Do trials of perpetrators retraumatize crime victims? *Journal of Interpersonal Violence*, 19, 2, 212–227.

Orth, U. (2002). Secondary Victimization of Crime Victims by Criminal Proceedings, *Social Justice Research*, 15, (4), 313–325.

Orth, U. (2003). Punishment goals of Crime Victims, *Law and Human Behavior*, 27 (2), 173–186.

Pemberton, A. (2005). Het spreekrecht. Vergelding of herstel? *Tijdschrift voor Herstelrecht*, 5 (3), 34–44. (in Dutch, with an English summary).

Pemberton, A. (2007). De Nederlandse slachtoffer-dader gesprekken: een theoretische verkenning. Tijdschrift voor Herstelrecht, 7(4), 37–52. (in Dutch, with an English summary).

Pemberton, A., Winkel, F.W., and Groenhuijsen, M.S. (2007). Taking victims seriously in restorative justice. *International Perspectives in Victimology*, 3, 1, 4–14.

Pemberton, A., Winkel, F.W., and Groenhuijsen, M.S. (2008). Evaluating victims' experiences in restorative justice. *British Journal of Community Justice*, 6 (2), 98–119.

Pemberton, A. (2008a). Victim Support and the International Crime Victim Survey: a consumer perspective. In Aromaa, K. and Heiskanen, M. (Eds.). *Victimization surveys in comparative perspective.* Helsinki, HEUNI.

Pemberton, A. (2008b). Over egels, vliegen vangen en herstelrecht. *Tijdschrift voor Herstelrecht*, 8(4), 53–65. (in Dutch, with an English summary).

Pemberton, A. (2009). The needs of victims of terrorism. In: Letschert, R.M., Staiger, I., and Pemberton, A. (Eds.). *Assistance to victims of terrorism.* Dordrecht, the Netherlands: Springer.

Pennebaker, J.W. (1990). *Opening up: The healing power of confiding in others.* New York: Morrow.

Reeves, H. and Mulley, K. (2000). The New Status of Victims in the UK: Oppurtunities and Threats. In Crawford, A. and Goodey, J. (Eds.). *Integrating a victim perspective within criminal justice.* Aldershot: Dartmouth Publishing.

Renssen, M. (2002) Traumatherapie na verkeersongevallen. Eyemovement Desensitization and Reprocessing (EMDR). Dissertation. Amsterdam: Free University.

Roberts, J.V., and Erez, E. (2004). Communication in sentencing: exploring the expressive function of Victim Impact Statements. *International review of Victimology*, 10, 223–244.

Rock, P. (1998). *After homicide.* Oxford. Clarendon Press.

Röhl, K. (1997). Procedural Justice: introduction and overview. In Röhl, K. F. and Machura, S. (Eds.). *Procedural Justice*. Aldershot: Ashgate.

Sanders, A., Hoyle, H. Morgan, R. and Cape, E. (2001). Victim Impact Statements: Don't Work, Can't Work, Criminal Law Review, June, 447–458.

Sarat, A. (1997). Vengeance, Victims and the Identities of Law, *Social and Legal Studies*, 6(2), 163–190.

Strang, H. (2002). *Repair or revenge: Victims and restorative justice*. Oxford: Oxford University Press.

Tedeschi, R.G. and Calhoun, L.G. (1996) The Posttraumatic Growth Inventory. Measuring the positive legacy of trauma. *Journal of Traumatic Stress*, 9, 455–471.

Tripp, T.M., Bies, R.J., and Aquino, K. (2007) A vigilante model of justice. Revenge, reconciliation, forgiveness and avoidance. *Social Justice Research*, 20(1), 10–34.

Tyler, T.R. (1990). *Why people obey the law*. New Haven, USA: Yale University Press.

Tyler, T.R. and Huo, Y.J. (2002). *Trust in the Law*. New York: Sage.

Van Stokkom, B. (2008). The expressive function of restorative punishment: a 'public' interest perspectives. In: Mackay, R. et al. (Eds.). *Images of Restorative Justice Theory*. Frankfurt am Main. Verlag fur Polizeiwissenschaft.

Vidmar, N. (2001). Retribution and revenge. In: Sanders, J. and Hamilton, V. L. (Ed.) Handbook of Justice Research in Law. New York. Kluwer.

Wade, N.G., Worthington, E.L., and Meyer, J.E. (2005). But do they work? A Meta-Analysis of Group Interventions to promote forgiveness. In: Worthington, E.L. (Ed.), *Handbook of Forgiveness*. New York. Routledge.

Walgrave, L. (2008). *Restorative justice, self-interest and responsible citizenship*. Cullumpton, UK. Willan Publishing.

Wemmers, J.M. (1996). *Victims in the criminal justice system*. Amsterdam: The Netherlands, Kugler.

Wemmers, J.M. (2002). Restorative justice for victims of crime: A victim-oriented approach to restorative justice. *International Review of Victimology*, 9, 43–59.

Wemmers, J.M. and Cyr, K. (2004). Victims' perspective on restorative justice. How much involvement are victims looking for? *International Review of Victimology*, 11: 1–16.

Wenzel, M., Okimoto, T.G., Feather, N.T., and Platow, M.J. (2008). Retributive and restorative justice. *Law and Human Behavior*, 32(5), 375–389.

Winick, B. (2008). *Therapeutic jurisprudence and victims of crime*. Downloaded from: http://papers.ssrn.com/sol3/papers.cfm?abstract_id=1102350.

Winkel, F.W. (2007). *Posttraumatic anger. Missing link in the wheel of misfortune*. Inaugural lecture Tilburg University. Nijmegen. Wolf Legal Publishers.

Worthington, E.L., Jr. and Scherer, M. (2004). Forgiveness as an emotion focused coping strategy that can reduce health risks and promote health resilience: Theory, review and hypotheses. *Psychology and Health,* 19, 385–405.

Zech, E. and Rime, B. (2005). Is talking about an emotional experience helpful? Effects on emotional recovery and perceived benefits. *Clinical Psychology and Psychotherapy*, 12, 270–287.

12

Empowerment through Emotion: The Use and Abuse of Victim Impact Evidence

Carolyn Hoyle

Abstract

This chapter considers the introduction of victim impact statements into criminal trials and describes some of its drawbacks. Focusing on the most controversial examples—victim impact statements in cases of murder and manslaughter—it analyses the threat posed by such statements to a defendant's right to a fair trial, and considers more broadly the place for and role of human emotions in criminal trials. The chapter concludes with recognition that we cannot hope to banish emotion from criminal justice, but the challenge is to admit it in ways that do not compromise the broader interests of justice, and are not instrumental, a means of making sentencing more punitive. Post-sentence victim impact statements would preserve the principle of just deserts, and allow sentencers to return to their prior reliance on more objective sources to judge a crime's severity.

1. Introduction

Two hundred years ago, criminal prosecutions in England and Wales were usually undertaken by private individuals, commercial firms or special Associations for the Prosecution of Felons formed for this sole purpose. Other than in cases where its interests were directly concerned, such as treason or sedition, and sometimes in murders, the State rarely intervened. Of course, this system had severe disadvantages, and was not, in general, equitable. However, it was always clear who the victim was, and what he or she wanted. Prosecutions and trials were visibly directed at resolving and repairing the harms caused by criminal acts. As in civil litigation, which the criminal process resembled, the two main parties in a criminal case, the victim and offender, had an opportunity to replay their conflict in the controlled arena of the court.

During the 19th century, as new State police forces began to regularize law enforcement, victims increasingly sought police assistance in the prosecution of offences. By the start of the 20th century, the police had assumed the prosecutorial role in almost every case (Hoyle & Young, 2002).[1] More than a century later, there have been many further changes, from the formation of police prosecuting solicitors' departments in the 1960s to the establishment, in 1986, of the Crown Prosecution Service (CPS), whose remit now extends to almost every aspect of decision-making with regard to charging, summonses and cautions. Beneath the details, the place of the victim in the design of each adversarial contest has remained stable for many years. In all but a handful of private prosecutions, events so rare as to warrant extensive media attention when they do occur, the State, in the shape of the police and the CPS, has become the intermediary between the victim and the court. Crime control mechanisms which used to be local and personal have become bureaucratic, centralized institutions. The State has secured ownership of offences and disputes that were once the preserve of private citizens and communities.

Critics of this transformation have argued that State-funded professionals and their agencies now 'steal conflicts' from both victims and offenders (Christie, 1977). Thus, it is claimed, they usurp the rights of victims to seek reparation for harms suffered, and to exercise a broad and central role in the criminal justice process. Whilst formerly the prosecutor-victim had rights—to decide on charges and to give information to the court—by the end of the twentieth century these had been assumed by the CPS, which had no corresponding duties to meet victims' needs.

Over the course of the twentieth century, criminal justice in the United States was also transformed from a private to a State-led process (Gewirtz, 1996). On both sides of the Atlantic, the role of victims had been relegated to that of witnesses, and they had been excluded from meaningful participation and decision-making (Christie, 1977). Both government surveys and academic empirical research showed the resultant dissatisfaction amongst victims through-

1. Although Rock (2004) has argued that the ideological and practical remnants of that early state of affairs remained largely in place throughout the nineteenth and much of the twentieth centuries, with prosecutions remaining largely private in law and in practice. Rock also takes issue with the romanticised view of victims as pathetic, heroic or admirable, arguing that many mounted prosecutions motivated by vengeance, greed or avoidance of charges against themselves.

out the Anglo-American system of adversarial criminal justice.[2] For example, a study by Shapland, Wilmore and Duff carried out in England between 1979 and 1982 found that victims' needs and feelings were ignored by criminal justice professionals, leading the authors to conclude that the system had lost sight of one of its crucial members (Shapland, Willmore & Duff, 1985). Towards the end of the 1980s, there was increasing criticism both within the academy and victim support organizations of the treatment of victims by all criminal justice agencies. Joanna Shapland (1988) referred to those agencies as 'fiefs,' which relegated the victims to the status of 'peasants.'

The stage, however, was being set for a further significant shift. From the 1980s on, in the light of mounting evidence of marginalization, emerging victims' rights movements sought to enhance the place of victims in the criminal process and began to advocate that specific legal rules be introduced to give greater weight to victims' interests, and to provide them with restitution and compensation. Their demands soon found a legislative response. Since 1985, the U.S. and UK, as well as many inquisitorial jurisdictions in Europe, have established institutions, legal frameworks and policies aimed at providing redress, justice and restitution to victims of crime. Reforms have been made with the explicit aim of ensuring that the victim is no longer the forgotten actor in the criminal process.

One such reform is the introduction of victim rights of allocution, in particular the introduction of victim impact statements into criminal trials. This chapter will consider this development in detail, set it in a broader context, and describe some of its drawbacks. It will describe the various international declarations and recommendations, which allow for, and encourage, victim impact evidence (VIE), and consider the most controversial examples—victim impact statements in cases of murder and manslaughter. It will also analyze the threat VIE may pose to a defendant's right to a fair trial, and consider the place for and role of human emotions in criminal trials.

2. The Re-Emergence of the Victim

The victims' movement on both sides of the Atlantic emerged against a steady and apparently inexorable rise in recorded offending, that became increasingly difficult to disparage as an over-inflated social problem. Recorded crime in England and Wales grew ten-fold between the 1950s and the 1990s to

2. For the U.S., see Knudten et al., 1977; for the UK, see Sparks, Genn and Dodd 1977.

five million a year, and from 1.1 offences per 100 population in 1950 to 9.5 in 1996. Similar rises were seen in most parts of America. Over the same period, both the U.S. and UK experienced sporadic outbreaks of urban rioting and street violence. In the U.S., a series of official reports into these phenomena recognized the extents of the harms inflicted on victims by rising violent crime. They were followed by national crime surveys, which were later introduced in the UK and Canada as well. Such surveys detailed the losses sustained by victims, their fear of crime, and the factors that made them reluctant to report certain offences. They also showed the disproportionate impact of crime on the working classes, minority ethnic groups and other vulnerable populations such as women and children in the home.

By the mid-1980s, the 'rediscovery' of poor, proletarian, female and black victims had energized the fledgling victims' movement, and given it a realistic claim to represent widespread social needs. Within the academy, the influence of radical criminology, and its Marxian narrative that saw the criminal process as a species of class-based State oppression, was in rapid decline. It was being replaced by what Jock Young called 'left realism,' a school whose concern was not only with offenders and offending, but also with disadvantaged victims (Young, 1994).

At the same time, practitioners and policy makers were coming to recognize that that the criminal justice system needed victims' cooperation if it was to succeed in identifying, prosecuting and convicting offenders. Victims were at last deemed necessary to the administration of justice. Since the first UK Victims' Charter in 1990, a series of official initiatives has sought to increase the system's effectiveness by offering witnesses and victims an enhanced role in the criminal process. Their instrumental purpose was perhaps at its most explicit in the 2004 government publication, 'No Witness No Justice.' This states on its cover page: 'At least 22,000 cases were abandoned in 2002/03 because of prosecution witness issues.' It continues, on the first page: 'Many victims and witnesses do not receive the level of information and support they need when participating in the criminal justice process. This neglect can often lead to a withdrawal of support for the prosecution, non-attendance at court and dissatisfaction with the process, which can result in failed cases and a reluctance by witnesses to re-engage in the criminal justice process on future occasions.'

These developments in Britain were mirrored internationally. In 1985 two influential documents were issued to enhance the status of victims: The United Nations Declaration of Basic Principles of Justice for Victims of Crime and Abuse of Power,[3] and the Council of Europe Recommendation on the Posi-

3. A/res/40/34, adopted by the General Assembly in 1985.

tion of the Victim in the Framework of Criminal Law and Procedure.[4] Both expressed similar sentiments and aims, calling for an enhanced role for victims. This, they stated, should extend to VIE, an opportunity for the both primary and secondary victims of crime to describe the personal effect of the alleged offence(s) at trial. Subsequent documents, such as the Statement of Victims' Rights in the Process of Criminal Justice,[5] the European Union Framework Decision on the Standing of Victims in Criminal Proceedings,[6] and, most recently, the 2006 Council of Europe Recommendation on Assistance to Crime Victims,[7] all adopt much the same approach. VIE, they state, is inherently desirable. However, it is important to note that none of these international statements of principle argue that victim statements should help to determine criminal sentences.

The first of these documents, the 1985 UN Declaration, capably sets out what ought to be the parameters for considering VIE, stating that while this was desirable, it also had the potential to harm the due process rights of defendants:

> The responsiveness of judicial and administrative processes to the needs of victims should be facilitated by ... (b) Allowing the views and concerns of victims to be presented and considered at appropriate stages of the proceedings where their personal interests are affected, *without prejudice to the accused* and consistent with the relevant national criminal justice system (my emphasis).[8]

The Rome Statute of the International Criminal Court, which, unlike the recommendations and guidelines discussed above, is legally binding for those States that have ratified or acceded to it, is explicit in laying down a legal system that respects the rights of victims without prejudicing the defendant's right to a fair trial. Article 68 of the Rome Statute states:

> Where the personal interests of the victims are affected, the Court shall permit their views and concerns to be presented and considered at stages of the proceedings determined to be appropriate by the Court and *in a manner which is not prejudicial to or inconsistent with the rights*

4. R(85)11, adopted in 1985.
5. Issued by the European Forum for Victim Services in 1996.
6. Council Framework Decision of 15 March 2001 (2001/220/JHA).
7. Adopted June 14, 2006.
8. A/RES/40/34, 29 November 1985, Para 6 (b).

> *of the accused and a fair and impartial trial.* Such views and concerns may be presented by the legal representatives of the victims where the Court considers it appropriate, in accordance with the Rules of Procedure and Evidence (my emphasis).[9]

International guidelines and legal frameworks which envisage an enhanced role for victims without impinging on fair procedures and outcomes for defendants have received support from national victim support organizations in Europe and their umbrella organization, the European Forum for Victim Services. In 1996, the European Forum published its Statement of Victims' Rights in the Process of Criminal Justice. It is worth quoting in some detail from this Statement, as it is clear from its recommendations regarding VIE that it does not condone the use of such statements by sentencers in determining the appropriate type or length of sentence:

> In all jurisdictions, victims should be able to provide information, in their own words, directly to the police and prosecution services who are responsible for decisions. The information may include the extent of the financial, physical or emotional damage caused by the crime, the existence or otherwise of any prior or continuing relationship with the offender, and any fears for personal safety or intimidation from the offender.
>
> The purpose of the statement should be to:
>
> - ensure that the victim has a right to be heard
> - provide information needed for any award of financial compensation
> - alert the authorities to any continuing risk to the victim which could affect release from custody
> - enable the professional parties involved to take the victim's interests into account at any stage at which the public interest may be relevant to a decision
> - inform the prosecutor about the wider circumstances of the case, which may alert him to potential secondary victimization during the management of the case both before and during the court hearing
> - provide the prosecutor with information which could be used to refute misleading statements made by the defense

9. Rome Statute of the International Criminal Court, Article 68, Para 3. The Statute entered into force on 1 July 2002. Rules 89–93 of the Rules of Procedure and Evidence describe the procedures which have to be following before victims and their representatives can be involved.

- enable the prosecutor to provide additional relevant information to the court for example, prior to sentence. (Para 3)

In Britain, the largest victims' movement group, Victim Support, has, since its establishment in 1974, maintained a relatively low-key political profile. The main thrust of its endeavor has been to campaign for emotional support, practical services, and information to individual victims at a local level (Maguire & Kynch, 2000). More recently it has adopted a proactive role promoting service rights for victims, though not rights of allocution, arguing that victims should 'be free of the burden of decisions relating to the offender.'[10] Other groups, such as the Victims of Crime Trust, have been more confrontational and exigent in their promotion of victims' interests, and less mindful of the need to balance these against the rights of offenders (Rock, 1998: 218). Some, such as Support After Murder and Manslaughter (SAMM), strongly advocate the use of VIE in the sentencing phase of trials.[11] Such groups have invoked the victim as a potent rhetorical device or symbolic tool, so levering up demands for harsher punishment in what Andrew Ashworth has called 'victims in the service of severity' (Ashworth, 2000: 186; see also, Garland, 2001: 143; MacCormick & Garland, 1998). Here, British victim interest groups are more like their counterparts across the Atlantic.

In the United States, a rights-based victim movement emerged in the 1960s and 1970s. Dissatisfied with the existing responses to victims, the movement demanded a reorientation of the criminal justice system in their favor. Initially it was largely homogeneous, being conservative in outlook and often seeking more punitive responses to offenders,[12] but more recently it has become variegated, with groups such as 'Parents of Murdered Children' eschewing political involvement. Nonetheless, lobbying by American victim interest groups has resulted in an explosion of federal and state action to establish and interpret victims' rights at critical stages of the criminal process. In the U.S., prosecutors will now commonly consult victims before plea bargains are finalized, for example, while there will almost invariably be an opportunity to give VIE (Tobolowsky, 1999).

In America, whilst VIE was first introduced by local initiatives, it was endorsed by the President's Task Force on Victims of Crime as early as 1982. This recommended that federal and state legislatures require victim impact statements at sentencing, and that prosecutors consult with victims and inform the court

10. www.victimsupport.org.uk.

11. *BBC News*, September 1, 2005.

12. For example, it was in some states associated with demands for the retention or reintroduction of the death penalty, see Hodgkinson, 2004.

of their wishes regarding bail, pleas, sentencing and restitution. It set the scene for widespread federal and state activity (Tobolowsky, 1999).

Overall, it is clear that victims have become accepted as key players in the criminal justice process in both America and England. Acknowledgement of their status, both as parties to the dispute (Christie, 1977), and as actors without whose cooperation most crime would remain unknown and unpunished, has been a powerful driver of reform.

VIE has proven to be politically popular in the U.S. and the UK. Many victims' rights groups and prosecutors argue that it promotes more informed and proportionate sentencing decisions by enabling the court to appreciate the extent of the harms inflicted by the defendant. Transferring some of the thinking of the restorative justice movement to the very different context of the sentencing phase of the adversarial trial, they have claimed that VIE assists the sentencing goals of rehabilitation, by confronting the offender with the reality of the impact of his crime, and of retribution, by identifying the degree of harm done (see Cassell, 1999; Erez & Rogers, 1999; Tobolowsky, 1999).

However, the main potential benefit stressed by advocates of VIE in homicide cases has been the psychotherapeutic effect on secondary victims (Mosteller, 2003; Cassell, 1999; Beloof, 1999). It is argued that with proper safeguards, the overall experience of providing victim impact evidence can be positive and empowering (Erez, 1999). Starkweather (1992), for example, writes that allowing families to have a say in the defendant's sentence might be seen as a type of 'psychic restitution,' in which the defendant can compensate for the loss to the victim and his or her survivors. Indeed it is argued that a justice system that fails to recognize a victim's right to participate threatens further 'secondary harm' (Cassell, 1999; Beloof, 1999).

There is no doubt that those bereaved by homicide experience extreme grief, feelings of pain, trauma, anger, guilt, isolation, confusion, and powerlessness.[13] Their emotional and psychological stress has been compared to that of rape victims and prisoners who have been tortured (Schlosser, 1997), and defined by many as a manifestation of post-traumatic stress disorder. They also often feel they have been overlooked by the criminal justice system (Vandiver, 2003). The academic literature is replete with empirical evidence of the ways in which the criminal justice response can aggravate and prolong families' distress (Vandiver, 2003). Numerous studies have pointed to the need for such victims to be kept informed about the progress of the case—what has been

13. For authoritative personal accounts, see Part 1 of Acker and Karp, 2006; Thompson, 2007; Rock, 1998: 185–200.

referred to as 'service needs' (Hoyle & Zedner, 2007). Meeting such needs is now widely accepted as essential, both in order to help such victims recover, and to encourage them to cooperate with the criminal process.

However, it is not a given that secondary victims also need and deserve a more active role in the criminal process, in particular the opportunity to tell the court directly how they were affected by the crime. The evidence that making an impact statement reduces significantly the distress experienced by victims and increases their satisfaction with the criminal process is tenuous to say the least (Tobolowsky, 1999). In some cases it appears that giving evidence *increases* the satisfaction of victims whilst in others it *decreases* it (Erez, 1994; Erez & Roberts, 2007), in particular by forcing victims to participate in the sentencing process against their wishes (Tobolowsky, 1999; Nadler & Rose, 2003), or by creating unmet expectations as to the effect of their input (Hoyle et al., 1998). Victims who make impact statements are likely to believe that their statements will make a difference to sentencing (statements are often made for instrumental reasons; Hoyle et al., 1998), and if the jury does not return the maximum sentence they may feel that the system has belittled the victim and their loss, or experience guilt that they have not adequately portrayed the worth of the victim (Bandes, 2000).

While giving VIE may provide some form of psychological catharsis for some individuals, there is evidence that others experience no such benefit. For example, it appears to have given no relief to the parents of Joe Geeling, an 11-year-old cystic fibrosis sufferer stabbed to death by a teenager from his school in England. After the killer, Michael Hamer, received a life sentence (with a requirement to serve a minimum of 12 years), they told journalists that they felt let down by the legal system despite the life sentence.[14] Furthermore, they were not only of the opinion that the outcome was too lenient, they also complained that the process did not serve them well. They spoke of their frustration that as relatives of a victim of crime they were 'impotent' in court proceedings, left looking on and feeling like 'voyeurs.' They had issued a moving and eloquent victim impact statement about how they had been affected by their son's death, which was read to the court before the defendant was sentenced, but felt that this had not given them the role they wanted. The boy's father explained:

> What a lot of parents won't understand is that you're very impotent ... You can help, but you've no control over anything. You've no rights

14. Months later the Court of Appeal increased Michael Hamer's minimum life tariff from 12 to 15 years, although accepting that the killing itself was not premeditated: *Reuters*, January 30, 2007.

> to any files or witness statements. You're treated as a third party. You can't instruct a QC. It's your child that's been murdered but it's not you that's taking the killer to court. You're like a voyeur.[15]

For these bereaved parents, the trauma of homicide had not been alleviated by VIE at all. They could have been speaking in the 1970s—in the era when the State is said to have 'stolen the conflict' and deprived victims of any sense of belonging in the criminal process.

Whatever the claims made about the satisfaction experienced by the relatives of some homicide victims as a result of VIE, the issue—in so far as UN Safeguards which protect the rights of defendants are concerned—is whether such evidence prejudices the possibility of a fair trial and a fair consideration at the sentencing stage of all factors that might be weighed in mitigation, particularly in jurisdictions that retain the death sentence (Mosteller, 2003). Opponents of victim impact statements argue that they reduce the objectivity of the process by shifting the focus away from legitimate sentencing factors and towards inappropriate considerations of victim retaliation and vengeance. Hence, they can lead to inequitable, disparate, or harsher sentencing. Austin Sarat has argued that such statements legitimize vengeance. Referring to the Supreme Court case that first allowed VIE in the sentencing phase of death penalty trials, he writes: '[It] brought revenge out of the shadows and accorded it an honored place in the jurisprudence of capital punishment.' (Sarat, 2001: 45).

Giving VIE may provide psychological help for victims. The possible accompanying risk—that it may also prejudice the case against the defendant—requires further examination.

3. Rights of Allocution in the UK

As we have seen, the enhanced importance of victims in public rhetoric and consequent policy is a recent development. Unfortunately, in their haste to satisfy the victims' movement's aspirations and their perceived support among the electorate, policy makers failed to address some vital questions, and their responses have often been marked by confusion and muddled thinking. Beyond a general wish to make victims' 'feel' more central to the criminal process,

---

15. *The Daily Mail*, November 9, 2006.

their objectives have not been clear. Nowhere is this more apparent than in the case of VIE.

Arguably, VIE has a greater capacity to affect other areas and actors within the criminal justice system than any conceivable measure devised for victims' needs. Improving the service the system provides for victims through innovations such as the quicker dissemination of information about a case, better facilities at court, closer consultation about trial dates and simplifying access to criminal injuries compensation are all desirable ends, and all have been at least partly achieved. However, none of them much affect alleged perpetrators. VIE is different. Whilst compensation orders impact on the finances of those found guilty of criminal offences, as indeed fines do, they do not impact on judicial decision making. Once a judge of facts or punishment has access to direct evidence about the consequences of a criminal action on an individual victim, the system's most crucial decisions as to conviction and sentence may potentially be altered. None of the international statements of principle published by the United Nations, Council of Europe and the European Union (discussed above) argue that victim statements should help to determine criminal sentences. In practice, however, it may be impossible to prevent such an outcome, and there is at least a risk that punishment may become tailored to the impact on the victim, not the crime's 'objective' severity, so creating anomalous or disproportionate sentences and eroding the principle of just deserts. VIE before a court reaches its verdict might have a still less desirable result—decisions as to guilt or innocence that are colored by the depth of a victim's emotional trauma.

Edwards identifies four separate, and at times conflicting rationales that have been publicly advanced for the introduction of VIE in the UK. These are: improving sentencing outcomes by making sentences proportionate to the harms done; enhancing system efficiency by making victims more likely to cooperate with the prosecution; and psychological benefits to victims. A fourth rationale, he argues, 'emphasizes process values, citizenship and rights.' (Edwards, 2001: 41).

In the 1990s, my colleagues and I experienced what Edwards terms the 'incoherence' of policy in this area firsthand, when we held a series of discussions with Home Office officials prior to and during a research project on the first pilot VIE schemes. We repeatedly asked for clarification on the purpose of making a victim personal statement, only to be told that this was an empirical question that was ours to answer, rather than a policy issue that ought to be determined in advance. Truly, this was the cart pulling the horse: having introduced the schemes without deciding what VIE was for, the Home Office was asking us to supply the answer by observing the schemes in the field. Our insistence that this approach was inappropriate was ignored, and the results were soon seen on the ground. The victims we interviewed had no clue about how or whether their statements might affect sentencing, and neither did those policy makers who had designed the scheme. It came as no surprise to discover that approximately 90 per cent of victims did not know what had happened to their statement months after the case had closed.

We published our findings in 1999. We had found that practitioners were split about equally on whether VIE should influence sentencing decisions. Defense solicitors were a little more hostile. The information provided was regarded as often irrelevant, exaggerated or unverifiable. Judges were concerned about the danger of VIE crossing the boundary from factual information to opinion about what should happen, and criticized Court of Appeal guidance as vague and unhelpful. We concluded: 'Objectives were unclear and need to be identified. If they are mainly expressive, victims should not be led to expect that victim statements will have any concrete effects. If primarily instrumental, there should be guidelines for taking them into account consistently and victims should be informed of the uses to which their VSs have been put.' Nine years later, the position remains equally muddled (Hoyle, Morgan & Sanders, 1999: 4).

When the Home Office announced in 2001 that VIE would be implemented nationally, the then-Home Secretary Jack Straw failed to provide the much-needed clarification, saying that it would be an opportunity for information given by victims' to be 'taken into account' (Home Office, 2000). This expression simply repeated the equally vague description in the Victims' Charters and it was then reiterated, without proper explanation, in the Home Office guidance for victims and for practitioners, both published in 2001. 'Taking into account' can be interpreted in many ways. The Court of Appeal has been equally opaque. Its judgment in *R v. Perks* (2000) laid down general guidelines, making clear that the courts should not take into account victims' opinions on the severity of the appropriate sentence. However, it did not specify how exactly they should interpret their duty to 'take into account' information on harms caused to victims.

In 2001 the Lord Chief Justice issued a Practice Direction (an authoritative judicial declaration), and so rolled out the 'Victim Personal Statement Scheme' across England and Wales. Under this scheme, when a police officer takes an evidential statement from a victim, the victim will be told about the chance to make a victim personal statement, which may be made or updated at any time prior to the trial. If the court is presented with a victim personal statement it should be 'considered', and served upon the defendant's solicitor or the defendant prior to sentence. Once again, the parameters were vague:

> The court must pass what it judges to be the appropriate sentence having regard to the circumstances of the offence and of the offender, taking into account, so far as the court considers it appropriate, the consequences to the victim. The opinions of the victim or the victim's close relatives as to what the sentence should be are therefore not relevant, unlike the consequence of the offence on them. Victims should be advised of this. If, despite the advice, opinions as to sentence are included in the statement, the court should pay no attention to them.[16]

It may be observed that this direction attempted to distinguish between a victim's 'opinion' as to what a sentence should be, and the proper disposal by the court. But as to the risks of disproportionally in the case of the victim who has been unusually traumatized, it is silent. VIE may substantially affect the sentence of a court without ever mentioning a specific prison term in years. Without a clear rationale for VIE, it is impossible to evaluate its efficacy. It is also difficult to put in place effective measures to prevent it being abused.

Under the Victims Code of Practice, the police are no longer *required* to solicit victim personal statements,[17] although they are still routinely gathering them and they are being presented to the courts. They are often reported by the media, which have recorded VIE in cases ranging from serious assaults, through burglaries, down to criminal damage to a 1 penny plastic carrier bag.[18]

In 2006, a new scheme was piloted to enable relatives of victims of murder and manslaughter to make a personal statement in court (in person or via a public advocate) before sentence on how they have been affected by the crime (Home Office, 2005: 28). On October 1, 2007, after the scheme had been tested under the umbrella of the Victims' Advocate pilots,[19] this scheme was rolled

---

16. President of the Queen's Bench Division, The Procedure To Be Followed In The Victims' Advocate Pilot Areas, 3 May 2006, describing the appropriate procedures for the Victim Personal Statements rolled out in 2001: http://www.judiciary.gov.uk/docs/victims_advocate_protocol_030506.pdf.

17. Personal communication with Lisa Vernon, Home Office October 2005.

18. In this bizarre case, a girl of 13 made a victim impact statement after the conviction of a 16-year-old boy for snatching a plastic bag from her hand, breaking the handles and returning it to her: *The Daily Mail*, September 25, 2007.

19. The Pilot catchment areas were: the Old Bailey, Birmingham, Manchester Crown Square, Cardiff and Winchester. The pilot scheme was confined to cases of murder and manslaughter, including familial homicide and corporate manslaughter, and excluded cases of death by dangerous driving: Queen's Bench Division: A Protocol Issued by the President of the Queen's Bench Division Setting Out the Procedure to be Followed in the Victims' Advocate Pilot Areas, 3 May 2006, http://www.judiciary.gov.uk/docs/victims_advocate_protocol_030506.pdf.

out across England and Wales as part of a wider scheme called 'Victim Focus.'[20] Through police Family Liaison officers, the relatives of victims (now including those killed by dangerous driving) have direct access to the prosecutor, who helps them to understand the trial process, and the various decisions taken along the way. In particular, prosecutors help them to prepare victim impact statements telling the court about their family member, and what the loss has meant to them.[21] These statements are formally known as 'Family Impact Statements,' although most press reports still refer to them as 'victim impact statements,'[22] and are typically read out in court by the prosecutor, but the family can read it themselves or request that it is read out by an independent advocate or a lay friend. Since their inception, at least 63 such statements have been delivered by the families themselves. The family is free, within the normal requirements of court procedure, to choose how best to express its views (i.e., whether the statement should be in oral or written form) and to update its statement on the effect of the crime after conviction. As with the Victim Personal Statements, the defendant is made aware of the contents of the statement in advance to ensure fairness. Statements are read out post conviction but before mitigation evidence is presented to the court. If the statement goes beyond the effect or impact of the murder or manslaughter the judge should intervene. Furthermore, in certain circumstances the defense will have the right to cross examine.

Nevertheless, only a small proportion of victims will normally get the opportunity to present VIE in court. Of course, most recorded crimes do not result in prosecution. However, even when someone has been prosecuted, there is a strong probability that varies with the crime alleged, that the defendant will plead guilty. And even when defendants plead not-guilty and the case goes to trial, most UK victims have chosen not to make a victim impact statement: the take up rate in Scotland is about fifteen per cent (Chalmers, Duff & Leverick, 2001). A small study carried out in 2004 suggests that take up in England and Wales was just 2 per cent before efforts were put in place to increase

20. The Victim Focus scheme was announced by the then Attorney General, Lord Goldsmith, in June 2007. The enhanced role and service to victims that the Crown Prosecution Service provides under this scheme is set out at http://www.cps.gov.uk/victims_witnesses/focus_scheme.html.

21. Home Office, News Release, 1 October 2007.

22. A 'Google search' of the term 'Family Impact Statements' produces only a few relevant articles using this term, whereas a search of 'Victim Impact Statements,' restricted to the UK, scores hundreds of hits.

it, when it rose only to around 19 per cent after this (CPS/ACPO, 2004). (The take-up rate in cases of murder or manslaughter to date is much higher.)

Meanwhile, more than 10 years since my colleagues and I conducted the first pilot studies, there is still no consensus or clear legal indication about whether or not victim personal statements or family impact statements are supposed to influence sentencing. As the law currently stands, the harm to the victim that results from the offence is already taken into account in the structure of the relevant sentencing guideline, and in order not to impose a disproportionate offence, more punishment should not be imposed on account of what the victim says. However, when the pilot scheme for the Family Impact Statements was launched, the consultation document suggested that they *were* designed to have an impact on sentencing: 'This should provide a better basis for the judge to take account of the effect of the crime on the bereaved relatives when sentencing.' (Home Office, 2005: 28).

Furthermore, whilst the CPS guidance on Victim Personal Statements states that sentencing should be offender-focused, it goes on to echo earlier official policy circulars in saying that the impact on the victim, although not their opinion as to the sentence, should be 'taken into account':

> Under the Victim Personal Statement scheme, the Practice Direction states that the court must pass what it judges to be the appropriate sentence having regard to the circumstances of the offence and of the offender (key principles are the seriousness of the offence and the culpability of the offender having regard to foreseeable consequences). The court should take into account, so far as it considers it appropriate, the consequences to the victim. The court will not take into account views on sentence (CPS, 2007: Para 22).

CPS guidance about Family Impact Statements in homicide trials is similarly equivocal:

> The Family Impact Statement cannot affect the sentence that the Judge may pass and the family will not be able to comment on what they think the sentence should be. However, the Family Impact Statement may help to provide a fuller understanding of the nature and impact of the crime when passing sentence (CPS, 2007: Para 23).

The following paragraph of this CPS guidance shows that the organization, along with everyone else, is still not clear whether or not such statements are supposed to impact on sentencing. Reflecting on the possibilities of unduly raising victims' expectations, only to disappoint them, it states: 'Prosecutors are advised to adopt a conservative view when advising the family—namely that the VPS is very unlikely to affect the sentence.' (CPS, 2007: Para 24).

Empirical research suggests that in fact, victim impact evidence seldom significantly influences sentencing decisions. Some studies suggest no significant relation between the introduction of victim impact evidence and sentencing outcomes, (Eisenberg, Garvey & Wells, 2003) with other studies showing only a minimal influence. Research in England and Wales and Scotland showed no impact on sentencing (Morgan & Sanders, 1999; Chalmers, Duff & Leverick, 2001). This, of course, explains—at least in part—why many victims are still dissatisfied. They make a statement for instrumental reasons and then either learn nothing about its impact or discover that it had no effect on sentencing (Sanders et al., 2001). It is unclear whether this is a product of resistance by criminal justice professionals to victims' influence (Erez, 1999; Erez & Rogers, 1999), or because they are 'misconceived in principle and unsatisfactory in practice' (Sanders et al., 2001: 447).

However, while aggregate data in some studies suggest little impact overall, this does not mean that victim impact statements do not influence sentencing decisions in individual cases. This is certainly the case in other parts of the criminal process. For example, empirical studies show that victim participation has an impact on parole decision making. A methodologically sophisticated American study by Morgan and Smith, which controlled for all of the relevant variables, found that victim participation—both victim allocution at hearings and written victim statements—was the second strongest predicting factor of parole dispositions (Morgan & Smith, 2005; see also, Parsonage, Bernat & Helfgott, 1992). Furthermore, research shows that in *some* cases where victims make an impact statement before sentencing such evidence does influence the sentence. Whilst in Scotland this may mean that the judge is more likely to impose a compensation order (Chalmers, Duff & Leverick, 2001), in some U.S. states (of which more later), it can mean the difference between life (in prison) and death (Luginbuhl & Burkhead, 1995).

Clearly, there is the potential, at least, for these statements to make sentencers more punitive and to create indefensible disparities in sentencing similar cases. This is certainly the public perception. In June 2007 a report in the English newspaper, *The Times,* discussed the introduction of Family Impact Statements, saying: 'Relatives will have the opportunity to draw up an "impact statement" with the help of prosecutors in a move that could lead to offenders being given tougher sentences.'[23]

---

23. *The Times,* June 25, 2007.

This article included a comment by the then-Attorney General, Lord Goldsmith, QC, which sums up the continuing vagueness as to VIE's proper role. 'Where the impact has been significant then that will affect the sentence,' the Government official in charge of the entire prosecution system said. 'In some other cases,' he added, 'it may not.' Goldsmith went on to assert that this would not create a 'two-tier system of punishment, in which offenders would get stiffer sentences if they killed someone whose friend and relatives happened to be more eloquent.'[24] He could not however, adduce any evidence in support of this belief.

4. Rights of Allocution in the U.S.

In America, as we have seen, the victims' rights movement to which policy makers began to devise responses was markedly more radical, and from the 1960s, unlike in Britain, its more influential advocates put one demand above any other—that for tougher sentences. The law has steadily evolved in an apparent attempt to meet it, with baleful implications for the due process rights of defendants, especially in capital murder cases.

In Canada, where a good deal of research into VIE has been carried out, statements are allowed to affect sentencing,[25] but in the United States there is variation on the permissibility of this. Prosecutors in the American federal system[26] and most states today enjoy virtual free reign in the introduction of VIE. They have broad discretion over how impact evidence is conveyed, who is permitted to testify, and the number of witnesses (Blume, 2003; Logan, 2005). In some form or other, a victim has a right to speak at sentencing in all fifty states.[27] There are few substantive limits or procedural protections regulating the admission of victim impact evidence; as Blume has argued, it is politically popular, largely unregulated and not likely to go away (Blume, 2003). Victim statements are allowed in all cases, but are most likely to be presented in homicide cases and attract most controversy in murders, which are eligible for the death penalty.

24. *Ibid.*

25. Canadian Criminal Code, Art 722.1, see further Roach (2005).

26. The federal criminal justice system set the precedent for the use of victim impact statements in sentencing with the passage of the Victim and Witness Protection Act of 1982 (see also the 1995 Attorney General Guidelines for Victim and Witness Assistance).

27. The constitutions or statutes of forty states either explicitly or implicitly grant victims the right to give recommendations at sentencing. Twenty-three of these states grant victims the constitutional right to address the sentencing authority, with seventeen granting the right by statute (Beloof, 2003).

Here, at least, the courts at first offered some initial resistance. In the 1987 case of *Booth v Maryland,* the U.S. Supreme Court ruled that VIE was not relevant or admissible in the unique circumstance of a capital sentencing hearing, where the jury's function is to 'express the conscience of the community on the ultimate question of life or death.'[28] To admit VIE at such hearings, the Court ruled, would be cruel and unusual under the U.S. Constitution's Eighth Amendment (Beloof, 2003).

Two years later, in the 1989 case of *South Carolina v Gathers,*[29] the Court again ruled that VIE was inadmissible. This time, however, it left open the possibility that there could, in cases other than the one it was considering, be circumstances where VIE *would* be admissible, so long as it related directly to the fact of the offence. In 1991, with *Payne v Tennessee*[30] a reconstituted Court reversed the decision in *Booth.* Henceforth, evidence of both the victim's unique personal characteristics and the crime's impact on the victim's family and community would be admissible. Only the admissibility of a secondary victim's opinion about the appropriate sentence was left unclear.[31] *Payne* effectively cleared the way for capital sentencing juries to consider VIE in the punishment phase of capital trials. According to Chief Justice Rehnquist, this was 'simply another form or method of informing the sentencing authority about the specific harm caused by the crime' and provided 'a quick glimpse of the life [the defendant] chose to extinguish.'

Since *Payne,* state and federal courts have allowed extensive use of VIE, in ordinary as well as capital cases. (As in the UK, no court has revisited the issue of the victim's opinion on the appropriate sentence, and here the earlier *Booth* holding that opinion evidence is prohibited by the Eighth Amendment law remains undisturbed.) A few states, including Oklahoma, Alabama, and Kansas, do however expressly allow victims' opinions as to the appropriate sentence for capital defendants, statements typically referred to as 'Victim Statements of Opinion,' although most jurisdictions deem this inadmissible (Beloof, 2003).

The federal Crime Victims Rights Act of 2004[32] gave victims further rights, and placed a duty on the federal courts to enforce them. Henceforth, victims were to have the right to be 'reasonably heard' at any public proceeding involving release, plea, or sentencing. On January 20, 2006 the United States

---

28. *Booth v Maryland*, 482 U.S. 496, 502 (1987) at 504.

29. *South Carolina v Gathers*, 490 U.S. 805 (1989) at 810.

30. 501 U.S. 808, 827 (1991).

31. The *Payne* court expressly avoided re-examination of its earlier (*Booth*) bar on opinion evidence because, according to the Court, no evidence of the sort was presented in *Payne's* sentencing (Logan, 2005).

32. 18 U.S.C. §3771.

Court of Appeals for the Ninth Circuit issued an opinion upholding the right of crime victims to give oral evidence at the convicted criminal's sentencing hearing, rather than merely to provide written victim impact statements. The Court added that this right applied even in cases where there was more than one criminal sentencing, saying: 'The District Court must consider the effects of the crime on the victims at the time it makes its decision with respect to punishment, not as they were at some point in the past.' The remedy where this right was not observed was to vacate the sentence and to hold a new sentencing hearing in which the victims would be allowed to speak.[33]

As in the UK, the prosecution is required to provide the defendant with notice of its intent to use VIE, unless the prosecution introduces the statement directly to rebut mitigating evidence introduced by the defendant. Whilst VIE is nearly always presented at the sentencing phase of proceedings (a few states also permit it at the first phase of the trial), prosecutors have broad discretion over how it is conveyed (e.g. videos, photos, poems, etc); who is permitted to testify (e.g. family, friends, co-workers, neighbors, rescue personnel); and the number of witnesses. For example, there were 55 victim witnesses at the trial of Oklahoma City bombing conspirator Terry Nichols, and 38 at the trial of his accomplice Timothy McVeigh (Logan, 2006; Blume, 2003). When Zacharias Moussaui stood trial in Alexandria, Virginia for his role in the plotting of the September 11 terrorist attacks, no fewer than 45 people gave VIE for the prosecution, starting with New York's former mayor, Rudy Giuliani.[34]

There is now mounting evidence that VIE in American death penalty cases is being used to provide far more than a mere 'quick glimpse' of victims and the loss resulting from a murder, as authorized by *Payne*: 'Jurors now regularly receive highly emotional, gripping evidence, with precious little in the way of substantive limits and procedural controls, or guidance on how the potent evidence should influence their death decisions' (Logan, 2006).

In December 2007, the California Supreme Court found admissible the presentation of victim impact evidence in a capital trial that included a 22-minute videotape montage, prepared and narrated by the victim's mother, composed of dozens of still photographs and video clips and set to haunting music.[35] Beginning with pictures of the victim, Sara Weir, as a baby, the images documented milestones in her life—sitting up for the first time, birthdays, high school proms and graduation—as well as holidays and family gatherings,

33. *Kenna v. California*, D.C. No. CR-03-00568-JFW.

34. CNN.com, 'Giving victims a voice in court' 15 May 2006, http://www.sentencing.nj.gov/downloads/pdf/articles/2006/May2006/story13.pdf.

35. *People of the State of California v. Douglas Oliver Kelly*, S049973, No. LA015339.

where she is shown with various members of her extended family. This videotape had followed an oral statement where the mother described in heart-wrenching terms the devastating effect of Sara's death—at age 19—on her and her family. The defense, on appeal, had argued that:

> The emotions evoked by this videotape are obvious and easily anticipated and they have no place in a capital sentencing trial. A juror could not help but feel tremendous pity and sorrow for the victim and her family and rage and loathing for the source of this pain—appellant Kelly.... the videotape tribute to Ms. Weir in this case was so highly inflammatory and emotional that its admission violated the constitutional guarantees of due process, fundamental fairness and a fair and reliable penalty determination.

California permits VIE as a circumstance of the crime, but in a previous case—*Edwards*—the state Supreme Court stated that evidence which 'invites an irrational, purely subjective response should be curtailed.'[36] The Weir video, the defense argued, did exactly that, and could in no sense be said to be limited to the 'quick glimpse' of the victim's life approved by the U.S. Supreme Court in *Payne*. The prosecutor, counsel said, had sought 'not merely to let the jury know who the victim was, but rather to urge the jury to return a sentence of death *because of* who the victim was,' thus rendering the penalty phase trial unconstitutionally unreliable and unfair. Furthermore, the appellant argued that the evidence created an intolerable risk of improper comparisons between the victim and the defendant:

> The quantity and emotional quality of the victim impact evidence was so out of proportion to the utter lack of mitigation evidence presented [on the appellant's behalf] as to completely shift the focus of the jury's deliberative task from the appropriate sentence, considering the defendant and the circumstances of the crime, to a wholly inconsistent and constitutionally unauthorized task—responding to the sorrow of the victim's family ... [rendering] the jury's death verdict a product of emotion rather than reason.

The Court did not agree. In its majority opinion, it stated that the video VIE was not unduly emotional, and that it was relevant to the penalty determination: 'It has more probative value than any prejudicial effect.' By a 5 to 4 majority, the judges had taken a very different stance to the Texas Court of

36. Penal Code section 190.2, subd. (a) [factor (a)] (*People v. Edwards, supra*, 54 Cal.3d at p. 835 at p. 836.

Criminal Appeals—a body normally thought to be much more conservative—just five years earlier. In *Salazar v. State*,[37] having viewed a similar video montage of the victim's life, the Texas court had held that 'the punishment phase of a criminal trial is not a memorial service for the victim. What may be entirely appropriate eulogies to celebrate the life and accomplishments of a unique individual are not necessarily admissible in a criminal trial.' Such highly wrought sentiments often leave no doubt as to what the victims believe to be the appropriate sentence (Hoffmann, 2003). As Logan has argued:

> "... fifteen years after Payne was decided, it is clear that victim impact evidence is being used to provide far more than a mere 'quick glimpse' of victims and the loss resulting from a murder. Jurors now regularly receive highly emotional, gripping evidence, with precious little in the way of substantive limits and procedural controls, or guidance on how the potent evidence should influence their death decisions."(Logan, 2006: 169).

Perusal of the many cases where the over-emotional nature of victim impact evidence in capital cases has been subject to appeals shows that appellate courts both within and across states are highly inconsistent in their interpretation of what is acceptable and what prejudicial.[38] But the trend seems unmistakable: little by little, the limits are being pushed back.

5. Victim Statements: Threats to a Fair Trial

Advocates of victim impact statements often suggest that it is only fair to allow evidence of the sympathetic nature of the victim, given that the defense introduces such information about the defendant:

> (T)he Supreme Court's constitutional rule [is that] in death penalty sentencing defendants must be allowed to introduce any and all mitigating evidence—any and all particularized evidence about their background, upbringing, and so forth, that might lead a jury to conclude that a death sentence would not be appropriate. Permitting similar particularization in victim impact evidence likewise encourages empathetic concern for the victim and the victim's survivors, as well as a complex understanding of the defendant's crime.... in the context of sentencing [the defendant's story and the victim or survivor's

37. Tex. Crim. App. 2002; 90 S.W.3d 330 at pp. 335–336.

38. Kelly's Appeal (filed 12/6/07) provides a thorough discussion of some of these cases.

> story] can be seen as counter-stories, which should both be available to the decision maker (Gewirtz, 1996: 873).

Cassell similarly argues that the rights of defendants and victims must be balanced: 'Given that our current system allows almost unlimited mitigation evidence on the part of the defendant, an argument for equal justice requires, if anything, that victim statements be allowed. Equality demands fairness not only *between* cases, but also *within* cases' (emphasis in original) (Cassell, 1999: 494).

However, many academics with expertise in this area argue that victim impact evidence skews, rather than levels, the forensic playing field. Susan Bandes, one of VIE's most ardent critics, suggests that it interferes with the court's ability to discharge its duty, deflecting it from its task of focusing on the defendant as an individual, and exacerbating inequalities in attitudes towards the prosecution and the defendant (Bandes, 1996). Certainly, some studies, using controlled experimental simulations, suggest that in American capital murder cases, VIE that communicates a greater sense of harm endured by the 'survivors' increases the chance that the jury will impose a death sentence (Greene, Koehring & Quiat 1998; Myers & Arbuthnot, 1999; Nadler & Rose, 2003). Research also suggests that VIE encourages irrelevant or invidious distinctions about the comparative worth of different victims, based on their relative social position, the degree to which they are articulate and their race. Defendants in cases where victims are perceived by juries as 'worthy' are more likely to receive the death penalty (Sundby, 2003). Of course, most sentences in adversarial jurisdictions are imposed by judges, not juries. Some judges, as trained legal professionals, may be less amenable to being swayed by VIE when determining the level of punishment. It does not, however, seem unreasonable to suggest that with some judges at least, the 'worthiness' of the victim as described by VIE will play a significant, perhaps subconscious part. It is difficult to see how this risk can be eliminated.

Victim impact statements represent an attempt to allow the horrific, chaotic and unrestrained impact of serious crime to be given clear expression within the avowedly cool and rational legal process. It can seem admirable that victims should find the courage to present their inner turmoil and pain to a court. However, it is also problematic. Some victim impact statements, as we have seen from the Californian example discussed above, are visceral and prejudicial, rather than probative and relevant and hence difficult to constrain by due process protections (Mosteller, 2003). Even less emotive statements can, when presented in court, sound remarkably like statements of opinion as to the appropriate sentence. For example, Logan quotes the wife of a murdered police officer who said the following in her VIE, the admissibility of which was upheld by the Illinois Supreme Court:

> My family and I are very confident that all of you will return a quick verdict which will send a message to my children, society, and the law enforcement community that we simply will not tolerate or accept our last means of protection being annihilated on our streets. Renew our faith in the criminal justice system and bring a phase of closure to this ongoing nightmare that fills our lives.[39]

As mentioned above, some U.S. states already allow VIE containing express opinions as to the appropriate sentence. In other jurisdictions, such as England and Wales, the lack of clarity as to VIE's purpose and proper limits means the courts sometime seem unable to distinguish between opinion testimony and the highly personalized accounts of victim impact statements (Blume, 2003: 272–3).

As stated above, the guidance in England and Wales says that sentencers should take into account the interests, but not the views of victims. Not only is this distinction blurred, it is not clear that it is always observed in practice.

In one of the first instances of a Family Impact Statement being read out in an English court, Adele Eastman spoke eloquently and very movingly about her grief at losing her fiancé, Tom ap Rhys Pryce, a lawyer who was stabbed to death during a mugging in northwest London by Donnel Carty, aged 19, and Delano Brown, aged 18. Lawyers read statements prepared by Adele, Tom's brother and his mother after the verdict but prior to sentencing. Adele's statement, reproduced in full by various national newspapers, ran to 1,479 words, and was both a celebration of Tom's life, qualities and successes, and an unflinching declaration of love. Like many other such statements from partners, parents and children of murder victims, it is both beautiful and harrowing to read. But the statement also describes the 'indescribable'; the 'pain and horror at losing Tom … in such a brutal way.' Adele's words make clear the devastation that the defendants have wrought:

> I feel as though Carty and Brown have ripped out my heart with their bare hands and torn it very slowly into pieces.… The waves of devastation caused by Carty and Brown's greed and bravado roll on and on. The attack which they carried out on Tom was barbaric, they showed him no mercy and have shown absolutely no remorse since.… Greed fuelled Carty and Brown's attack on Tom but it is obvious, particularly from the trademark injury which they inflicted on his left leg, that they were also trying to play the "big man".[40]

39. *People v. Williams*: 1124, cited in Logan, 2006.

40. *The Daily Telegraph*, 30 November 2006.

The statement is dignified and controlled and does not go beyond its remit. The same is true of the statement made by Tom's mother who, quite remarkably, calls for crime prevention, rather than retribution. However, Tom's brother's statement speculates on the crime in a way that goes beyond the evidence presented in court: 'It could be that at the point that he stopped defending himself he was even more vulnerable and that was possibly when they stabbed him twice more even after he had handed over his goods. If that is the case it is more of an execution than a murder. I do not forgive them.' Nor, it is reasonable to argue, should he. But, nor should he be allowed to speculate in a statement on the nature of the killing in ways plainly intended to increase the sentence tariff.

In sentencing the two defendants to life in prison (to serve minimums of 21 years for the older and 17 years for the younger) the judge was almost certainly influenced only by the history of offences presented to the court (both defendants were prolific offenders who had been involved in a series of muggings) and their non-guilty plea. However, it is possible that he was also influenced by the inflammatory reference to 'execution' in this statement.

In May 2007, the Court of Appeal ruled that the 17-year term imposed in the case of Delano Brown was 'unduly lenient' and raised it to 20 years. The defense lawyers had tried to get these minimum terms reduced, arguing that they had been disproportionately long as a direct result of the victim impact statements. The Lord Chief Justice, Lord Phillips, sitting with two other judges, said the court rejected defense submissions that 'the sentences in this case were influenced by the fact that the victim was a professional man engaged to be married to a professional woman'. Nonetheless, he said, explaining his decision to increase the tariff, the judges had found Adele Eastman's VIE 'heart-rending.' To disaggregate the impact of the VIE from other factors in the appellate judges' minds is impossible. But it seems evident that they exercised at least some influence, leading one to the uncomfortable inference that if the victim had been less loved by his fiancée, his killers might have served a shorter term in prison.

As the legal journalist Marcel Berlins wrote in response to Adele Eastman's statement:

> My two main objections to the 'victim's advocate' scheme were amply proved. It gives victims (or their representatives) an influence over sentencing, and it is hugely unfair as between different classes and categories of victims.... judges are human. To suggest that they will remain immune to a highly emotional account of the grief felt by the survivor—and of the wonderfulness of the victim—is unrealistic and absurd. I have spoken to a number of judges, in confidence; not one of them could guarantee that he or she would remain unmoved when

> calculating the sentence (or, in cases of life imprisonment, the minimum term). The discriminatory aspect of the scheme is obvious. The articulate, the educated and the attractive will be able to put up a quality performance; those with lesser advantages—and whose loved ones could not be painted in saintly colors—will be even more disadvantaged at the trial.[41]

Another British columnist echoed this concern:

> No judge who heard Adele Eastman's heart-breaking Victim Impact Statement at the trial of her murdered fiancé, Tom ap Rhys Price, could have remained unmoved. But Ms. Eastman's plangent statement was the best argument for their abolition. What if there had been no one to speak for Mr. Rhys Price? What if he had been a loner, a tramp, an elderly person with no family? Would this life have meant fewer years in prison for his murderers? Sentencing, once judged on the gravity of the offence, may now be assessed on the gravity of the offence's emotional residue.[42]

In a debate published by *The Observer* newspaper in the week following the sentencing of Tom's killers, various contributors expressed concerns about partiality and lesser sentences for less worthy victims. As one put it, 'The tramp attacked by thugs and left to die without a friend in the world is as much part of our society as those with vocal relatives and friends.'[43]

Just 12 weeks before Adele Eastman's statement was read out, a court sentencing a teenager, convicted of death by dangerous driving, heard an equally emotional statement from the victim's mother, Elizabeth Davidson. It made the judge cry and when the mother was invited to read it out on BBC Radio 4's Today program, it made listeners in England and beyond cry too. No one should deny Elizabeth Davidson or Adele Eastman the right to make public their grief, but what—beyond catharsis—is the purpose and the what are costs? As another journalist wrote of this judge: 'His tears had the positive effect of demonstrating his humanity. But they did nothing to instill faith in his ability to make a decision based purely on the facts … the expression of such raw emotion is inappropriate in a context where clear-headedness is all-important'.[44] In the

41. *The Guardian*, December 4, 2006.
42. *The Independent*, April 23, 2007.
43. *The Observer*, December 3, 2006.
44. *Scotland on Sunday*, December 3, 2006.

words of the conservative *Daily Telegraph*: '[It] is becoming worryingly clear ... that the victim statement is leading quite literally to one law for the rich and another for the poor.'[45]

Many victims will manage heroically to constrain their statements within the necessary parameters. Others, inevitably, will not. With appropriate support and guidance they may manage to prepare a statement, which does not stray beyond the impact on their lives of the loss of a loved one, but in delivering personally such a statement they may be unable to control themselves to stick to what the courts have deemed to be admissible. In addition, even if they do not stray beyond the agreed, admissible text, their delivery may well be highly emotional, intensifying the statement's impact in a way that cannot be conveyed merely by the words, and which, arguably, ought not to influence the outcome of a criminal tribunal. The risk is that once given a voice, victims may be able to voice thoughts and emotions that while tragic and understandable, prejudice both the defendant and justice more generally.

An Irish case in 2006 provides one such example. Majella Holohan had prepared a victim impact statement to read out in court upon the conviction of her son's killer. However, the defendant was not convicted of murder, as she had hoped, but of manslaughter. Clearly disappointed, once inside the witness box she went well beyond the agreed statement and introduced evidence—of semen allegedly found on the victim's body—that the prosecution had already decided not to call, as it was prejudicial, inconclusive and even misleading. To introduce this allegation in the way that she did was certainly provocative, and arguably contemptuous of the court. Not surprisingly, it was reproduced the following day in media reports, which branded the defendant a 'pedophile killer' solely because of the VIE given by Holohan.

It was plain that Holohan went far beyond what was admissible in a victim statement under Irish law (which, in essence, conforms to the position as described above in England and Wales). However, the judge failed to intervene and chose not to censure her behavior. It is not hard to see why. Once a devastated mother has found the courage and has been given a public forum to speak out about such unimaginable loss, it is going to be almost impossible to interrupt and shut her down. As in England, the rules are clear in Ireland: no new evidence should be introduced in a victim impact statement, and if it is, the judge should disregard it in sentencing. Understandably, the defendant's lawyers in this case were anxious that it would, nevertheless, influence the court's deci-

45. *The Telegraph*, December 3, 2006.

sion.[46] Just over a year after the trial, the judge reflected on the case in an address to the Law Society:

> The tabloids stirred up such hatred for the accused that he has no future in this country when his time is served. This was not the intention of the sentencing judge and it is not acceptable that a sentencing objective of the High Court, upheld by the Court of Criminal Appeal, should be frustrated by an unwitting coalition between the victim and the tabloid press.[47]

This case shows that VIE, even when supposedly hedged with restrictions, can put judges in a difficult and compromising position that does little to serve the interests of justice. In an evaluation of Scottish pilot projects, Chalmers and his colleagues concluded that VIE's benefits, measured in terms of victim satisfaction with the criminal process, far outweighed any potential for prejudicing defendants' due process rights. They argue:

> By and large, victims commented solely on the impact of the offence. There clearly were some statements that strayed beyond the scope of the offence of which the offender was convicted, but never to the extent that a proof of mitigation was required. These instances were dealt with by the sentencing judge simply disregarding the irrelevant information when passing sentence (Chalmers, Duff & Leverick, 2001: 379).

The authors provide no evidence that, in reality, judges can or do disregard inadmissible or prejudicial information. Their assertion is that because judges *should* do this, they always will. This, it seems to me, is a dangerous act of faith.

6. What Place for Emotions in Criminal Justice?

Two hundred years ago, in the era when the State's role in the criminal process remained very limited, raw emotional responses to crime were the stock in trade of the court process, and public displays of grief and vengeance the norm. Punishment was often highly visible: defendants were still being hurt and humiliated in the stocks, and executed on public gallows.

---

46. This case was reported in most Irish newspapers; see, for example, *The (Irish) Sunday Times*, January 29, 2006 and May 7, 2006.

47. Mr. Justice Paul Carney, quoted in *The Irish Times*, October 11, 2007.

The State's takeover of criminal justice went a long way towards silencing victims and airbrushing their pain from public discourse. Very recently, the mood has changed. Anglo-American society has sought ways to give a voice to victims, by the introduction of restorative justice and victim statement schemes in particular and through the victims' movement more generally. These changes represent a 're-emotionalization of law'—an increased willingness to admit into the criminal process, and into decision making, emotional responses to crime, whether they be from the public in general or from specific victims (Karstedt, 2002: 299–301). The public, more than ever before, comments on criminal justice, whether on legislation or on decision making in specific cases. Through victims' rights groups, the media, and directly via electronic communications such as blogs and e-discussion pages, the public speaks to judges, policy makers and politicians, and their messages are often angry and retributive.

Deeming, probably correctly, that it will bring electoral advantage, politicians on both sides of the Atlantic are explicit in expressing their regard for such public emotion, as is evident by the 'heightened emotional tone' within contemporary Anglo-American political discourse and public policy on crime (De Hann & Loader, 2002: 247). They are also keen to allow these emotions into the courtroom. Today, more than ever in recent history, emotion is not only welcome in the court room, it is encouraged. The courts, as well as other criminal justice institutions 'are becoming more attuned to, and minded to accept, the claims for recognition made by angry, vengeful or traumatized victims'(De Hann & Loader, 2002: 247).

Of course, to some extent, emotions have always had a place within the court. Certain crimes are defined according to emotion: hate crimes, for example, where emotion is the aggravator, or the euthanasia of terminal patients, popularly termed 'mercy killings,' where emotion is presented in mitigation. It might be said that over many decades, the criminal court has been better equipped than any other forum to deal with emotions, largely because it has controlled them (Karstedt, 2002). In the guilt phase of a trial, it has allowed only emotions from those actors directly affected by the offence, and only then when mediated through the appropriate channels. The court has also regulated emotion by limiting its expression to those factors directly relevant to deciding what the offence is, and the offender's culpability. Barristers have had to demonstrate the relevance of information that does not clearly fit into these categories.

Victim impact evidence, as it has been introduced in adversarial jurisdictions on both sides of the Atlantic, seriously challenges this management of emotion. In both Britain and America the guidelines are equivocal, evolving, and, in practice, becoming ever more flexible. They also depend on a dubious psychological assertion that should have been problematized before VIE was ever given in a court of law—the claim that sentencing decisions will not be influenced if victims refrain from stating direct opinions. Moreover, there is some evidence that those working within the criminal justice system think that victim impact statements *should* influence sentences and actively try to bring this about. For example, a senior British police officer recently said that officers in his force, when helping victims to make an impact statement, sometimes suggested that they should make clear how much they have been harmed *in order* to increase the likelihood of a custodial sentence. He saw the main aim of victim impact statements as being instrumental, rather than cathartic or expressive and was unapologetic about that.[48] Similarly, the current Chair of Magistrates Association has said that magistrates like to have access to victim impact statements so that the victim's emotions and personal experiences of and responses to the crime could inform sentencing. When asked in an interview whether victims who were forgiving would have the same impact as those full of vengeance she was unequivocal: the 'offence against society' model took precedence when the victim was forgiving or did not feel much harmed, so that milder impact statements would not be taken as mitigation. However, in a case where the VIE suggested that the victim had been seriously harmed, the 'offence against victim' model took precedence, with the impact statement serving as an aggravator.[49]

Academics who argue in favor of VIE can also be ambivalent. Chalmers et al. argue that because the majority of victims in their evaluation of the Scottish pilot schemes thought that their decision to make a victim impact statement had been the correct one, this justifies any risk that the statement might have an unacceptable influence on the sentencing judge. They see this risk as small, stating most of the victims in their study made statements to achieve an emotional catharsis, not to influence the sentence. So why not conclude that in order to remove the risk altogether, VIE should only be allowed post sen-

48. Detective Superintendent Matt Sarti, Head of Prison Intelligence Unit of the Metropolitan Police speaking at a consultation meeting for the Howard League Commission on English Prisons Today (on which the author serves), 29 October 2007.

49. Cindy Barnett, Chair of Magistrates Association, Consultation Meeting, 29 October 2007 for the Howard League Commission on English Prisons Today. Examples of this can be found at all points of the criminal process in the U.S. For example the American victims organisation, Murder Victims Families for Reconciliation, claims that in some states prosecutors try to prevent victims who are opposed to the death penalty from making a victim impact statement http://www.mvfr.org/about.

tence? Here lies the equivocal rub. According to Chalmers et al., the reason is precisely in order to leave open the possibility of influencing sentences. As they write:

> ... victim statement did sometimes add *valuable* information to that already held be sentencers and, in some cases, caused the sentencing judge to impose a different sentence ... to that which they would otherwise have imposed (my emphasis) (Chalmers, Duff & Leverick, 2001: 378).

Some of the core issues in the debate that should have been held 20 years ago, when VIE made its debut, have been well put by Burr. Although he is writing about the specific context of the penalty phase in capital murder trials, his conclusions are more broadly applicable:

> Victim impact evidence is lethal for capital defendants and often illusory for the witnesses who provide it ... At best, victim impact testimony provides a momentary opportunity for survivors to give voice to their loss, be heard, and feel less isolated. At worst, victim impact testimony exploits the immense pain suffered by survivors—using the emotional reaction to their circumstances as a lever to produce a death sentence, while leaving them as onlookers in a criminal justice process whose focus is punishing the offender, not meeting the needs of survivors (Burr, 2003: 517).

In other words, 'the restoration of the conflict,' the transfer of power from the State to victims that advocates argue is represented by the use of VIE is at best extremely restricted, and at worst largely illusory. And just when it seems to be most effective, when sentencing authorities do appear to be swayed, this will embody a grave and unjustified inroad into defendants' due process rights, as what ought to be dispassionate decisions become subsumed by public passion, the expression of uncontrolled emotion.

It is probably too late to put the genie back into the bottle: too much to hope that politicians and policy makers on either side of the Atlantic will recognize this danger, and in the name of due process, end the production of VIE altogether. There is, however, one recourse that would leave the vaunted psychological benefits to victims intact, while alleviating the risk of unjust disproportionally: to retain VIE, but only to admit it *after* sentencing is complete.

To allow victims to make an impact statement immediately after sentencing would serve their needs for closure without unfairly affecting the defendant's rights. If victim impact evidence does confer cathartic benefits, as it may well do, it is difficult to see why this effect should be any weaker if confined to the period when it can no longer influencing the sentencing decision —indeed, it already is in capital cases in a few American states, such as Indiana and Wyoming.

Once institutionalized, post-sentence VIE could retain the full solemnity of the judicial proceeding. The judge should insist that the court remains seated (even if a brief adjournment is needed for the family to console themselves) and that the jury, legal teams and the defendant listen to the statement. No one should be allowed to interrupt or challenge the family's statement, and they should be allowed to read it themselves or opt for another to do so.

To banish emotion from criminal justice is unrealistic. We cannot lock it out of the court room, nor should we. The challenge—which should, as I have argued, have been met many years ago—is to admit it in ways that do not compromise the broader interests of justice, and are not instrumental, a means of making sentencing more punitive. Post-sentence VIE would preserve the principle of just deserts, and allow sentencers to return to their prior reliance on more objective sources to judge a crime's severity, such as financial statements or medical reports. Punishment, it cannot be sufficiently emphasized, should be tailored to fit the crime, not the victims.

References

Acker, J.R. and Karp, D.R. (Eds.) (2006). *Wounds that do not Bind: Victim-Based Perspectives on the Death Penalty* (Durham, NC: Carolina Academic Press).

Ashworth, A. (2000). 'Victims' Rights, Defendants' Rights and Criminal Procedure', in A. Crawford and J. Goodey (Eds.), *Integrating a Victim Perspective within Criminal Justice* (Aldershot: Ashgate Dartmouth).

Bandes, S. (1996). 'Empathy, Narrative, and Victim Impact Statements', *University of Chicago Law Review* 63 at 361–412.

Bandes, S. (2000). 'When Victims Seek Closure: Forgiveness, Vengeance, and the Role of Government', *Fordham Urban Law Journal* 27: 1599–1606.

Beloof, D.E. (1999). *Victims in Criminal Procedure.* (Durham, NC: Carolina Academic Press).

Beloof, D.E. (2003). 'Constitutional Implications of Crime Victims as Participants'. *Cornell Law Review* 88(2) at 282–305.

Blume, J.H. (2003). 'Ten Years of *Payne*: Victim Impact Evidence in Capital Cases' *Cornell Law Review* 88 at 257–281.

Burr, R. (2003). 'Litigating with Victim Impact Testimony: The Serendipity That Has Come from *Payne v Tennessee*' *Cornell Law Review* 88 at 517–529.

Cassell, P.G. (1999). 'Barbarians at the Gates? A Reply to the Critics of the Victims' Rights Amendment' *Utah Law Review* 2 at 479–544.

Chalmers, J., Duff, P., and Leverick, F. (2001). 'Victim Impact Statements: Can Work, Do Work (For Those Who Bother To Make Them), *Criminal Law Review* at 360–379.

Christie, N., (1977). 'Conflicts as Property', *British Journal of Criminology*, 17(1) at 1–15.

CPS (2007). Victim Focus Scheme: Guidance on enhanced CPS service for bereaved families, Para 22 http://www.cps.gov.uk/victims_witnesses/focus_ scheme.html.

CPS/ACPO (2004). *No Witness, No Justice Pilot Evaluation*, Executive Summary http://www.cps.gov.uk/publications/reports/nwnjevaluation291004.htm.

Beloof, D.E. (2003). 'Constitutional Implications of Crime Victims as Participants' *Cornell Law Review* 88 at 282–305.

De Hann, W. and Loader, I. (2002). 'On the Emotions of Crime, Punishment and Social Control', *Theoretical Criminology*, 6, at 243–353.

Edwards, I. (2001). 'Victim Participation in Sentencing: The Problems of Incoherence', *The Howard Journal*, 40(1), 39–54.

Eisenberg, T., Garvey, S.P., and Wells, M.T. (2003). 'Victim Characteristics and Victim Impact Evidence in South Carolina Capital Cases'. *Cornell Law Review* 88(2) at 306–342.

Erez, E. (1999). 'Who's Afraid of The Big Bad Victim? Victim Impact Statements as Victim Empowerment and Enhancement of Justice', *Criminal Law Review*, at 545–556.

Erez, E. (1994). 'Victim Participation in Sentencing: And the Debate Goes On ...' *International Review of Victimology* (3) at 17–32.

Erez, E. and Roberts, J. (2007). 'Victim Participation in the Criminal Justice System', in R.C. Davis, A.J. Lurigio, and S. Herman (Eds.), *Victims of Crime* (Los Angeles: Sage, 3rd ed.).

Erez, E. and Rogers, L. (1999). 'Victim Impact Statements and Sentencing Outcomes and Processes: The Perspectives of Legal Professionals' *British Journal of Criminology* 39 at 216–239.

Garland, D. (2001). *The Culture of Control: Crime and Social Order in Contemporary Society.* (Oxford: Oxford University Press).

Gewirtz, P. (1996). 'Victims and Voyeurs at the Criminal Trial' *Northwestern University Law Review*, 90(3) at 863–897.

Greene, E., Koehring, H., and Quiat, M., (1998). 'Victim Impact Evidence in Capital Cases: Does the Victim's Character Matter?' *Journal of Applied Social Psychology* 28(2) at 145–156.

Hodgkinson, P. (2004). 'Victims: meeting the needs of the families of the homicide victim and the condemned', in P. Hodgkinson and W. Schabas, (Eds.), *Capital Punishment: Strategies for Abolition* (Cambridge: Cambridge University Press).

Hoffmann, J.L. (2003). 'Revenge or Mercy? Some Thoughts About Survivor Opinion Evidence in Death Penalty Cases' *Cornell Law Review* 88(2) at 530–542.

Home Office. (2000). 'Home Secretary announces national victim statements', Home Office Press Release 147/2000.

Home Office. (2005). *Hearing the Relatives of Murder and Manslaughter Victims: Consultation Document*. London, Home Office, CJS: 28.

Hoyle, C., Cape, E., Morgan, R., and Sanders, A. (1998). *Evaluation of the "one-stop shop" and victim statement pilot projects*. (London: Home Office Research Development and Statistics Directorate).

Hoyle, C., Morgan, R., and Sanders, A. (1999). *The Victim's Charter—An Evaluation of Pilot Projects*, HORS, Research Findings No. 107 (London: Home Office).

Hoyle, C. and Young, R., (2002). 'Restorative Justice: Assessing the Prospects and Pitfalls' in M. McConville and G. Wilson (Eds.) *The Handbook of the Criminal Justice Process*, (Oxford: Oxford University Press).

Hoyle, C. and Zedner, L. (2007). 'Victims, Victimization and Criminal Justice' in M. Maguire, R. Morgan, and R. Reiner (Eds.), *The Oxford Handbook of Criminology* (Oxford: Oxford University Press, 4th ed.), pp. 461–495.

Karstedt, S. (2002). 'Emotions and Criminal Justice', *Theoretical Criminology*, 6(3), at 299–318.

Knudten, R.D., Meade, A.C., Knudten, M.S., and Doerner, W.G. (1977). *Victims and Witnesses: Their Experiences with Crime and the Criminal Justice System*, Executive Summary, (National Institute of Law Enforcement and Criminal Justice, LEAA, U.S. Department of Justice).

Logan, W.A. (2005). 'Victims, Survivors and the Decisions to Seek and Impose Death' in Acker, J.R. and Karp, D.R. (Eds.), *Wounds That Do Not Bind: Victim-Based Perspectives on the Death Penalty*, (Durham, NC: Carolina Academic Press).

Luginbuhl, J. and Burkhead, M. (1995). 'Victim Impact Evidence in a Capital Trial: Encouraging Votes for Death' *American Journal of Criminal Justice* 20 at 1–16.

MacCormick, N. and Garland, D. (1998). 'Sovereign States and Vengeful Victims: The Problem of the Right to Punish' in A. Ashworth and M. Wasik, (Eds.), *The Fundamentals of Sentencing Theory*. (Oxford: Oxford University Press).

Maguire, M. and Kynch, J., (2000). *Public Perceptions and Victims' Experiences of Victim Support: Findings from the 1998 British Crime Survey* HO Occasional Paper. (London: Home Office).

Morgan, K. and Smith, B.L. (2005). 'Victims, Punishment, and Parole: The Effect of Victim Participation on Parole Hearings', *Criminology and Public Policy*, 4 (2) at 333–360.

Morgan, R. and Sanders, A. (1999). *The Uses of Victim Statements* (London: Home Office).

Mosteller, R.P. (2003). 'Victim Impact Evidence: Hard to Find the Real Rules' *Cornell Law Review* 88 at 543–554.

Myers, B. and Arbuthnot, J. (1999). 'The Effects of Victim Impact Evidence on the Verdicts and Sentencing Judgments of Mock Jurors' *Journal of Offender Rehabilitation* 29(3/4) at 95–112.

Nadler, J. and Rose, M.R. (2003). 'Victim Impact Testimony and the Psychology of Punishment.' *Cornell Law Review* 88(2) at 419–456.

Parsonage, W.H., Bernat, F.P., and Helfgott, J. (1992). 'Victim Impact Testimony and Pennsylvania's Parole Decision Making Process: A pilot study', *Criminal Justice Policy Review* 6, 187–206.

Roach, K. (2005). Victims' Rights and the Charter, *Criminal Law Quarterly* (49) at 474–516.

Rock, P. (1998). 'Murderers, Victims and "Survivors": The Social Construction of Deviance' *British Journal of Criminology* 38, at 185–200.

Rock, P. (1998). *After Homicide: Practical and Political Responses to Bereavement.* (Oxford: Oxford University Press).

Rock, P. (2004). 'Victims, Prosecutors and the State in nineteenth century England and Wales', Criminal Justice, 4(4) at 331–54.

Sanders, A., Hoyle, C., Morgan, R., and Cape, E. (2001). 'Victim Impact Statements: Don't Work, Can't Work', *Criminal Law Review*, at 447–458.

Sarat, A. (2001). *When the State Kills: Capital Punishment and the American Condition* (Princeton University Press).

Schlosser, E. (1997). 'A grief like no other' *Atlantic Monthly* at 37–76.

Shapland, J. (1988). 'Fiefs and peasants: accomplishing change for victims in the criminal justice system', in Maguire, M. and Pointing, J. (Eds.) *Victims of Crime: A New Deal?*, (Milton Keynes, Open University Press).

Shapland, J., Willmore, D., and Duff, P. (1985). *Victims in the Criminal Justice System*, (Aldershot: Gower Publishing).

Sparks, R., Genn, H., and Dodd, D. (1977). *Surveying Victims*, (London: John Wiley).

Starkweather, D.A. (1992). 'The Retributive Theory of "Just Deserts" and Victim Participation in Plea Bargaining', *Indiana Law Journal* 67, at 864–67.

Sundby, S.E. (2003). 'The Capital Jury and Empathy: The Problem of Worthy and Unworthy Victims' *Cornell Law Review* 88 at 343–381.

Thompson, M.P. (2007). 'Homicide Survivors: A summary of the research' in R.C. Davis, A.J. Lurigio, and S. Herman (Eds.), *Victims of Crime* (Los Angeles: Sage, 3rd ed.).

Tobolowsky, P. (1999). 'Victim Participation in the Criminal Justice Process: Fifteen Years After the President's Task Force on Victims of Crime', *New England Journal on Criminal and Civil Confinement*, 25(1) at 21–106.

Vandiver, M. (2003). 'The Impact of the Death Penalty on the Families of Homicide Victims and of Condemned Prisoners' in J. R. Acker, R. M. Bohm, and C. S. Lanier (Eds.), *America's Experiment with Capital Punishment* (Durham, North Carolina: Carolina Academic Press, 2nd edn).

Young, J. (1994). 'Incessant Chatter: Recent Paradigms in Criminology' in Maguire, M., Morgan, R. and Reiner, R. (Eds.) *The Oxford Handbook of Criminology* (Oxford: Oxford University Press).

Author Biographies

Fran Buntman is an Assistant Professor of Sociology at The George Washington University. She researches, writes, and teaches about prisons and other aspects of criminal justice, power, and resistance, focusing mostly on the United States and South Africa. In addition to her 2003 book, *Robben Island and Prisoner Resistance to Apartheid* (Cambridge University Press), she has published numerous articles, chapters, reviews, and editorials including the 2009 "Prison and Democracy: Lessons Learned, and Not Learned, from 1989 to 2009" (*International Journal of Politics, Culture, and Society*), the 2010 "'Old Synagogue' and Apartheid Court: Constructing a South African Heritage Site" (*South African Historical Journal*, with Barbara Buntman), and, earlier in 2001, focusing on the United States, race, and law, "Race, Reputation, and the Supreme Court: Valuing Blackness and Whiteness" in the *University of Miami Law Review.*

Daniel Downs is the research coordinator for the Loss Prevention Research Council and he also serves as a part-time professor in the Department of Criminology and Sociology at the University of Florida. His work includes offender interviewing, advanced statistical modelling and randomized controlled trials as it relates to situational crime prevention. Dr. Downs has a PhD in Criminology, Law and Justice from the University of Illinois at Chicago and an MA in Experimental Psychology from California State University, San Bernardino. His research interests include environmental criminology, youth attitudes toward the law, legal cynicism, quantitative methodology and youth delinquency. For his dissertation, he created and validated a new measure of legal cynicism.

Edna Erez is Professor in the Department of Criminology, Crime, and Justice at the University of Illinois at Chicago. She has a Law degree from the Hebrew University of Jerusalem, and MA in Criminology and PhD in Sociology from the University of Pennsylvania. Her research interests include comparative justice, victims in the justice system, violence against women and victimization in the context of transnational crime and terrorism. She serves on the editorial board of several major professional journals and she is a co-editor of *International Review of Victimology* and Associate Editor of *Violence and Vic-*

tims. Professor Erez was Visiting Professor at Warsaw University, University of Melbourne and Haifa University, and a resident scholar at the Max Planck Institute for International and Comparative Criminal Law (Freiburg) and the Australian Institute of Criminology.

Tali Gal teaches, writes and advocates in the fields of children's rights, restorative justice and victims' rights. While acting as the staff lawyer and later as Legal Advisor for the Israel National Council for the Child, she founded in 1999 the Child Victims Assistant Project and was a co-founding member of the Israeli Victims' Rights Coalition. She was also a Board Member at Bizchut: a non-governmental organization promoting the rights of people with disabilities; and a member at the governmental Rotlevi Subcommittee reviewing Israel's implementation of the UN Convention on the Rights of the Child in the criminal justice process. She holds an LL.B (Hebrew University 1996); an LL.M (American University 2000); and a PhD (Law, the Australian National University 2006). Her book *Child Victims and Restorative Justice: A Needs-Rights Model* is forthcoming (June 2011) in Oxford University Press.

Helmut Hirtenlehner obtained his doctorate in sociology at the University of Linz, Austria, in 2000. In 2008, he finished his *habilitation* (post-doctorate) in criminology. He is currently Associate Professor at the Institute for Criminal Sciences at the University of Linz. His research interests include quantitative methods, fear of crime, punitiveness and victimology. Recent publications are: *Kultur, Institutionen und Kriminalität. Eine Prüfung der Institutionellen Anomietheorie mit Viktimisierungsdaten aus Europa* [Culture, Institutions and Crime: Testing Institutional Anomie Theory with Victimization Data From Europe], *Monatsschrift für Kriminologie und Strafrechtsreform* 2010 (together with Johann Bacher, Dietrich Oberwittler, Dina Hummelsheim and Jonathan Jackson), *Gestalkt! Eine empirische Analyse der Erfahrungen und Bedürfnisse von Stalking-Opfern in Oberösterreich* [Stalked! An empirical analysis of the experiences and needs of victims of stalking in Upper Austria] (together with Barbara Starzer, Innsbruck 2011).

Carolyn Hoyle is Reader in Criminology at the Centre for Criminology and Green Templeton College, University of Oxford. She has published empirical and theoretical research on a number of criminological topics including policing, domestic violence, restorative justice and the death penalty. Her publications include: *What is Criminology?* (with Mary Bosworth, Oxford University Press, 2011); *Debating Restorative Justice* (with Chris Cunneen, Hart Publishing, 2010); *Restorative Justice: Critical Concepts in Criminology* (Routledge Major Works, 2009); *The Death Penalty: A Worldwide Perspective* (with Roger Hood, Oxford University Press, 2008); *New Visions of Crime Victims* (with Richard Young, Hart Publishing, 2002); *Negotiating Domestic Violence: Police,*

Criminal Justice and Victims (Oxford University Press, 2000). She teaches undergraduate and graduate courses on: 'Restorative Justice'; 'The Death Penalty'; 'Victims'; 'Race, Gender and Criminal Justice' and 'Qualitative Methods', and supervises DPhil, MPhil and MSc students on a range of topics, including: victims, domestic violence, death penalty, and restorative justice.

Peter R. Ibarra is an Associate Professor in the Department of Criminology, Law, and Justice at the University of Illinois at Chicago. He received his PhD in Sociology from the University of California at Santa Cruz and was a postdoctoral fellow in the Department of Sociology at the University of California at Los Angeles. His interests are in the sociology of crime, deviance and control, social problems theory, community policing (especially in urban immigrant neighborhoods), technology and criminal justice and qualitative research methods. He is currently working on a NIJ funded research project on how courts are using GPS for domestic violence cases during the pre-adjudication period. He is also involved in the writing of a team ethnography based on extensive fieldwork conducted in Hollywood, California neighborhoods that centered on crime, community, and life histories. Other writing projects include work in the areas of social problems theory and electronic monitoring.

Michael Kilchling, Dr. jur., is a senior researcher at the Department of Criminology of the Max Planck Institute for Foreign and International Criminal Law in Freiburg, Germany (MPI) and lecturer at the University of Freiburg. His research interests include penal sanctions and sanctioning systems, victim/offender mediation and other forms of restorative justice and victimology. He was a member of several expert groups at the Council of Europe and the EU Commission such as, the *Group of Specialists on Assistance to Victims and Prevention of Victimization* at the Council of Europe which prepared the Recommendation R(2006)8 on Assistance to Crime Victims. Currently he is secretary of the board of the European Forum for Restorative Justice (EFRJ). Recent publications include: *Victims of Terrorism Policies—Should Victims of Terrorism be Treated Differently*? (European Journal on Criminal Policy and Research 2007, with Hans-Jörg Albrecht); *Restorative Justice Developments in Germany* (in: Miers/Aertsen, Regulating Restorative Justice: A Comparative Study of Legislative Provisions in European Countries, 2011).

Helmut Kury, Prof. Dr., studied psychology at the University of Freiburg, Germany. He was lecturer at the University in Freiburg (1970–1973), senior researcher at the Department of Criminology of the Max-Planck-Institute for Foreign and International Criminal Law (MPI) in Freiburg (1973–1980 and 1989–2006) and the first Director of the Criminological Research Institute of Lower Saxony (KFN) in Hannover (1980–1989). He conducted various studies on the rehabilitation of offenders, methodology of empirical research, victimization, mediation, crime prevention, alternatives to imprisonment. Main publications include: *Crime Prevention: New Approaches* (co-edited with Joachim Obergfell-Fuchs, Mainz 2003); *Gewalt in der Familie* [Violence in the Family] (co-edited with Joachim Obergfell-Fuchs, Freiburg 2005); *Fear of Crime—Punitivity: New Developments in Theory and Research* (Bochum 2008); *International Perspectives on Punitivity* (co-edited with Theodore N. Ferdinand, Bochum 2008); *Punitivity—International Developments* (co-edited with Evelyn Shea, Bochum 2011, 3 vols.).

Antony Pemberton, PhD is a senior researcher and research coordinator at the International Victimology Institute at Tilburg University in the Netherlands. His research concerns victims of a variety of crimes, with a particular focus on interdisciplinary studies into the experience of victims in (criminal) justice processes. Amongst others he has co-authored a book on victims of terrorism, has published a series of articles connecting social and clinical psychology to victimology in theories of restorative justice and has completed evaluations of the Dutch law on victim impact statements and the European Union Framework Decision on the standing of victims in criminal proceedings. He is currently co-editing a volume on victims of international crimes (including genocide) and is involved in a European Union project on victims and restorative justice.

Sandra Reynaers is a lawyer from the Netherlands who is currently finishing her PhD at Intervict—The International Victimology Institute of Tilburg—which is set within the Law Faculty of Tilburg University in the Netherlands. Her doctoral thesis is about victims' rights and the role of the public prosecution service. The aim of this study is to develop a set of recommendations, which will enable the public prosecution service to use a victim-focused approach without prejudicing other values of the criminal justice system in both civil (inquisitorial) and common (adversarial) law-based systems. The two jurisdictions included in her research are the Netherlands and England & Wales. For this reason, she was a Visiting Fellow at the Centre for Criminology, Oxford University, in 2008/2009. Her main fields of interest are criminal justice, victimology, human rights, and international and European law.

Lyane Sautner, PD Dr. jur., is Associate Professor and Head of the Department of Criminal Law and Victimology at the Johannes Kepler University, Linz, Austria. She studied law and finished her *habilitation* (post-doctorate) in 2009. Lyane Sautner is member of the board of the *Weisser Ring* in Austria and of Victim Support Europe (VSE). Recent publications include: *Opferinteressen und Strafrechtstheorien: Zugleich ein Beitrag zum restorativen Umgang mit*

Straftaten [Victims' Interests and Penal Theories] (Innsbruck/Wien/Bozen, 2010); *Überlegungen zur Einführung einer Wiedergutmachungsstrafe in das österreichische Strafrecht* [Considering the Implementation of a Compensation Order Into Austrian Criminal Law] (Juristische Blätter 2010).

Vered Shidlo-Hezroni is a lawyer and a member of the Israeli Bar Association. She has practiced law in Israel for over a decade. Currently, she is a PhD student (ABD) in the Department of Criminology, Law and Justice at the University of Illinois at Chicago. Her dissertation focuses on the construction of Organ Trafficking as a social problem in Israel. Vered has a Masters of Law (LLM) from the University of Houston Law School with concentration in International and Comparative law. Her Master thesis examined military responses to terrorist attacks under international law. Vered also holds a Bachelors of Law degree (LLB) from the College of Management in Israel and Bachelors of Arts (BA, Cum Laude) with a major in Criminology from Bar-Ilan University.

Bas van Stokkom is research fellow at the Centre for Ethics, Radboud University Nijmegen and lecturer at the Faculty of Social Sciences, Free University Amsterdam, in the Netherlands. His research concentrates on the fields of deliberative democracy, restorative justice and punishment ethics. He is Secretary of the Dutch-Flemish journal *Tijdschrift voor Herstelrecht* (Journal of Restorative Justice) and co-editor of the studies *Images of Restorative Justice Theory* (2008), *Reflections on Reassurance Policing in the Low Countries* (2008) and *Restorative Policing* (Journal of Police Studies 2009, no. 11).

Susanne Walther, Prof. Dr., is a Professor of criminal law, criminal procedure and comparative criminal law at the University of Cologne, Germany. She received her legal education in Freiburg (Germany), Geneva (Switzerland) and Georgetown University Law Center in Washington, D.C. (USA). She received her LL.M. in Common Law Studies in 1989, followed by her doctorate in 1990 and her *habilitation* (post-doctorate) in 1998. A considerable part of her publications deal with victim issues. Her *habilitation* thesis focused on the theory of reparation (*Vom Rechtsbruch zum Realkonflikt*, Berlin 2000). Other publications include: *Reparation in the German Criminal Justice System* (International Review of Victimology 2000); *Victims' Rights in the German Court System* (Federal Sentencing Reporter 2006); *Zum Anspruch des Deliktsopfers auf rechtliches Gehör und auf ein faires Verfahren* [On Victims' Rights to be Heard and to a Fair Trial] (Goltdammers Archiv 2007); *Interessen und Rechtsstellung des Verletzten im Strafverfahren* [Interests and Legal Position of the Victim at Criminal Proceedings] (Juristische Rundschau 2008).

Jo-Anne Wemmers PhD, is a Professor at the School of Criminology of the Université de Montréal, Canada as well as Head of the Research Group Victimology and Restorative Justice at the International Centre for Comparative Criminology. She has published many articles and books in the area of victimology, including *Introduction à la victimologie* (Les Presses de l'Université de Montréal), *Caring for Victims of Crime* (Criminal Justice Press) and *Victims in the Criminal Justice System* (Kugler Publications). Former Secretary General of the World Society of Victimology, she is currently President of the Elizabeth Fry Society of Quebec as well as Editor of the *International Review of Victimology* and the *Journal international de victimologie.*

David B. Wexler is Professor of Law and Director, International Network on Therapeutic Jurisprudence at the University of Puerto Rico and Distinguished Research Professor of Law Emeritus, University of Arizona. He first named and explicated the therapeutic jurisprudence perspective in a paper delivered in 1987 to a Law and Mental Health workshop sponsored by the National Institute of Mental Health. Wexler is the author of seven books, the most recent of which is *Rehabilitating Lawyers: Principles of Therapeutic Jurisprudence for Criminal Law Practice* (Carolina Academic Press, 2008). He has served as a Fulbright Senior Specialist in Australia and New Zealand, is a consultant to the National Judicial Institute of Canada and the Judicial Academy of Puerto Rico, and has addressed audiences around the world. His work has been translated to Spanish, Portuguese, Hebrew, and Urdu.

Bruce J. Winick, who passed away in August 2010, was the Silvers-Rubenstein Distinguished Professor of Law and Professor of Psychiatry and Behavioral Sciences at the University of Miami in Coral Gables, Florida, where he has taught since 1974. The co-founder of the school of social enquiry known as therapeutic jurisprudence, Winick was Director of the University of Miami School of Law's recently established Therapeutic Jurisprudence Center. Winick has authored numerous books, including *Civil Commitment: A Therapeutic Jurisprudence Model* (2005), *Judging in a Therapeutic Key: Therapeutic Jurisprudence and the Courts* (2003), *and Protecting Society from Sexually Dangerous Offenders: Law, Justice, and Therapy* (2003). He served on the editorial boards of *Psychology, Public Policy & Law*, *Law & Human Behavior,* and *Psychiatry, Psychology & Law.* He received the Philippe Pinel Award of the International Academy of Law and Mental Health, an honorary distinguished membership in the American Psychology-Law Society, the University of Miami Provost's Award for Outstanding Scholarship, the Thurgood Marshall Award of the Association of the Bar of the City of New York, and the Human Rights Award of the American Immigration Lawyers Association.

Index